25-12-87

Merry Christmas
&
Happy New Year to all!
Love always,
Mary Lynn

D1315955

THE
OFFICIAL
BICENTENNIAL
DIARY

The
Official
Bicentennial
Diary
has been
created to
celebrate
Australia's
first
200 years

1988

PUBLISHERS

SUNSHINE DIARIES PTY LTD
Chief Executive .... IAN M. McDONALD
Editor-in-Chief .... HARRY GORDON
Production Co-ordinator .... GORDON MILTON
Editorial/Research Assistant ....MARION GITTUS
Production Assistant .... TRUDY UPTON

RESEARCH	**DESIGN**
HARRY GORDON	DAN BREADEN
TOM BAIN	
TIM HANNA	**ART PRODUCTION**
LAWRENCE FYSH	CORPORATE GRAPHICS

PHOTOGRAPHY	**PHOTOGRAPHIC**
BARRY GREEN	**CO-ORDINATOR**
RON RATCLIFFE	HELEN BARNARD
CHARLES BARRON	

COMPUTER TYPESETTING	**COLOUR SEPARATIONS**
Press Etching (Qld)	Press Etching (Qld)
Pty Ltd	Pty Ltd
ADDITIONAL	**ADDITIONAL FILM**
TYPESETTING	**PRODUCTION**
Savage Type Pty Ltd	Savage Colour Pty Ltd
PRINTING	**BINDING**
Wilke and Company Ltd (Vic)	Podlich Enterprises
Prestige Litho Pty Ltd	Pty Ltd

First published in 1987 by Sunshine Diaries Pty Ltd,
25 Wellington Street, Petrie Terrace, Brisbane, Qld.

Copyright © Sunshine Diaries Pty Ltd

This book is copyright. Apart from any fair dealing for the purposes of private study, research, criticism or review, as permitted under the Copyright Act, no part may be reproduced by any
process without written permission. Inquiries should be addressed to the Publishers.

All rights reserved.

Whilst every care has been taken in compiling the information
in this Volume the Publishers cannot accept responsibility for
any errors, inadvertent or not, that may be found or may occur
at some time in the future owing to changes in legislation, or
for any other reason.

Proudly produced in Australia by Sunshine Diaries Pty Ltd under
Exclusive Licence to the Australian Bicentennial Authority.

National Library of Australia
Cataloguing-in-Publication data
  The Official Bicentennial diary.

  Bibliography.
  Includes index.
  ISBN 0 9587714 1 3.

  1. Diaries (Blank-books). 2. Australia —
  History.

994.

THE
OFFICIAL
BICENTENNIAL
DIARY

Australia
1788-1988

PUBLISHER'S NOTE

The Official Bicentennial Diary was created to fulfil the objective of lifting the normally dull, everyday diary to something truly appropriate to the year 1988. It contains everything a normal working diary should, but is enhanced by design, colour and many historical features.

We were very fortunate to attract a team of dedicated professionals who shared our desires and enthusiasm for the project.

There are too many to name individually but three deserve special mention.

Mr. Harry Gordon, who wrote the group of historical essays, is one of them. His imaginative words, his distinctive style and his refreshing point-of-view inspired all of us to greater efforts.

Another is Mr. Tom Bain, whose brainchild it was so many months ago.

And the third, Mr. Ian Kerr, who had the vision and the drive to make the project a reality.

We sincerely hope that you derive as much pleasure from using this volume as we derived from producing it.

IAN M. McDONALD
Sunshine Diaries Pty Ltd

CONTENTS

The daily "quotes" featured have been, in some respects, edited to improve clarity whilst carefully preserving the spirit of the original Journals.

All Bicentennial Events listed were correct at time of printing. Please check any revisions and additional events in your State Bicentennial Information Programme, or with the many Bicentennial Information Centres throughout Australia.

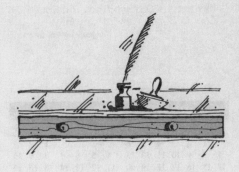

SUNSHINE DIARIES

MONDAY 28 DECEMBER

On this day in 1836
Governor Hindmarsh proclaims
Colony of South Australia

9.00	
9.30	
10.00	
10.30	
11.00	
11.30	
12.00	
12.30	
1.00	
1.30	
2.00	
2.30	
3.00	
3.30	
4.00	
4.30	
5.00	
5.30	
6.00	

NOTES

"A Gluorious Breas Contineus.
But. the Weather Hasey; a brest. the
Land of Lions on New Holland this
Day."

James Scott

TUESDAY 29 DECEMBER

On this day in 1916
Floods in Clermont, Qld claim 67 lives

9.00	
9.30	
10.00	
10.30	
11.00	
11.30	
12.00	
12.30	
1.00	
1.30	
2.00	
2.30	
3.00	
3.30	
4.00	
4.30	
5.00	
5.30	
6.00	

NOTES

"The bilge water very offensive
in mine and Mr Collins's Cabins
oblig'd to keep our doors open — it
spoil'd two Mezzatinted Prints in my
Cabin . . . We reckon ourselves this
day abt 1000 miles from the South
Cape & 2000 from Botany Bay."

Surgeon Bowes Smyth

WEDNESDAY 30 DECEMBER

On this day in 1821
N.S.W. Government issues first permits
for private distilleries

9.00	
9.30	
10.00	
10.30	
11.00	
11.30	
12.00	
12.30	
1.00	
1.30	
2.00	
2.30	
3.00	
3.30	
4.00	
4.30	
5.00	
5.30	
6.00	

NOTES

"It rain'd great part of the night
& the sea very high — We
sometimes ship'd Seas fore & aft the
water was sometimes ankle deep on
the quarter deck. This day by the
Log we Sail'd 200 miles."

Surgeon Bowes Smyth

JANUARY

M	T	W	T	F	S	S
				1	2	3
4	5	6	7	8	9	10
11	12	13	14	15	16	17
18	19	20	21	22	23	24
25	26	27	28	29	30	31

FEBRUARY

M	T	W	T	F	S	S
1	2	3	4	5	6	7
8	9	10	11	12	13	14
15	16	17	18	19	20	21
22	23	24	25	26	27	28
29						

MARCH

M	T	W	T	F	S	S
1	2	3	4	5	6	
7	8	9	10	11	12	13
14	15	16	17	18	19	20
21	22	23	24	25	26	27
28	29	30	31			

APRIL

M	T	W	T	F	S	S
				1	2	3
4	5	6	7	8	9	10
11	12	13	14	15	16	17
18	19	20	21	22	23	24
25	26	27	28	29	30	

MAY

M	T	W	T	F	S	S
30	31					1
2	3	4	5	6	7	8
9	10	11	12	13	14	15
16	17	18	19	20	21	22
23	24	25	26	27	28	29

JUNE

M	T	W	T	F	S	S
	1	2	3	4	5	
6	7	8	9	10	11	12
13	14	15	16	17	18	19
20	21	22	23	24	25	26
27	28	29	30			

THURSDAY 31 DECEMBER

On this day in 1908
Broken Hill miners begin six-month
strike over wage reductions

9.00	
9.30	
10.00	
10.30	
11.00	
11.30	
12.00	
12.30	
1.00	
1.30	
2.00	
2.30	
3.00	
3.30	
4.00	
4.30	
5.00	
5.30	
6.00	

NOTES

"This day many of the Women
were wash'd out of their Births by
the seas we ship'd . . . The Chicken
Coops which were on the Round
house & fasten'd very securely as It
was thought, gave way & came with
such violence against the side as to
drive the Goat house all in pieces &
lamed the Goat & Kidd."

Surgeon Bowes Smyth

FRIDAY 1 JANUARY

On this day in 1901
Commonwealth of Australia proclaimed:
Edmund Barton first Prime Minister

9.00	
9.30	
10.00	
10.30	
11.00	
11.30	
12.00	
12.30	
1.00	
1.30	
2.00	
2.30	
3.00	
3.30	
4.00	
4.30	
5.00	
5.30	
6.00	

NOTES

"Very heavy gales — violent
tumbling seas — as SUPPLY fights
her way into the New Year, our
position being close to the southern
tip of Van Diemen's Land". To
understand the conditions a remark
by Clark . . . "Oh I wish I had never
come . . . New Year's Day, hard salt
beef and musty pancakes."

Captain Phillip

SATURDAY 2 JANUARY

On this day in 1798
George Bass discovers the most southerly
point of mainland, Wilson's Promontory

"I see no further sight of land
and the gales and heavy seas are
growing worse, King reports that
SUPPLY was obliged for the first
time since leaving England to furl
her topsails as the brig now labours
very much and ships a great
quantity of water."

Captain Phillip

SUNDAY 3 JANUARY

On this day in 1941
AIF 6th Division attacks Bardia,
Libya, in WWII

EVENTS OF THE WEEK

QLD: Brisbane.
Tall Ships in port,
some open to the
public. 30th Dec. to
2nd Jan.

NSW/VIC: Albury-
Wodonga.
The Travelling
Australian
Bicentennial

Exhibition opens.
1st to 5th Jan.

VIC: Melbourne. Tall
Ships in Port
Melbourne. Open to
the public. 31st Dec.
and 1st Jan.

JULY								AUGUST						
M	T	W	T	F	S	S		M	T	W	T	F	S	S
		1	2	3									1	
4	5	6	7	8	9	10		8	9	10	11	12	13	14
11	12	13	14	15	16	17		15	16	17	18	19	20	21
18	19	20	21	22	23	24		22	23	24	25	26	27	28
25	26	27	28	29	30	31		29	30	31				

SEPTEMBER								OCTOBER						
M	T	W	T	F	S	S		M	T	W	T	F	S	S
			1	2	3	4		31					1	2
5	6	7	8	9	10	11		3	4	5	6	7	8	9
12	13	14	15	16	17	18		10	11	12	13	14	15	16
19	20	21	22	23	24	25		17	18	19	20	21	22	23
26	27	28	29	30				24	25	26	27	28	29	30

NOVEMBER								DECEMBER						
M	T	W	T	F	S	S		M	T	W	T	F	S	S
	1	2	3	4	5	6				1	2	3	4	
7	8	9	10	11	12	13		5	6	7	8	9	10	11
14	15	16	17	18	19	20		12	13	14	15	16	17	18
21	22	23	24	25	26	27		19	20	21	22	23	24	25
28	29	30						26	27	28	29	30	31	

On this day in 1688
William Dampier sights north-west
coast of Australia

9.00
9.30
10.00
10.30
11.00
11.30
12.00
12.30
1.00
1.30
2.00
2.30
3.00
3.30
4.00
4.30
5.00
5.30
6.00

NOTES

"King gave me a description of
the new land we were passing, Sir,
it is of good heighth but uneven.
Being obliged to make best use of
the westerly wind which then blew,
we could not explore this part of
the coast more than Captain Cook
has already done."

Captain Phillip

On this day in 1843
New South Wales Constitution proclaimed

9.00
9.30
10.00
10.30
11.00
11.30
12.00
12.30
1.00
1.30
2.00
2.30
3.00
3.30
4.00
4.30
5.00
5.30
6.00

NOTES

"The long trek north to Botany
Bay would now be much more
difficult than anticipated for we had
now lost our favourable winds"
Bradley reported from *SIRIUS*;
"There are now in the cabin,
Geraniums in full blossom, grape
vines, Bananas and several other
sorts of plants brought from Rio de
Janeiro."

Lieutenant Bradley

On this day in 1932
J.A. Lyons becomes Prime Minister

9.00
9.30
10.00
10.30
11.00
11.30
12.00
12.30
1.00
1.30
2.00
2.30
3.00
3.30
4.00
4.30
5.00
5.30
6.00

NOTES

It was reported from *SUPPLY* as
she moves up the East Coast that
the wind shifted suddenly to S.W. in
a very heavy squall which gave but
little warning. From the deck of the
SIRIUS, far behind the *SUPPLY*,
Bradley remarked that night, "the
Aurora Australis was very
bright . . ."

Lieutenant Bradley

JANUARY							FEBRUARY						
M	T	W	T	F	S	S	M	T	W	T	F	S	S
				1	2	3	1	2	3	4	5	6	7
4	5	6	7	8	9	10	8	9	10	11	12	13	14
11	12	13	14	15	16	17	15	16	17	18	19	20	21
18	19	20	21	22	23	24	22	23	24	25	26	27	28
25	26	27	28	29	30	31	29						

MARCH							APRIL						
M	T	W	T	F	S	S	M	T	W	T	F	S	S
1	2	3	4	5	6					1	2	3
7	8	9	10	11	12	13	4	5	6	7	8	9	10
14	15	16	17	18	19	20	11	12	13	14	15	16	17
21	22	23	24	25	26	27	18	19	20	21	22	23	24
28	29	30	31				25	26	27	28	29	30	

MAY							JUNE						
M	T	W	T	F	S	S	M	T	W	T	F	S	S
30	31					1			1	2	3	4	5
2	3	4	5	6	7	8	6	7	8	9	10	11	12
9	10	11	12	13	14	15	13	14	15	16	17	18	19
16	17	18	19	20	21	22	20	21	22	23	24	25	26
23	24	25	26	27	28	29	27	28	29	30			

THURSDAY 7 JANUARY

On this day in 1933
Aviation pioneer Bert Hinkler presumed
killed in plane crash near Florence, Italy.

9.00	
9.30	
10.00	
10.30	
11.00	
11.30	
12.00	
12.30	
1.00	
1.30	
2.00	
2.30	
3.00	
3.30	
4.00	
4.30	
5.00	
5.30	
6.00	

NOTES

SUPPLY is now making reasonable headway towards Botany Bay. The sighting of land inspired Surgeon White to praise Captain Hunter, "I believe a convoy was never conducted with more care, or made the land with more accuracy and certainty, than this. Indeed, ability and experienced nautical knowledge were never more evidenced on all occasions than by Captain Hunter . . ."
Surgeon White

FRIDAY 8 JANUARY

On this day in 1789
First child born on Norfolk Island:
named Norfolk

9.00	
9.30	
10.00	
10.30	
11.00	
11.30	
12.00	
12.30	
1.00	
1.30	
2.00	
2.30	
3.00	
3.30	
4.00	
4.30	
5.00	
5.30	
6.00	

NOTES

"Uncertain of what was beneath the ships in this unchartered stretch of coastline I ordered soundings to be frequently taken with 120 fathoms but could not get any ground. Collins believed the danger of accidents had been lessened because the convoy behaved well . . ."
Captain Phillip

SATURDAY 9 JANUARY

On this day in 1826
First Executive Council for
Van Diemen's Land appointed

"*SUPPLY* was now experiencing head on fresh gales from the northward. The fleet was sailing in very bad weather conditions and in fact were between 6 or 11 miles behind yesterday's position."
Captain Phillip

SUNDAY 10 JANUARY

On this day in 1868
Last convict ship to Australia arrives
in Western Australia

EVENTS OF THE WEEK

NSW: Sydney. Australasian Rotaract Conference. University of New South Wales. 9th to 16th Jan.

NSW: Sydney. Australian Bicentenary Baptist Celebration.

University of Sydney. 9th to 17th Jan.

TAS: Hobart. Tall Ships in port, some open to the public. 10th to 14th Jan.

JULY						
M	T	W	T	F	S	S
				1	2	3
4	5	6	7	8	9	10
11	12	13	14	15	16	17
18	19	20	21	22	23	24
25	26	27	28	29	30	31

AUGUST						
M	T	W	T	F	S	S
1	2	3	4	5	6	7
8	9	10	11	12	13	14
15	16	17	18	19	20	21
22	23	24	25	26	27	28
29	30	31				

SEPTEMBER						
M	T	W	T	F	S	S
	1	2	3	4		
5	6	7	8	9	10	11
12	13	14	15	16	17	18
19	20	21	22	23	24	25
26	27	28	29	30		

OCTOBER						
M	T	W	T	F	S	S
31					1	2
3	4	5	6	7	8	9
10	11	12	13	14	15	16
17	18	19	20	21	22	23
24	25	26	27	28	29	30

NOVEMBER						
M	T	W	T	F	S	S
1	2	3	4	5	6	
7	8	9	10	11	12	13
14	15	16	17	18	19	20
21	22	23	24	25	26	27
28	29	30				

DECEMBER						
M	T	W	T	F	S	S
		1	2	3	4	
5	6	7	8	9	10	11
12	13	14	15	16	17	18
19	20	21	22	23	24	25
26	27	28	29	30	31	

MONDAY 11 JANUARY

On this day in 1902
Fingerprinting of criminals
introduced in Sydney

9.00	
9.30	
10.00	
10.30	
11.00	
11.30	
12.00	
12.30	
1.00	
1.30	
2.00	
2.30	
3.00	
3.30	
4.00	
4.30	
5.00	
5.30	
6.00	

NOTES

"The ships of the fleet were recovering from the storm of the terrible tenth and spent the day repairing sails and reinforcing the rigging in anticipation of worse to come. *SUPPLY* was still having her progress severely retarded."

Captain Phillip

TUESDAY 12 JANUARY

On this day in 1799
Bass and Flinders return to Sydney after
circumnavigating Van Diemen's Land.

9.00	
9.30	
10.00	
10.30	
11.00	
11.30	
12.00	
12.30	
1.00	
1.30	
2.00	
2.30	
3.00	
3.30	
4.00	
4.30	
5.00	
5.30	
6.00	

NOTES

"*SUPPLY* was by now at the end of her tether, as she was within striking distance of Botany Bay, but could make little headway against the cruel north winds that chose to block her progress."

Captain Phillip

WEDNESDAY 13 JANUARY

On this day in 1933
Third, and most controversial, Test of the
"Bodyline" series commences in Adelaide

9.00	
9.30	
10.00	
10.30	
11.00	
11.30	
12.00	
12.30	
1.00	
1.30	
2.00	
2.30	
3.00	
3.30	
4.00	
4.30	
5.00	
5.30	
6.00	

NOTES

"I saw the land very clearly, but it was a case of so near and yet so far, as the winds blowing against us together with a strong tide we could no more approach Botany Bay and pass through the heads to anchor than a man can climb a greasy pole."

Captain Phillip

JANUARY
M	T	W	T	F	S	S
				1	2	3
4	5	6	7	8	9	10
11	12	13	14	15	16	17
18	19	20	21	22	23	24
25	26	27	28	29	30	31

FEBRUARY
M	T	W	T	F	S	S
1	2	3	4	5	6	7
8	9	10	11	12	13	14
15	16	17	18	19	20	21
22	23	24	25	26	27	28
29						

MARCH
M	T	W	T	F	S	S
1	2	3	4	5	6	
7	8	9	10	11	12	13
14	15	16	17	18	19	20
21	22	23	24	25	26	27
28	29	30	31			

APRIL
M	T	W	T	F	S	S
				1	2	3
4	5	6	7	8	9	10
11	12	13	14	15	16	17
18	19	20	21	22	23	24
25	26	27	28	29	30	

MAY
M	T	W	T	F	S	S
30	31				1	
2	3	4	5	6	7	8
9	10	11	12	13	14	15
16	17	18	19	20	21	22
23	24	25	26	27	28	29

JUNE
M	T	W	T	F	S	S
	1	2	3	4	5	
6	7	8	9	10	11	12
13	14	15	16	17	18	19
20	21	22	23	24	25	26
27	28	29	30			

THURSDAY 14 JANUARY

9.00	
9.30	
10.00	
10.30	
11.00	
11.30	
12.00	
12.30	
1.00	
1.30	
2.00	
2.30	
3.00	
3.30	
4.00	
4.30	
5.00	
5.30	
6.00	

NOTES

"Never has so great a difficulty been had in attempting to enter a bay, for today there was not a breeze sufficiently strong to rundown the distance to Botany Bay."

Lieutenant King

FRIDAY 15 JANUARY

9.00	
9.30	
10.00	
10.30	
11.00	
11.30	
12.00	
12.30	
1.00	
1.30	
2.00	
2.30	
3.00	
3.30	
4.00	
4.30	
5.00	
5.30	
6.00	

NOTES

"Though we tacked the SUPPLY four times in the course of the day, our little brig gained, then lost ground on trying to approach the elusive Botany Bay entrance, the winds and the currents are still against us. We have experienced 24 hours of sheer frustration."

Captain Phillip

SATURDAY 16 JANUARY

"We repeated the pattern of approach and fall back on the SUPPLY but once again could not go forward to our destination. The rest of the fleet, also experiencing bad conditions were still struggling up the east coast unaware of the frustrations of the SUPPLY".

Captain Phillip

SUNDAY 17 JANUARY

EVENTS OF THE WEEK

VIC: Bendigo. The Travelling Australian Bicentennial Exhibition opens. 11th to 14th Jan.
TAS: Hobart. The Tall Ships Race commences, the ships race to Sydney. 14th Jan.

SA: Noarlunga. International Long Distance Swimming Championships commence. Port Noarlunga Beach. 16th to 17th Jan.

JULY							AUGUST						
M	T	W	T	F	S	S	M	T	W	T	F	S	S
				1	2	3	1	2	3	4	5	6	7
4	5	6	7	8	9	10	8	9	10	11	12	13	14
11	12	13	14	15	16	17	15	16	17	18	19	20	21
18	19	20	21	22	23	24	22	23	24	25	26	27	28
25	26	27	28	29	30	31	29	30	31				

SEPTEMBER							OCTOBER						
M	T	W	T	F	S	S	M	T	W	T	F	S	S
		1	2	3	4	31						1	2
5	6	7	8	9	10	11	3	4	5	6	7	8	9
12	13	14	15	16	17	18	10	11	12	13	14	15	16
19	20	21	22	23	24	25	17	18	19	20	21	22	23
26	27	28	29	30			24	25	26	27	28	29	30

NOVEMBER							DECEMBER						
M	T	W	T	F	S	S	M	T	W	T	F	S	S
1	2	3	4	5	6				1	2	3	4
7	8	9	10	11	12	13	5	6	7	8	9	10	11
14	15	16	17	18	19	20	12	13	14	15	16	17	18
21	22	23	24	25	26	27	19	20	21	22	23	24	25
28	29	30					26	27	28	29	30	31	

MONDAY 18 JANUARY

On this day in 1788
Governor Arthur Phillip enters Botany Bay

9.00	
9.30	
10.00	
10.30	
11.00	
11.30	
12.00	
12.30	
1.00	
1.30	
2.00	
2.30	
3.00	
3.30	
4.00	
4.30	
5.00	
5.30	
6.00	

NOTES

"Today the long awaited day eventually came as *SUPPLY* hauled in for Botany Bay. At three Lt. Dawes, King, myself and some officers on *SUPPLY* landed on the northerly side . . . We observed some natives, I think it is easy to conceive the ridiculous figure we must appear to these poor creatures, who are perfectly naked."

Captain Phillip

TUESDAY 19 JANUARY

On this day in 1790
Second Fleet sails for New South Wales
carrying 1006 convicts

9.00	
9.30	
10.00	
10.30	
11.00	
11.30	
12.00	
12.30	
1.00	
1.30	
2.00	
2.30	
3.00	
3.30	
4.00	
4.30	
5.00	
5.30	
6.00	

NOTES

"The *SUPPLY* sailing very badly . . . I began to examine the bay as soon as we were anchored. We left in longboats at 11 o'clock returning at 6 o'clock, having not sited natives, only their huts, did not find any suitable area to establish the colony."

Captain Phillip

WEDNESDAY 20 JANUARY

On this day in 1966
Sir Robert Menzies retires as P.M. after
record term of 17 years

9.00	
9.30	
10.00	
10.30	
11.00	
11.30	
12.00	
12.30	
1.00	
1.30	
2.00	
2.30	
3.00	
3.30	
4.00	
4.30	
5.00	
5.30	
6.00	

NOTES

"On shore today we had people from the *SUPPLY, FRIENDSHIP, SCARBOROUGH* and *ALEXANDER* hurriedly cut grass for the remaining livestock, catch fish for the humans, make peace with the natives and try to find running water and good soil for a land base, but none seemed suitable."

Captain Phillip

JANUARY
M	T	W	T	F	S	S
				1	2	3
4	5	6	7	8	9	10
11	12	13	14	15	16	17
18	19	20	21	22	23	24
25	26	27	28	29	30	31

FEBRUARY
M	T	W	T	F	S	S
1	2	3	4	5	6	7
8	9	10	11	12	13	14
15	16	17	18	19	20	21
22	23	24	25	26	27	28
29						

MARCH
M	T	W	T	F	S	S
1	2	3	4	5	6	
7	8	9	10	11	12	13
14	15	16	17	18	19	20
21	22	23	24	25	26	27
28	29	30	31			

APRIL
M	T	W	T	F	S	S
				1	2	3
4	5	6	7	8	9	10
11	12	13	14	15	16	17
18	19	20	21	22	23	24
25	26	27	28	29	30	

MAY
M	T	W	T	F	S	S
30	31					1
2	3	4	5	6	7	8
9	10	11	12	13	14	15
16	17	18	19	20	21	22
23	24	25	26	27	28	29

JUNE
M	T	W	T	F	S	S
		1	2	3	4	5
6	7	8	9	10	11	12
13	14	15	16	17	18	19
20	21	22	23	24	25	26
27	28	29	30			

THURSDAY 21 JANUARY

On this day in 1788
Governor Phillip enters Port Jackson and lands at Camp Cove

9.00	
9.30	
10.00	
10.30	
11.00	
11.30	
12.00	
12.30	
1.00	
1.30	
2.00	
2.30	
3.00	
3.30	
4.00	
4.30	
5.00	
5.30	
6.00	

NOTES

"We . . . had the satisfaction of finding the finest harbour in the world, in which a thousand sail-of-the-line may ride in the most perfect security." Phillip, happy with this location and the particular cove he named Sydney, camped overnight and next morning commenced the return to Botany Bay.

Captain Phillip

FRIDAY 22 JANUARY

On this day in 1931
Sir Isaac Isaacs, first Australian-born Governor-General takes up office.

9.00	
9.30	
10.00	
10.30	
11.00	
11.30	
12.00	
12.30	
1.00	
1.30	
2.00	
2.30	
3.00	
3.30	
4.00	
4.30	
5.00	
5.30	
6.00	

NOTES

"I have given the name Manly Cove to this place today, because of the confidence and manly behaviour shown by the natives. They seemed desirous of our hats and attempted to seize some. Like King, Bowes had to order pants to be pulled down for the 'Indians'. They expressed a wish to know of what sex we were."

Captain Phillip

SATURDAY 23 JANUARY

On this day in 1982
Colin Hayes trains seven of the eight winners at Victoria Park: an Australian record

"We arrived back in our little boats in the evening and I immediately sent a signal from *SIRIUS* for the agent and the masters of all the transports to come aboard. They were ordered to prepare their ships for sea immediately. Clark delighted with the projected move to Port Jackson."

Captain Phillip

SUNDAY 24 JANUARY

On this day in 1788
French explorer Jean La Perouse arrives off Botany Bay, six days after Phillip.

EVENTS OF THE WEEK

NSW: Sydney. Tall Ships in port, some open to the public. 19th to 26th Jan.

VIC: Geelong. The Travelling Australian Bicentennial Exhibition opens. 21st to 26th Jan.

ACT: Canberra. Australian Bicentennial Dog Show commences. Australian National University. 23rd to 26th Jan.

JULY							AUGUST						
M	T	W	T	F	S	S	M	T	W	T	F	S	S
				1	2	3	1	2	3	4	5	6	7
4	5	6	7	8	9	10	8	9	10	11	12	13	14
11	12	13	14	15	16	17	15	16	17	18	19	20	21
18	19	20	21	22	23	24	22	23	24	25	26	27	28
25	26	27	28	29	30	31	29	30	31				

SEPTEMBER							OCTOBER						
M	T	W	T	F	S	S	M	T	W	T	F	S	S
			1	2	3	4	31					1	2
5	6	7	8	9	10	11	3	4	5	6	7	8	9
12	13	14	15	16	17	18	10	11	12	13	14	15	16
19	20	21	22	23	24	25	17	18	19	20	21	22	23
26	27	28	29	30			24	25	26	27	28	29	30

NOVEMBER							DECEMBER						
M	T	W	T	F	S	S	M	T	W	T	F	S	S
1	2	3	4	5	6				1	2	3	4
7	8	9	10	11	12	13	5	6	7	8	9	10	11
14	15	16	17	18	19	20	12	13	14	15	16	17	18
21	22	23	24	25	26	27	19	20	21	22	23	24	25
28	29	30					26	27	28	29	30	31	

MONDAY 25 JANUARY

On this day in 1974
Devastating floods hit Brisbane: 13 lives lost

9.00	
9.30	
10.00	
10.30	
11.00	
11.30	
12.00	
12.30	
1.00	
1.30	
2.00	
2.30	
3.00	
3.30	
4.00	
4.30	
5.00	
5.30	
6.00	

NOTES

"At 6 am the *SIRIUS* made the signal for all ships to weigh. Mr Clark expressed his views to me on the transfer to Port Jackson in unmistakable terms, 'I am very happy that we are not to stay here, for if we had stayed here, it would have been the grave of all of us'."

Captain Phillip

TUESDAY 26 JANUARY

On this day in 1788
Governor Phillip takes formal possession of colony of New South Wales

9.00	
9.30	
10.00	
10.30	
11.00	
11.30	
12.00	
12.30	
1.00	
1.30	
2.00	
2.30	
3.00	
3.30	
4.00	
4.30	
5.00	
5.30	
6.00	

NOTES

"A flagstaff was erected at Sydney Cove and possession was taken for His Majesty. In the evening the whole of the party that came round in *SUPPLY* were assembled at the point where they had landed and a Union Jack displayed, I and my officers drank the health of His Majesty and success to the new colony."

Captain Phillip

WEDNESDAY 27 JANUARY

On this day in 1859
The paddle steamer "Albury" pioneers Darling River, N.S.W.

9.00	
9.30	
10.00	
10.30	
11.00	
11.30	
12.00	
12.30	
1.00	
1.30	
2.00	
2.30	
3.00	
3.30	
4.00	
4.30	
5.00	
5.30	
6.00	

NOTES

"I gave strict orders that the natives should not be offended, or molested on any account, and advised that wherever they were met with, they were to be treated with every mark of friendship. In case of their stealing anything, mild means were to be used to recover it, but on no account to fire at them with ball or shot."

Captain Phillip

JANUARY							FEBRUARY						
M	T	W	T	F	S	S	M	T	W	T	F	S	S
				1	2	3	1	2	3	4	5	6	7
4	5	6	7	8	9	10	8	9	10	11	12	13	14
11	12	13	14	15	16	17	15	16	17	18	19	20	21
18	19	20	21	22	23	24	22	23	24	25	26	27	28
25	26	27	28	29	30	31	29						

MARCH							APRIL						
M	T	W	T	F	S	S	M	T	W	T	F	S	S
1	2	3	4	5	6					1	2	3
7	8	9	10	11	12	13	4	5	6	7	8	9	10
14	15	16	17	18	19	20	11	12	13	14	15	16	17
21	22	23	24	25	26	27	18	19	20	21	22	23	24
28	29	30	31				25	26	27	28	29	30	

MAY							JUNE						
M	T	W	T	F	S	S	M	T	W	T	F	S	S
30	31					1			1	2	3	4	5
2	3	4	5	6	7	8	6	7	8	9	10	11	12
9	10	11	12	13	14	15	13	14	15	16	17	18	19
16	17	18	19	20	21	22	20	21	22	23	24	25	26
23	24	25	26	27	28	29	27	28	29	30			

THURSDAY 28 JANUARY

On this day in 1893
Federal Bank of Australia closes in
Melbourne starting bank crash

9.00	
9.30	
10.00	
10.30	
11.00	
11.30	
12.00	
12.30	
1.00	
1.30	
2.00	
2.30	
3.00	
3.30	
4.00	
4.30	
5.00	
5.30	
6.00	

NOTES

"I note the native women keep at a distance and stand near the man with the spears. This mark of attention showing us that, although they met us unarmed they had arms ready to protect them, increased my favourable opinion of them. My plan with respect to the natives was, if possible, to cultivate an aquaintance with them."

Captain Phillip

FRIDAY 29 JANUARY

On this day in 1854
First Australian cotton exported to England

9.00	
9.30	
10.00	
10.30	
11.00	
11.30	
12.00	
12.30	
1.00	
1.30	
2.00	
2.30	
3.00	
3.30	
4.00	
4.30	
5.00	
5.30	
6.00	

NOTES

"Today my Judge Advocate David Collins reflected, 'if only it were possible that on taking possession of nature as we had thus done, in her simplest, purest garb, we might not sully that purity by the introduction of vice, profaneness and immorality.' But this though much to be wished, was little to be expected."

Phillip quoting Judge Advocate Collins

SATURDAY 30 JANUARY

On this day in 1897
Tasmania has first election under
Hare-Clark System — proportional voting

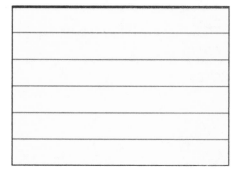

"The natives are all entirely naked . . . The men had their beards long and very bushy . . . Their noses are somewhat flat, and all those that we noticed had a hole bored through which they sometimes put a stick or small bone. Most of these natives had lost one of their front teeth, their skins are much scarred. They walk very upright . . ."

Captain Phillip

SUNDAY 31 JANUARY

On this day in 1942
Government mobilizes Australian workforce;
manpower regulations implemented

EVENTS OF THE WEEK

NSW: Sydney. First Fleet Re-Enactment. Farm Cove. 26th Jan.

NSW: Sydney. Tall Ships Grand Parade out of Sydney Harbour. 26th Jan.

NSW: Sydney. Bicentennial Collection 1988 — International Wool Event. Opera House. 31st Jan.

JULY							AUGUST						
M	T	W	T	F	S	S	M	T	W	T	F	S	S
				1	2	3	1	2	3	4	5	6	7
4	5	6	7	8	9	10	8	9	10	11	12	13	14
11	12	13	14	15	16	17	15	16	17	18	19	20	21
18	19	20	21	22	23	24	22	23	24	25	26	27	28
25	26	27	28	29	30	31	29	30	31				

SEPTEMBER							OCTOBER						
M	T	W	T	F	S	S	M	T	W	T	F	S	S
		1	2	3	4		31					1	2
5	6	7	8	9	10	11	3	4	5	6	7	8	9
12	13	14	15	16	17	18	10	11	12	13	14	15	16
19	20	21	22	23	24	25	17	18	19	20	21	22	23
26	27	28	29	30			24	25	26	27	28	29	30

NOVEMBER							DECEMBER						
M	T	W	T	F	S	S	M	T	W	T	F	S	S
1	2	3	4	5	6				1	2	3	4	
7	8	9	10	11	12	13	5	6	7	8	9	10	11
14	15	16	17	18	19	20	12	13	14	15	16	17	18
21	22	23	24	25	26	27	19	20	21	22	23	24	25
28	29	30					26	27	28	29	30	31	

MONDAY 1 FEBRUARY

On this day in 1858
William Dean makes first balloon
ascent in Australia

9.00	
9.30	
10.00	
10.30	
11.00	
11.30	
12.00	
12.30	
1.00	
1.30	
2.00	
2.30	
3.00	
3.30	
4.00	
4.30	
5.00	
5.30	
6.00	

NOTES

"The start of our first full month on shore, I realise that I will have little help and a lot of hindrance from Major Ross, the man appointed to be my Lieutenant-Governor and Commander of the Marines . . . I had not been asked to choose any of the personnel for the settlement."

Captain Phillip

TUESDAY 2 FEBRUARY

On this day in 1829
Sturt discovers the Darling River

9.00	
9.30	
10.00	
10.30	
11.00	
11.30	
12.00	
12.30	
1.00	
1.30	
2.00	
2.30	
3.00	
3.30	
4.00	
4.30	
5.00	
5.30	
6.00	

NOTES

"I am beginning to realise that the marine soldiers are becoming discontented and bored as there is little soldiering to be done and it seems their main pastime is quarrelling. The permanent strain of having to be careful that I do not offend any of the military officers . . . at times becomes intolerable."

Captain Phillip

WEDNESDAY 3 FEBRUARY

On this day in 1788
First church service in Australia
at Sydney Cove

9.00	
9.30	
10.00	
10.30	
11.00	
11.30	
12.00	
12.30	
1.00	
1.30	
2.00	
2.30	
3.00	
3.30	
4.00	
4.30	
5.00	
5.30	
6.00	

NOTES

"The Rev. Richard Johnson, our official chaplain to the settlement conducted the first divine service in Sydney preached in the open air on a text from Psalm 116."

Captain Phillip

JANUARY							FEBRUARY						
M	T	W	T	F	S	S	M	T	W	T	F	S	S
				1	2	3	1	2	3	4	5	6	7
4	5	6	7	8	9	10	8	9	10	11	12	13	14
11	12	13	14	15	16	17	15	16	17	18	19	20	21
18	19	20	21	22	23	24	22	23	24	25	26	27	28
25	26	27	28	29	30	31	29						

MARCH							APRIL						
M	T	W	T	F	S	S	M	T	W	T	F	S	S
1	2	3	4	5	6						1	2	3
7	8	9	10	11	12	13	4	5	6	7	8	9	10
14	15	16	17	18	19	20	11	12	13	14	15	16	17
21	22	23	24	25	26	27	18	19	20	21	22	23	24
28	29	30	31				25	26	27	28	29	30	

MAY							JUNE						
M	T	W	T	F	S	S	M	T	W	T	F	S	S
30	31					1			1	2	3	4	5
2	3	4	5	6	7	8	6	7	8	9	10	11	12
9	10	11	12	13	14	15	13	14	15	16	17	18	19
16	17	18	19	20	21	22	20	21	22	23	24	25	26
23	24	25	26	27	28	29	27	28	29	30			

THURSDAY 4 FEBRUARY

On this day in 1874
Mark Bell becomes first Australian-born
winner of Victoria Cross

9.00	
9.30	
10.00	
10.30	
11.00	
11.30	
12.00	
12.30	
1.00	
1.30	
2.00	
2.30	
3.00	
3.30	
4.00	
4.30	
5.00	
5.30	
6.00	

NOTES

"We are now 9 days since original settlement and some of the animals we have seen include Kangaroos about as big as large sheep; a very large species of Lizard, Dogs, Rats, Raccoons, Flying Squirrels, very large Snakes, a Bird of a new genus, as large as an Ostrich. Many species of Cockatoos . . . great quantities of Ants . . . many Flies and Musquito's."

Captain Phillip

FRIDAY 5 FEBRUARY

On this day in 1869
"Welcome Stranger" gold nugget,
weighing 2284 ounces, found

9.00	
9.30	
10.00	
10.30	
11.00	
11.30	
12.00	
12.30	
1.00	
1.30	
2.00	
2.30	
3.00	
3.30	
4.00	
4.30	
5.00	
5.30	
6.00	

NOTES

". . . we found fish aplenty, although the harbour is full of sharks . . . oysters very large."

Lieutenant Bradley

". . . all the tents of the battalion have been pitched, likewise those for the convicts, my tent house up and some culinary seeds put in . . . a few beans, peas, small salad that was sown on our arrival have come up . . ."

Surgeon Worgan

SATURDAY 6 FEBRUARY

On this day in 1952
Queen Elizabeth II succeeds her father,
King George VI

"All the convicts are now disembarked and at night when the last of the women convicts were landed, the blackening skies released a most terrible tropical storm. The male convicts unleashed frustrations built up in the twelve months they had been chained below decks, broke loose from their temporary gaol-yard and into the women's camps."

Captain Phillip

SUNDAY 7 FEBRUARY

On this day in 1788
Colony of New South Wales proclaimed

EVENTS OF THE WEEK

NSW: Sydney. Navigation Congress commences. University of New South Wales. 2nd to 5th Feb.

TAS: Deloraine. The Bicentennial Cattle Drive on the Borradaile Plain. 5th to 7th Feb.

SA: Mt. Gambier. The Travelling Australian Bicentennial Exhibition opens. 1st to 4th Feb.

JULY							AUGUST						
M	T	W	T	F	S	S	M	T	W	T	F	S	S
			1	2	3		1	2	3	4	5	6	7
4	5	6	7	8	9	10	8	9	10	11	12	13	14
11	12	13	14	15	16	17	15	16	17	18	19	20	21
18	19	20	21	22	23	24	22	23	24	25	26	27	28
25	26	27	28	29	30	31	29	30	31				

SEPTEMBER							OCTOBER						
M	T	W	T	F	S	S	M	T	W	T	F	S	S
		1	2	3	4		31					1	2
5	6	7	8	9	10	11	3	4	5	6	7	8	9
12	13	14	15	16	17	18	10	11	12	13	14	15	16
19	20	21	22	23	24	25	17	18	19	20	21	22	23
26	27	28	29	30			24	25	26	27	28	29	30

NOVEMBER							DECEMBER						
M	T	W	T	F	S	S	M	T	W	T	F	S	S
1	2	3	4	5	6				1	2	3	4
7	8	9	10	11	12	13	5	6	7	8	9	10	11
14	15	16	17	18	19	20	12	13	14	15	16	17	18
21	22	23	24	25	26	27	19	20	21	22	23	24	25
28	29	30					26	27	28	29	30	31	

MONDAY 8 FEBRUARY

On this day in 1952
"The Northern Territory News" first
published in Darwin

9.00	
9.30	
10.00	
10.30	
11.00	
11.30	
12.00	
12.30	
1.00	
1.30	
2.00	
2.30	
3.00	
3.30	
4.00	
4.30	
5.00	
5.30	
6.00	

NOTES

"Worgan, with others, visited Botany Bay by land (about ten miles) to pay a visit to the French Officers (serving with La Perouse, who had anchored at Botany Bay after Phillip had left). The French told how some convicts had been over and applied earnestly to be taken on board. The French did not entertain them."

Captain Phillip

TUESDAY 9 FEBRUARY

On this day in 1923
S.M. Bruce becomes Prime Minister

9.00	
9.30	
10.00	
10.30	
11.00	
11.30	
12.00	
12.30	
1.00	
1.30	
2.00	
2.30	
3.00	
3.30	
4.00	
4.30	
5.00	
5.30	
6.00	

NOTES

". . . my attitude enables me to stand before you as one human being to another, I appeal to whatever goodness is in you to face this new opportunity and to accept the necessary discipline to make something more of yourselves. The laws affecting this colony are English laws, they are not Phillip's laws."

Captain Phillip in a speech to the convicts

WEDNESDAY 10 FEBRUARY

On this day in 1964
82 dead after collision between
HMAS "Voyager" and HMAS "Melbourne".

9.00	
9.30	
10.00	
10.30	
11.00	
11.30	
12.00	
12.30	
1.00	
1.30	
2.00	
2.30	
3.00	
3.30	
4.00	
4.30	
5.00	
5.30	
6.00	

NOTES

"Despite the number of weddings Mr Clark reported that he was troubled by the immorality in the settlement. He was sure that some of the people getting married had spouses in England and regards his surroundings as most unsavoury."

Captain Phillip

JANUARY							FEBRUARY						
M	T	W	T	F	S	S	M	T	W	T	F	S	S
				1	2	3	1	2	3	4	5	6	7
4	5	6	7	8	9	10	8	9	10	11	12	13	14
11	12	13	14	15	16	17	15	16	17	18	19	20	21
18	19	20	21	22	23	24	22	23	24	25	26	27	28
25	26	27	28	29	30	31	29						

MARCH							APRIL						
M	T	W	T	F	S	S	M	T	W	T	F	S	S
1	2	3	4	5	6					1	2	3	
7	8	9	10	11	12	13	4	5	6	7	8	9	10
14	15	16	17	18	19	20	11	12	13	14	15	16	17
21	22	23	24	25	26	27	18	19	20	21	22	23	24
28	29	30	31				25	26	27	28	29	30	

MAY							JUNE						
M	T	W	T	F	S	S	M	T	W	T	F	S	S
30	31					1			1	2	3	4	5
2	3	4	5	6	7	8	6	7	8	9	10	11	12
9	10	11	12	13	14	15	13	14	15	16	17	18	19
16	17	18	19	20	21	22	20	21	22	23	24	25	26
23	24	25	26	27	28	29	27	28	29	30			

THURSDAY 11 FEBRUARY

On this day in 1861
Burke and Wills reach Gulf of Carpentaria

9.00	
9.30	
10.00	
10.30	
11.00	
11.30	
12.00	
12.30	
1.00	
1.30	
2.00	
2.30	
3.00	
3.30	
4.00	
4.30	
5.00	
5.30	
6.00	

NOTES

"Bramwell, a marine has been sentenced to 200 lashes for striking a female convict, and Barsby, a convict to only 150 lashes for striking a sentry, Bowes noted that this severity shown to the marines and lenity to the convicts has already excited great . . . discontent among the corps . . . shot a Kangaroo . . . it is nearly equal in goodness to venison."

Captain Phillip

FRIDAY 12 FEBRUARY

On this day in 1851
E.H. Hargraves discovers gold

9.00	
9.30	
10.00	
10.30	
11.00	
11.30	
12.00	
12.30	
1.00	
1.30	
2.00	
2.30	
3.00	
3.30	
4.00	
4.30	
5.00	
5.30	
6.00	

NOTES

"At the request of several officers who had not been present on the 7th my commission were read a second time. My Lieutenant-Governor and Judge Advocate were sworn in as Justices of the peace and Lt. King took the oath as Superintendant and Commanding Officer of Norfolk Island. I have signed all instructions and commission for Lt. King."

Captain Phillip

SATURDAY 13 FEBRUARY

On this day in 1832
King's School at Parramatta opens.

Phillip took the oath of Abjuration and Assurance and further made this declaration, "I, Arthur Phillip, do declare, that I do believe that there is not any transubstantiation in the sacrement of the Lord's supper, or in the elements of bread and wine, at or after the consecration thereof by any person . . ."

Captain Phillip

SUNDAY 14 FEBRUARY

On this day in 1966
Decimal currency introduced

EVENTS OF THE WEEK

QLD: Toowoomba. The National Concours — A tribute to 200 years of transport. Toowoomba Showground. 12th to 14th Feb.

VIC: Mildura. The Travelling Australian

Bicentennial Exhibition opens. 11th to 14th Feb.

WA: Perth. The Festival of Perth commences. 12th Feb. to 5th Mar.

JULY							AUGUST						
M	T	W	T	F	S	S	M	T	W	T	F	S	S
				1	2	3	1	2	3	4	5	6	7
4	5	6	7	8	9	10	8	9	10	11	12	13	14
11	12	13	14	15	16	17	15	16	17	18	19	20	21
18	19	20	21	22	23	24	22	23	24	25	26	27	28
25	26	27	28	29	30	31	29	30	31				

SEPTEMBER							OCTOBER						
M	T	W	T	F	S	S	M	T	W	T	F	S	S
			1	2	3	4	31					1	2
5	6	7	8	9	10	11	3	4	5	6	7	8	9
12	13	14	15	16	17	18	10	11	12	13	14	15	16
19	20	21	22	23	24	25	17	18	19	20	21	22	23
26	27	28	29	30			24	25	26	27	28	29	30

NOVEMBER							DECEMBER						
M	T	W	T	F	S	S	M	T	W	T	F	S	S
1	2	3	4	5	6				1	2	3	4
7	8	9	10	11	12	13	5	6	7	8	9	10	11
14	15	16	17	18	19	20	12	13	14	15	16	17	18
21	22	23	24	25	26	27	19	20	21	22	23	24	25
28	29	30					26	27	28	29	30	31	

MONDAY 15 FEBRUARY

On this day in 1942
Japanese capture Singapore: over 15,000
Australian troops imprisoned

9.00	
9.30	
10.00	
10.30	
11.00	
11.30	
12.00	
12.30	
1.00	
1.30	
2.00	
2.30	
3.00	
3.30	
4.00	
4.30	
5.00	
5.30	
6.00	

NOTES

"The cook of the *PRINCE OF WALES* (a negro) going on shore by the hawser rope was shacked off it and drowned. My Judge Advocate Collins sentenced two women to receive 25 lashes each for theft, and one man 45 lashes for theft. The *SUPPLY* cleared the heads at 8 am bound for Norfolk Island."

Captain Phillip

TUESDAY 16 FEBRUARY

On this day in 1983
"Ash Wednesday" bushfires sweep
southern Australia: 73 die

9.00	
9.30	
10.00	
10.30	
11.00	
11.30	
12.00	
12.30	
1.00	
1.30	
2.00	
2.30	
3.00	
3.30	
4.00	
4.30	
5.00	
5.30	
6.00	

NOTES

Clark gave the following graphic picture in a letter to his wife. "I was very ill with a toothache and had it out by Mr Consident. I thought that half my head would have come off, there is a piece of the jawbone remaining to the tooth. The pain was so great, that I fainted away, I would not let Consident report to Major Ross but rather did my picket . . ."

2nd Lieutenant Clark

WEDNESDAY 17 FEBRUARY

On this day in 1788
Lt. H.L. Ball sights Lord Howe Island during
HMS "Supply" trip to Norfolk Island

9.00	
9.30	
10.00	
10.30	
11.00	
11.30	
12.00	
12.30	
1.00	
1.30	
2.00	
2.30	
3.00	
3.30	
4.00	
4.30	
5.00	
5.30	
6.00	

NOTES

"Reverend Richard Johnson celebrated the first Holy Communion in the Colony at Sydney today."

Captain Phillip

JANUARY							FEBRUARY						
M	T	W	T	F	S	S	M	T	W	T	F	S	S
			1	2	3		1	2	3	4	5	6	7
4	5	6	7	8	9	10	8	9	10	11	12	13	14
11	12	13	14	15	16	17	15	16	17	18	19	20	21
18	19	20	21	22	23	24	22	23	24	25	26	27	28
25	26	27	28	29	30	31	29						

MARCH							APRIL						
M	T	W	T	F	S	S	M	T	W	T	F	S	S
1	2	3	4	5	6					1	2	3	
7	8	9	10	11	12	13	4	5	6	7	8	9	10
14	15	16	17	18	19	20	11	12	13	14	15	16	17
21	22	23	24	25	26	27	18	19	20	21	22	23	24
28	29	30	31				25	26	27	28	29	30	

MAY							JUNE						
M	T	W	T	F	S	S	M	T	W	T	F	S	S
30	31				1				1	2	3	4	5
2	3	4	5	6	7	8	6	7	8	9	10	11	12
9	10	11	12	13	14	15	13	14	15	16	17	18	19
16	17	18	19	20	21	22	20	21	22	23	24	25	26
23	24	25	26	27	28	29	27	28	29	30			

THURSDAY 18 FEBRUARY

On this day in 1793
Rev. Richard Johnson opens first
church school in Sydney

9.00	
9.30	
10.00	
10.30	
11.00	
11.30	
12.00	
12.30	
1.00	
1.30	
2.00	
2.30	
3.00	
3.30	
4.00	
4.30	
5.00	
5.30	
6.00	

NOTES

Phillip made special note today
by recording, "Today I left the
SIRIUS to take up permanent
residence on shore in, as we now
call it, Sydney."

Captain Phillip

FRIDAY 19 FEBRUARY

On this day in 1942
Darwin bombed by Japanese:
approximately 250 killed

9.00	
9.30	
10.00	
10.30	
11.00	
11.30	
12.00	
12.30	
1.00	
1.30	
2.00	
2.30	
3.00	
3.30	
4.00	
4.30	
5.00	
5.30	
6.00	

NOTES

"I have allocated a small piece
of land to each convict to grow
things for himself, I am trying to
give some interest and incentive by
setting them all a certain time in
which to complete their jobs for the
day. If they finish early I will allow
them to work on their own plots of
land. The main concern I have for
the settlement is still clearing and
building."

Captain Phillip

SATURDAY 20 FEBRUARY

On this day in 1960
Sir Frank MacFarlane Burnet awarded
Nobel Prize for medicine

"I am doing everything possible
to stop the situation turning into an
uncontrollable scramble for survival.
I have encouraged marriage so that
some sort of stability might be
brought into the chaotic situation. I
feel that it is everyone for himself
and that I am the only one for all."

Captain Phillip

SUNDAY 21 FEBRUARY

On this day in 1929
Peacetime compulsory military
training abolished

EVENTS OF THE WEEK

NSW: Sydney.
International Youth
Skill Olympics.
Darling Harbour
Exhibition Centre.
18th to 22nd Feb.
SA: Port Pirie.
The Travelling
Australian
Bicentennial
Exhibition opens.
20th to 23rd Feb.

NT: Darwin. The
Territory Connection
— a convoy of
veteran and vintage
cars leaves Darwin
for Adelaide. 21st
Feb.

JULY							AUGUST						
M	T	W	T	F	S	S	M	T	W	T	F	S	S
				1	2	3	1	2	3	4	5	6	7
4	5	6	7	8	9	10	8	9	10	11	12	13	14
11	12	13	14	15	16	17	15	16	17	18	19	20	21
18	19	20	21	22	23	24	22	23	24	25	26	27	28
25	26	27	28	29	30	31	29	30	31				

SEPTEMBER							OCTOBER						
M	T	W	T	F	S	S	M	T	W	T	F	S	S
			1	2	3	4	31					1	2
5	6	7	8	9	10	11	3	4	5	6	7	8	9
12	13	14	15	16	17	18	10	11	12	13	14	15	16
19	20	21	22	23	24	25	17	18	19	20	21	22	23
26	27	28	29	30			24	25	26	27	28	29	30

NOVEMBER							DECEMBER						
M	T	W	T	F	S	S	M	T	W	T	F	S	S
	1	2	3	4	5	6			1	2	3	4	
7	8	9	10	11	12	13	5	6	7	8	9	10	11
14	15	16	17	18	19	20	12	13	14	15	16	17	18
21	22	23	24	25	26	27	19	20	21	22	23	24	25
28	29	30					26	27	28	29	30	31	

MONDAY 22 FEBRUARY

On this day in 1791
First Australian land grant
issued to James Ruse

9.00	
9.30	
10.00	
10.30	
11.00	
11.30	
12.00	
12.30	
1.00	
1.30	
2.00	
2.30	
3.00	
3.30	
4.00	
4.30	
5.00	
5.30	
6.00	

NOTES

"Many of the colony are in the business of catching possums and are doing a brisk trade with ships crews in exchange for food and rum."

Captain Phillip

TUESDAY 23 FEBRUARY

On this day in 1931
Dame Nellie Melba dies

9.00	
9.30	
10.00	
10.30	
11.00	
11.30	
12.00	
12.30	
1.00	
1.30	
2.00	
2.30	
3.00	
3.30	
4.00	
4.30	
5.00	
5.30	
6.00	

NOTES

"I have endeavoured to lay out my first plan for the settlement, . . . The ground marked for Government House will include the main guard, civil, and criminal courts . . . Land will be granted with a clause that will ever prevent more than one house being built in the allotment which will be 50 ft in front and 150 ft in depth."

Captain Phillip

WEDNESDAY 24 FEBRUARY

On this day in 1817
Barron Field, first Supreme Court judge,
arrives in Sydney

9.00	
9.30	
10.00	
10.30	
11.00	
11.30	
12.00	
12.30	
1.00	
1.30	
2.00	
2.30	
3.00	
3.30	
4.00	
4.30	
5.00	
5.30	
6.00	

NOTES

"Many convicts are coming in from the bush where they should not have been, telling me tales about the natives, but I suspect that it might have been the convicts who provoked the natives . . . I have issued a law to prevent people buying from the convicts or selling to them and I will give harsh punishment to offenders."

Captain Phillip

JANUARY								FEBRUARY						
M	T	W	T	F	S	S		M	T	W	T	F	S	S
				1	2	3		1	2	3	4	5	6	7
4	5	6	7	8	9	10		8	9	10	11	12	13	14
11	12	13	14	15	16	17		15	16	17	18	19	20	21
18	19	20	21	22	23	24		22	23	24	25	26	27	28
25	26	27	28	29	30	31		29						

MARCH								APRIL						
M	T	W	T	F	S	S		M	T	W	T	F	S	S
1	2	3	4	5	6							1	2	3
7	8	9	10	11	12	13		4	5	6	7	8	9	10
14	15	16	17	18	19	20		11	12	13	14	15	16	17
21	22	23	24	25	26	27		18	19	20	21	22	23	24
28	29	30	31					25	26	27	28	29	30	

MAY								JUNE						
M	T	W	T	F	S	S		M	T	W	T	F	S	S
30	31				1					1	2	3	4	5
2	3	4	5	6	7	8		6	7	8	9	10	11	12
9	10	11	12	13	14	15		13	14	15	16	17	18	19
16	17	18	19	20	21	22		20	21	22	23	24	25	26
23	24	25	26	27	28	29		27	28	29	30			

THURSDAY 25 FEBRUARY

On this day in 1825
Aboriginal known as "Mosquito"
executed in Van Diemen's Land.

9.00	
9.30	
10.00	
10.30	
11.00	
11.30	
12.00	
12.30	
1.00	
1.30	
2.00	
2.30	
3.00	
3.30	
4.00	
4.30	
5.00	
5.30	
6.00	

NOTES

"I record this night very heavy tempest with thunder and lightning. At half past eight at night a flash of lightning struck with such force to a huge tree adjacent to my tent that it split it down the middle to the ground. No other damage."

Captain Phillip

JULY								AUGUST						
M	T	W	T	F	S	S		M	T	W	T	F	S	S
			1	2	3			1	2	3	4	5	6	7
4	5	6	7	8	9	10		8	9	10	11	12	13	14
11	12	13	14	15	16	17		15	16	17	18	19	20	21
18	19	20	21	22	23	24		22	23	24	25	26	27	28
25	26	27	28	29	30	31		29	30	31				

FRIDAY 26 FEBRUARY

On this day in 1830
First major game of cricket; Civilians defeat
57th Regiment in Hyde Park

9.00	
9.30	
10.00	
10.30	
11.00	
11.30	
12.00	
12.30	
1.00	
1.30	
2.00	
2.30	
3.00	
3.30	
4.00	
4.30	
5.00	
5.30	
6.00	

NOTES

" . . . rations for 7 days for each marine and male convict — 7 pounds of flour or in lieu thereof 7 pounds of bread, 7 pounds of beef or in lieu thereof 4lb of pork, 3 pints of peas, 6 ounces of butter, half pound of rice. Two thirds of the above for the women but no spirits."

Captain Phillip

SEPTEMBER								OCTOBER						
M	T	W	T	F	S	S		M	T	W	T	F	S	S
		1	2	3	4			31					1	2
5	6	7	8	9	10	11		3	4	5	6	7	8	9
12	13	14	15	16	17	18		10	11	12	13	14	15	16
19	20	21	22	23	24	25		17	18	19	20	21	22	23
26	27	28	29	30				24	25	26	27	28	29	30

SATURDAY 27 FEBRUARY

On this day in 1928
Bert Hinkler completes solo flights from
England to his home town, Bundaberg, Qld

"We have made some discoveries this week. One is that the tree which I have said grows something like the fir, answers very well for the making of shingles. Our other acquisition is the lighting on a soil which is seemingly fitted for making bricks, and about 8 or 10 convicts of the trade are now employed in the business."

Captain Phillip

SUNDAY 28 FEBRUARY

On this day in 1851
Pressure to end convict system: "Anti-Transportation League" formed in Hobart

EVENTS OF THE WEEK

VIC: Melbourne. 1988 National Arts and Crafts Exhibition opens. Royal Melbourne Showground. 25th to 28th Feb.

ACT: Canberra. 1988 Bicentennial Royal Canberra Show opens.

National Exhibition Centre, Mitchell. 26th to 28th Feb.

SA: Adelaide. Festival Fringe; activities and events for all. 26th Feb. to 27th Mar.

NOVEMBER								DECEMBER						
M	T	W	T	F	S	S		M	T	W	T	F	S	S
1	2	3	4	5	6					1	2	3	4	
7	8	9	10	11	12	13		5	6	7	8	9	10	11
14	15	16	17	18	19	20		12	13	14	15	16	17	18
21	22	23	24	25	26	27		19	20	21	22	23	24	25
28	29	30						26	27	28	29	30	31	

MONDAY 29 FEBRUARY

9.00	
9.30	
10.00	
10.30	
11.00	
11.30	
12.00	
12.30	
1.00	
1.30	
2.00	
2.30	
3.00	
3.30	
4.00	
4.30	
5.00	
5.30	
6.00	

NOTES

"Lieutenant Ball Commander of *SUPPLY*, made Norfolk Island today but it was to be 5 days before a place could be found . . . to land the provisions. A small island being seen on the passage . . . Lt. Ball examined it on his return . . . he named it after Lord Howe . . . sickness increased — dysentery caused some deaths . . . some sheep were killed supposedly by a dog (dingo)."

Captain Phillip

TUESDAY 1 MARCH

9.00	
9.30	
10.00	
10.30	
11.00	
11.30	
12.00	
12.30	
1.00	
1.30	
2.00	
2.30	
3.00	
3.30	
4.00	
4.30	
5.00	
5.30	
6.00	

NOTES

"Today I pardoned five convicts, one of them being convict Freeman on the condition of his becoming the public executioner for and during the term for which he was transported to this country, and of his residing within the limits of this Government for and during the term of his natural life."

Captain Phillip

WEDNESDAY 2 MARCH

9.00	
9.30	
10.00	
10.30	
11.00	
11.30	
12.00	
12.30	
1.00	
1.30	
2.00	
2.30	
3.00	
3.30	
4.00	
4.30	
5.00	
5.30	
6.00	

NOTES

"At daylight, together with my first Lt. of *SIRIUS* and others set out to further examine Broken Bay, we were victualled for 7 days. We came into contact with many other natives, one very excessively ugly female, heavy with child, exchanged a straw hat for one of their spears. The natives were everywhere, mainly standing on high ground."

Captain Phillip

JANUARY

M	T	W	T	F	S	S
			1	2	3
4	5	6	7	8	9	10
11	12	13	14	15	16	17
18	19	20	21	22	23	24
25	26	27	28	29	30	31

FEBRUARY

M	T	W	T	F	S	S
1	2	3	4	5	6	7
8	9	10	11	12	13	14
15	16	17	18	19	20	21
22	23	24	25	26	27	28
29						

MARCH

M	T	W	T	F	S	S
	1	2	3	4	5	6
7	8	9	10	11	12	13
14	15	16	17	18	19	20
21	22	23	24	25	26	27
28	29	30	31			

APRIL

M	T	W	T	F	S	S
				1	2	3
4	5	6	7	8	9	10
11	12	13	14	15	16	17
18	19	20	21	22	23	24
25	26	27	28	29	30	

MAY

M	T	W	T	F	S	S
30	31					1
2	3	4	5	6	7	8
9	10	11	12	13	14	15
16	17	18	19	20	21	22
23	24	25	26	27	28	29

JUNE

M	T	W	T	F	S	S
	1	2	3	4	5
6	7	8	9	10	11	12
13	14	15	16	17	18	19
20	21	22	23	24	25	26
27	28	29	30			

THURSDAY 3 MARCH

On this day in 1885
New South Wales Contingent leaves
Sydney to fight in the Sudan

9.00	
9.30	
10.00	
10.30	
11.00	
11.30	
12.00	
12.30	
1.00	
1.30	
2.00	
2.30	
3.00	
3.30	
4.00	
4.30	
5.00	
5.30	
6.00	

NOTES

"A very large Alligator said to be seen near the tents 14ft long . . . shot a remarkably large bird today — as big as an Ostrich. Worgan made a notation about the bird, . . . which answers the description given by Dr Goldsmith of the Emew. It resembles the Ostrich. Its flesh proved very good eating and four of us dined off it from one of the sidebones."

Captain Phillip

FRIDAY 4 MARCH

On this day in 1899
Cyclone hits Cooktown area: 307 lives lost

9.00	
9.30	
10.00	
10.30	
11.00	
11.30	
12.00	
12.30	
1.00	
1.30	
2.00	
2.30	
3.00	
3.30	
4.00	
4.30	
5.00	
5.30	
6.00	

NOTES

". . . we found a straw hat and some strings of beads which favours the opinion of the natives not having any fixed residence as nothing of that kind had been given them here, and several were, both at Botany Bay and Port Jackson . . . We do not go far without seeing the natives, they are all about the bay."

Captain Phillip

SATURDAY 5 MARCH

On this day in 1803
Australia's first newspaper
"The Sydney Gazette" published

"We had help today from an old man and a youth (natives) in preparing ground for us to sleep on, he tried to entise us into a cave, we declined, and this was unfortunate for it rained hard overnight and the cave was found the next day to be large and dry."

Captain Phillip

SUNDAY 6 MARCH

On this day in 1788
First settlement of Norfolk Island

EVENTS OF THE WEEK

VIC: Melbourne. Moomba Festival commences. 4th to 14th Mar.

SA: Adelaide. The Travelling Australian Bicentennial Exhibition opens. 29th Feb. to 6th Mar.

NATIONAL: Australian Bicentennial Everest Expedition, a world first attempt at a double traverse of the mountain. 1st Mar. to 10th May.

JULY							AUGUST						
M	T	W	T	F	S	S	M	T	W	T	F	S	S
			1	2	3		1	2	3	4	5	6	7
4	5	6	7	8	9	10	8	9	10	11	12	13	14
11	12	13	14	15	16	17	15	16	17	18	19	20	21
18	19	20	21	22	23	24	22	23	24	25	26	27	28
25	26	27	28	29	30	31	29	30	31				

SEPTEMBER							OCTOBER						
M	T	W	T	F	S	S	M	T	W	T	F	S	S
		1	2	3	4		31					1	2
5	6	7	8	9	10	11	3	4	5	6	7	8	9
12	13	14	15	16	17	18	10	11	12	13	14	15	16
19	20	21	22	23	24	25	17	18	19	20	21	22	23
26	27	28	29	30			24	25	26	27	28	29	30

NOVEMBER							DECEMBER						
M	T	W	T	F	S	S	M	T	W	T	F	S	S
	1	2	3	4	5	6				1	2	3	4
7	8	9	10	11	12	13	5	6	7	8	9	10	11
14	15	16	17	18	19	20	12	13	14	15	16	17	18
21	22	23	24	25	26	27	19	20	21	22	23	24	25
28	29	30					26	27	28	29	30	31	

MONDAY 7 MARCH

On this day in 1836
Surveyor-General Robert Hoddle lays out the main streets of Melbourne

9.00	
9.30	
10.00	
10.30	
11.00	
11.30	
12.00	
12.30	
1.00	
1.30	
2.00	
2.30	
3.00	
3.30	
4.00	
4.30	
5.00	
5.30	
6.00	

NOTES

"We landed on a small island about two miles up SW arm of bay, we secured for the night — caught a great deal of mullet so I have called it Mullet Island. Clark reported that he felt better today as Arundell gave him some stuff which worked him both ways and had done him a great deal of good."
Captain Phillip

TUESDAY 8 MARCH

On this day in 1965
Qantas makes first non-stop aerial crossing from U.S.A. to Australia

9.00	
9.30	
10.00	
10.30	
11.00	
11.30	
12.00	
12.30	
1.00	
1.30	
2.00	
2.30	
3.00	
3.30	
4.00	
4.30	
5.00	
5.30	
6.00	

NOTES

"I am suffering a pain in my side, I think it has come about by the combination of extreme fatigue and having to remain in wet clothes for so long. The Lieutenant-Governor, back at the cove, is reported as referring to my expedition 'as a party of pleasure'."
Captain Phillip

WEDNESDAY 9 MARCH

On this day in 1836
Temperance campaigner John Tawell orders 600 gals. of rum emptied into Sydney Cove

9.00	
9.30	
10.00	
10.30	
11.00	
11.30	
12.00	
12.30	
1.00	
1.30	
2.00	
2.30	
3.00	
3.30	
4.00	
4.30	
5.00	
5.30	
6.00	

NOTES

"I am authorised to emancipate the convicts for good behaviour, for being industrious and I am further authorised to grant land to them. Authority being withheld for my granting land to the marines is just, for their endeavours are required elsewhere. Today the first reference to the first court martial convened to hear charges against two marines . . ."
Captain Phillip

JANUARY								FEBRUARY						
M	T	W	T	F	S	S		M	T	W	T	F	S	S
				1	2	3		1	2	3	4	5	6	7
4	5	6	7	8	9	10		8	9	10	11	12	13	14
11	12	13	14	15	16	17		15	16	17	18	19	20	21
18	19	20	21	22	23	24		22	23	24	25	26	27	28
25	26	27	28	29	30	31		29						

MARCH								APRIL						
M	T	W	T	F	S	S		M	T	W	T	F	S	S
1	2	3	4	5	6						1	2	3
7	8	9	10	11	12	13		4	5	6	7	8	9	10
14	15	16	17	18	19	20		11	12	13	14	15	16	17
21	22	23	24	25	26	27		18	19	20	21	22	23	24
28	29	30	31					25	26	27	28	29	30	

MAY								JUNE						
M	T	W	T	F	S	S		M	T	W	T	F	S	S
30	31					1				1	2	3	4	5
2	3	4	5	6	7	8		6	7	8	9	10	11	12
9	10	11	12	13	14	15		13	14	15	16	17	18	19
16	17	18	19	20	21	22		20	21	22	23	24	25	26
23	24	25	26	27	28	29		27	28	29	30			

THURSDAY 10 MARCH

On this day in 1794
Rev. Samuel Marsden arrives in Sydney

9.00	
9.30	
10.00	
10.30	
11.00	
11.30	
12.00	
12.30	
1.00	
1.30	
2.00	
2.30	
3.00	
3.30	
4.00	
4.30	
5.00	
5.30	
6.00	

NOTES

"La Perouse, five days earlier than he had planned, slipped out of Botany Bay and he and his two beautiful ships and all who had so far survived the journey sailed into the unknown never to be seen again." (It was not until 1826 that the wreckage of the two ships was sighted on a reef in the Santa Cruz group of islands in the Pacific.)

Captain Phillip

FRIDAY 11 MARCH

On this day in 1843
Tin discovered near Beechworth, Victoria

9.00	
9.30	
10.00	
10.30	
11.00	
11.30	
12.00	
12.30	
1.00	
1.30	
2.00	
2.30	
3.00	
3.30	
4.00	
4.30	
5.00	
5.30	
6.00	

NOTES

"I have ordered a start on Hospital Accomodation, other than tents to start immediately. There will be a ward for the troops and one for the convicts and a dispensary for the few medical supplies that were brought out. In all the building will be 84 ft by 23 ft, situated on the west side of the cove." (Today this location is George Street North, near Circular Quay.)

Captain Phillip

SATURDAY 12 MARCH

On this day in 1913
Canberra named capital city of Australia.

"This morning *FYSHBURN* delivered two casks of wine to the hospital. I have ordered *SIRIUS* to air her small sails and send two field pieces ashore for the garrison. This day Peter Dargon tryed for a breach of trust. This night, at 5 o'clock Easty and Clayton received 150 lashes each and Dargon 100."

Captain Phillip

SUNDAY 13 MARCH

On this day in 1944
Commonwealth Government introduces unemployment and sickness benefits

EVENTS OF THE WEEK

SA: Whyalla.
The Travelling Australian Bicentennial Exhibition opens. 12th to 15th Mar.

SA: Adelaide.
1988 Women's 15 km World Road Race Championships. 13th March.

ACT: Canberra.
The Great Australian Balloon Gathering commences. National Library Grounds. 12th to 21st Mar.

JULY							AUGUST						
M	T	W	T	F	S	S	M	T	W	T	F	S	S
				1	2	3	1	2	3	4	5	6	7
4	5	6	7	8	9	10	8	9	10	11	12	13	14
11	12	13	14	15	16	17	15	16	17	18	19	20	21
18	19	20	21	22	23	24	22	23	24	25	26	27	28
25	26	27	28	29	30	31	29	30	31				

SEPTEMBER							OCTOBER						
M	T	W	T	F	S	S	M	T	W	T	F	S	S
			1	2	3	4	31					1	2
5	6	7	8	9	10	11	3	4	5	6	7	8	9
12	13	14	15	16	17	18	10	11	12	13	14	15	16
19	20	21	22	23	24	25	17	18	19	20	21	22	23
26	27	28	29	30			24	25	26	27	28	29	30

NOVEMBER							DECEMBER						
M	T	W	T	F	S	S	M	T	W	T	F	S	S
	1	2	3	4	5	6				1	2	3	4
7	8	9	10	11	12	13	5	6	7	8	9	10	11
14	15	16	17	18	19	20	12	13	14	15	16	17	18
21	22	23	24	25	26	27	19	20	21	22	23	24	25
28	29	30					26	27	28	29	30	31	

MONDAY 14 MARCH

On this day in 1968
First liver transplant operation in Australia
performed in Sydney

9.00	
9.30	
10.00	
10.30	
11.00	
11.30	
12.00	
12.30	
1.00	
1.30	
2.00	
2.30	
3.00	
3.30	
4.00	
4.30	
5.00	
5.30	
6.00	

NOTES

"It is interesting to note that I saw some natives who seemed to be more shy than usual. When I coaxed one to come near me, he used signs to let me know that he had been hit on the shoulder. I am convinced it is another case of aggression by the convicts."

Captain Phillip

TUESDAY 15 MARCH

On this day in 1877
First cricket Test match between Australia
and England starts in Melbourne

9.00	
9.30	
10.00	
10.30	
11.00	
11.30	
12.00	
12.30	
1.00	
1.30	
2.00	
2.30	
3.00	
3.30	
4.00	
4.30	
5.00	
5.30	
6.00	

NOTES

"We have found three sorts of stone in this country: Freestone; which appears equal to Portland stone, a bad firestone, and a stone that appears to contain a large proportion of iron. We have found clay for bricks, but no chalk or limestone has yet been found."

Captain Phillip

WEDNESDAY 16 MARCH

On this day in 1787
First Fleet begins assembling at
Mother Bank off the Isle of Wight

9.00	
9.30	
10.00	
10.30	
11.00	
11.30	
12.00	
12.30	
1.00	
1.30	
2.00	
2.30	
3.00	
3.30	
4.00	
4.30	
5.00	
5.30	
6.00	

NOTES

"It is not possible to determine with any accuracy the number of natives, but I think that in Botany Bay, Port Jackson, Broken Bay and the intermediate coast they cannot be less than one thousand five hundred."

Captain Phillip

JANUARY							FEBRUARY						
M	T	W	T	F	S	S	M	T	W	T	F	S	S
				1	2	3	1	2	3	4	5	6	7
4	5	6	7	8	9	10	8	9	10	11	12	13	14
11	12	13	14	15	16	17	15	16	17	18	19	20	21
18	19	20	21	22	23	24	22	23	24	25	26	27	28
25	26	27	28	29	30	31	29						

MARCH							APRIL						
M	T	W	T	F	S	S	M	T	W	T	F	S	S
1	2	3	4	5	6						1	2	3
7	8	9	10	11	12	13	4	5	6	7	8	9	10
14	15	16	17	18	19	20	11	12	13	14	15	16	17
21	22	23	24	25	26	27	18	19	20	21	22	23	24
28	29	30	31				25	26	27	28	29	30	

MAY							JUNE						
M	T	W	T	F	S	S	M	T	W	T	F	S	S
30	31					1			1	2	3	4	5
2	3	4	5	6	7	8	6	7	8	9	10	11	12
9	10	11	12	13	14	15	13	14	15	16	17	18	19
16	17	18	19	20	21	22	20	21	22	23	24	25	26
23	24	25	26	27	28	29	27	28	29	30			

THURSDAY 17 MARCH

On this day in 1942
General Douglas MacArthur arrives in Australia

9.00	
9.30	
10.00	
10.30	
11.00	
11.30	
12.00	
12.30	
1.00	
1.30	
2.00	
2.30	
3.00	
3.30	
4.00	
4.30	
5.00	
5.30	
6.00	

NOTES

"One of my servants who often went hunting for me and had been missing for some five days returned and reported that he had been carried off by natives. He had killed a kangaroo, they took it from him, broiled and ate it, I think him lucky to be returned complete."

Captain Phillip

FRIDAY 18 MARCH

On this day in 1923
John Campbell Miles discovers silver and lead at Mt. Isa

9.00	
9.30	
10.00	
10.30	
11.00	
11.30	
12.00	
12.30	
1.00	
1.30	
2.00	
2.30	
3.00	
3.30	
4.00	
4.30	
5.00	
5.30	
6.00	

NOTES

"The *SCARBOROUGH* landed five thousand bricks . . . I ordered Major Ross to suspend the officers of the court martial from all duty and to place them under arrest. Easty stated that, 'the court confined themselves . . . and said they would go home to England'."

Captain Phillip

SATURDAY 19 MARCH

On this day in 1932
Sydney Harbour Bridge opens

"It is good to see the return of *SUPPLY* today, she has anchored in Port Jackson in close to Sydney Cove. It is 34 days since her departure to Norfolk Island: The chief acquisition that we hope may accrue to our settlement from this island is the turtle, of which we hope to have many a feast."

Captain Phillip

SUNDAY 20 MARCH

On this day in 1917
Frank McNamara first Australian airman to win Victoria Cross

EVENTS OF THE WEEK

NSW: Sydney. Chicago Symphony Orchestra, one of the world's best. Sydney Opera House. 15th to 18th Mar.

ACT: Canberra. World Polocross Test Series commences. 14th to 29th Mar.

ACT: Canberra. Fifth National Philatelic Convention commences. 19th to 21st Mar.

JULY							AUGUST						
M	T	W	T	F	S	S	M	T	W	T	F	S	S
				1	2	3	1	2	3	4	5	6	7
4	5	6	7	8	9	10	8	9	10	11	12	13	14
11	12	13	14	15	16	17	15	16	17	18	19	20	21
18	19	20	21	22	23	24	22	23	24	25	26	27	28
25	26	27	28	29	30	31	29	30	31				

SEPTEMBER							OCTOBER						
M	T	W	T	F	S	S	M	T	W	T	F	S	S
			1	2	3	4	31					1	2
5	6	7	8	9	10	11	3	4	5	6	7	8	9
12	13	14	15	16	17	18	10	11	12	13	14	15	16
19	20	21	22	23	24	25	17	18	19	20	21	22	23
26	27	28	29	30			24	25	26	27	28	29	30

NOVEMBER							DECEMBER						
M	T	W	T	F	S	S	M	T	W	T	F	S	S
1	2	3	4	5	6					1	2	3	4
7	8	9	10	11	12	13	5	6	7	8	9	10	11
14	15	16	17	18	19	20	12	13	14	15	16	17	18
21	22	23	24	25	26	27	19	20	21	22	23	24	25
28	29	30					26	27	28	29	30	31	

On this day in 1931
A.N.A.'s flagship "Southern Cloud" disappears
on Sydney-Melbourne flight: eight die

9.00	
9.30	
10.00	
10.30	
11.00	
11.30	
12.00	
12.30	
1.00	
1.30	
2.00	
2.30	
3.00	
3.30	
4.00	
4.30	
5.00	
5.30	
6.00	

NOTES

Collins recorded difficulties with the animals, "Great inconvenience was found from the necessity . . . of suffering the stock of individuals to run loose amongst the tents and huts; much damage in particular was sustained by hogs, who frequently forced their way into them while their owners were at labour . . ."

Captain Phillip

On this day in 1880
Women admitted to universities for
the first time; in Melbourne

9.00	
9.30	
10.00	
10.30	
11.00	
11.30	
12.00	
12.30	
1.00	
1.30	
2.00	
2.30	
3.00	
3.30	
4.00	
4.30	
5.00	
5.30	
6.00	

NOTES

"We have seen very heavy thunderstorms, and I believe the Gum-tree strongly attracts the lightning, but the natives always make their fire, if not before their own huts, at the root of a Gum Tree, which burns very freely, and they never put a fire out when they leave the place."

Captain Phillip

On this day in 1922
Queensland abolishes Legislative Council,
only State without Upper House

9.00	
9.30	
10.00	
10.30	
11.00	
11.30	
12.00	
12.30	
1.00	
1.30	
2.00	
2.30	
3.00	
3.30	
4.00	
4.30	
5.00	
5.30	
6.00	

NOTES

"I record the catching of a great shark this day, 13 feet long and 6½ feet round. After his jaws were taken out they passed over the largest man in the ship without touching; the liver gave us 26 gallons of oil; he had four hooks cut from within him besides that which caught him."

Captain Phillip

JANUARY							FEBRUARY						
M	T	W	T	F	S	S	M	T	W	T	F	S	S
				1	2	3	1	2	3	4	5	6	7
4	5	6	7	8	9	10	8	9	10	11	12	13	14
11	12	13	14	15	16	17	15	16	17	18	19	20	21
18	19	20	21	22	23	24	22	23	24	25	26	27	28
25	26	27	28	29	30	31	29						

MARCH							APRIL						
M	T	W	T	F	S	S	M	T	W	T	F	S	S
1	2	3	4	5	6						1	2	3
7	8	9	10	11	12	13	4	5	6	7	8	9	10
14	15	16	17	18	19	20	11	12	13	14	15	16	17
21	22	23	24	25	26	27	18	19	20	21	22	23	24
28	29	30	31				25	26	27	28	29	30	

MAY							JUNE						
M	T	W	T	F	S	S	M	T	W	T	F	S	S
30	31					1			1	2	3	4	5
2	3	4	5	6	7	8	6	7	8	9	10	11	12
9	10	11	12	13	14	15	13	14	15	16	17	18	19
16	17	18	19	20	21	22	20	21	22	23	24	25	26
23	24	25	26	27	28	29	27	28	29	30			

THURSDAY 24 MARCH

On this day in 1925
First-ever broadcast of parliamentary debate

9.00	
9.30	
10.00	
10.30	
11.00	
11.30	
12.00	
12.30	
1.00	
1.30	
2.00	
2.30	
3.00	
3.30	
4.00	
4.30	
5.00	
5.30	
6.00	

NOTES

"I had Bradley organise Lt. Dawes of the marines, a corporal and eight privates to be loaned from *SIRIUS* to do duty on shore, as the battalion is sadly weakened by scurvy and other sickness. Ground is still being cleared but it is a slow task."

Captain Phillip

FRIDAY 25 MARCH

On this day in 1935
Pearling fleet anchored at Lacepede
hit by cyclone: 142 lives lost

9.00	
9.30	
10.00	
10.30	
11.00	
11.30	
12.00	
12.30	
1.00	
1.30	
2.00	
2.30	
3.00	
3.30	
4.00	
4.30	
5.00	
5.30	
6.00	

NOTES

"At 7 pm John Fisher, a seaman, died of dysentery on board *LADY PENRHYN*. He was only 20 and Bowes attributed his death to his own imprudence in swimming to shore naked in the middle of the night to one of the convict women with whom he had formed a connection . . ."

Captain Phillip

SATURDAY 26 MARCH

On this day in 1856
First inter-Colonial cricket played on MCG:
N.S.W. beats Victoria

" . . . cut on the rocks; on the top of a mountain I saw the figure of a man in the attitude they put themselves in when they are going to dance, which was much better done than I had seen before, and the figure of a large lizard was sufficiently well executed to satisfy everyone what animal was meant."

Captain Phillip

SUNDAY 27 MARCH

On this day in 1939
Australia's first military aircraft, the
"Wirraway", test-flown

EVENTS OF THE WEEK

QLD: Gold Coast. Rescue '88 — Australia. World Life Saving General Assembly, medical congress and inter-club championships. Conrad International Hotel. 22nd to 30th Mar.
WA: Kalgoorlie. The Travelling

Australian Bicentennial Exhibition opens. 25th to 28th Mar.
NSW: Sydney. Royal Easter Show. 25th Mar. to 5th Apr.

JULY							AUGUST						
M	T	W	T	F	S	S	M	T	W	T	F	S	S
				1	2	3	1	2	3	4	5	6	7
4	5	6	7	8	9	10	8	9	10	11	12	13	14
11	12	13	14	15	16	17	15	16	17	18	19	20	21
18	19	20	21	22	23	24	22	23	24	25	26	27	28
25	26	27	28	29	30	31	29	30	31				

SEPTEMBER							OCTOBER						
M	T	W	T	F	S	S	M	T	W	T	F	S	S
			1	2	3	4	31					1	2
5	6	7	8	9	10	11	3	4	5	6	7	8	9
12	13	14	15	16	17	18	10	11	12	13	14	15	16
19	20	21	22	23	24	25	17	18	19	20	21	22	23
26	27	28	29	30			24	25	26	27	28	29	30

NOVEMBER							DECEMBER						
M	T	W	T	F	S	S	M	T	W	T	F	S	S
	1	2	3	4	5	6				1	2	3	4
7	8	9	10	11	12	13	5	6	7	8	9	10	11
14	15	16	17	18	19	20	12	13	14	15	16	17	18
21	22	23	24	25	26	27	19	20	21	22	23	24	25
28	29	30					26	27	28	29	30	31	

MONDAY 28 MARCH

On this day in 1791
Mary Bryant and eight male convicts escape
from colony in open boat

9.00	
9.30	
10.00	
10.30	
11.00	
11.30	
12.00	
12.30	
1.00	
1.30	
2.00	
2.30	
3.00	
3.30	
4.00	
4.30	
5.00	
5.30	
6.00	

NOTES

"I am determined that this colony will thrive; there is good country near us, and I will have it settled and cultivated early in the spring . . . trouble is still occurring between the convicts and the natives."

Captain Phillip

TUESDAY 29 MARCH

On this day in 1901
First federal elections held

9.00	
9.30	
10.00	
10.30	
11.00	
11.30	
12.00	
12.30	
1.00	
1.30	
2.00	
2.30	
3.00	
3.30	
4.00	
4.30	
5.00	
5.30	
6.00	

NOTES

" . . . went with the steward of the *GOLDEN GROVE* to the hills near Botany Bay . . . shot a female kangaroo, with a young one in its false belly. The young I preserved in spirit, and the other he stuffed for himself. I collected seeds from a plant in blossom which was exceedingly handsome and different from any shrub I ever saw."

Captain Phillip

WEDNESDAY 30 MARCH

On this day in 1942
Food rationing introduced for
tea, sugar and butter

9.00	
9.30	
10.00	
10.30	
11.00	
11.30	
12.00	
12.30	
1.00	
1.30	
2.00	
2.30	
3.00	
3.30	
4.00	
4.30	
5.00	
5.30	
6.00	

NOTES

"The surgeon wounded and brought down a crow in sight of the natives . . . The surgeon picked up and threw the bird toward them, which having recovered itself flew away and joined others in a tree close by. This uncommon circumstance, which could not appear to them short of our having power to give and take life, astonished them . . ."

Captain Phillip

JANUARY							FEBRUARY						
M	T	W	T	F	S	S	M	T	W	T	F	S	S
				1	2	3	1	2	3	4	5	6	7
4	5	6	7	8	9	10	8	9	10	11	12	13	14
11	12	13	14	15	16	17	15	16	17	18	19	20	21
18	19	20	21	22	23	24	22	23	24	25	26	27	28
25	26	27	28	29	30	31	29						

MARCH							APRIL						
M	T	W	T	F	S	S	M	T	W	T	F	S	S
1	2	3	4	5	6					1	2	3	
7	8	9	10	11	12	13	4	5	6	7	8	9	10
14	15	16	17	18	19	20	11	12	13	14	15	16	17
21	22	23	24	25	26	27	18	19	20	21	22	23	24
28	29	30	31				25	26	27	28	29	30	

MAY							JUNE						
M	T	W	T	F	S	S	M	T	W	T	F	S	S
30	31					1			1	2	3	4	5
2	3	4	5	6	7	8	6	7	8	9	10	11	12
9	10	11	12	13	14	15	13	14	15	16	17	18	19
16	17	18	19	20	21	22	20	21	22	23	24	25	26
23	24	25	26	27	28	29	27	28	29	30			

THURSDAY 31 MARCH

On this day in 1921
Royal Australian Air Force founded

9.00	
9.30	
10.00	
10.30	
11.00	
11.30	
12.00	
12.30	
1.00	
1.30	
2.00	
2.30	
3.00	
3.30	
4.00	
4.30	
5.00	
5.30	
6.00	

NOTES

"Because the run of water that supplies this settlement is only a drain from a swamp at the head of it; to protect it, therefore as much as possible from the sun, I have ordered that it is forbidden to cut down trees within fifty feet of the run, as there had not yet been found a finer run in any of the coves of the harbour."

Captain Phillip

FRIDAY 1 APRIL

On this day in 1955
Hobart becomes first Australian city to introduce parking metres.

9.00	
9.30	
10.00	
10.30	
11.00	
11.30	
12.00	
12.30	
1.00	
1.30	
2.00	
2.30	
3.00	
3.30	
4.00	
4.30	
5.00	
5.30	
6.00	

NOTES

"The steward of *GOLDEN GROVE* killed a large snake among rushes in a swampy place. It was nearly as big as my arm, upwards of 8 ft long, a very wide mouth with two rows of sharp pointed teeth in the upper jaw and two in the under one. It was of a very dark colour . . . with large bright yellow spots . . ."

Surgeon Bowes Smyth

SATURDAY 2 APRIL

On this day in 1918
Australian divisions in France formed into single corps under Monash's command

"I find the great labour in clearing the ground will not permit more than eight acres to be sown this year with wheat and barley. At the same time the immense number of ants and field mice will render our crops very uncertain."

Captain Phillip

SUNDAY 3 APRIL

On this day in 1954
Russian diplomat, Vladimir Petrov, defects, admits he was a spy

EVENTS OF THE WEEK

ACT: Canberra. Gemboree '88 — National Assembly of Lapidaries. National Exhibition Centre. 1st to 4th Apr.

VIC: Stawell. Stawell Gift. Professional athletics meeting.

Central Park. 2nd to 4th Apr.

NSW: Sydney. Spirit of Australia 1150km Endurance Horse Ride. Begins RAS Showgrounds.

JULY								AUGUST						
M	T	W	T	F	S	S		M	T	W	T	F	S	S
				1	2	3		1	2	3	4	5	6	7
4	5	6	7	8	9	10		8	9	10	11	12	13	14
11	12	13	14	15	16	17		15	16	17	18	19	20	21
18	19	20	21	22	23	24		22	23	24	25	26	27	28
25	26	27	28	29	30	31		29	30	31				

SEPTEMBER								OCTOBER						
M	T	W	T	F	S	S		M	T	W	T	F	S	S
			1	2	3	4		31					1	2
5	6	7	8	9	10	11		3	4	5	6	7	8	9
12	13	14	15	16	17	18		10	11	12	13	14	15	16
19	20	21	22	23	24	25		17	18	19	20	21	22	23
26	27	28	29	30				24	25	26	27	28	29	30

NOVEMBER								DECEMBER						
M	T	W	T	F	S	S		M	T	W	T	F	S	S
	1	2	3	4	5	6					1	2	3	4
7	8	9	10	11	12	13		5	6	7	8	9	10	11
14	15	16	17	18	19	20		12	13	14	15	16	17	18
21	22	23	24	25	26	27		19	20	21	22	23	24	25
28	29	30						26	27	28	29	30	31	

MONDAY 4 APRIL

On this day in 1883
Queensland government annexes New Guinea;
disallowed by British government

9.00	
9.30	
10.00	
10.30	
11.00	
11.30	
12.00	
12.30	
1.00	
1.30	
2.00	
2.30	
3.00	
3.30	
4.00	
4.30	
5.00	
5.30	
6.00	

NOTES

" . . . part of the livestock brought from the Cape, small as it was, has been lost, and our resource in fish is also uncertain. Some days great quantities are caught never sufficient to save any of the provisions; and I find at times fish to be very scarce."

Captain Phillip

TUESDAY 5 APRIL

On this day in 1932
Champion racehorse Phar Lap dies in U.S.A.

9.00	
9.30	
10.00	
10.30	
11.00	
11.30	
12.00	
12.30	
1.00	
1.30	
2.00	
2.30	
3.00	
3.30	
4.00	
4.30	
5.00	
5.30	
6.00	

NOTES

"I see the necessity of a regular supply of provisions for four or five years, and of clothing, shoes, and frocks in the greatest proportion. More females are needed in the colony if it is to thrive as they are at present a very small proportion."

Captain Phillip

WEDNESDAY 6 APRIL

On this day in 1830
William Hamilton becomes Australia's first
full-time paid bank manager

9.00	
9.30	
10.00	
10.30	
11.00	
11.30	
12.00	
12.30	
1.00	
1.30	
2.00	
2.30	
3.00	
3.30	
4.00	
4.30	
5.00	
5.30	
6.00	

NOTES

"I have ordered an inscription be made on a piece of copper to replace an inscribed piece of timber torn down by the natives at Botany Bay. It was to mark the place the French Abbe who died, was buried."

Captain Phillip

JANUARY
M	T	W	T	F	S	S
				1	2	3
4	5	6	7	8	9	10
11	12	13	14	15	16	17
18	19	20	21	22	23	24
25	26	27	28	29	30	31

FEBRUARY
M	T	W	T	F	S	S
1	2	3	4	5	6	7
8	9	10	11	12	13	14
15	16	17	18	19	20	21
22	23	24	25	26	27	28
29						

MARCH
M	T	W	T	F	S	S
1	2	3	4	5	6
7	8	9	10	11	12	13
14	15	16	17	18	19	20
21	22	23	24	25	26	27
28	29	30	31			

APRIL
M	T	W	T	F	S	S
				1	2	3
4	5	6	7	8	9	10
11	12	13	14	15	16	17
18	19	20	21	22	23	24
25	26	27	28	29	30	

MAY
M	T	W	T	F	S	S
30	31					1
2	3	4	5	6	7	8
9	10	11	12	13	14	15
16	17	18	19	20	21	22
23	24	25	26	27	28	29

JUNE
M	T	W	T	F	S	S
	1	2	3	4	5
6	7	8	9	10	11	12
13	14	15	16	17	18	19
20	21	22	23	24	25	26
27	28	29	30			

THURSDAY 7 APRIL

On this day in 1939
Sir Earle Page becomes Prime Minister
for just 19 days

9.00	
9.30	
10.00	
10.30	
11.00	
11.30	
12.00	
12.30	
1.00	
1.30	
2.00	
2.30	
3.00	
3.30	
4.00	
4.30	
5.00	
5.30	
6.00	

NOTES

" . . . the stealing of food is now punishable by execution. If I had not made it so then I would have encouraged those who would steal food to bring about the slow death by starvation of those who would not steal."

Captain Phillip

FRIDAY 8 APRIL

On this day in 1817
Australia's first bank, the Bank of
New South Wales, established

9.00	
9.30	
10.00	
10.30	
11.00	
11.30	
12.00	
12.30	
1.00	
1.30	
2.00	
2.30	
3.00	
3.30	
4.00	
4.30	
5.00	
5.30	
6.00	

NOTES

"The sense of urgency about our need for better soil is growing greater day by day. So though I feel my absence from the Cove could lead to more trouble, I have decided to explore further inland and will leave with a small party one week from today."

Captain Phillip

SATURDAY 9 APRIL

On this day in 1844
William Clarke reveals his gold discoveries
to NSW legislature

"One very bad quality of the timber of this country puts us to great inconvenience; I mean the large gum-tree which splits and warps in such a manner when used green, and to which necessity obliged us, that a storehouse boarded up with this wood is rendered useless."

Captain Phillip

SUNDAY 10 APRIL

On this day in 1837
Governor Bourke proclaims the
site of Melbourne

EVENTS OF THE WEEK

WA: Albany. The Travelling Australian Bicentennial Exhibition opens. 5th to 8th Apr.

NSW: Sydney. Standard Chartered Dragon Boat Race. International Championship 1988. Darling Harbour. 9th and 10th Apr.

SA: Adelaide. The Great Eastern Steeplechase. Onkaparinga Racing Club. 4th Apr.

JULY							AUGUST						
M	T	W	T	F	S	S	M	T	W	T	F	S	S
				1	2	3	1	2	3	4	5	6	7
4	5	6	7	8	9	10	8	9	10	11	12	13	14
11	12	13	14	15	16	17	15	16	17	18	19	20	21
18	19	20	21	22	23	24	22	23	24	25	26	27	28
25	26	27	28	29	30	31	29	30	31				

SEPTEMBER							OCTOBER						
M	T	W	T	F	S	S	M	T	W	T	F	S	S
		1	2	3	4		31					1	2
5	6	7	8	9	10	11	3	4	5	6	7	8	9
12	13	14	15	16	17	18	10	11	12	13	14	15	16
19	20	21	22	23	24	25	17	18	19	20	21	22	23
26	27	28	29	30			24	25	26	27	28	29	30

NOVEMBER							DECEMBER						
M	T	W	T	F	S	S	M	T	W	T	F	S	S
	1	2	3	4	5	6				1	2	3	4
7	8	9	10	11	12	13	5	6	7	8	9	10	11
14	15	16	17	18	19	20	12	13	14	15	16	17	18
21	22	23	24	25	26	27	19	20	21	22	23	24	25
28	29	30					26	27	28	29	30	31	

MONDAY **11** APRIL

On this day in 1941
Siege of Tobruk begins

9.00	
9.30	
10.00	
10.30	
11.00	
11.30	
12.00	
12.30	
1.00	
1.30	
2.00	
2.30	
3.00	
3.30	
4.00	
4.30	
5.00	
5.30	
6.00	

NOTES

"My principal surgeon suggested to me that the expediency of another supply of Turtle from Lord Howe Island was necessary as our small settlement began to wear the aspect of distress from the great number of Scorbutic patients that were daily seen creeping to and from hospital tents."

Captain Phillip

TUESDAY **12** APRIL

On this day in 1924
The battle-cruiser HMAS "Australia"
ceremoniously scuttled

9.00	
9.30	
10.00	
10.30	
11.00	
11.30	
12.00	
12.30	
1.00	
1.30	
2.00	
2.30	
3.00	
3.30	
4.00	
4.30	
5.00	
5.30	
6.00	

NOTES

" . . . sometimes very hot, sometimes very cold, sometimes very wet. I have no way of avoiding the full effects of the weather on bodies that were feeling the results of the continual eating of stale salted meat and flour in which weevils had taken a long-term interest."

Captain Phillip

WEDNESDAY **13** APRIL

On this day in 1954
Prime Minister Menzies announces Vladimir
Petrov granted political asylum

9.00	
9.30	
10.00	
10.30	
11.00	
11.30	
12.00	
12.30	
1.00	
1.30	
2.00	
2.30	
3.00	
3.30	
4.00	
4.30	
5.00	
5.30	
6.00	

NOTES

" . . . sighted more kangaroos near the settlement than in any other part of the country. The kangaroo, though it resembles the Jerboa in the peculiarity of using only the hinder legs in progression, does not belong to that genus . . . I visited the caves in the lower part of the harbour."

Captain Phillip

JANUARY	FEBRUARY
M T W T F S S	M T W T F S S

JANUARY						
M	T	W	T	F	S	S
					1	2	3
4	5	6	7	8	9	10
11	12	13	14	15	16	17
18	19	20	21	22	23	24
25	26	27	28	29	30	31

FEBRUARY						
M	T	W	T	F	S	S
1	2	3	4	5	6	7
8	9	10	11	12	13	14
15	16	17	18	19	20	21
22	23	24	25	26	27	28
29						

MARCH						
M	T	W	T	F	S	S
1	2	3	4	5	6	
7	8	9	10	11	12	13
14	15	16	17	18	19	20
21	22	23	24	25	26	27
28	29	30	31			

APRIL						
M	T	W	T	F	S	S
				1	2	3
4	5	6	7	8	9	10
11	12	13	14	15	16	17
18	19	20	21	22	23	24
25	26	27	28	29	30	

MAY						
M	T	W	T	F	S	S
30	31					1
2	3	4	5	6	7	8
9	10	11	12	13	14	15
16	17	18	19	20	21	22
23	24	25	26	27	28	29

JUNE						
M	T	W	T	F	S	S
		1	2	3	4	5
6	7	8	9	10	11	12
13	14	15	16	17	18	19
20	21	22	23	24	25	26
27	28	29	30			

On this day in 1933
Maude Bonney begins first solo flight by woman from Australia to England

9.00	
9.30	
10.00	
10.30	
11.00	
11.30	
12.00	
12.30	
1.00	
1.30	
2.00	
2.30	
3.00	
3.30	
4.00	
4.30	
5.00	
5.30	
6.00	

NOTES

"The natives have no kind of clothing, they appear to be sensible of the cold, and to dislike the rain very much, I do smile, when they put on their heads, when it rains, a piece of bark, under which I have seen them shiver. I still cannot make them eat with us though they seldom refused bread or meat if offered."

Captain Phillip

JULY							AUGUST						
M	T	W	T	F	S	S	M	T	W	T	F	S	S
				1	2	3	1	2	3	4	5	6	7
4	5	6	7	8	9	10	8	9	10	11	12	13	14
11	12	13	14	15	16	17	15	16	17	18	19	20	21
18	19	20	21	22	23	24	22	23	24	25	26	27	28
25	26	27	28	29	30	31	29	30	31				

On this day in 1928
G.H. Wilkins and C.B. Eilson begin first transpolar flight

9.00	
9.30	
10.00	
10.30	
11.00	
11.30	
12.00	
12.30	
1.00	
1.30	
2.00	
2.30	
3.00	
3.30	
4.00	
4.30	
5.00	
5.30	
6.00	

NOTES

"I am anxious to acquire all the knowledge of the country within my power, in the shortest time. Dr. White, Lt. Ball, Lt. Johnson, the Judge Advocate, myself, 3 soldiers and 2 seamen set out for and landed safely at Manly Cove . . . I intend to trace to its source a river which was discovered a few days before."

Captain Phillip

SEPTEMBER							OCTOBER						
M	T	W	T	F	S	S	M	T	W	T	F	S	S
			1	2	3	4	31					1	2
5	6	7	8	9	10	11	3	4	5	6	7	8	9
12	13	14	15	16	17	18	10	11	12	13	14	15	16
19	20	21	22	23	24	25	17	18	19	20	21	22	23
26	27	28	29	30			24	25	26	27	28	29	30

On this day in 1826
Sydney Female School of Industry established to educate female servants

"We continued westward, proceeding many miles inland and I note we cannot trace, by a single vestige, that the natives had been recently in these parts . . . here in the most desert, wild and solitary seclusion that the imagination can form any idea of, we took up our abode for the night . . ."

Chief Surgeon White

On this day in 1944
Police stop publication of Sydney Daily Telegraph at gunpoint in censorship dispute

EVENTS OF THE WEEK

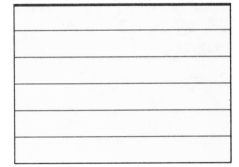

WA: Bunbury. The Travelling Australian Bicentennial Exhibition opens. 14th to 17th Apr.

VIC: Melbourne. The Pacific Asia Travel Association 1988 Annual Conference. The Hyatt on Collins. 17th to 21st Apr.

NATIONAL: Heritage Week — coordinated by the National Trust in each State. 17th to 24th Apr.

NOVEMBER							DECEMBER						
M	T	W	T	F	S	S	M	T	W	T	F	S	S
	1	2	3	4	5	6				1	2	3	4
7	8	9	10	11	12	13	5	6	7	8	9	10	11
14	15	16	17	18	19	20	12	13	14	15	16	17	18
21	22	23	24	25	26	27	19	20	21	22	23	24	25
28	29	30					26	27	28	29	30	31	

MONDAY 18 APRIL

On this day in 1970
VFL Park football ground opens in Melbourne

9.00	
9.30	
10.00	
10.30	
11.00	
11.30	
12.00	
12.30	
1.00	
1.30	
2.00	
2.30	
3.00	
3.30	
4.00	
4.30	
5.00	
5.30	
6.00	

NOTES

" . . . began our progress down the river, some places where the tide had flowed . . . we were obliged to ford; and, at times, under the necessity of climbing heights nearly inaccessible. At length, after undergoing much fatigue, we were agreeably surprised, and cheered, with the sight of two boats, sent by Captain Hunter to meet us . . ."

Chief Surgeon White

TUESDAY 19 APRIL

On this day in 1984
"Advance Australia Fair" proclaimed
Australia's National Anthem

9.00	
9.30	
10.00	
10.30	
11.00	
11.30	
12.00	
12.30	
1.00	
1.30	
2.00	
2.30	
3.00	
3.30	
4.00	
4.30	
5.00	
5.30	
6.00	

NOTES

"We arrived safe back at Sydney Cove last night . . . about fifteen miles from the sea coast we had a fine view of the mountains inland, the northmost I named Carmarthen Hills, the southernmost Landsdowne Hills. A mountain between I called Richmond Hill; from the rising of these mountains I did not doubt that a large river would be found."

Captain Phillip

WEDNESDAY 20 APRIL

On this day in 1770
Lt. Zachary Hicks, of Cook's ship
"Endeavour", sights Australian east coast

9.00	
9.30	
10.00	
10.30	
11.00	
11.30	
12.00	
12.30	
1.00	
1.30	
2.00	
2.30	
3.00	
3.30	
4.00	
4.30	
5.00	
5.30	
6.00	

NOTES

"Bowes applied to me for my letter to the Secretary of State respecting his superintending the convicts and Mr. White the surgeon of the settlement for his certificate. I have promised the letter and certificate for tomorrow."

Captain Phillip

JANUARY							FEBRUARY						
M	T	W	T	F	S	S	M	T	W	T	F	S	S
				1	2	3	1	2	3	4	5	6	7
4	5	6	7	8	9	10	8	9	10	11	12	13	14
11	12	13	14	15	16	17	15	16	17	18	19	20	21
18	19	20	21	22	23	24	22	23	24	25	26	27	28
25	26	27	28	29	30	31	29						

MARCH							APRIL						
M	T	W	T	F	S	S	M	T	W	T	F	S	S
	1	2	3	4	5	6					1	2	3
7	8	9	10	11	12	13	4	5	6	7	8	9	10
14	15	16	17	18	19	20	11	12	13	14	15	16	17
21	22	23	24	25	26	27	18	19	20	21	22	23	24
28	29	30	31				25	26	27	28	29	30	

MAY							JUNE						
M	T	W	T	F	S	S	M	T	W	T	F	S	S
30	31					1			1	2	3	4	5
2	3	4	5	6	7	8	6	7	8	9	10	11	12
9	10	11	12	13	14	15	13	14	15	16	17	18	19
16	17	18	19	20	21	22	20	21	22	23	24	25	26
23	24	25	26	27	28	29	27	28	29	30			

THURSDAY 21 APRIL

On this day in 1856
First eight-hour working day procession in Melbourne

9.00	
9.30	
10.00	
10.30	
11.00	
11.30	
12.00	
12.30	
1.00	
1.30	
2.00	
2.30	
3.00	
3.30	
4.00	
4.30	
5.00	
5.30	
6.00	

NOTES

"Captain Hunter went with Lieutenant Bradley and the master of *SIRIUS* in two boats to survey the branches of the Middle Harbour: A party in boats from the *FRIENDSHIP* went to collect cabbage trees for buildings."

Captain Phillip

FRIDAY 22 APRIL

On this day in 1860
John McDouall Stuart becomes first explorer to reach centre of continent

9.00	
9.30	
10.00	
10.30	
11.00	
11.30	
12.00	
12.30	
1.00	
1.30	
2.00	
2.30	
3.00	
3.30	
4.00	
4.30	
5.00	
5.30	
6.00	

NOTES

"The country was so rugged . . . as we set out on another expedition, as to render it almost impossible to explore our way by the assistance of a compass. Therefore we took a small hand hatchet in order to mark the trees as we went on being our only guide to direct us in our return."

Chief Surgeon White

SATURDAY 23 APRIL

On this day in 1788
Gov. Phillip selects site of Rose Hill, renamed Parramatta 1791

" . . . though the Governor suffered much pain he would not relinquish the object of his pursuit of the expeditions . . . we made a kettle of excellent soup out of a white cockatoo and two crows which I had shot."

Chief Surgeon White

SUNDAY 24 APRIL

On this day in 1804
St. David's cemetery established; first in Van Diemen's Land

EVENTS OF THE WEEK

WA: Perth. The Travelling Australian Bicentennial Exhibition opens. 23rd to 29th Apr.

NSW: Sydney. Trans-Tasman Challenge. International yacht race begins. Sydney Harbour. 23rd to 30th Apr.

QLD: Brisbane. Spirit of Australia 1150km Endurance Horse Ride concludes. Samford Valley. 24th Apr.

JULY							AUGUST						
M	T	W	T	F	S	S	M	T	W	T	F	S	S
				1	2	3	1	2	3	4	5	6	7
4	5	6	7	8	9	10	8	9	10	11	12	13	14
11	12	13	14	15	16	17	15	16	17	18	19	20	21
18	19	20	21	22	23	24	22	23	24	25	26	27	28
25	26	27	28	29	30	31	29	30	31				

SEPTEMBER							OCTOBER						
M	T	W	T	F	S	S	M	T	W	T	F	S	S
			1	2	3	4	31					1	2
5	6	7	8	9	10	11	3	4	5	6	7	8	9
12	13	14	15	16	17	18	10	11	12	13	14	15	16
19	20	21	22	23	24	25	17	18	19	20	21	22	23
26	27	28	29	30			24	25	26	27	28	29	30

NOVEMBER							DECEMBER						
M	T	W	T	F	S	S	M	T	W	T	F	S	S
1	2	3	4	5	6					1	2	3	4
7	8	9	10	11	12	13	5	6	7	8	9	10	11
14	15	16	17	18	19	20	12	13	14	15	16	17	18
21	22	23	24	25	26	27	19	20	21	22	23	24	25
28	29	30					26	27	28	29	30	31	

9.00	
9.30	
10.00	
10.30	
11.00	
11.30	
12.00	
12.30	
1.00	
1.30	
2.00	
2.30	
3.00	
3.30	
4.00	
4.30	
5.00	
5.30	
6.00	

NOTES

"Having sowed some seeds we pursued our route three or four miles west . . . we saw a tree in flames without the least appearance of any natives; we suspected it had been set on fire by lightning . . . The ground about was very dry and parched, that it was with some difficulty we could drive tent pegs or poles into it."

Chief Surgeon White

TUESDAY 26 APRIL

On this day in 1890
A.B. (Banjo) Paterson first publishes
"The Man from Snowy River"

9.00	
9.30	
10.00	
10.30	
11.00	
11.30	
12.00	
12.30	
1.00	
1.30	
2.00	
2.30	
3.00	
3.30	
4.00	
4.30	
5.00	
5.30	
6.00	

NOTES

"We still continue Westward . . . beyond the chasm, we came to a pleasant hill, the top of which was totally clear of trees, and perfectly free from underwood. His Excellency gave it the name of Belle Veue . . . a short distance further on, finding our provisions to run short, our return was concluded though with great reluctance . . ."

Chief Surgeon White

WEDNESDAY 27 APRIL

On this day in 1869
Electric telegraph submarine cable from
Melbourne to Tasmania opens

9.00	
9.30	
10.00	
10.30	
11.00	
11.30	
12.00	
12.30	
1.00	
1.30	
2.00	
2.30	
3.00	
3.30	
4.00	
4.30	
5.00	
5.30	
6.00	

NOTES

"We now find ourselves obliged to make a forced march back, as our provisions were quite exhausted . . . by our calculation we had penetrated into the country, to the westward, not less than 32 or 33 miles."

Chief Surgeon White

JANUARY							FEBRUARY						
M	T	W	T	F	S	S	M	T	W	T	F	S	S
				1	2	3	1	2	3	4	5	6	7
4	5	6	7	8	9	10	8	9	10	11	12	13	14
11	12	13	14	15	16	17	15	16	17	18	19	20	21
18	19	20	21	22	23	24	22	23	24	25	26	27	28
25	26	27	28	29	30	31	29						

MARCH							APRIL						
M	T	W	T	F	S	S	M	T	W	T	F	S	S
1	2	3	4	5	6					1	2	3	
7	8	9	10	11	12	13	4	5	6	7	8	9	10
14	15	16	17	18	19	20	11	12	13	14	15	16	17
21	22	23	24	25	26	27	18	19	20	21	22	23	24
28	29	30	31				25	26	27	28	29	30	

MAY							JUNE						
M	T	W	T	F	S	S	M	T	W	T	F	S	S
30	31				1				1	2	3	4	5
2	3	4	5	6	7	8	6	7	8	9	10	11	12
9	10	11	12	13	14	15	13	14	15	16	17	18	19
16	17	18	19	20	21	22	20	21	22	23	24	25	26
23	24	25	26	27	28	29	27	28	29	30			

THURSDAY 28 APRIL

On this day in 1965
Australia commits combat troops to Vietnam

9.00	
9.30	
10.00	
10.30	
11.00	
11.30	
12.00	
12.30	
1.00	
1.30	
2.00	
2.30	
3.00	
3.30	
4.00	
4.30	
5.00	
5.30	
6.00	

NOTES

"The Governor and his party returned to Sydney Cove in the evening, after examining various inlets in the upper part of the harbour on the way." The Governor remarked "I believe, no country can be more difficult to penetrate into than this is".

Chief Surgeon White

FRIDAY 29 APRIL

On this day in 1770
James Cook lands in Botany Bay

9.00	
9.30	
10.00	
10.30	
11.00	
11.30	
12.00	
12.30	
1.00	
1.30	
2.00	
2.30	
3.00	
3.30	
4.00	
4.30	
5.00	
5.30	
6.00	

NOTES

"The carpenter was employed fixing new skirting boards under the whales . . . while the ship was on the heel the white composition bolts and nails which had been driven for experiment at Rio de Janiero were found to be much decayed, being eaten into the copper. Some of the iron bolts in the butts also examined and found but little touched."

Lieutenant Bradley

SATURDAY 30 APRIL

On this day in 1810
First horse-race meeting in Australia at Parramatta

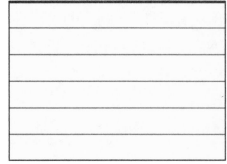

" . . . convict Peter Hopley was charged with the suspicion of stealing a quart tin pot, the property of Margaret Stewart. Hopley said he found it on the beach and admitted he did wrong in not finding an owner for it. He was found guilty and sentenced to receive 100 lashes. This I approved of."

Captain Phillip

SUNDAY 1 MAY

On this day in 1849
Transportation of convicts to Western Australia approved by British Government

EVENTS OF THE WEEK

VIC: Melbourne. The 11th Public Relations World Congress. The Hyatt on Collins. 26th to 29th Apr.
QLD: Brisbane. World Expo 88 commences. South Bank of Brisbane River. 30th Apr. to 30th Oct.

NSW: Sydney. 31st International Advertising Association World Congress. Opera House. 1st to 5th May.

JULY							AUGUST						
M	T	W	T	F	S	S	M	T	W	T	F	S	S
				1	2	3	1	2	3	4	5	6	7
4	5	6	7	8	9	10	8	9	10	11	12	13	14
11	12	13	14	15	16	17	15	16	17	18	19	20	21
18	19	20	21	22	23	24	22	23	24	25	26	27	28
25	26	27	28	29	30	31	29	30	31				

SEPTEMBER							OCTOBER						
M	T	W	T	F	S	S	M	T	W	T	F	S	S
			1	2	3	4	31					1	2
5	6	7	8	9	10	11	3	4	5	6	7	8	9
12	13	14	15	16	17	18	10	11	12	13	14	15	16
19	20	21	22	23	24	25	17	18	19	20	21	22	23
26	27	28	29	30			24	25	26	27	28	29	30

NOVEMBER							DECEMBER						
M	T	W	T	F	S	S	M	T	W	T	F	S	S
	1	2	3	4	5	6				1	2	3	4
7	8	9	10	11	12	13	5	6	7	8	9	10	11
14	15	16	17	18	19	20	12	13	14	15	16	17	18
21	22	23	24	25	26	27	19	20	21	22	23	24	25
28	29	30					26	27	28	29	30	31	

MONDAY 2 MAY

On this day in 1829
Captain Charles Fremantle takes possession
of Western Australia

9.00	
9.30	
10.00	
10.30	
11.00	
11.30	
12.00	
12.30	
1.00	
1.30	
2.00	
2.30	
3.00	
3.30	
4.00	
4.30	
5.00	
5.30	
6.00	

NOTES

"This morning John Bennett a convict received sentence of death for robbing the *CHARLOTTE*'s tent of bread, sugar and other articles to the value of 5/-, he was taken from the Court House to the place of execution and was hanged immediately."

Private John Easty

TUESDAY 3 MAY

On this day in 1841
New Zealand proclaimed a colony
independent of NSW

9.00	
9.30	
10.00	
10.30	
11.00	
11.30	
12.00	
12.30	
1.00	
1.30	
2.00	
2.30	
3.00	
3.30	
4.00	
4.30	
5.00	
5.30	
6.00	

NOTES

Thefts, efforts to escape and assaults and other forms of crime were taking place . . . "The endless punishment I have to witness is causing me great grief, but, I know that discipline is a necessity for the survival of the colony."

Captain Phillip

WEDNESDAY 4 MAY

On this day in 1842
Moreton Bay declared a free settlement

9.00	
9.30	
10.00	
10.30	
11.00	
11.30	
12.00	
12.30	
1.00	
1.30	
2.00	
2.30	
3.00	
3.30	
4.00	
4.30	
5.00	
5.30	
6.00	

NOTES

"The natives gave some of the officers fish and they in return shaved the natives which they appeared to be pleased with . . . Worgan found John Macneal on board *SIRIUS* with five or six wounds on his head and concussion. Though he did not despair of his life, he thought him to be in a desperate situation."

Lieutenant Bradley

JANUARY								FEBRUARY						
M	T	W	T	F	S	S		M	T	W	T	F	S	S
				1	2	3		1	2	3	4	5	6	7
4	5	6	7	8	9	10		8	9	10	11	12	13	14
11	12	13	14	15	16	17		15	16	17	18	19	20	21
18	19	20	21	22	23	24		22	23	24	25	26	27	28
25	26	27	28	29	30	31		29						

MARCH								APRIL						
M	T	W	T	F	S	S		M	T	W	T	F	S	S
1	2	3	4	5	6							1	2	3
7	8	9	10	11	12	13		4	5	6	7	8	9	10
14	15	16	17	18	19	20		11	12	13	14	15	16	17
21	22	23	24	25	26	27		18	19	20	21	22	23	24
28	29	30	31					25	26	27	28	29	30	

MAY								JUNE						
M	T	W	T	F	S	S		M	T	W	T	F	S	S
30	31					1				1	2	3	4	5
2	3	4	5	6	7	8		6	7	8	9	10	11	12
9	10	11	12	13	14	15		13	14	15	16	17	18	19
16	17	18	19	20	21	22		20	21	22	23	24	25	26
23	24	25	26	27	28	29		27	28	29	30			

THURSDAY 5 MAY

On this day in 1966
First Australian National Servicemen arrive
at Vietnam battle zone

9.00	
9.30	
10.00	
10.30	
11.00	
11.30	
12.00	
12.30	
1.00	
1.30	
2.00	
2.30	
3.00	
3.30	
4.00	
4.30	
5.00	
5.30	
6.00	

NOTES

"The *LADY PENRHYN* leaves the colony. Southwell (of the *SIRIUS*) dated a long detailed letter to his mother . . . he commented very favourably on the amount of fish available and thought his state of good health was due to this supplement to the rations. He also commented on the amount of fresh water for drinking and washing."
Surgeon Bowes Smyth

FRIDAY 6 MAY

On this day in 1886
Broken Hill Proprietary Ltd. smelters
open at Broken Hill

9.00	
9.30	
10.00	
10.30	
11.00	
11.30	
12.00	
12.30	
1.00	
1.30	
2.00	
2.30	
3.00	
3.30	
4.00	
4.30	
5.00	
5.30	
6.00	

NOTES

"The *SCARBOROUGH* sailed for China. The *SUPPLY* having completed caulking sailed for Lord Howe Island to convoy the transports clear of the coast and to procure Turtle. I approved of William Parr to receive 200 lashes for groundlessly insinuating to the sentinal that the worst provisions were issued to them, and for attempting to sow discontent amongst the battalion." **Captain Phillip**

SATURDAY 7 MAY

On this day in 1770
James Cook sails from Botany Bay and sights
entrance to Port Jackson

"I note some convicts have no idea how to make their rations spin out over the week, rations being given out weekly. Some ate almost all theirs at once and then stole because they were hungry."
Captain Phillip

SUNDAY 8 MAY

On this day in 1942
Battle of Coral Sea smashes Japanese
invasion force

EVENTS OF THE WEEK

QLD: Brisbane. Beef '88 Exhibition. Expo 88 site. 4th to 7th May.

ACT: Canberra. Bicentennial Carriage Driving Championships and National Harness Show. National Exhibition Centre. 4th to 8th May.

WA: Geraldton. The Travelling Australian Bicentennial Exhibition opens. 6th to 9th May.

JULY							AUGUST						
M	T	W	T	F	S	S	M	T	W	T	F	S	S
				1	2	3	1	2	3	4	5	6	7
4	5	6	7	8	9	10	8	9	10	11	12	13	14
11	12	13	14	15	16	17	15	16	17	18	19	20	21
18	19	20	21	22	23	24	22	23	24	25	26	27	28
25	26	27	28	29	30	31	29	30	31				

SEPTEMBER							OCTOBER						
M	T	W	T	F	S	S	M	T	W	T	F	S	S
			1	2	3	4	31					1	2
5	6	7	8	9	10	11	3	4	5	6	7	8	9
12	13	14	15	16	17	18	10	11	12	13	14	15	16
19	20	21	22	23	24	25	17	18	19	20	21	22	23
26	27	28	29	30			24	25	26	27	28	29	30

NOVEMBER							DECEMBER						
M	T	W	T	F	S	S	M	T	W	T	F	S	S
	1	2	3	4	5	6				1	2	3	4
7	8	9	10	11	12	13	5	6	7	8	9	10	11
14	15	16	17	18	19	20	12	13	14	15	16	17	18
21	22	23	24	25	26	27	19	20	21	22	23	24	25
28	29	30					26	27	28	29	30	31	

MONDAY 9 MAY

On this day in 1901
First Federal Parliament meets in Exhibition
Buildings, Melbourne

9.00	
9.30	
10.00	
10.30	
11.00	
11.30	
12.00	
12.30	
1.00	
1.30	
2.00	
2.30	
3.00	
3.30	
4.00	
4.30	
5.00	
5.30	
6.00	

NOTES

The *SIRIUS* "sent a party on shore to build huts for female convicts". After four months and because of the lack of suitable building material and the difficulty of acquiring it, only two officers were in huts.

Captain Phillip

TUESDAY 10 MAY

On this day in 1824
Sir John Pedder takes office as
Chief Justice of Van Diemen's Land

9.00	
9.30	
10.00	
10.30	
11.00	
11.30	
12.00	
12.30	
1.00	
1.30	
2.00	
2.30	
3.00	
3.30	
4.00	
4.30	
5.00	
5.30	
6.00	

NOTES

Bradley described an episode with a shark. "Many natives, men and women about our fishing boat. A shark followed this boat coming up the harbour. He got hold of one of the blades of one of the oars and when shook from that, he went to the rudder, and did not quit it till struck with the tiller."

Lieutenant Bradley

WEDNESDAY 11 MAY

On this day in 1813
Blaxland, Wentworth and Lawson set out
to cross the Blue Mountains

9.00	
9.30	
10.00	
10.30	
11.00	
11.30	
12.00	
12.30	
1.00	
1.30	
2.00	
2.30	
3.00	
3.30	
4.00	
4.30	
5.00	
5.30	
6.00	

NOTES

"I have ordered the marines to spend more time building their own huts instead of so much parading."

Captain Phillip

JANUARY							FEBRUARY						
M	T	W	T	F	S	S	M	T	W	T	F	S	S
				1	2	3	1	2	3	4	5	6	7
4	5	6	7	8	9	10	8	9	10	11	12	13	14
11	12	13	14	15	16	17	15	16	17	18	19	20	21
18	19	20	21	22	23	24	22	23	24	25	26	27	28
25	26	27	28	29	30	31	29						

MARCH							APRIL						
M	T	W	T	F	S	S	M	T	W	T	F	S	S
1	2	3	4	5	6						1	2	3
7	8	9	10	11	12	13	4	5	6	7	8	9	10
14	15	16	17	18	19	20	11	12	13	14	15	16	17
21	22	23	24	25	26	27	18	19	20	21	22	23	24
28	29	30	31				25	26	27	28	29	30	

MAY							JUNE						
M	T	W	T	F	S	S	M	T	W	T	F	S	S
30	31					1			1	2	3	4	5
2	3	4	5	6	7	8	6	7	8	9	10	11	12
9	10	11	12	13	14	15	13	14	15	16	17	18	19
16	17	18	19	20	21	22	20	21	22	23	24	25	26
23	24	25	26	27	28	29	27	28	29	30			

THURSDAY 12 MAY

On this day in 1810
Gov. William Bligh finally sails for England
after "Rum Rebellion"

9.00	
9.30	
10.00	
10.30	
11.00	
11.30	
12.00	
12.30	
1.00	
1.30	
2.00	
2.30	
3.00	
3.30	
4.00	
4.30	
5.00	
5.30	
6.00	

NOTES

"White and Worgan stressed the opinion that 1st Lieut. James Maxwell should return to Europe as soon as possible, as it is absolutely necessary, being the only chance he has of recovering from a dysentoric complaint."

Captain Phillip

FRIDAY 13 MAY

On this day in 1787
First Fleet sails from Portsmouth

9.00	
9.30	
10.00	
10.30	
11.00	
11.30	
12.00	
12.30	
1.00	
1.30	
2.00	
2.30	
3.00	
3.30	
4.00	
4.30	
5.00	
5.30	
6.00	

NOTES

"Walked out today as far as the brickgrounds. A pleasant road through the wood about two miles from the village . . . I see they have made between 20 and 30,000 bricks and are employed digging out a kiln for the burning of them."

Surgeon Worgan

SATURDAY 14 MAY

On this day in 1900
Commonwealth Bill introduced to
House of Commons

Hunter, Bradley and Worgan went in a boat about 12 miles up the harbour . . . "having extended our land excursion as far as we wished, we returned to the place where we landed regaling ourselves with a cold kangaroo pie, plum pudding, a bottle of wine, all which comforts we brought from the ships."

Surgeon Worgan

SUNDAY 15 MAY

On this day in 1928
Royal Flying Doctor Service begins,
first such service in the world

EVENTS OF THE WEEK

NATIONAL:
Bicentennial Around Australia Relay commences from New Parliament House, Canberra. 9th May to 13th December.

NSW: Sydney. Lions Club

International 36th Multiple District 201 Convention. 15th to 20th May.

ACT: Canberra. World Polocrosse Test Series. 14th to 29th May.

JULY							AUGUST						
M	T	W	T	F	S	S	M	T	W	T	F	S	S
				1	2	3	1	2	3	4	5	6	7
4	5	6	7	8	9	10	8	9	10	11	12	13	14
11	12	13	14	15	16	17	15	16	17	18	19	20	21
18	19	20	21	22	23	24	22	23	24	25	26	27	28
25	26	27	28	29	30	31	29	30	31				

SEPTEMBER							OCTOBER						
M	T	W	T	F	S	S	M	T	W	T	F	S	S
		1	2	3	4		31					1	2
5	6	7	8	9	10	11	3	4	5	6	7	8	9
12	13	14	15	16	17	18	10	11	12	13	14	15	16
19	20	21	22	23	24	25	17	18	19	20	21	22	23
26	27	28	29	30			24	25	26	27	28	29	30

NOVEMBER							DECEMBER						
M	T	W	T	F	S	S	M	T	W	T	F	S	S
1	2	3	4	5	6					1	2	3	4
7	8	9	10	11	12	13	5	6	7	8	9	10	11
14	15	16	17	18	19	20	12	13	14	15	16	17	18
21	22	23	24	25	26	27	19	20	21	22	23	24	25
28	29	30					26	27	28	29	30	31	

On this day in 1837
Construction begins on St. Andrews,
first C of E Cathedral in Australia

On this day in 1963
Government approves set up of U.S. naval
base at N.W. Cape, Western Australia

On this day in 1901
First wireless transmission in Australia
from Queenscliff, Vic.

9.00	9.00	9.00
9.30	9.30	9.30
10.00	10.00	10.00
10.30	10.30	10.30
11.00	11.00	11.00
11.30	11.30	11.30
12.00	12.00	12.00
12.30	12.30	12.30
1.00	1.00	1.00
1.30	1.30	1.30
2.00	2.00	2.00
2.30	2.30	2.30
3.00	3.00	3.00
3.30	3.30	3.30
4.00	4.00	4.00
4.30	4.30	4.30
5.00	5.00	5.00
5.30	5.30	5.30
6.00	6.00	6.00

NOTES

NOTES

NOTES

"I signed my second despatch to Lord Sydney in which I make mention that the sitting as members of the criminal court is thought a hardship by the officers, and of which they say, they were not informed before they left England."

Captain Phillip

"I will not take convicts from the public works which were far behind in construction to help the marines clear and cultivate their land. The carrying out of public works was already hampered by the quality of the wood, the difficulty of getting it and the shortage of men skilled in the art of carpentry."

Captain Phillip

Bradley described the shortage of food among the natives . . . "They were all friendly, but seemed they were badly off for food, most of them chewed a root much like fern . . . two natives so intent upon fishing did not notice us, nor were fish caught the whole of the time we were near them."

Lieutenant Bradley

JANUARY							FEBRUARY						
M	T	W	T	F	S	S	M	T	W	T	F	S	S
				1	2	3	1	2	3	4	5	6	7
4	5	6	7	8	9	10	8	9	10	11	12	13	14
11	12	13	14	15	16	17	15	16	17	18	19	20	21
18	19	20	21	22	23	24	22	23	24	25	26	27	28
25	26	27	28	29	30	31	29						

MARCH							APRIL						
M	T	W	T	F	S	S	M	T	W	T	F	S	S
	1	2	3	4	5	6					1	2	3
7	8	9	10	11	12	13	4	5	6	7	8	9	10
14	15	16	17	18	19	20	11	12	13	14	15	16	17
21	22	23	24	25	26	27	18	19	20	21	22	23	24
28	29	30	31				25	26	27	28	29	30	

MAY							JUNE						
M	T	W	T	F	S	S	M	T	W	T	F	S	S
30	31				1				1	2	3	4	5
2	3	4	5	6	7	8	6	7	8	9	10	11	12
9	10	11	12	13	14	15	13	14	15	16	17	18	19
16	17	18	19	20	21	22	20	21	22	23	24	25	26
23	24	25	26	27	28	29	27	28	29	30			

THURSDAY 19 MAY

On this day in 1861
Dame Nellie Melba (Helen
Porter Mitchell) born

9.00	
9.30	
10.00	
10.30	
11.00	
11.30	
12.00	
12.30	
1.00	
1.30	
2.00	
2.30	
3.00	
3.30	
4.00	
4.30	
5.00	
5.30	
6.00	

NOTES

"They have begun to unlade the
transports, and land the stores, and
it has this day been publickly
announced that some of the
transports will sail for England in 6
weeks, so a scribbling we will go."
Surgeon Worgan

FRIDAY 20 MAY

On this day in 1929
First airmail stamp issued:
costs threepence

9.00	
9.30	
10.00	
10.30	
11.00	
11.30	
12.00	
12.30	
1.00	
1.30	
2.00	
2.30	
3.00	
3.30	
4.00	
4.30	
5.00	
5.30	
6.00	

NOTES

"Much excitement in the colony,
the opportunity of writing home
and sending news back — who is
the King? the Queen? the Ministers?
whats the whim? our whim will
soon be to go naked, for you know,
my clothes are all torn to pieces by
going into the woods . . ."
Surgeon Worgan

SATURDAY 21 MAY

On this day in 1906
Japanese naval squadron visits Australia

"I had seen that the soil is
better and the trees further apart
at the head of the harbour; I think
it will be a good place to make
another settlement. I would like to
explore this area again soon, but the
pressure of work at the cove
prevents me . . ."
Captain Phillip

SUNDAY 22 MAY

On this day in 1860
First Queensland Parliament elections held.

EVENTS OF THE WEEK

NSW: Sydney.
57th ANZAAS
Bicentennial
Congress. University
of Sydney. 16th to
20th May.

WA: Port Hedland.
The Travelling
Australian
Bicentennial

Exhibition opens
17th to 19th May.

NSW: Sydney.
1988 National
Bicentennial
Congress including a
Bicentennial
Musicale. 22nd to
30th May.

JULY								AUGUST						
M	T	W	T	F	S	S		M	T	W	T	F	S	S
				1	2	3		1	2	3	4	5	6	7
4	5	6	7	8	9	10		8	9	10	11	12	13	14
11	12	13	14	15	16	17		15	16	17	18	19	20	21
18	19	20	21	22	23	24		22	23	24	25	26	27	28
25	26	27	28	29	30	31		29	30	31				

SEPTEMBER								OCTOBER						
M	T	W	T	F	S	S		M	T	W	T	F	S	S
		1	2	3	4		31						1	2
5	6	7	8	9	10	11		3	4	5	6	7	8	9
12	13	14	15	16	17	18		10	11	12	13	14	15	16
19	20	21	22	23	24	25		17	18	19	20	21	22	23
26	27	28	29	30				24	25	26	27	28	29	30

NOVEMBER								DECEMBER						
M	T	W	T	F	S	S		M	T	W	T	F	S	S
1	2	3	4	5	6					1	2	3	4
7	8	9	10	11	12	13		5	6	7	8	9	10	11
14	15	16	17	18	19	20		12	13	14	15	16	17	18
21	22	23	24	25	26	27		19	20	21	22	23	24	25
28	29	30						26	27	28	29	30	31	

MONDAY 23 MAY

On this day in 1883
Adelaide Zoo established

9.00	
9.30	
10.00	
10.30	
11.00	
11.30	
12.00	
12.30	
1.00	
1.30	
2.00	
2.30	
3.00	
3.30	
4.00	
4.30	
5.00	
5.30	
6.00	

NOTES

"The *PRINCE OF WALES* was cleared of stores . . . some canoes landed at Major Ross's garden up the harbour. They stole a jacket and several other things which were afterwards found in one of the canoes by some of the convicts."

Lieutenant Bradley

TUESDAY 24 MAY

On this day in 1930
Amy Johnson, first woman to fly solo from England, arrives at Darwin

9.00	
9.30	
10.00	
10.30	
11.00	
11.30	
12.00	
12.30	
1.00	
1.30	
2.00	
2.30	
3.00	
3.30	
4.00	
4.30	
5.00	
5.30	
6.00	

NOTES

" . . . There is something singular in these Evites (female natives) . . . if ever they deign to come near you to take a present they appear as coy, shy and timorous as a maid on her wedding night, but when they are, as they think, out of reach, they hollow to you, frisk, flirt and play a hundred wanton pranks . . ."

Surgeon Worgan

WEDNESDAY 25 MAY

On this day in 1896
South Australian women first exercise their right to vote

9.00	
9.30	
10.00	
10.30	
11.00	
11.30	
12.00	
12.30	
1.00	
1.30	
2.00	
2.30	
3.00	
3.30	
4.00	
4.30	
5.00	
5.30	
6.00	

NOTES

"The *SUPPLY* tender arrived in this Cove to-day from Lord Howe Island but O Woeful news, for our Alderman like stomachs, not a single turtle so, for having for this 10 days past, liquorish chops from the idea of 4 or 5 turtle feasts on her arrival, we are now all chop-fallen."

Surgeon Worgan

JANUARY							FEBRUARY						
M	T	W	T	F	S	S	M	T	W	T	F	S	S
				1	2	3	1	2	3	4	5	6	7
4	5	6	7	8	9	10	8	9	10	11	12	13	14
11	12	13	14	15	16	17	15	16	17	18	19	20	21
18	19	20	21	22	23	24	22	23	24	25	26	27	28
25	26	27	28	29	30	31	29						

MARCH							APRIL						
M	T	W	T	F	S	S	M	T	W	T	F	S	S
	1	2	3	4	5	6					1	2	3
7	8	9	10	11	12	13	4	5	6	7	8	9	10
14	15	16	17	18	19	20	11	12	13	14	15	16	17
21	22	23	24	25	26	27	18	19	20	21	22	23	24
28	29	30	31				25	26	27	28	29	30	

MAY							JUNE						
M	T	W	T	F	S	S	M	T	W	T	F	S	S
30	31					1			1	2	3	4	5
2	3	4	5	6	7	8	6	7	8	9	10	11	12
9	10	11	12	13	14	15	13	14	15	16	17	18	19
16	17	18	19	20	21	22	20	21	22	23	24	25	26
23	24	25	26	27	28	29	27	28	29	30			

On this day in 1853
Last convict arrives in Hobart after
50 years of transportation

9.00	
9.30	
10.00	
10.30	
11.00	
11.30	
12.00	
12.30	
1.00	
1.30	
2.00	
2.30	
3.00	
3.30	
4.00	
4.30	
5.00	
5.30	
6.00	

NOTES

"John Trace was charged with feloniously and fraudulently stealing, taking, and carrying away one pound and a half of flour, value threepence, the property of Thomas Till on Sunday 18th May, between four and five in the afternoon. We found Trace guilty. He was sentenced to 200 lashes, and to repay the deficiency. Sentence signed by Collins and self."

Captain Phillip

On this day in 1967
Referendum allows Federal Parliament
to legislate for Aboriginals

9.00	
9.30	
10.00	
10.30	
11.00	
11.30	
12.00	
12.30	
1.00	
1.30	
2.00	
2.30	
3.00	
3.30	
4.00	
4.30	
5.00	
5.30	
6.00	

NOTES

"In future barracks, store houses and all buildings, will be covered with shingles, which we now make from a tree like the pine-tree in appearance, the wood resembling the English oak, I am sure these will be more secure from the danger of fire . . ."

Captain Phillip

On this day in 1838
Adelaide Theatre Royal, first theatre
in S.A., opens

"We let an old native observe the fatal effects of our gun, by showing him a bird in a tree and then shooting it. On seeing the bird fall dead, he looked at the gun with astonishment and seemed as afraid of it and thinks it may go off loaded or unloaded."

Surgeon Worgan

On this day in 1835
John Batman arrives at Port Phillip Bay

EVENTS OF THE WEEK

NSW: Sydney. Pacific Basin Economic Council 21st International General Meeting. Sheraton Wentworth Hotel. 23rd to 26th May.

NSW: Sydney. Toastmasters Down Under Convention.

Sheraton Wentworth Hotel. 26th to 29th May.

NT: Newcastle Waters. Droving Australia commences. 28th May.

JULY							AUGUST						
M	T	W	T	F	S	S	M	T	W	T	F	S	S
				1	2	3	1	2	3	4	5	6	7
4	5	6	7	8	9	10	8	9	10	11	12	13	14
11	12	13	14	15	16	17	15	16	17	18	19	20	21
18	19	20	21	22	23	24	22	23	24	25	26	27	28
25	26	27	28	29	30	31	29	30	31				

SEPTEMBER							OCTOBER						
M	T	W	T	F	S	S	M	T	W	T	F	S	S
		1	2	3	4		31					1	2
5	6	7	8	9	10	11	3	4	5	6	7	8	9
12	13	14	15	16	17	18	10	11	12	13	14	15	16
19	20	21	22	23	24	25	17	18	19	20	21	22	23
26	27	28	29	30			24	25	26	27	28	29	30

NOVEMBER							DECEMBER						
M	T	W	T	F	S	S	M	T	W	T	F	S	S
1	2	3	4	5	6					1	2	3	4
7	8	9	10	11	12	13	5	6	7	8	9	10	11
14	15	16	17	18	19	20	12	13	14	15	16	17	18
21	22	23	24	25	26	27	19	20	21	22	23	24	25
28	29	30					26	27	28	29	30	31	

MONDAY 30 MAY

On this day in 1848
Edmund Kennedy begins expedition
to Cape York Peninsula

9.00	
9.30	
10.00	
10.30	
11.00	
11.30	
12.00	
12.30	
1.00	
1.30	
2.00	
2.30	
3.00	
3.30	
4.00	
4.30	
5.00	
5.30	
6.00	

NOTES

"Two convicts who had been left on their own to cut rushes were later found dead — one had three spears in him the other a blow on the forehead. I intend to investigate these killings for it is my opinion, with many others, that the natives are not the aggressors."

Captain Phillip

TUESDAY 31 MAY

On this day in 1942
Three Japanese midget submarines
enter Sydney Harbour

9.00	
9.30	
10.00	
10.30	
11.00	
11.30	
12.00	
12.30	
1.00	
1.30	
2.00	
2.30	
3.00	
3.30	
4.00	
4.30	
5.00	
5.30	
6.00	

NOTES

"There being no other shelter for the guard but tents, great inconvenience was found in placing under its charge one or two prisoners together. The convicts, therefore . . . were sent to the Bare Island at the entrance of this cove (Botany Bay) where they were to be supplied weekly with provisions."

Captain Phillip

WEDNESDAY 1 JUNE

On this day in 1850
First convict ship arrives in Western Australia
carrying 75 male convicts

9.00	
9.30	
10.00	
10.30	
11.00	
11.30	
12.00	
12.30	
1.00	
1.30	
2.00	
2.30	
3.00	
3.30	
4.00	
4.30	
5.00	
5.30	
6.00	

NOTES

" . . . the native who seemed to be the leader came towards us making signs for us to get away but, when he saw me advancing alone and unarmed, he dropped his spear and we met in a friendly way. In no time we were surrounded by about 200 natives."

Surgeon Worgan

JANUARY								FEBRUARY						
M	T	W	T	F	S	S		M	T	W	T	F	S	S
				1	2	3		1	2	3	4	5	6	7
4	5	6	7	8	9	10		8	9	10	11	12	13	14
11	12	13	14	15	16	17		15	16	17	18	19	20	21
18	19	20	21	22	23	24		22	23	24	25	26	27	28
25	26	27	28	29	30	31		29						

MARCH								APRIL						
M	T	W	T	F	S	S		M	T	W	T	F	S	S
1	2	3	4	5	6						1	2	3	
7	8	9	10	11	12	13		4	5	6	7	8	9	10
14	15	16	17	18	19	20		11	12	13	14	15	16	17
21	22	23	24	25	26	27		18	19	20	21	22	23	24
28	29	30	31					25	26	27	28	29	30	

MAY								JUNE						
M	T	W	T	F	S	S		M	T	W	T	F	S	S
30	31				1					1	2	3	4	5
2	3	4	5	6	7	8		6	7	8	9	10	11	12
9	10	11	12	13	14	15		13	14	15	16	17	18	19
16	17	18	19	20	21	22		20	21	22	23	24	25	26
23	24	25	26	27	28	29		27	28	29	30			

THURSDAY 2 JUNE

On this day in 1846
Melbourne newspaper "Argus" first issued:
runs until 1957

9.00	
9.30	
10.00	
10.30	
11.00	
11.30	
12.00	
12.30	
1.00	
1.30	
2.00	
2.30	
3.00	
3.30	
4.00	
4.30	
5.00	
5.30	
6.00	

NOTES

FRIDAY 3 JUNE

On this day in 1790
"Lady Juliana", first ship of Second Fleet,
arrives in Port Jackson

9.00	
9.30	
10.00	
10.30	
11.00	
11.30	
12.00	
12.30	
1.00	
1.30	
2.00	
2.30	
3.00	
3.30	
4.00	
4.30	
5.00	
5.30	
6.00	

NOTES

SATURDAY 4 JUNE

On this day in 1819
Convict barracks at Hyde Park opens:
able to hold 600 convicts

"Being His Majesty's Birthday, the same was observed with every demonstration of joy permitted. *SIRIUS* and *SUPPLY* fired each 21 guns . . . The soldiers drank their sovereign's health in porter. Convicts were allowed half a pint of Rum a man . . . Three convicts condemned to die received full pardon, and all cheerfully joined in singing God Save The King round their bonfires."

Captain Phillip

SUNDAY 5 JUNE

On this day in 1827
Allan Cunningham discovers Darling
Downs in Queensland

The criminal court sat,
" . . . two men were charged with feloniously, with force of arms, stealing 20 pounds weight of goat's flesh, of the value of ten shillings . . . and the next day two more persons were charged with stealing 12 pounds weight of the said goat's flesh."

Surgeon Worgan

" . . . we perceived that the Governor was in great pain, from a return of his complaint. Though his countenance too plainly indicated his torture which he suffered, he took every method in his power to conceal it."

Chief Surgeon White

EVENTS OF THE WEEK

NT: Darwin. The Travelling Australian Bicentennial Exhibition opens. 1st to 4th June.

ACT: Canberra. International Training in Communications National Conference. Lakeside Hotel. 2nd to 6th June.

NORFOLK ISLAND: Bounty Week Celebrations, celebrating arrival of mutineers. 4th to 12th June.

	JULY							AUGUST					
M	T	W	T	F	S	S	M	T	W	T	F	S	S
				1	2	3	1	2	3	4	5	6	7
4	5	6	7	8	9	10	8	9	10	11	12	13	14
11	12	13	14	15	16	17	15	16	17	18	19	20	21
18	19	20	21	22	23	24	22	23	24	25	26	27	28
25	26	27	28	29	30	31	29	30	31				

	SEPTEMBER							OCTOBER					
M	T	W	T	F	S	S	M	T	W	T	F	S	S
			1	2	3	4	31					1	2
5	6	7	8	9	10	11	3	4	5	6	7	8	9
12	13	14	15	16	17	18	10	11	12	13	14	15	16
19	20	21	22	23	24	25	17	18	19	20	21	22	23
26	27	28	29	30			24	25	26	27	28	29	30

	NOVEMBER							DECEMBER					
M	T	W	T	F	S	S	M	T	W	T	F	S	S
	1	2	3	4	5	6				1	2	3	4
7	8	9	10	11	12	13	5	6	7	8	9	10	11
14	15	16	17	18	19	20	12	13	14	15	16	17	18
21	22	23	24	25	26	27	19	20	21	22	23	24	25
28	29	30					26	27	28	29	30	31	

MONDAY 6 JUNE

On this day in 1859
Queensland granted Separation
from New South Wales

9.00	
9.30	
10.00	
10.30	
11.00	
11.30	
12.00	
12.30	
1.00	
1.30	
2.00	
2.30	
3.00	
3.30	
4.00	
4.30	
5.00	
5.30	
6.00	

NOTES

"A party of gentlemen with their servants and 4 soldiers were walking to Botany Bay . . . met with a body of 300 natives all armed with spears and targets. They did not seem to feel their superiority but walked out of the track of our people and let them pass without showing any mischevious intention."
David Blackburn

TUESDAY 7 JUNE

On this day in 1917
Attack on Messines Ridge during WWI;
nearly 7000 Australian casualties

9.00	
9.30	
10.00	
10.30	
11.00	
11.30	
12.00	
12.30	
1.00	
1.30	
2.00	
2.30	
3.00	
3.30	
4.00	
4.30	
5.00	
5.30	
6.00	

NOTES

"Signed a precept for a court for 9 am on Tuesday 10th June and addressed it to the Judge Advocate, Hunter, Ball, Campbell, Shea, Maitland-Shairp, and Davey. Collins and Hunter sat as magistrates and tried two cases. I ordered the *FRIENDSHIP* to send a longboat and 5 hands for wood for the women's houses."
Captain Phillip

WEDNESDAY 8 JUNE

On this day in 1805
John Macarthur arrives in Sydney
with first merino sheep

9.00	
9.30	
10.00	
10.30	
11.00	
11.30	
12.00	
12.30	
1.00	
1.30	
2.00	
2.30	
3.00	
3.30	
4.00	
4.30	
5.00	
5.30	
6.00	

NOTES

" . . . if I could send 50 farmers out with their families into the open country they would do more in one year in rendering this colony independent of the mother country, as to provisions, than a thousand convicts."
Captain Phillip

JANUARY							FEBRUARY						
M	T	W	T	F	S	S	M	T	W	T	F	S	S
				1	2	3	1	2	3	4	5	6	7
4	5	6	7	8	9	10	8	9	10	11	12	13	14
11	12	13	14	15	16	17	15	16	17	18	19	20	21
18	19	20	21	22	23	24	22	23	24	25	26	27	28
25	26	27	28	29	30	31	29						

MARCH							APRIL						
M	T	W	T	F	S	S	M	T	W	T	F	S	S
1	2	3	4	5	6						1	2	3
7	8	9	10	11	12	13	4	5	6	7	8	9	10
14	15	16	17	18	19	20	11	12	13	14	15	16	17
21	22	23	24	25	26	27	18	19	20	21	22	23	24
28	29	30	31				25	26	27	28	29	30	

MAY							JUNE						
M	T	W	T	F	S	S	M	T	W	T	F	S	S
30	31					1			1	2	3	4	5
2	3	4	5	6	7	8	6	7	8	9	10	11	12
9	10	11	12	13	14	15	13	14	15	16	17	18	19
16	17	18	19	20	21	22	20	21	22	23	24	25	26
23	24	25	26	27	28	29	27	28	29	30			

THURSDAY 9 JUNE

On this day in 1928
Charles Kingsford-Smith and crew complete
first Pacific air crossing; USA to Aust.

9.00	
9.30	
10.00	
10.30	
11.00	
11.30	
12.00	
12.30	
1.00	
1.30	
2.00	
2.30	
3.00	
3.30	
4.00	
4.30	
5.00	
5.30	
6.00	

NOTES

"... accordingly, we made up a
wigwam of gum boughs, cut some
dry ferns for a bed, lit 2 or 3
roaring fires near our hut and set
down to dinner. We sung the
evening away and about 9 o'clock
retired to rest, taking it by turns to
keep watch, and supply the fires
with fuel."

Surgeon Worgan

FRIDAY 10 JUNE

On this day in 1835
William Wentworth founds first political
party — Australian Patriotic Association

9.00	
9.30	
10.00	
10.30	
11.00	
11.30	
12.00	
12.30	
1.00	
1.30	
2.00	
2.30	
3.00	
3.30	
4.00	
4.30	
5.00	
5.30	
6.00	

NOTES

"... we walked over a vast
extent of rich land and through
some pleasant valleys, the soil
seemed fit for producing any kind
of grain, but from its situation, the
quantity of heavy timber growing
upon it, to render it fit for
cultivation would require a vast
number of people, teams of cattle
and a great length of time."

Surgeon Worgan

SATURDAY 11 JUNE

On this day in 1863
First public use of electricity in Australia

"Several parties were sent in
quest of the bull and cows which
belonged to the settlement, they
having been missing some days: one
of the convicts having absented
himself about the same time, it was
supposed he had driven them
away."

Surgeon Worgan

SUNDAY 12 JUNE

On this day in 1872
Royal Mint opens in Melbourne

EVENTS OF THE WEEK

NSW: Sydney. Quilt
Australia '88.
Centrepoint. 12th to
15th June.

NSW: Sydney.
The 35th Sydney
Film Festival. State
Theatre. 10th to
24th June.

NT: Darwin.
Australian Cat
Federation. National
Cat Show. Foskey
Pavilion —
Showgrounds. 11th
to 13th June.

JULY								AUGUST						
M	T	W	T	F	S	S		M	T	W	T	F	S	S
				1	2	3		1	2	3	4	5	6	7
4	5	6	7	8	9	10		8	9	10	11	12	13	14
11	12	13	14	15	16	17		15	16	17	18	19	20	21
18	19	20	21	22	23	24		22	23	24	25	26	27	28
25	26	27	28	29	30	31		29	30	31				

SEPTEMBER								OCTOBER						
M	T	W	T	F	S	S		M	T	W	T	F	S	S
			1	2	3	4		31					1	2
5	6	7	8	9	10	11		3	4	5	6	7	8	9
12	13	14	15	16	17	18		10	11	12	13	14	15	16
19	20	21	22	23	24	25		17	18	19	20	21	22	23
26	27	28	29	30				24	25	26	27	28	29	30

NOVEMBER								DECEMBER						
M	T	W	T	F	S	S		M	T	W	T	F	S	S
1	2	3	4	5	6						1	2	3	4
7	8	9	10	11	12	13		5	6	7	8	9	10	11
14	15	16	17	18	19	20		12	13	14	15	16	17	18
21	22	23	24	25	26	27		19	20	21	22	23	24	25
28	29	30						26	27	28	29	30	31	

MONDAY 13 JUNE

On this day in 1942
Rationing of clothing begins in Australia

9.00	
9.30	
10.00	
10.30	
11.00	
11.30	
12.00	
12.30	
1.00	
1.30	
2.00	
2.30	
3.00	
3.30	
4.00	
4.30	
5.00	
5.30	
6.00	

NOTES

" . . . I hope few convicts will be sent out for one year at least, except carpenters, masons, and bricklayers or farmers, who can support themselves and assist in supporting others. Numbers of those now here are a burthen and incapable of any kind of hard labour."

Captain Phillip

TUESDAY 14 JUNE

On this day in 1893
Paddy Hannan discovers gold at Kalgoorlie, W.A.

9.00	
9.30	
10.00	
10.30	
11.00	
11.30	
12.00	
12.30	
1.00	
1.30	
2.00	
2.30	
3.00	
3.30	
4.00	
4.30	
5.00	
5.30	
6.00	

NOTES

Bradley noted that the Governor made known his intentions of sending the PRINCE OF WALES transport to England. This ship had been fitting for sea for several days and was said to be going to Norfolk Island, until the question was asked by Captain Tench.

WEDNESDAY 15 JUNE

On this day in 1862
Frank Gardiner, bushranger, leads gold escort robbery near Forbes, N.S.W.

9.00	
9.30	
10.00	
10.30	
11.00	
11.30	
12.00	
12.30	
1.00	
1.30	
2.00	
2.30	
3.00	
3.30	
4.00	
4.30	
5.00	
5.30	
6.00	

NOTES

" . . . clothing, particularly the womens, is very bad, most of the axes, spades, and shovels the worst that ever were seen. The provision is as good. Of the seed and corn sent from England part has been destroyed by weevil; the rest in very good order."

Captain Phillip

JANUARY								FEBRUARY						
M	T	W	T	F	S	S		M	T	W	T	F	S	S
				1	2	3		1	2	3	4	5	6	7
4	5	6	7	8	9	10		8	9	10	11	12	13	14
11	12	13	14	15	16	17		15	16	17	18	19	20	21
18	19	20	21	22	23	24		22	23	24	25	26	27	28
25	26	27	28	29	30	31		29						

MARCH								APRIL						
M	T	W	T	F	S	S		M	T	W	T	F	S	S
1	2	3	4	5	6							1	2	3
7	8	9	10	11	12	13		4	5	6	7	8	9	10
14	15	16	17	18	19	20		11	12	13	14	15	16	17
21	22	23	24	25	26	27		18	19	20	21	22	23	24
28	29	30	31					25	26	27	28	29	30	

MAY								JUNE						
M	T	W	T	F	S	S		M	T	W	T	F	S	S
30	31					1				1	2	3	4	5
2	3	4	5	6	7	8		6	7	8	9	10	11	12
9	10	11	12	13	14	15		13	14	15	16	17	18	19
16	17	18	19	20	21	22		20	21	22	23	24	25	26
23	24	25	26	27	28	29		27	28	29	30			

THURSDAY 16 JUNE

On this day in 1982
Tasmanian Government passes Act for
construction of Gordon River dam

9.00	
9.30	
10.00	
10.30	
11.00	
11.30	
12.00	
12.30	
1.00	
1.30	
2.00	
2.30	
3.00	
3.30	
4.00	
4.30	
5.00	
5.30	
6.00	

NOTES

" . . . I have no account of the
time for which the convicts are
sentenced, or the dates of the
conviction, some of them, by their
own account, have a little more
than a year to remain, and, I am
told, will apply for permission to
return to England, or to go to
India."

Captain Phillip

FRIDAY 17 JUNE

On this day in 1788
First official use of "Sydney" as name
of settlement.

9.00	
9.30	
10.00	
10.30	
11.00	
11.30	
12.00	
12.30	
1.00	
1.30	
2.00	
2.30	
3.00	
3.30	
4.00	
4.30	
5.00	
5.30	
6.00	

NOTES

"Until I receive instructions
arising from matters of the 16th,
none will be permitted to leave the
settlement; but if, when the time
for which they were sentenced
expires, the most abandoned and
useless were permitted to go to
China, in any ships that may stop
here, it would be a great advantage
to the settlement."

Captain Phillip

SATURDAY 18 JUNE

On this day in 1829
Governor James Stirling proclaims
colony at Swan River, W.A.

"The number of convicts now
employed in erecting the necessary
building and cultivating the lands
only amounts to 320 — and the
whole number of people victualled
amounts to 966 — consequently we
have only the labour of a part, to
provide for the whole."

Captain Phillip

SUNDAY 19 JUNE

On this day in 1931
Depression riots in Sydney between
police and anti-evictionists

EVENTS OF THE WEEK

WA: Perth.
Highpoint City
Trans-Australia Bike
Race begins. 19th
June.

NATIONAL Queen's
Birthday Holiday —
all States except
Western Australia.
13th June.

NT: Alice Springs.
The Travelling
Australian
Bicentennial
Exhibition opens.
14th to 16th June.

JULY							AUGUST						
M	T	W	T	F	S	S	M	T	W	T	F	S	S
				1	2	3	1	2	3	4	5	6	7
4	5	6	7	8	9	10	8	9	10	11	12	13	14
11	12	13	14	15	16	17	15	16	17	18	19	20	21
18	19	20	21	22	23	24	22	23	24	25	26	27	28
25	26	27	28	29	30	31	29	30	31				

SEPTEMBER							OCTOBER						
M	T	W	T	F	S	S	M	T	W	T	F	S	S
		1	2	3	4		31					1	2
5	6	7	8	9	10	11	3	4	5	6	7	8	9
12	13	14	15	16	17	18	10	11	12	13	14	15	16
19	20	21	22	23	24	25	17	18	19	20	21	22	23
26	27	28	29	30			24	25	26	27	28	29	30

NOVEMBER							DECEMBER						
M	T	W	T	F	S	S	M	T	W	T	F	S	S
1	2	3	4	5	6					1	2	3	4
7	8	9	10	11	12	13	5	6	7	8	9	10	11
14	15	16	17	18	19	20	12	13	14	15	16	17	18
21	22	23	24	25	26	27	19	20	21	22	23	24	25
28	29	30					26	27	28	29	30	31	

MONDAY 20 JUNE

On this day in 1969
Arbitration Court accepts principle
of equal pay for women

9.00	
9.30	
10.00	
10.30	
11.00	
11.30	
12.00	
12.30	
1.00	
1.30	
2.00	
2.30	
3.00	
3.30	
4.00	
4.30	
5.00	
5.30	
6.00	

NOTES

"I observe the natives had lit a fire on each side of a very old man found nearly dead. He was laying on his back and appeared worn out with age."

Captain Phillip

TUESDAY 21 JUNE

On this day in 1954
John Landy becomes first Australian
to break 4-minute mile

9.00	
9.30	
10.00	
10.30	
11.00	
11.30	
12.00	
12.30	
1.00	
1.30	
2.00	
2.30	
3.00	
3.30	
4.00	
4.30	
5.00	
5.30	
6.00	

NOTES

"A kind of fruit had been discovered here, a pure ascid, and found very good in scorbutic cases. A party was employed to get those berries for many people were down with the scurvy."

Lieutenant Bradley

WEDNESDAY 22 JUNE

On this day in 1863
Adelaide's first gaslights operate

9.00	
9.30	
10.00	
10.30	
11.00	
11.30	
12.00	
12.30	
1.00	
1.30	
2.00	
2.30	
3.00	
3.30	
4.00	
4.30	
5.00	
5.30	
6.00	

NOTES

"Corbett, who survived for nineteen days, finally came back to camp because life was too difficult to subsist in the woods . . . earthquake so frightened Corbett he gave himself up to justice."

Captain Phillip

JANUARY								FEBRUARY						
M	T	W	T	F	S	S		M	T	W	T	F	S	S
				1	2	3		1	2	3	4	5	6	7
4	5	6	7	8	9	10		8	9	10	11	12	13	14
11	12	13	14	15	16	17		15	16	17	18	19	20	21
18	19	20	21	22	23	24		22	23	24	25	26	27	28
25	26	27	28	29	30	31		29						

MARCH								APRIL						
M	T	W	T	F	S	S		M	T	W	T	F	S	S
1	2	3	4	5	6						1	2	3
7	8	9	10	11	12	13		4	5	6	7	8	9	10
14	15	16	17	18	19	20		11	12	13	14	15	16	17
21	22	23	24	25	26	27		18	19	20	21	22	23	24
28	29	30	31					25	26	27	28	29	30	

MAY								JUNE						
M	T	W	T	F	S	S		M	T	W	T	F	S	S
30	31					1				1	2	3	4	5
2	3	4	5	6	7	8		6	7	8	9	10	11	12
9	10	11	12	13	14	15		13	14	15	16	17	18	19
16	17	18	19	20	21	22		20	21	22	23	24	25	26
23	24	25	26	27	28	29		27	28	29	30			

THURSDAY 23 JUNE

On this day in 1980
Australia's first test-tube baby born

9.00	
9.30	
10.00	
10.30	
11.00	
11.30	
12.00	
12.30	
1.00	
1.30	
2.00	
2.30	
3.00	
3.30	
4.00	
4.30	
5.00	
5.30	
6.00	

NOTES

" . . . the Governor revoked the decree by which Corbett was outlawed, and he was tried by the criminal court, simply for the theft he had committed, and sentenced to be hanged."

Chief Surgeon White

FRIDAY 24 JUNE

On this day in 1915
Albert Jacka awarded first
Australian VC of WWI

9.00	
9.30	
10.00	
10.30	
11.00	
11.30	
12.00	
12.30	
1.00	
1.30	
2.00	
2.30	
3.00	
3.30	
4.00	
4.30	
5.00	
5.30	
6.00	

NOTES

" . . . having received orders from Governor Phillip to gitt the ship in readiness to proceed to England, with Lieut. Shortland as soon as our goods was landed . . . ship to be careened."

Log of FRIENDSHIP

SATURDAY 25 JUNE

On this day in 1950
Communist-controlled North Korea
invades South Korea

" . . . Corbett was executed at 11.30 am and died penitent. When brought to the fatal tree he addressed the convicts in a pathetic, eloquent and well directed speech."

Sergeant James Scott

SUNDAY 26 JUNE

On this day in 1880
Kelly gang execute police informer Aaron
Sherritt near Beechworth

EVENTS OF THE WEEK

VIC: Melbourne.
Highpoint City
Trans-Australia Bike
Race ends. 25th
June.
NATIONAL: Mormon
Tabernacle Choir
Tour of Australia.
25th June to 4th
July.

QLD: Mt. Isa.
The Travelling
Australian
Bicentennial
Exhibition opens.
24th to 27th June.

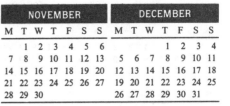

JULY							AUGUST						
M	T	W	T	F	S	S	M	T	W	T	F	S	S
				1	2	3	1	2	3	4	5	6	7
4	5	6	7	8	9	10	8	9	10	11	12	13	14
11	12	13	14	15	16	17	15	16	17	18	19	20	21
18	19	20	21	22	23	24	22	23	24	25	26	27	28
25	26	27	28	29	30	31	29	30	31				

SEPTEMBER							OCTOBER						
M	T	W	T	F	S	S	M	T	W	T	F	S	S
			1	2	3	4	31					1	2
5	6	7	8	9	10	11	3	4	5	6	7	8	9
12	13	14	15	16	17	18	10	11	12	13	14	15	16
19	20	21	22	23	24	25	17	18	19	20	21	22	23
26	27	28	29	30			24	25	26	27	28	29	30

NOVEMBER							DECEMBER						
M	T	W	T	F	S	S	M	T	W	T	F	S	S
1	2	3	4	5	6					1	2	3	4
7	8	9	10	11	12	13	5	6	7	8	9	10	11
14	15	16	17	18	19	20	12	13	14	15	16	17	18
21	22	23	24	25	26	27	19	20	21	22	23	24	25
28	29	30					26	27	28	29	30	31	

MONDAY 27 JUNE

On this day in 1876
Edward Trickett wins Australia's first world
sporting title, for sculling

9.00	
9.30	
10.00	
10.30	
11.00	
11.30	
12.00	
12.30	
1.00	
1.30	
2.00	
2.30	
3.00	
3.30	
4.00	
4.30	
5.00	
5.30	
6.00	

NOTES

"Tho' we have had heavy rains
at the change of the moon, this
cannot be called a rainy season. The
climate is a very fine one, and the
country will, I make no doubt, when
the woods are cleared away, be as
healthy as any in the world . . ."

Captain Phillip

TUESDAY 28 JUNE

On this day in 1919
Treaty of Versailles signed by Australia

9.00	
9.30	
10.00	
10.30	
11.00	
11.30	
12.00	
12.30	
1.00	
1.30	
2.00	
2.30	
3.00	
3.30	
4.00	
4.30	
5.00	
5.30	
6.00	

NOTES

"I have given orders for a cellar
to be built on the west side of the
cove for the storage of the spirits
on board the *FYSHBURN* as I hope to
send her away by the middle of
August."

Captain Phillip

WEDNESDAY 29 JUNE

On this day in 1880
Ned Kelly captured at Glenrowan

9.00	
9.30	
10.00	
10.30	
11.00	
11.30	
12.00	
12.30	
1.00	
1.30	
2.00	
2.30	
3.00	
3.30	
4.00	
4.30	
5.00	
5.30	
6.00	

NOTES

"No tidings of our cows and
bulls yet . . . Their loss if it proves
one, will be rather a misfortune for
our Colony, and, as an additional
calamity, the sheep, both of the
public and private stocks, die very
fast."

Surgeon Worgan

JANUARY							FEBRUARY						
M	T	W	T	F	S	S	M	T	W	T	F	S	S
				1	2	3	1	2	3	4	5	6	7
4	5	6	7	8	9	10	8	9	10	11	12	13	14
11	12	13	14	15	16	17	15	16	17	18	19	20	21
18	19	20	21	22	23	24	22	23	24	25	26	27	28
25	26	27	28	29	30	31	29						

MARCH							APRIL						
M	T	W	T	F	S	S	M	T	W	T	F	S	S
	1	2	3	4	5	6					1	2	3
7	8	9	10	11	12	13	4	5	6	7	8	9	10
14	15	16	17	18	19	20	11	12	13	14	15	16	17
21	22	23	24	25	26	27	18	19	20	21	22	23	24
28	29	30	31				25	26	27	28	29	30	

MAY							JUNE						
M	T	W	T	F	S	S	M	T	W	T	F	S	S
30	31				1				1	2	3	4	5
2	3	4	5	6	7	8	6	7	8	9	10	11	12
9	10	11	12	13	14	15	13	14	15	16	17	18	19
16	17	18	19	20	21	22	20	21	22	23	24	25	26
23	24	25	26	27	28	29	27	28	29	30			

THURSDAY 30 JUNE

On this day in 1926
A. Cobham begins first Australia-
England-Australia flight

9.00	
9.30	
10.00	
10.30	
11.00	
11.30	
12.00	
12.30	
1.00	
1.30	
2.00	
2.30	
3.00	
3.30	
4.00	
4.30	
5.00	
5.30	
6.00	

NOTES

"Exemplary punishments
seemed during June to be growing
daily more necessary. Stock was
often killed, huts and tents broken
open and provisions constantly
stolen . . . daily routine continued in
the SIRIUS."

Judge Advocate Collins

FRIDAY 1 JULY

On this day in 1930
Don Bradman establishes record score in
England v Australia Test; 334 runs

9.00	
9.30	
10.00	
10.30	
11.00	
11.30	
12.00	
12.30	
1.00	
1.30	
2.00	
2.30	
3.00	
3.30	
4.00	
4.30	
5.00	
5.30	
6.00	

NOTES

". . . standing on the sea face at
South Head we had a good view of
the sea, and of all that part of the
harbour open to it . . . if the flat
round this rock was not a perfect
smooth bottom, I am confident with
the sea that was running, it would
break."

Lieutenant Bradley

SATURDAY 2 JULY

On this day in 1811
George Johnston cashiered from N.S.W. Corps
for action in deposing Governor Bligh

"My orders of June 20 were
carried out. The corporal and 8
marines ashore rejoined and three
marines were transferred from
SIRIUS. George Flemming joined
Captain Campbell's company, Isaac
Farr joined Captain Shea's, and
James Angell joined Captain
Merideth's. I wrote letters to Sir
Joseph Banks, describing the plants
and seeds of the country and the
animals and natives." **Captain Phillip**

SUNDAY 3 JULY

On this day in 1872
"Sydney Morning Herald" receives first direct
news cable from London

EVENTS OF THE WEEK

NT: Statewide.
Tenth Anniversary
— Self Government.
1st Jul.

QLD: Brisbane.
International
Trombone Seminar.
Queensland
Conservatorium of
Music.
2nd to 7th Jul.

ACT: Canberra.
ICASE World
Conference on
Science Education.
National Convention
Centre.
3rd to 9th Jul.

JULY							AUGUST						
M	T	W	T	F	S	S	M	T	W	T	F	S	S
				1	2	3	1	2	3	4	5	6	7
4	5	6	7	8	9	10	8	9	10	11	12	13	14
11	12	13	14	15	16	17	15	16	17	18	19	20	21
18	19	20	21	22	23	24	22	23	24	25	26	27	28
25	26	27	28	29	30	31	29	30	31				

SEPTEMBER							OCTOBER						
M	T	W	T	F	S	S	M	T	W	T	F	S	S
			1	2	3	4	31					1	2
5	6	7	8	9	10	11	3	4	5	6	7	8	9
12	13	14	15	16	17	18	10	11	12	13	14	15	16
19	20	21	22	23	24	25	17	18	19	20	21	22	23
26	27	28	29	30			24	25	26	27	28	29	30

NOVEMBER							DECEMBER						
M	T	W	T	F	S	S	M	T	W	T	F	S	S
	1	2	3	4	5	6				1	2	3	4
7	8	9	10	11	12	13	5	6	7	8	9	10	11
14	15	16	17	18	19	20	12	13	14	15	16	17	18
21	22	23	24	25	26	27	19	20	21	22	23	24	25
28	29	30					26	27	28	29	30	31	

MONDAY 4 JULY

On this day in 1930
Charles Kingsford-Smith completes the first
London to New York flight

9.00	
9.30	
10.00	
10.30	
11.00	
11.30	
12.00	
12.30	
1.00	
1.30	
2.00	
2.30	
3.00	
3.30	
4.00	
4.30	
5.00	
5.30	
6.00	

NOTES

"I received a letter from Surgeon White who states that the want of necessaries to aid the operations of medicine including the observance and attention of cleanliness, has been most materially and sensibly felt."

Captain Phillip

TUESDAY 5 JULY

On this day in 1905
Alfred Deakin commences second term
as Prime Minister

9.00	
9.30	
10.00	
10.30	
11.00	
11.30	
12.00	
12.30	
1.00	
1.30	
2.00	
2.30	
3.00	
3.30	
4.00	
4.30	
5.00	
5.30	
6.00	

NOTES

"I am sad that Lieut Collins will return to England on account of his very bad state of health, and I will take the liberty of mentioning him to Lord Sydney as an officer and a gentleman I should not have parted with under any other considerations."

Captain Phillip

WEDNESDAY 6 JULY

On this day in 1813
John Macarthur ships 36 bales
of wool to England

9.00	
9.30	
10.00	
10.30	
11.00	
11.30	
12.00	
12.30	
1.00	
1.30	
2.00	
2.30	
3.00	
3.30	
4.00	
4.30	
5.00	
5.30	
6.00	

NOTES

"I hope after the ships have sailed to be able to persuade some of the natives to live near us and every possible means shall be used to reconcile them to us & to render their situation more comfortable."

Captain Phillip

JANUARY							FEBRUARY						
M	T	W	T	F	S	S	M	T	W	T	F	S	S
				1	2	3	1	2	3	4	5	6	7
4	5	6	7	8	9	10	8	9	10	11	12	13	14
11	12	13	14	15	16	17	15	16	17	18	19	20	21
18	19	20	21	22	23	24	22	23	24	25	26	27	28
25	26	27	28	29	30	31	29						

MARCH							APRIL						
M	T	W	T	F	S	S	M	T	W	T	F	S	S
	1	2	3	4	5	6					1	2	3
7	8	9	10	11	12	13	4	5	6	7	8	9	10
14	15	16	17	18	19	20	11	12	13	14	15	16	17
21	22	23	24	25	26	27	18	19	20	21	22	23	24
28	29	30	31				25	26	27	28	29	30	

MAY							JUNE						
M	T	W	T	F	S	S	M	T	W	T	F	S	S
30	31					1			1	2	3	4	5
2	3	4	5	6	7	8	6	7	8	9	10	11	12
9	10	11	12	13	14	15	13	14	15	16	17	18	19
16	17	18	19	20	21	22	20	21	22	23	24	25	26
23	24	25	26	27	28	29	27	28	29	30			

THURSDAY 7 JULY

On this day in 1960
Graeme Thorne kidnapped. The first child
kidnapping ever in Australia

9.00	
9.30	
10.00	
10.30	
11.00	
11.30	
12.00	
12.30	
1.00	
1.30	
2.00	
2.30	
3.00	
3.30	
4.00	
4.30	
5.00	
5.30	
6.00	

NOTES

"I today set down rules for new convicts whose sentence is for a term of 14 years or more. One, a yearly fine to be paid for the lands granted, two, after the fifth year; the fine to be in grain and in proportion to the crop; this I should hope will be the only tax on the crops."

Captain Phillip

FRIDAY 8 JULY

On this day in 1799
Matthew Flinders begins exploration
of N.E. coast of Australia

9.00	
9.30	
10.00	
10.30	
11.00	
11.30	
12.00	
12.30	
1.00	
1.30	
2.00	
2.30	
3.00	
3.30	
4.00	
4.30	
5.00	
5.30	
6.00	

NOTES

"A party of hungry natives came to the place where the *SIRIUS'S* boat had been to haul the seine, and, having beaten the crew, took from them by force a part of the fish they had caught."

Chief Surgeon White

SATURDAY 9 JULY

On this day in 1900
Commonwealth of Australia Constitution Act
given Royal assent

" . . . as I have ever since my arrival here, entered my son, John Ross, as a volunteer, serving without pay would you do me the honour of appointing him to the vacancy in the detachment."

Major Ross
Commander of the marines

SUNDAY 10 JULY

On this day in 1842
Sydney incorporated as Australia's first city

EVENTS OF THE WEEK

NSW: Sydney.
Fourth International
Piano Competition of
Australia.
8th to 23rd Jul.

QLD: Cairns.
The Travelling
Australian
Bicentennial
Exhibition opens.
7th to 10th Jul.

ACT: Canberra.1988
International
Mathematical
Olympiad. CAE
Belconnen.
8th to 21st Jul.

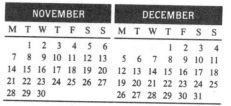

JULY							AUGUST						
M	T	W	T	F	S	S	M	T	W	T	F	S	S
				1	2	3	1	2	3	4	5	6	7
4	5	6	7	8	9	10	8	9	10	11	12	13	14
11	12	13	14	15	16	17	15	16	17	18	19	20	21
18	19	20	21	22	23	24	22	23	24	25	26	27	28
25	26	27	28	29	30	31	29	30	31				

SEPTEMBER							OCTOBER						
M	T	W	T	F	S	S	M	T	W	T	F	S	S
			1	2	3	4	31					1	2
5	6	7	8	9	10	11	3	4	5	6	7	8	9
12	13	14	15	16	17	18	10	11	12	13	14	15	16
19	20	21	22	23	24	25	17	18	19	20	21	22	23
26	27	28	29	30			24	25	26	27	28	29	30

NOVEMBER							DECEMBER						
M	T	W	T	F	S	S	M	T	W	T	F	S	S
	1	2	3	4	5	6				1	2	3	4
7	8	9	10	11	12	13	5	6	7	8	9	10	11
14	15	16	17	18	19	20	12	13	14	15	16	17	18
21	22	23	24	25	26	27	19	20	21	22	23	24	25
28	29	30					26	27	28	29	30	31	

MONDAY 11 JULY

On this day in 1940
Petrol rationing introduced; 2000 miles
per year per motorist

9.00	
9.30	
10.00	
10.30	
11.00	
11.30	
12.00	
12.30	
1.00	
1.30	
2.00	
2.30	
3.00	
3.30	
4.00	
4.30	
5.00	
5.30	
6.00	

NOTES

" . . . the seasons had changed and I feel these first twenty four weeks a very long time and I record on this day 'a white frost in the morning which was priety sharp'."

Captain Phillip

TUESDAY 12 JULY

On this day in 1826
British Government rules that English
sterling currency be used in Australia

9.00	
9.30	
10.00	
10.30	
11.00	
11.30	
12.00	
12.30	
1.00	
1.30	
2.00	
2.30	
3.00	
3.30	
4.00	
4.30	
5.00	
5.30	
6.00	

NOTES

" . . . but I am myself fully convinced that the nation would save money by feeding their convicts at home, upon venison & claret, clothing them in purple & gold, rather than provide for them here (Sydney Cove) the worst fare that can be thought of."

Captain J. Campbell

WEDNESDAY 13 JULY

On this day in 1945
J.B. Chifley becomes Prime Minister
till 19 December 1949

9.00	
9.30	
10.00	
10.30	
11.00	
11.30	
12.00	
12.30	
1.00	
1.30	
2.00	
2.30	
3.00	
3.30	
4.00	
4.30	
5.00	
5.30	
6.00	

NOTES

"The ALEXANDER, FRIENDSHIP, and PRINCE OF WALES with the BORROWDALE prepared to sail for England. The SUPPLY to sail at the same time for Norfolk Island . . . There is no less than thirty one long letters in the different ships."

Chief Surgeon White

JANUARY							FEBRUARY						
M	T	W	T	F	S	S	M	T	W	T	F	S	S
				1	2	3	1	2	3	4	5	6	7
4	5	6	7	8	9	10	8	9	10	11	12	13	14
11	12	13	14	15	16	17	15	16	17	18	19	20	21
18	19	20	21	22	23	24	22	23	24	25	26	27	28
25	26	27	28	29	30	31	29						

MARCH							APRIL						
M	T	W	T	F	S	S	M	T	W	T	F	S	S
	1	2	3	4	5	6					1	2	3
7	8	9	10	11	12	13	4	5	6	7	8	9	10
14	15	16	17	18	19	20	11	12	13	14	15	16	17
21	22	23	24	25	26	27	18	19	20	21	22	23	24
28	29	30	31				25	26	27	28	29	30	

MAY							JUNE						
M	T	W	T	F	S	S	M	T	W	T	F	S	S
30	31				1				1	2	3	4	5
2	3	4	5	6	7	8	6	7	8	9	10	11	12
9	10	11	12	13	14	15	13	14	15	16	17	18	19
16	17	18	19	20	21	22	20	21	22	23	24	25	26
23	24	25	26	27	28	29	27	28	29	30			

THURSDAY 14 JULY

On this day in 1842
First building allotments sold in Brisbane

9.00	
9.30	
10.00	
10.30	
11.00	
11.30	
12.00	
12.30	
1.00	
1.30	
2.00	
2.30	
3.00	
3.30	
4.00	
4.30	
5.00	
5.30	
6.00	

NOTES

" . . . it is impossible to behold without emotion the departure of the first fleet of ships for Europe. On their speedy arrival in England perhaps hangs our fate; by hastening supplies to us."

Captain W. Tench

FRIDAY 15 JULY

On this day in 1964
The "Australian", first national daily newspaper, published

9.00	
9.30	
10.00	
10.30	
11.00	
11.30	
12.00	
12.30	
1.00	
1.30	
2.00	
2.30	
3.00	
3.30	
4.00	
4.30	
5.00	
5.30	
6.00	

NOTES

"Boards of direction were sent to Botany Bay to be fixed on Bare Island, which is near the entrance, so that any ships that may arrive would be directed to Port Jackson."

Lieutenant Bradley

SATURDAY 16 JULY

On this day in 1910
John Duigan flies first Australian-made aeroplane

"Major Ross is demanding of me that his men be paid extra for doing artisan's work. I agreed that all those soldiers that did carpenter's work be paid at the rate of three shillings a day."

Captain Phillip

SUNDAY 17 JULY

On this day in 1964
Donald Campbell sets land speed record of 648.6km/h on Lake Eyre

EVENTS OF THE WEEK

NT: Statewide.
The Eddie Connellan Memorial Air Rally.
13th and 14th Jul.

ACT: Canberra.
Bicentennial Coca-Cola World Netball Youth Cup.
Australian Institute of Sport.
16th to 30th Jul.

QLD: Townsville.
The Travelling Australian Bicentennial Exhibition opens.
16th to 19th Jul.

	JULY							AUGUST						
M	T	W	T	F	S	S	M	T	W	T	F	S	S
				1	2	3	1	2	3	4	5	6	7
4	5	6	7	8	9	10	8	9	10	11	12	13	14
11	12	13	14	15	16	17	15	16	17	18	19	20	21
18	19	20	21	22	23	24	22	23	24	25	26	27	28
25	26	27	28	29	30	31	29	30	31				

	SEPTEMBER							OCTOBER						
M	T	W	T	F	S	S	M	T	W	T	F	S	S
			1	2	3	4	31					1	2
5	6	7	8	9	10	11	3	4	5	6	7	8	9
12	13	14	15	16	17	18	10	11	12	13	14	15	16
19	20	21	22	23	24	25	17	18	19	20	21	22	23
26	27	28	29	30			24	25	26	27	28	29	30

	NOVEMBER							DECEMBER						
M	T	W	T	F	S	S	M	T	W	T	F	S	S
	1	2	3	4	5	6				1	2	3	4
7	8	9	10	11	12	13	5	6	7	8	9	10	11
14	15	16	17	18	19	20	12	13	14	15	16	17	18
21	22	23	24	25	26	27	19	20	21	22	23	24	25
28	29	30					26	27	28	29	30	31	

MONDAY 18 JULY

On this day in 1801
Matthew Flinders leaves England to
circumnavigate and map Australia

9.00	
9.30	
10.00	
10.30	
11.00	
11.30	
12.00	
12.30	
1.00	
1.30	
2.00	
2.30	
3.00	
3.30	
4.00	
4.30	
5.00	
5.30	
6.00	

NOTES

"Lieutenant Kellow has asked to be relieved at the end of his term. In a report from Bradley I note that several of the women convicts met with a party of the natives in a cove where they were employed. The natives did not appear to notice the difference of dress, but soon found which sex they were."

Captain Phillip

TUESDAY 19 JULY

On this day in 1826
Australia's first recorded use of gaslight;
in a Sydney shop

9.00	
9.30	
10.00	
10.30	
11.00	
11.30	
12.00	
12.30	
1.00	
1.30	
2.00	
2.30	
3.00	
3.30	
4.00	
4.30	
5.00	
5.30	
6.00	

NOTES

"Three major questions are being continually asked, 'how shall we shelter ourselves?' was the simplest, 'what shall we eat?' was more vital, and 'how shall we live to-gether?' was the most persistent, and is still a question of burning importance."

Captain Phillip

WEDNESDAY 20 JULY

On this day in 1861
"Sydney Morning Herald" reports anti-
Chinese riots by gold miners at Lambing Flat

9.00	
9.30	
10.00	
10.30	
11.00	
11.30	
12.00	
12.30	
1.00	
1.30	
2.00	
2.30	
3.00	
3.30	
4.00	
4.30	
5.00	
5.30	
6.00	

NOTES

"Anything shot went into the pot . . . an emu seven feet two inches tall was served at my vice regal table . . . young kangaroos eat tender with good flavour, but the old ones eat tough . . . even crows stew well."

Captain Phillip

JANUARY							FEBRUARY						
M	T	W	T	F	S	S	M	T	W	T	F	S	S
				1	2	3	1	2	3	4	5	6	7
4	5	6	7	8	9	10	8	9	10	11	12	13	14
11	12	13	14	15	16	17	15	16	17	18	19	20	21
18	19	20	21	22	23	24	22	23	24	25	26	27	28
25	26	27	28	29	30	31	29						

MARCH							APRIL						
M	T	W	T	F	S	S	M	T	W	T	F	S	S
	1	2	3	4	5	6					1	2	3
7	8	9	10	11	12	13	4	5	6	7	8	9	10
14	15	16	17	18	19	20	11	12	13	14	15	16	17
21	22	23	24	25	26	27	18	19	20	21	22	23	24
28	29	30	31				25	26	27	28	29	30	

MAY							JUNE						
M	T	W	T	F	S	S	M	T	W	T	F	S	S
30	31				1				1	2	3	4	5
2	3	4	5	6	7	8	6	7	8	9	10	11	12
9	10	11	12	13	14	15	13	14	15	16	17	18	19
16	17	18	19	20	21	22	20	21	22	23	24	25	26
23	24	25	26	27	28	29	27	28	29	30			

THURSDAY 21 JULY

On this day in 1858
Adelaide and Melbourne linked by first
intercolonial electric telegraph line

9.00	
9.30	
10.00	
10.30	
11.00	
11.30	
12.00	
12.30	
1.00	
1.30	
2.00	
2.30	
3.00	
3.30	
4.00	
4.30	
5.00	
5.30	
6.00	

NOTES

" . . . there was trouble with
Major Ross too over the ration —
what Major Ross said about the
reduction is happily unknown to me.
The trouble at present is rather one
of anxiety than actual starvation."

Captain Phillip

FRIDAY 22 JULY

On this day in 1925
First regular Sydney-Melbourne
airmail service established

9.00	
9.30	
10.00	
10.30	
11.00	
11.30	
12.00	
12.30	
1.00	
1.30	
2.00	
2.30	
3.00	
3.30	
4.00	
4.30	
5.00	
5.30	
6.00	

NOTES

"At one time or another almost
every officer found himself under
arrest, the charge generally being
the mysterious one of "Conduct
unbecoming an Officer" — Major
Ross was a man of difficult and very
aggravating disposition."

Judge Advocate Collins

SATURDAY 23 JULY

On this day in 1910
Australia's first nationwide
penny postage established

"The blacksmith's shop has
been destroyed by fire . . .
fortunately, through the exertion of
the people, the bellows and other
tools were saved, this was no easy
point as within several minutes the
wooden structure was totally in
flames."

Chief Surgeon White

SUNDAY 24 JULY

On this day in 1907
Australasia wins Davis Cup tennis
championship for first time

EVENTS OF THE WEEK

VIC: Melbourne.
The Australian
Bicentennial
International Trade
Fair '88. Royal
Exhibition Building.
23rd to 31st Jul.

QLD: Pomona.
World Thong
Throwing
Championships.

Cooroora Park.
24th Jul.

NT: Darwin.
The Royal Darwin
Show.
Showgrounds,
Winnellie.
21st to 23rd Jul.

	JULY								AUGUST					
M	T	W	T	F	S	S	M	T	W	T	F	S	S
			1	2	3		1	2	3	4	5	6	7
4	5	6	7	8	9	10	8	9	10	11	12	13	14
11	12	13	14	15	16	17	15	16	17	18	19	20	21
18	19	20	21	22	23	24	22	23	24	25	26	27	28
25	26	27	28	29	30	31	29	30	31				

	SEPTEMBER								OCTOBER					
M	T	W	T	F	S	S	M	T	W	T	F	S	S
		1	2	3	4		31					1	2
5	6	7	8	9	10	11	3	4	5	6	7	8	9
12	13	14	15	16	17	18	10	11	12	13	14	15	16
19	20	21	22	23	24	25	17	18	19	20	21	22	23
26	27	28	29	30			24	25	26	27	28	29	30

	NOVEMBER								DECEMBER					
M	T	W	T	F	S	S	M	T	W	T	F	S	S
1	2	3	4	5	6					1	2	3	4
7	8	9	10	11	12	13	5	6	7	8	9	10	11
14	15	16	17	18	19	20	12	13	14	15	16	17	18
21	22	23	24	25	26	27	19	20	21	22	23	24	25
28	29	30					26	27	28	29	30	31	

MONDAY 25 JULY

On this day in 1924
Government introduces compulsory
voting in Federal elections

9.00	
9.30	
10.00	
10.30	
11.00	
11.30	
12.00	
12.30	
1.00	
1.30	
2.00	
2.30	
3.00	
3.30	
4.00	
4.30	
5.00	
5.30	
6.00	

NOTES

"Oh how valiant are my colonists to experiment gastronomically with the few edible plants found in this country . . . a most useful anti-scorbutic was a little vine from which they decocted a tea."

Captain Phillip

TUESDAY 26 JULY

On this day in 1818
Phillip Parker King returns to Sydney after
surveying north coast of continent

9.00	
9.30	
10.00	
10.30	
11.00	
11.30	
12.00	
12.30	
1.00	
1.30	
2.00	
2.30	
3.00	
3.30	
4.00	
4.30	
5.00	
5.30	
6.00	

NOTES

"It is difficult to keep hungry people from devouring the seed and the stud animals on the spot . . . to plant crops and raise stock is the natural answer to food problems, but I despair."

Captain Phillip

WEDNESDAY 27 JULY

On this day in 1972
Tasmanian Attorney-General resigns over
Tasmanian hydro scheme

9.00	
9.30	
10.00	
10.30	
11.00	
11.30	
12.00	
12.30	
1.00	
1.30	
2.00	
2.30	
3.00	
3.30	
4.00	
4.30	
5.00	
5.30	
6.00	

NOTES

"I find it no longer desirable or even possible, to bring women from the Friendly Islands for the convicts. They would have to be fed, and as things are it would be bringing them to misery."

Captain Phillip

JANUARY
M	T	W	T	F	S	S
				1	2	3
4	5	6	7	8	9	10
11	12	13	14	15	16	17
18	19	20	21	22	23	24
25	26	27	28	29	30	31

FEBRUARY
M	T	W	T	F	S	S
1	2	3	4	5	6	7
8	9	10	11	12	13	14
15	16	17	18	19	20	21
22	23	24	25	26	27	28
29						

MARCH
M	T	W	T	F	S	S
1	2	3	4	5	6	
7	8	9	10	11	12	13
14	15	16	17	18	19	20
21	22	23	24	25	26	27
28	29	30	31			

APRIL
M	T	W	T	F	S	S
				1	2	3
4	5	6	7	8	9	10
11	12	13	14	15	16	17
18	19	20	21	22	23	24
25	26	27	28	29	30	

MAY
M	T	W	T	F	S	S
30	31					1
2	3	4	5	6	7	8
9	10	11	12	13	14	15
16	17	18	19	20	21	22
23	24	25	26	27	28	29

JUNE
M	T	W	T	F	S	S
		1	2	3	4	5
6	7	8	9	10	11	12
13	14	15	16	17	18	19
20	21	22	23	24	25	26
27	28	29	30			

On this day in 1902
Noted Aboriginal artist,
Albert Namatjira, born

9.00	
9.30	
10.00	
10.30	
11.00	
11.30	
12.00	
12.30	
1.00	
1.30	
2.00	
2.30	
3.00	
3.30	
4.00	
4.30	
5.00	
5.30	
6.00	

NOTES

"When not required for labour, convicts of both sexes visited a friendly family of natives nearby. They danced, and sung with apparent good humour, exchanged presents . . . but the natives would not venture back with the convicts."

Judge Advocate Collins

On this day in 1942
Japanese move down Kokoda Trail
towards Port Moresby

9.00	
9.30	
10.00	
10.30	
11.00	
11.30	
12.00	
12.30	
1.00	
1.30	
2.00	
2.30	
3.00	
3.30	
4.00	
4.30	
5.00	
5.30	
6.00	

NOTES

"I catalogue the natives military implements — their spears they throw 30 or 40 yards with unerring precision, a bark shield to ward off things thrown at them, a humble kind of scymitar, a bludgeon or club about 20 inches long and a stone hatchet."

Chief Surgeon White

On this day in 1842
System of representative government
begins in N.S.W.

"I need leather for the soals for the men's shooes, and materials for mending them. Shooes here last but for a very short time and further more as a postscript we have a much wanted need for vinegar."

Chief Surgeon White

On this day in 1900
Western Australia votes to join the
Commonwealth of Australia

EVENTS OF THE WEEK

QLD: Rockhampton. The Travelling Australian Bicentennial Exhibition opens. 26th to 29th Jul.

QLD: Cairns. Bicentenary Stage Coach Run from Melbourne to Cairns. 29th Jul.

ACT: Canberra. Watercolours and Drawings in Australia. Australian National Gallery. 30th Jul. to 23rd Oct.

JULY							AUGUST						
M	T	W	T	F	S	S	M	T	W	T	F	S	S
				1	2	3	1	2	3	4	5	6	7
4	5	6	7	8	9	10	8	9	10	11	12	13	14
11	12	13	14	15	16	17	15	16	17	18	19	20	21
18	19	20	21	22	23	24	22	23	24	25	26	27	28
25	26	27	28	29	30	31	29	30	31				

SEPTEMBER							OCTOBER						
M	T	W	T	F	S	S	M	T	W	T	F	S	S
		1	2	3	4	31						1	2
5	6	7	8	9	10	11	3	4	5	6	7	8	9
12	13	14	15	16	17	18	10	11	12	13	14	15	16
19	20	21	22	23	24	25	17	18	19	20	21	22	23
26	27	28	29	30			24	25	26	27	28	29	30

NOVEMBER							DECEMBER						
M	T	W	T	F	S	S	M	T	W	T	F	S	S
1	2	3	4	5	6					1	2	3	4
7	8	9	10	11	12	13	5	6	7	8	9	10	11
14	15	16	17	18	19	20	12	13	14	15	16	17	18
21	22	23	24	25	26	27	19	20	21	22	23	24	25
28	29	30					26	27	28	29	30	31	

MONDAY 1 AUGUST

On this day in 1840
Transportation of convicts to
New South Wales ceases

9.00	
9.30	
10.00	
10.30	
11.00	
11.30	
12.00	
12.30	
1.00	
1.30	
2.00	
2.30	
3.00	
3.30	
4.00	
4.30	
5.00	
5.30	
6.00	

NOTES

"Living with the natives . . . to the officers they were an amusement and an alleviation of the post's tedium. To the convicts they were people inferior even to themselves. They all tried to take their own wrongs out on the blackman or to make what profit they could out of him."

Captain Phillip

TUESDAY 2 AUGUST

On this day in 1857
Hobart and Launceston linked
by electric telegraph

9.00	
9.30	
10.00	
10.30	
11.00	
11.30	
12.00	
12.30	
1.00	
1.30	
2.00	
2.30	
3.00	
3.30	
4.00	
4.30	
5.00	
5.30	
6.00	

NOTES

"Patrick Gray was charged with stealing 1½ pounds of pork. The prisoner acknowledged the theft and was found guilty. He was sentenced to receive 500 lashes, to repay 1½ lbs. of pork, and to work for six months in heavy irons, at such a place as there may be the heaviest labour."

Judge Advocate Collins

WEDNESDAY 3 AUGUST

On this day in 1846
"Hutchins", Australia's oldest extant
boy's school, opens in Hobart

9.00	
9.30	
10.00	
10.30	
11.00	
11.30	
12.00	
12.30	
1.00	
1.30	
2.00	
2.30	
3.00	
3.30	
4.00	
4.30	
5.00	
5.30	
6.00	

NOTES

"This country requires warm clothing, the rains are frequent and the nights very cold."

Captain Phillip

JANUARY								FEBRUARY						
M	T	W	T	F	S	S	M	T	W	T	F	S	S
				1	2	3	1	2	3	4	5	6	7
4	5	6	7	8	9	10	8	9	10	11	12	13	14
11	12	13	14	15	16	17	15	16	17	18	19	20	21
18	19	20	21	22	23	24	22	23	24	25	26	27	28
25	26	27	28	29	30	31	29						

MARCH								APRIL						
M	T	W	T	F	S	S	M	T	W	T	F	S	S
1	2	3	4	5	6					1	2	3	
7	8	9	10	11	12	13	4	5	6	7	8	9	10
14	15	16	17	18	19	20	11	12	13	14	15	16	17
21	22	23	24	25	26	27	18	19	20	21	22	23	24
28	29	30	31				25	26	27	28	29	30	

MAY								JUNE						
M	T	W	T	F	S	S	M	T	W	T	F	S	S
30	31			1					1	2	3	4	5
2	3	4	5	6	7	8	6	7	8	9	10	11	12
9	10	11	12	13	14	15	13	14	15	16	17	18	19
16	17	18	19	20	21	22	20	21	22	23	24	25	26
23	24	25	26	27	28	29	27	28	29	30			

THURSDAY 4 AUGUST

On this day in 1914
Great Britain declares war on Germany

9.00	
9.30	
10.00	
10.30	
11.00	
11.30	
12.00	
12.30	
1.00	
1.30	
2.00	
2.30	
3.00	
3.30	
4.00	
4.30	
5.00	
5.30	
6.00	

NOTES

"It will be interesting to hear how King is faring on Norfolk Island with the cold and the persistent wet that we are experiencing."
Captain Phillip

FRIDAY 5 AUGUST

On this day in 1944
1,100 Japanese attempt breakout
from Cowra POW camp

9.00	
9.30	
10.00	
10.30	
11.00	
11.30	
12.00	
12.30	
1.00	
1.30	
2.00	
2.30	
3.00	
3.30	
4.00	
4.30	
5.00	
5.30	
6.00	

NOTES

"I have suspended all public labour whilst this heavy rain persists . . . it is fruitless to continue any work under these terrible conditions."
Captain Phillip

SATURDAY 6 AUGUST

On this day in 1914
First shot fired by Australia in WWI;
at Queenscliff , Vic

"It has rained continuously for four days, with damage to many of the huts. I fear for the life of the colony."
Captain Phillip

SUNDAY 7 AUGUST

On this day in 1858
Scotch College plays Melbourne Grammar
in first game of Australian Rules

EVENTS OF THE WEEK

QLD: Brisbane. International Festival of Youth Orchestras. 1st to 11th Aug.

QLD: Maryborough. The Travelling Australian Bicentennial Exhibition opens. 5th to 8th Aug.

NT: Alice Springs. Re-opening of the old Ghan passenger railway line. 6th Aug.

NSW: Sydney. Bicentennial Round Australia Yacht Race. 6th Aug.

JULY							AUGUST						
M	T	W	T	F	S	S	M	T	W	T	F	S	S
				1	2	3	1	2	3	4	5	6	7
4	5	6	7	8	9	10	8	9	10	11	12	13	14
11	12	13	14	15	16	17	15	16	17	18	19	20	21
18	19	20	21	22	23	24	22	23	24	25	26	27	28
25	26	27	28	29	30	31	29	30	31				

SEPTEMBER							OCTOBER						
M	T	W	T	F	S	S	M	T	W	T	F	S	S
			1	2	3	4	31					1	2
5	6	7	8	9	10	11	3	4	5	6	7	8	9
12	13	14	15	16	17	18	10	11	12	13	14	15	16
19	20	21	22	23	24	25	17	18	19	20	21	22	23
26	27	28	29	30			24	25	26	27	28	29	30

NOVEMBER							DECEMBER						
M	T	W	T	F	S	S	M	T	W	T	F	S	S
	1	2	3	4	5	6				1	2	3	4
7	8	9	10	11	12	13	5	6	7	8	9	10	11
14	15	16	17	18	19	20	12	13	14	15	16	17	18
21	22	23	24	25	26	27	19	20	21	22	23	24	25
28	29	30					26	27	28	29	30	31	

MONDAY 8 AUGUST

On this day in 1789
First police force in colony established
consisting of 12 well-behaved convicts

9.00	
9.30	
10.00	
10.30	
11.00	
11.30	
12.00	
12.30	
1.00	
1.30	
2.00	
2.30	
3.00	
3.30	
4.00	
4.30	
5.00	
5.30	
6.00	

NOTES

"The rains have caused the brick kiln to fall in once more, and bricks to a large amount are destroyed; all roads about the settlement are rendered impassable."

Captain Phillip

TUESDAY 9 AUGUST

On this day in 1870
Melbourne Town Hall opens

9.00	
9.30	
10.00	
10.30	
11.00	
11.30	
12.00	
12.30	
1.00	
1.30	
2.00	
2.30	
3.00	
3.30	
4.00	
4.30	
5.00	
5.30	
6.00	

NOTES

"The convicts are taking advantage of the bad weather, thefts are frequent, sheep are being stolen and although a proclamation has been issued offering a pardon to any convict leading to the arrest of person concerned in the felonies, there was no response."

Judge Advocate Collins

WEDNESDAY 10 AUGUST

On this day in 1857
Gas lighting first used in Melbourne

9.00	
9.30	
10.00	
10.30	
11.00	
11.30	
12.00	
12.30	
1.00	
1.30	
2.00	
2.30	
3.00	
3.30	
4.00	
4.30	
5.00	
5.30	
6.00	

NOTES

"I asked Campbell does he know whom in the detachment would wish to remain in the country after the expiration of three years — he replied 'I believe four officers and four privates'."

Captain Phillip

JANUARY								FEBRUARY						
M	T	W	T	F	S	S		M	T	W	T	F	S	S
				1	2	3		1	2	3	4	5	6	7
4	5	6	7	8	9	10		8	9	10	11	12	13	14
11	12	13	14	15	16	17		15	16	17	18	19	20	21
18	19	20	21	22	23	24		22	23	24	25	26	27	28
25	26	27	28	29	30	31		29						

MARCH								APRIL						
M	T	W	T	F	S	S		M	T	W	T	F	S	S
	1	2	3	4	5	6						1	2	3
7	8	9	10	11	12	13		4	5	6	7	8	9	10
14	15	16	17	18	19	20		11	12	13	14	15	16	17
21	22	23	24	25	26	27		18	19	20	21	22	23	24
28	29	30	31					25	26	27	28	29	30	

MAY								JUNE						
M	T	W	T	F	S	S		M	T	W	T	F	S	S
30	31					1				1	2	3	4	5
2	3	4	5	6	7	8		6	7	8	9	10	11	12
9	10	11	12	13	14	15		13	14	15	16	17	18	19
16	17	18	19	20	21	22		20	21	22	23	24	25	26
23	24	25	26	27	28	29		27	28	29	30			

THURSDAY 11 AUGUST

On this day in 1824
New South Wales constituted a Crown Colony

9.00	
9.30	
10.00	
10.30	
11.00	
11.30	
12.00	
12.30	
1.00	
1.30	
2.00	
2.30	
3.00	
3.30	
4.00	
4.30	
5.00	
5.30	
6.00	

NOTES

"The whole detachment had now been on shore seven months and was victuled at full weight of every speacie except beef which was served, 3½ lb of beef 2lb of pork each man for one week. With the addition of one pound of flour on Sundays, no cheese but 6 oz butter per man per week."

James Scott

FRIDAY 12 AUGUST

On this day in 1829
City of Perth proclaimed

9.00	
9.30	
10.00	
10.30	
11.00	
11.30	
12.00	
12.30	
1.00	
1.30	
2.00	
2.30	
3.00	
3.30	
4.00	
4.30	
5.00	
5.30	
6.00	

NOTES

"In honour of the birthday of the Prince of Wales I gave a dinner to every gentleman in the settlement, they seemed to enjoy themselves much more than they did 4th June. Surgeon General White and Surgeon Balmain quarreled & went out in the middle of the night to decide it with pistols. They fired 5 rounds, without doing any injury."

Captain Phillip

SATURDAY 13 AUGUST

On this day in 1806
Captain William Bligh becomes colony's fourth Governor

"I record to day the catching of three sting-rays, two of which weighed each about three hundred weight, and were distributed throughout the colony."

Captain Phillip

SUNDAY 14 AUGUST

On this day in 1861
William Landsborough begins Burke and Wills relief expedition

EVENTS OF THE WEEK

QLD: Brisbane. The Royal National Show. Exhibition Grounds. 11th to 20th Aug.

NSW: Sydney. Military Tattoo. Entertainment Centre. 12th to 28th Aug.

QLD: Toowoomba. The Travelling Australian Bicentennial Exhibition opens. 14th to 17th Aug.

JULY							AUGUST						
M	T	W	T	F	S	S	M	T	W	T	F	S	S
				1	2	3	1	2	3	4	5	6	7
4	5	6	7	8	9	10	8	9	10	11	12	13	14
11	12	13	14	15	16	17	15	16	17	18	19	20	21
18	19	20	21	22	23	24	22	23	24	25	26	27	28
25	26	27	28	29	30	31	29	30	31				

SEPTEMBER							OCTOBER						
M	T	W	T	F	S	S	M	T	W	T	F	S	S
			1	2	3	4	31					1	2
5	6	7	8	9	10	11	3	4	5	6	7	8	9
12	13	14	15	16	17	18	10	11	12	13	14	15	16
19	20	21	22	23	24	25	17	18	19	20	21	22	23
26	27	28	29	30			24	25	26	27	28	29	30

NOVEMBER							DECEMBER						
M	T	W	T	F	S	S	M	T	W	T	F	S	S
1	2	3	4	5	6					1	2	3	4
7	8	9	10	11	12	13	5	6	7	8	9	10	11
14	15	16	17	18	19	20	12	13	14	15	16	17	18
21	22	23	24	25	26	27	19	20	21	22	23	24	25
28	29	30					26	27	28	29	30	31	

MONDAY 15 AUGUST

On this day in 1945
Japanese Government surrenders,
ending WWII

9.00	
9.30	
10.00	
10.30	
11.00	
11.30	
12.00	
12.30	
1.00	
1.30	
2.00	
2.30	
3.00	
3.30	
4.00	
4.30	
5.00	
5.30	
6.00	

NOTES

"Convict Daly, a designing miscreant, was given 300 lashes and condemned to wear a canvas coat branded with a large 'R' for rogue . . . his insane gold mine scheme has upset the whole detachment."

Chief Surgeon White

TUESDAY 16 AUGUST

On this day in 1853
William Randell pioneers steamboat
trade on Murray River.

9.00	
9.30	
10.00	
10.30	
11.00	
11.30	
12.00	
12.30	
1.00	
1.30	
2.00	
2.30	
3.00	
3.30	
4.00	
4.30	
5.00	
5.30	
6.00	

NOTES

"The scurvy was still prevaling with great violence, we at present cannot find any remedy against it, even though the country produces several tolerable vegetables . . . many suffer and we know not what to do."

Chief Surgeon White

WEDNESDAY 17 AUGUST

On this day in 1821
First large-scale auction of Australian
wool held in London

9.00	
9.30	
10.00	
10.30	
11.00	
11.30	
12.00	
12.30	
1.00	
1.30	
2.00	
2.30	
3.00	
3.30	
4.00	
4.30	
5.00	
5.30	
6.00	

NOTES

"Hunter asked for a survey to be taken of exactly as possible the number of canoes and natives within the harbour of Port Jackson . . . it was reported back to him — canoes 67, natives 137 — which is by no means a just account of the numbers."

Captain Phillip

JANUARY								FEBRUARY						
M	T	W	T	F	S	S		M	T	W	T	F	S	S
				1	2	3		1	2	3	4	5	6	7
4	5	6	7	8	9	10		8	9	10	11	12	13	14
11	12	13	14	15	16	17		15	16	17	18	19	20	21
18	19	20	21	22	23	24		22	23	24	25	26	27	28
25	26	27	28	29	30	31		29						

MARCH								APRIL						
M	T	W	T	F	S	S		M	T	W	T	F	S	S
1	2	3	4	5	6						1	2	3	
7	8	9	10	11	12	13		4	5	6	7	8	9	10
14	15	16	17	18	19	20		11	12	13	14	15	16	17
21	22	23	24	25	26	27		18	19	20	21	22	23	24
28	29	30	31					25	26	27	28	29	30	

MAY								JUNE						
M	T	W	T	F	S	S		M	T	W	T	F	S	S
30	31					1				1	2	3	4	5
2	3	4	5	6	7	8		6	7	8	9	10	11	12
9	10	11	12	13	14	15		13	14	15	16	17	18	19
16	17	18	19	20	21	22		20	21	22	23	24	25	26
23	24	25	26	27	28	29		27	28	29	30			

THURSDAY 18 AUGUST

On this day in 1786
Lord Sydney announces Britain's
plan to settle Australia

9.00	
9.30	
10.00	
10.30	
11.00	
11.30	
12.00	
12.30	
1.00	
1.30	
2.00	
2.30	
3.00	
3.30	
4.00	
4.30	
5.00	
5.30	
6.00	

NOTES

"We are being hampered when fishing as no matter what spot we choose to fish at the natives follow us and fish with great enthusiasm along side us."

Lieutenant Bradley

FRIDAY 19 AUGUST

On this day in 1820
Joseph Wild discovers Lake George;
near present site of Canberra

9.00	
9.30	
10.00	
10.30	
11.00	
11.30	
12.00	
12.30	
1.00	
1.30	
2.00	
2.30	
3.00	
3.30	
4.00	
4.30	
5.00	
5.30	
6.00	

NOTES

"Today I landed at the sand hills to walk along the shore to Botany Bay. I was restless to be on the move again in search of any resource that this country can offer."

Captain Phillip

SATURDAY 20 AUGUST

On this day in 1860
Burke and Wills set out from Melbourne
aiming to reach the Gulf of Carpentaria

"Though sighting many natives on my return journey from Botany Bay, one event was unusual in that, a large party of natives were on the beach feasting on the remains of a whale . . ."

Captain Phillip

SUNDAY 21 AUGUST

On this day in 1844
Mayor of Sydney holds first recorded
fancy-dress ball in Australia

EVENTS OF THE WEEK

QLD: Longreach. Droving Australia (Cattle Drive). Re-enactment. Estimated arrival date. 17th Aug.

NSW: Lismore. Australian Conference on Tree and Nut Crops.
Workers Club. 15th to 19th Aug.

VIC: Melbourne. Sun News-Pictorial International Home Show. Royal Exhibition Building. 20th to 28th Aug.

JULY							AUGUST						
M	T	W	T	F	S	S	M	T	W	T	F	S	S
				1	2	3	1	2	3	4	5	6	7
4	5	6	7	8	9	10	8	9	10	11	12	13	14
11	12	13	14	15	16	17	15	16	17	18	19	20	21
18	19	20	21	22	23	24	22	23	24	25	26	27	28
25	26	27	28	29	30	31	29	30	31				

SEPTEMBER							OCTOBER						
M	T	W	T	F	S	S	M	T	W	T	F	S	S
		1	2	3	4		31					1	2
5	6	7	8	9	10	11	3	4	5	6	7	8	9
12	13	14	15	16	17	18	10	11	12	13	14	15	16
19	20	21	22	23	24	25	17	18	19	20	21	22	23
26	27	28	29	30			24	25	26	27	28	29	30

NOVEMBER							DECEMBER						
M	T	W	T	F	S	S	M	T	W	T	F	S	S
1	2	3	4	5	6					1	2	3	4
7	8	9	10	11	12	13	5	6	7	8	9	10	11
14	15	16	17	18	19	20	12	13	14	15	16	17	18
21	22	23	24	25	26	27	19	20	21	22	23	24	25
28	29	30					26	27	28	29	30	31	

MONDAY 22 AUGUST

On this day in 1770
James Cook takes official possession
of east coast of Australia

9.00	
9.30	
10.00	
10.30	
11.00	
11.30	
12.00	
12.30	
1.00	
1.30	
2.00	
2.30	
3.00	
3.30	
4.00	
4.30	
5.00	
5.30	
6.00	

NOTES

"This morning was so cold that these poor wretches stood shivering on the beach, and appeared to be very sensible of the comfort and advantage of being clothed. One of them wore a skin of a reddish colour."

Lieutenant Bradley

TUESDAY 23 AUGUST

On this day in 1870
Last British troops leave Australia; colonies
to form own armed forces

9.00	
9.30	
10.00	
10.30	
11.00	
11.30	
12.00	
12.30	
1.00	
1.30	
2.00	
2.30	
3.00	
3.30	
4.00	
4.30	
5.00	
5.30	
6.00	

NOTES

"The expedition to the 'N' arm continues . . . All along the shore we met the natives, who seem to have no fixed residence or abode; but, indescriminately, whenever they meet with a hut, or, what is more common, a convenient excavation or hole in the rocks, take possession of it for the time."

Chief Surgeon White

WEDNESDAY 24 AUGUST

On this day in 1908
Tommy Burns defeats local Bill Squires in
first world title fight held in Australia

9.00	
9.30	
10.00	
10.30	
11.00	
11.30	
12.00	
12.30	
1.00	
1.30	
2.00	
2.30	
3.00	
3.30	
4.00	
4.30	
5.00	
5.30	
6.00	

NOTES

"I have observed that it is possible, when any of these uncivilized native beings happen to fall out, that instead of deciding the matter by fisticuffs, as with us boxing Britons, they instantly obey the first dictates of passionate resentment, aiming for the time at nothing less than the life of their immediate antagonist."

Chief Surgeon White

JANUARY

M	T	W	T	F	S	S
				1	2	3
4	5	6	7	8	9	10
11	12	13	14	15	16	17
18	19	20	21	22	23	24
25	26	27	28	29	30	31

FEBRUARY

M	T	W	T	F	S	S
1	2	3	4	5	6	7
8	9	10	11	12	13	14
15	16	17	18	19	20	21
22	23	24	25	26	27	28
29						

MARCH

M	T	W	T	F	S	S
1	2	3	4	5	6	
7	8	9	10	11	12	13
14	15	16	17	18	19	20
21	22	23	24	25	26	27
28	29	30	31			

APRIL

M	T	W	T	F	S	S
				1	2	3
4	5	6	7	8	9	10
11	12	13	14	15	16	17
18	19	20	21	22	23	24
25	26	27	28	29	30	

MAY

M	T	W	T	F	S	S
30	31			1		
2	3	4	5	6	7	8
9	10	11	12	13	14	15
16	17	18	19	20	21	22
23	24	25	26	27	28	29

JUNE

M	T	W	T	F	S	S
	1	2	3	4	5	
6	7	8	9	10	11	12
13	14	15	16	17	18	19
20	21	22	23	24	25	26
27	28	29	30			

THURSDAY 25 AUGUST

On this day in 1793
Reverend Richard Johnson completes
first church in colony

9.00	
9.30	
10.00	
10.30	
11.00	
11.30	
12.00	
12.30	
1.00	
1.30	
2.00	
2.30	
3.00	
3.30	
4.00	
4.30	
5.00	
5.30	
6.00	

NOTES

"The governor had the hawk
shot out of the tree . . . the natives
were highly pleased to see the hawk
presented by the governor to a
young girl, who appeared to be the
daughter of the most distinguished
amongst them."

Chief Surgeon White

FRIDAY 26 AUGUST

On this day in 1942
First land defeat of Japanese, by Australians
at Milne Bay, New Guinea

9.00	
9.30	
10.00	
10.30	
11.00	
11.30	
12.00	
12.30	
1.00	
1.30	
2.00	
2.30	
3.00	
3.30	
4.00	
4.30	
5.00	
5.30	
6.00	

NOTES

"After a long and rough
passage, the *SUPPLY* arrived from
Norfolk Island . . . the first report
was that Mr Cunningham and three
seamen have been lost at sea."

Chief Surgeon White

SATURDAY 27 AUGUST

On this day in 1908
Don Bradman, Australia's cricketing
legend, born

" . . . Norfolk Island affords
much in resources . . . The only
difficulty being the want of a good
landing place, Mr. King proposes
blowing up two or three of the
small rocks which make the reef
dangerous, thereby securing a safe
entrance."

Captain Phillip

SUNDAY 28 AUGUST

On this day in 1835
Convict William Buckley, an escapee for
32 years, granted free pardon

EVENTS OF THE WEEK

QLD: Brisbane.
Bicentennial Tour of
Australia by England
and New Zealand
rugby union teams.
Ballymore Oval.
27th Aug.

NSW: Grafton.
The Travelling
Australian
Bicentennial
Exhibition opens.
23rd to 26th Aug.

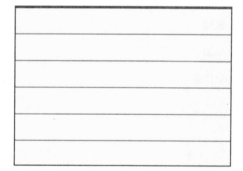

JULY								AUGUST						
M	T	W	T	F	S	S	M	T	W	T	F	S	S
				1	2	3	1	2	3	4	5	6	7
4	5	6	7	8	9	10	8	9	10	11	12	13	14
11	12	13	14	15	16	17	15	16	17	18	19	20	21
18	19	20	21	22	23	24	22	23	24	25	26	27	28
25	26	27	28	29	30	31	29	30	31				

SEPTEMBER								OCTOBER						
M	T	W	T	F	S	S	M	T	W	T	F	S	S
			1	2	3	4	31					1	2
5	6	7	8	9	10	11	3	4	5	6	7	8	9
12	13	14	15	16	17	18	10	11	12	13	14	15	16
19	20	21	22	23	24	25	17	18	19	20	21	22	23
26	27	28	29	30			24	25	26	27	28	29	30

NOVEMBER								DECEMBER						
M	T	W	T	F	S	S	M	T	W	T	F	S	S
1	2	3	4	5	6					1	2	3	4
7	8	9	10	11	12	13	5	6	7	8	9	10	11
14	15	16	17	18	19	20	12	13	14	15	16	17	18
21	22	23	24	25	26	27	19	20	21	22	23	24	25
28	29	30					26	27	28	29	30	31	

MONDAY **29** AUGUST	TUESDAY **30** AUGUST	WEDNESDAY **31** AUGUST
On this day in 1882 Australia defeats England to win first "Ashes" Test	On this day in 1837 Sir James Dowling appointed N.S.W. Chief Justice	On this day in 1846 Sydney committee established to organise relief appeal for Irish famine

29 August	30 August	31 August
9.00	9.00	9.00
9.30	9.30	9.30
10.00	10.00	10.00
10.30	10.30	10.30
11.00	11.00	11.00
11.30	11.30	11.30
12.00	12.00	12.00
12.30	12.30	12.30
1.00	1.00	1.00
1.30	1.30	1.30
2.00	2.00	2.00
2.30	2.30	2.30
3.00	3.00	3.00
3.30	3.30	3.30
4.00	4.00	4.00
4.30	4.30	4.30
5.00	5.00	5.00
5.30	5.30	5.30
6.00	6.00	6.00

NOTES

NOTES

NOTES

"The natives have been attacking our livestock . . . when ever an opportunity offered, they have seldom failed to destroy whatever stock they could seize upon unobserved."

Captain Phillip

"Equal to the attack on our stock the natives attacked the convicts on every occasion which presents itself; and some of them have become victims of these savages."

Captain Phillip

"I have already observed that the natives stand much in fear of a musquet they very seldom approach any persons by whom it is carried; and their apprehensions are almost equally great when they perceive a red garment."

Captain Phillip

JANUARY							FEBRUARY						
M	T	W	T	F	S	S	M	T	W	T	F	S	S
				1	2	3	1	2	3	4	5	6	7
4	5	6	7	8	9	10	8	9	10	11	12	13	14
11	12	13	14	15	16	17	15	16	17	18	19	20	21
18	19	20	21	22	23	24	22	23	24	25	26	27	28
25	26	27	28	29	30	31	29						

MARCH							APRIL						
M	T	W	T	F	S	S	M	T	W	T	F	S	S
1	2	3	4	5	6						1	2	3
7	8	9	10	11	12	13	4	5	6	7	8	9	10
14	15	16	17	18	19	20	11	12	13	14	15	16	17
21	22	23	24	25	26	27	18	19	20	21	22	23	24
28	29	30	31				25	26	27	28	29	30	

MAY							JUNE						
M	T	W	T	F	S	S	M	T	W	T	F	S	S
30	31					1			1	2	3	4	5
2	3	4	5	6	7	8	6	7	8	9	10	11	12
9	10	11	12	13	14	15	13	14	15	16	17	18	19
16	17	18	19	20	21	22	20	21	22	23	24	25	26
23	24	25	26	27	28	29	27	28	29	30			

THURSDAY 1 SEPTEMBER

On this day in 1951
ANZUS Pact signed for mutual defence of
Australia, New Zealand and U.S.A.

9.00	
9.30	
10.00	
10.30	
11.00	
11.30	
12.00	
12.30	
1.00	
1.30	
2.00	
2.30	
3.00	
3.30	
4.00	
4.30	
5.00	
5.30	
6.00	

NOTES

"It has been determined that
the *SIRIUS* should visit some of the
islands near the settlement, the
Friendly or Society Islands. Every
preparation was made for the
voyage."

Lieutenant Bradley

FRIDAY 2 SEPTEMBER

On this day in 1922
Henry Lawson, poet and
short-story writer, dies

9.00	
9.30	
10.00	
10.30	
11.00	
11.30	
12.00	
12.30	
1.00	
1.30	
2.00	
2.30	
3.00	
3.30	
4.00	
4.30	
5.00	
5.30	
6.00	

NOTES

"Some kind of covering will be
wanted for the children. This is not
an expense that will be necessary to
continue after a number of settlers
are in the colony, for then the
convicts will have some resources;
at present they have none."

Captain Phillip

SATURDAY 3 SEPTEMBER

On this day in 1939
Australia announces declaration of war
against Germany

"Our first sowing of seed had
failed . . . barley and many seeds
have rotted in the ground . . .
therefore I find the necessity to sow
the ground a second time with seed
which I had saved for the next
year . . ."

Captain Phillip

SUNDAY 4 SEPTEMBER

On this day in 1888
British New Guinea (Papua) becomes
a Crown Colony

EVENTS OF THE WEEK

NSW: Armidale.
The Travelling
Australian
Bicentennial
Exhibition opens.
1st to 4th Sep.

SA: Adelaide.
Royal Adelaide
Show. Wayville
Showgrounds.
2nd to 10th Sep.

ACT: Canberra.
Bicentennial Tour of
Australia by England
and New Zealand
rugby union teams.
Manuka Oval.
4th Sep.

JULY								AUGUST						
M	T	W	T	F	S	S		M	T	W	T	F	S	S
				1	2	3		1	2	3	4	5	6	7
4	5	6	7	8	9	10		8	9	10	11	12	13	14
11	12	13	14	15	16	17		15	16	17	18	19	20	21
18	19	20	21	22	23	24		22	23	24	25	26	27	28
25	26	27	28	29	30	31		29	30	31				

SEPTEMBER								OCTOBER						
M	T	W	T	F	S	S		M	T	W	T	F	S	S
			1	2	3	4		31					1	2
5	6	7	8	9	10	11		3	4	5	6	7	8	9
12	13	14	15	16	17	18		10	11	12	13	14	15	16
19	20	21	22	23	24	25		17	18	19	20	21	22	23
26	27	28	29	30				24	25	26	27	28	29	30

NOVEMBER								DECEMBER						
M	T	W	T	F	S	S		M	T	W	T	F	S	S
1	2	3	4	5	6						1	2	3	4
7	8	9	10	11	12	13		5	6	7	8	9	10	11
14	15	16	17	18	19	20		12	13	14	15	16	17	18
21	22	23	24	25	26	27		19	20	21	22	23	24	25
28	29	30						26	27	28	29	30	31	

MONDAY 5 SEPTEMBER

On this day in 1883
Charles Rasp discovers mineral wealth
at Broken Hill

9.00	
9.30	
10.00	
10.30	
11.00	
11.30	
12.00	
12.30	
1.00	
1.30	
2.00	
2.30	
3.00	
3.30	
4.00	
4.30	
5.00	
5.30	
6.00	

NOTES

"It is now my intention to despatch the *SIRIUS* to the Cape of Good Hope, in order to purchase such quantity of provisions as she might be capable of taking on board; I have given instructions to lighten the ship."

Captain Phillip

TUESDAY 6 SEPTEMBER

On this day in 1859
Brisbane incorporated as Queensland capital

9.00	
9.30	
10.00	
10.30	
11.00	
11.30	
12.00	
12.30	
1.00	
1.30	
2.00	
2.30	
3.00	
3.30	
4.00	
4.30	
5.00	
5.30	
6.00	

NOTES

"In consequence of my order to lighten ship, 8 guns with their carriages, 24 rounds of shot for each gun, 20 half barrels of powder, a spare anchor and various other articles were put on shore at Sydney Cove."

Captain Phillip

WEDNESDAY 7 SEPTEMBER

On this day in 1795
Aboriginal, Bennelong, returns to
Sydney from England

9.00	
9.30	
10.00	
10.30	
11.00	
11.30	
12.00	
12.30	
1.00	
1.30	
2.00	
2.30	
3.00	
3.30	
4.00	
4.30	
5.00	
5.30	
6.00	

NOTES

"I have ordered the carpenters with all haste to begin maintenance work on the *SIRIUS*, the ship has been much neglected in that department; as the carpenters have all been employed constantly since our arrival in this country with work in the settlement."

Captain Phillip

JANUARY								FEBRUARY						
M	T	W	T	F	S	S		M	T	W	T	F	S	S
				1	2	3		1	2	3	4	5	6	7
4	5	6	7	8	9	10		8	9	10	11	12	13	14
11	12	13	14	15	16	17		15	16	17	18	19	20	21
18	19	20	21	22	23	24		22	23	24	25	26	27	28
25	26	27	28	29	30	31		29						

MARCH								APRIL						
M	T	W	T	F	S	S		M	T	W	T	F	S	S
1	2	3	4	5	6							1	2	3
7	8	9	10	11	12	13		4	5	6	7	8	9	10
14	15	16	17	18	19	20		11	12	13	14	15	16	17
21	22	23	24	25	26	27		18	19	20	21	22	23	24
28	29	30	31					25	26	27	28	29	30	

MAY								JUNE						
M	T	W	T	F	S	S		M	T	W	T	F	S	S
30	31					1				1	2	3	4	5
2	3	4	5	6	7	8		6	7	8	9	10	11	12
9	10	11	12	13	14	15		13	14	15	16	17	18	19
16	17	18	19	20	21	22		20	21	22	23	24	25	26
23	24	25	26	27	28	29		27	28	29	30			

THURSDAY 8 SEPTEMBER

On this day in 1851
Significant gold discoveries
at Ballarat, Victoria

9.00	
9.30	
10.00	
10.30	
11.00	
11.30	
12.00	
12.30	
1.00	
1.30	
2.00	
2.30	
3.00	
3.30	
4.00	
4.30	
5.00	
5.30	
6.00	

NOTES

" . . . the *GOLDEN GROVE* store
ship is to prepare as soon as possible
for sea, she is to be employed in
taking provisions and stores,
together with a party of convicts to
Norfolk Island."

Captain Phillip

FRIDAY 9 SEPTEMBER

On this day in 1836
Governor Bourke formally declares Port
Phillip district open for settlement

9.00	
9.30	
10.00	
10.30	
11.00	
11.30	
12.00	
12.30	
1.00	
1.30	
2.00	
2.30	
3.00	
3.30	
4.00	
4.30	
5.00	
5.30	
6.00	

NOTES

"I have made it known of my
intention of establishing a
settlement on some ground which I
had seen at the head of this harbour
to the westward in April last, and
which, from its form, I had named it
the Crescent."

Captain Phillip

SATURDAY 10 SEPTEMBER

On this day in 1825
Moreton Bay Settlement formally
called Brisbane

"Store houses that will not be
in danger from fire will, if possible
be erected during the course of the
forthcoming summer; the necessary
building works would go faster if
we but had limestone . . . at present
we are obliged to lay bricks and
stones in clay."

Captain Phillip

SUNDAY 11 SEPTEMBER

On this day in 1795
Captain John Hunter becomes Governor
of New South Wales

EVENTS OF THE WEEK

QLD: Brisbane.
Military Tattoo.
Boondall
Entertainment
Centre.
10th to 18th Sep.

NSW: Newcastle.
The Travelling
Australian
Bicentennial

Exhibition opens.
10th to 14th Sep.

NSW: Sydney:
Bicentennial Tour by
England and New
Zealand rugby union
teams. Concord Oval.
11th Sep.

JULY								AUGUST						
M	T	W	T	F	S	S		M	T	W	T	F	S	S
				1	2	3		1	2	3	4	5	6	7
4	5	6	7	8	9	10		8	9	10	11	12	13	14
11	12	13	14	15	16	17		15	16	17	18	19	20	21
18	19	20	21	22	23	24		22	23	24	25	26	27	28
25	26	27	28	29	30	31		29	30	31				

SEPTEMBER								OCTOBER						
M	T	W	T	F	S	S		M	T	W	T	F	S	S
			1	2	3	4		31					1	2
5	6	7	8	9	10	11		3	4	5	6	7	8	9
12	13	14	15	16	17	18		10	11	12	13	14	15	16
19	20	21	22	23	24	25		17	18	19	20	21	22	23
26	27	28	29	30				24	25	26	27	28	29	30

NOVEMBER								DECEMBER						
M	T	W	T	F	S	S		M	T	W	T	F	S	S
1	2	3	4	5	6					1	2	3	4	
7	8	9	10	11	12	13		5	6	7	8	9	10	11
14	15	16	17	18	19	20		12	13	14	15	16	17	18
21	22	23	24	25	26	27		19	20	21	22	23	24	25
28	29	30						26	27	28	29	30	31	

MONDAY **12** SEPTEMBER	TUESDAY **13** SEPTEMBER	WEDNESDAY **14** SEPTEMBER
On this day in 1803 Lt. John Bowen establishes first settlement in Van Diemen's Land	On this day in 1915 Commonwealth first imposes income tax as wartime measure	On this day in 1801 First duel in colony: John Macarthur wounds Col. William Paterson

9.00	9.00	9.00
9.30	9.30	9.30
10.00	10.00	10.00
10.30	10.30	10.30
11.00	11.00	11.00
11.30	11.30	11.30
12.00	12.00	12.00
12.30	12.30	12.30
1.00	1.00	1.00
1.30	1.30	1.30
2.00	2.00	2.00
2.30	2.30	2.30
3.00	3.00	3.00
3.30	3.30	3.30
4.00	4.00	4.00
4.30	4.30	4.30
5.00	5.00	5.00
5.30	5.30	5.30
6.00	6.00	6.00

NOTES

NOTES

NOTES

"This country is supposed to have mines of Iron and Tin or Silver by those who have been used to work in mines; but I give no encouragement to search after what, if found in our present situation, would be the greatest evil that could befall the settlement."

Captain Phillip

"Collins and Hunter to hear a charge against William Boggis, accused by Lydia Munroe of wanting to have connection with her, against her will. John Owen charged with aiding and assisting. Boggis's defence was that it was not likely he should want to have connection with other people present. Boggis and Owen found guilty. Boggis 100 lashes, Owen 50."

Judge Advocate Collins

"Live stock raids continued on and off, the natives now came in large parties, they were always armed and most of the raids were for the purpose of taking our sheep."

Judge Advocate Collins

JANUARY							FEBRUARY						
M	T	W	T	F	S	S	M	T	W	T	F	S	S
				1	2	3	1	2	3	4	5	6	7
4	5	6	7	8	9	10	8	9	10	11	12	13	14
11	12	13	14	15	16	17	15	16	17	18	19	20	21
18	19	20	21	22	23	24	22	23	24	25	26	27	28
25	26	27	28	29	30	31	29						

MARCH							APRIL						
M	T	W	T	F	S	S	M	T	W	T	F	S	S
	1	2	3	4	5	6					1	2	3
7	8	9	10	11	12	13	4	5	6	7	8	9	10
14	15	16	17	18	19	20	11	12	13	14	15	16	17
21	22	23	24	25	26	27	18	19	20	21	22	23	24
28	29	30	31				25	26	27	28	29	30	

MAY							JUNE						
M	T	W	T	F	S	S	M	T	W	T	F	S	S
30	31					1			1	2	3	4	5
2	3	4	5	6	7	8	6	7	8	9	10	11	12
9	10	11	12	13	14	15	13	14	15	16	17	18	19
16	17	18	19	20	21	22	20	21	22	23	24	25	26
23	24	25	26	27	28	29	27	28	29	30			

On this day in 1870
Construction begins on overland telegraph
line from Adelaide to Darwin

9.00	
9.30	
10.00	
10.30	
11.00	
11.30	
12.00	
12.30	
1.00	
1.30	
2.00	
2.30	
3.00	
3.30	
4.00	
4.30	
5.00	
5.30	
6.00	

NOTES

"Some of the natives are not pleased with our remaining amongst them, as they see we deprive them of fish, which is almost their only support; but if they set fire to the corn, necessity will oblige me to drive them to a greater distance."

Captain Phillip

On this day in 1956
First regular television service
launched in Sydney

9.00	
9.30	
10.00	
10.30	
11.00	
11.30	
12.00	
12.30	
1.00	
1.30	
2.00	
2.30	
3.00	
3.30	
4.00	
4.30	
5.00	
5.30	
6.00	

NOTES

"The natives last summer would neither eat shark or stingray; but the scarcity of the fish in the winter, I believe, obliges them to eat anything that affords them the smallest nourishment. Trouble is still besetting the settlement from them."

Captain Phillip

On this day in 1864
Bendigo-Echuca railway line established;
opens up Riverina district

"Relations with the natives is deteriorating, unabated animosity continues to prevail between the natives and us; with sudden human losses and disappearances we were becoming more on our guard than ever."

Captain W. Tench

On this day in 1797
Coal discovered at Newcastle, N.S.W.

EVENTS OF THE WEEK

ACT: Canberra. Commonwealth Parliamentary Association Annual Conference — 1988. 12th to 25th Sep.

VIC: Melbourne. Royal Melbourne Show. Ascot Vale. 15th to 24th Sep.

QLD: Brisbane. Warana Festival. 16th Sep. to 2nd Oct.

NSW: Narromine. Around Australia Air Race — Day One. 18th Sep. to 1st Oct.

JULY							AUGUST						
M	T	W	T	F	S	S	M	T	W	T	F	S	S
				1	2	3	1	2	3	4	5	6	7
4	5	6	7	8	9	10	8	9	10	11	12	13	14
11	12	13	14	15	16	17	15	16	17	18	19	20	21
18	19	20	21	22	23	24	22	23	24	25	26	27	28
25	26	27	28	29	30	31	29	30	31				

SEPTEMBER							OCTOBER						
M	T	W	T	F	S	S	M	T	W	T	F	S	S
			1	2	3	4	31					1	2
5	6	7	8	9	10	11	3	4	5	6	7	8	9
12	13	14	15	16	17	18	10	11	12	13	14	15	16
19	20	21	22	23	24	25	17	18	19	20	21	22	23
26	27	28	29	30			24	25	26	27	28	29	30

NOVEMBER							DECEMBER						
M	T	W	T	F	S	S	M	T	W	T	F	S	S
	1	2	3	4	5	6				1	2	3	4
7	8	9	10	11	12	13	5	6	7	8	9	10	11
14	15	16	17	18	19	20	12	13	14	15	16	17	18
21	22	23	24	25	26	27	19	20	21	22	23	24	25
28	29	30					26	27	28	29	30	31	

On this day in 1798
Isaac Nichols becomes first recorded
hotel licensee in colony

9.00	
9.30	
10.00	
10.30	
11.00	
11.30	
12.00	
12.30	
1.00	
1.30	
2.00	
2.30	
3.00	
3.30	
4.00	
4.30	
5.00	
5.30	
6.00	

NOTES

" . . . the white clay with which the natives paint themselves is found in great abundance; and which if cleared of the sand (which may be done with little trouble), would make good china. I have sent specimuns to Sir Joseph Banks."

Captain Phillip

On this day in 1822
Eight convicts escape from Macquarie
Harbour; only one survives

9.00	
9.30	
10.00	
10.30	
11.00	
11.30	
12.00	
12.30	
1.00	
1.30	
2.00	
2.30	
3.00	
3.30	
4.00	
4.30	
5.00	
5.30	
6.00	

NOTES

"An eight oared boat, sent out in frame for use of the settlement, was got into the water today, and another of sixteen oars is being worked on."

Judge Advocate Collins

On this day in 1851
First Victorian gold mining licence issued

9.00	
9.30	
10.00	
10.30	
11.00	
11.30	
12.00	
12.30	
1.00	
1.30	
2.00	
2.30	
3.00	
3.30	
4.00	
4.30	
5.00	
5.30	
6.00	

NOTES

"As soon as the *SIRIUS* sails I intend going up the harbour with a small detatchment to the ground I had named the Crescent . . . it is more easily cultivated than the land round us."

Captain Phillip

JANUARY							FEBRUARY						
M	T	W	T	F	S	S	M	T	W	T	F	S	S
				1	2	3	1	2	3	4	5	6	7
4	5	6	7	8	9	10	8	9	10	11	12	13	14
11	12	13	14	15	16	17	15	16	17	18	19	20	21
18	19	20	21	22	23	24	22	23	24	25	26	27	28
25	26	27	28	29	30	31	29						

MARCH							APRIL						
M	T	W	T	F	S	S	M	T	W	T	F	S	S
1	2	3	4	5	6					1	2	3
7	8	9	10	11	12	13	4	5	6	7	8	9	10
14	15	16	17	18	19	20	11	12	13	14	15	16	17
21	22	23	24	25	26	27	18	19	20	21	22	23	24
28	29	30	31				25	26	27	28	29	30	

MAY							JUNE						
M	T	W	T	F	S	S	M	T	W	T	F	S	S
30	31					1			1	2	3	4	5
2	3	4	5	6	7	8	6	7	8	9	10	11	12
9	10	11	12	13	14	15	13	14	15	16	17	18	19
16	17	18	19	20	21	22	20	21	22	23	24	25	26
23	24	25	26	27	28	29	27	28	29	30			

On this day in 1918
First direct wireless message from
England to Australia

9.00	
9.30	
10.00	
10.30	
11.00	
11.30	
12.00	
12.30	
1.00	
1.30	
2.00	
2.30	
3.00	
3.30	
4.00	
4.30	
5.00	
5.30	
6.00	

NOTES

"The hutting of the detachment has been going on under the direction of the Major-Commandant. The officers have all separate houses, and except one or two are all under cover. The barracks are still in hand."

Captain Phillip

On this day in 1893
Electric traction tramway begins in Hobart;
first in southern hemisphere

9.00	
9.30	
10.00	
10.30	
11.00	
11.30	
12.00	
12.30	
1.00	
1.30	
2.00	
2.30	
3.00	
3.30	
4.00	
4.30	
5.00	
5.30	
6.00	

NOTES

"The good behaviour and industry of two convicts, both at Norfolk Island, have induced me to request to the under-secretary that their families may be sent to them from England as they do not wish to leave after the time for which they have been transported expires."

Captain Phillip

On this day in 1917
Herbert Klingberg passes driving test for
first Australian car licence

"When we first landed a great exertion of everyone was necessary, and I felt the disapointment, but not now, 20 acres of ground in cultivation, and those who have gardens and vegetables in plenty. I have no doubt that a very few years will make this settlement a very desirable one, and fully answer the end proposed by Government."

Captain Phillip

On this day in 1981
Federal government begins deregulation of
Builders Labourers Federation

EVENTS OF THE WEEK

VIC: Melbourne. VFL Grand Final. Melbourne Cricket Ground. 24th Sep.

WA: Perth. The Perth Royal Show. Claremont. 24th Sep. to 1st Oct.

NSW: Dubbo. The Travelling Australian Bicentennial Exhibition opens. 20th to 23rd Sep.

JULY							AUGUST						
M	T	W	T	F	S	S	M	T	W	T	F	S	S
				1	2	3	1	2	3	4	5	6	7
4	5	6	7	8	9	10	8	9	10	11	12	13	14
11	12	13	14	15	16	17	15	16	17	18	19	20	21
18	19	20	21	22	23	24	22	23	24	25	26	27	28
25	26	27	28	29	30	31	29	30	31				

SEPTEMBER							OCTOBER						
M	T	W	T	F	S	S	M	T	W	T	F	S	S
			1	2	3	4	31					1	2
5	6	7	8	9	10	11	3	4	5	6	7	8	9
12	13	14	15	16	17	18	10	11	12	13	14	15	16
19	20	21	22	23	24	25	17	18	19	20	21	22	23
26	27	28	29	30			24	25	26	27	28	29	30

NOVEMBER							DECEMBER						
M	T	W	T	F	S	S	M	T	W	T	F	S	S
	1	2	3	4	5	6				1	2	3	4
7	8	9	10	11	12	13	5	6	7	8	9	10	11
14	15	16	17	18	19	20	12	13	14	15	16	17	18
21	22	23	24	25	26	27	19	20	21	22	23	24	25
28	29	30					26	27	28	29	30	31	

MONDAY 26 SEPTEMBER

On this day in 1983
Australia wins America's Cup
yachting contest

9.00	
9.30	
10.00	
10.30	
11.00	
11.30	
12.00	
12.30	
1.00	
1.30	
2.00	
2.30	
3.00	
3.30	
4.00	
4.30	
5.00	
5.30	
6.00	

NOTES

"The children's allowance is, I think, too little, and I have been obliged in several instances recently to order children half the men's allowance, or two thirds, as the women are allowed."

Judge Advocate Collins

TUESDAY 27 SEPTEMBER

On this day in 1851
Sir Thomas Mitchell fights one of last duels in
N.S.W., with Stuart Donaldson

9.00	
9.30	
10.00	
10.30	
11.00	
11.30	
12.00	
12.30	
1.00	
1.30	
2.00	
2.30	
3.00	
3.30	
4.00	
4.30	
5.00	
5.30	
6.00	

NOTES

"The convicts who have had some little education, are the greatest villains we have. The Governor has been obliged to continue them in places for which they prove themselves very unfit subjects."

Judge Advocate Collins

WEDNESDAY 28 SEPTEMBER

On this day in 1950
Australian forces first see action
in Korean war

9.00	
9.30	
10.00	
10.30	
11.00	
11.30	
12.00	
12.30	
1.00	
1.30	
2.00	
2.30	
3.00	
3.30	
4.00	
4.30	
5.00	
5.30	
6.00	

NOTES

"The *GOLDEN GROVE* is now ready to sail . . . The persons on board will make the number of settlers on Norfolk Island 60, I am sending eighteen months provisions with them."

Captain Phillip

JANUARY							FEBRUARY						
M	T	W	T	F	S	S	M	T	W	T	F	S	S
				1	2	3	1	2	3	4	5	6	7
4	5	6	7	8	9	10	8	9	10	11	12	13	14
11	12	13	14	15	16	17	15	16	17	18	19	20	21
18	19	20	21	22	23	24	22	23	24	25	26	27	28
25	26	27	28	29	30	31	29						

MARCH							APRIL						
M	T	W	T	F	S	S	M	T	W	T	F	S	S
1	2	3	4	5	6					1	2	3
7	8	9	10	11	12	13	4	5	6	7	8	9	10
14	15	16	17	18	19	20	11	12	13	14	15	16	17
21	22	23	24	25	26	27	18	19	20	21	22	23	24
28	29	30	31				25	26	27	28	29	30	

MAY							JUNE						
M	T	W	T	F	S	S	M	T	W	T	F	S	S
30	31			1					1	2	3	4	5
2	3	4	5	6	7	8	6	7	8	9	10	11	12
9	10	11	12	13	14	15	13	14	15	16	17	18	19
16	17	18	19	20	21	22	20	21	22	23	24	25	26
23	24	25	26	27	28	29	27	28	29	30			

THURSDAY 29 SEPTEMBER

On this day in 1969
Start of "Poseidon" share boom:
80c shares reach $290

9.00	
9.30	
10.00	
10.30	
11.00	
11.30	
12.00	
12.30	
1.00	
1.30	
2.00	
2.30	
3.00	
3.30	
4.00	
4.30	
5.00	
5.30	
6.00	

NOTES

"I am sorry to have been so long without knowing more of the natives, but demands and pressures or work at the colony leaves me but little choice."

Captain Phillip

FRIDAY 30 SEPTEMBER

On this day in 1813
To alleviate currency shortages, "holey dollar" and "dump" circulated

9.00	
9.30	
10.00	
10.30	
11.00	
11.30	
12.00	
12.30	
1.00	
1.30	
2.00	
2.30	
3.00	
3.30	
4.00	
4.30	
5.00	
5.30	
6.00	

NOTES

"I believe in the necessity of having always two years provisions beforehand; a store-ship may be lost a very long time before it is known here or in England."

Captain Phillip

SATURDAY 1 OCTOBER

On this day in 1844
Ludwig Leichhardt sets out
for Port Essington

"There is great activity all round the *SIRIUS* and *GOLDEN GROVE* as I have indicated to both the masters, when dining on board with my family, that I would wish them to weigh anchor in the morning."

Captain Phillip

SUNDAY 2 OCTOBER

On this day in 1986
Sir Robert Helpmann, renowned ballet dancer and choreographer, dies

EVENTS OF THE WEEK

QLD: Townsville. Military Tattoo. Showground. 26th to 28th Sep.

NSW: Sydney. Bicentennial International Naval Review. Sydney Harbour. 1st Oct.

NSW: Orange. The Travelling Australian Bicentennial Exhibition opens. 29th Sep. to 2nd Oct.

JULY							AUGUST						
M	T	W	T	F	S	S	M	T	W	T	F	S	S
				1	2	3	1	2	3	4	5	6	7
4	5	6	7	8	9	10	8	9	10	11	12	13	14
11	12	13	14	15	16	17	15	16	17	18	19	20	21
18	19	20	21	22	23	24	22	23	24	25	26	27	28
25	26	27	28	29	30	31	29	30	31				

SEPTEMBER							OCTOBER						
M	T	W	T	F	S	S	M	T	W	T	F	S	S
			1	2	3	4	31					1	2
5	6	7	8	9	10	11	3	4	5	6	7	8	9
12	13	14	15	16	17	18	10	11	12	13	14	15	16
19	20	21	22	23	24	25	17	18	19	20	21	22	23
26	27	28	29	30			24	25	26	27	28	29	30

NOVEMBER							DECEMBER						
M	T	W	T	F	S	S	M	T	W	T	F	S	S
	1	2	3	4	5	6				1	2	3	4
7	8	9	10	11	12	13	5	6	7	8	9	10	11
14	15	16	17	18	19	20	12	13	14	15	16	17	18
21	22	23	24	25	26	27	19	20	21	22	23	24	25
28	29	30					26	27	28	29	30	31	

MONDAY 3 OCTOBER

On this day in 1985
First Australian Formula One
Grand Prix held; in Adelaide

9.00	
9.30	
10.00	
10.30	
11.00	
11.30	
12.00	
12.30	
1.00	
1.30	
2.00	
2.30	
3.00	
3.30	
4.00	
4.30	
5.00	
5.30	
6.00	

NOTES

"The rations are now cut until the return of the *SIRIUS*, one pound of flour from the weekly ration to each person. I expect the *SIRIUS* back within six months and the above reduction will be justified if there be any delay."

Captain Phillip

TUESDAY 4 OCTOBER

On this day in 1913
First ships of RAN arrive from England
to form Australian Fleet

9.00	
9.30	
10.00	
10.30	
11.00	
11.30	
12.00	
12.30	
1.00	
1.30	
2.00	
2.30	
3.00	
3.30	
4.00	
4.30	
5.00	
5.30	
6.00	

NOTES

"When only a few days out we sprung a serious leak — knowing how serious the food situation is back at the colony, I have decided to push on making what repairs I can at sea — we will have to pump continuously."

Captain Hunter aboard the *SIRIUS*

WEDNESDAY 5 OCTOBER

On this day in 1929
Hereward de Havilland wins Sydney-Perth
Transcontinental Air Race

9.00	
9.30	
10.00	
10.30	
11.00	
11.30	
12.00	
12.30	
1.00	
1.30	
2.00	
2.30	
3.00	
3.30	
4.00	
4.30	
5.00	
5.30	
6.00	

NOTES

"Scurvy has broken out. The ship is ill-found. The only anti-scorbutic on board is a little essence of malt. There is only twelve men left in each watch and they are so enfeebled as to be almost useless . . . This will be a brave voyage indeed . . ."

Captain Hunter aboard the *SIRIUS*

JANUARY							FEBRUARY						
M	T	W	T	F	S	S	M	T	W	T	F	S	S
				1	2	3	1	2	3	4	5	6	7
4	5	6	7	8	9	10	8	9	10	11	12	13	14
11	12	13	14	15	16	17	15	16	17	18	19	20	21
18	19	20	21	22	23	24	22	23	24	25	26	27	28
25	26	27	28	29	30	31	29						

MARCH							APRIL						
M	T	W	T	F	S	S	M	T	W	T	F	S	S
	1	2	3	4	5	6					1	2	3
7	8	9	10	11	12	13	4	5	6	7	8	9	10
14	15	16	17	18	19	20	11	12	13	14	15	16	17
21	22	23	24	25	26	27	18	19	20	21	22	23	24
28	29	30	31				25	26	27	28	29	30	

MAY							JUNE						
M	T	W	T	F	S	S	M	T	W	T	F	S	S
30	31					1			1	2	3	4	5
2	3	4	5	6	7	8	6	7	8	9	10	11	12
9	10	11	12	13	14	15	13	14	15	16	17	18	19
16	17	18	19	20	21	22	20	21	22	23	24	25	26
23	24	25	26	27	28	29	27	28	29	30			

THURSDAY 6 OCTOBER

On this day in 1911
Enrolment on national electoral rolls
becomes compulsory

9.00	
9.30	
10.00	
10.30	
11.00	
11.30	
12.00	
12.30	
1.00	
1.30	
2.00	
2.30	
3.00	
3.30	
4.00	
4.30	
5.00	
5.30	
6.00	

NOTES

"The first settlers have now
been ashore for thirty-six weeks or
nine months; children conceived on
shore were now being born in the
colony — The First White
Australians."

Judge Advocate Collins

FRIDAY 7 OCTOBER

On this day in 1897
Charles Chauvel, pioneer film maker, born

9.00	
9.30	
10.00	
10.30	
11.00	
11.30	
12.00	
12.30	
1.00	
1.30	
2.00	
2.30	
3.00	
3.30	
4.00	
4.30	
5.00	
5.30	
6.00	

NOTES

"I have ordered a gang of
convicts, 'to roll some logs together'
to make our First bridge over the
stream at the head of the cove."

Captain Phillip

SATURDAY 8 OCTOBER

On this day in 1908
Yass-Canberra chosen as site
for Federal capital

"It will be settlers, with the
assistance of the convicts, that will
put this country in a situation for
supporting its inhabitants."

Captain Phillip

SUNDAY 9 OCTOBER

On this day in 1803
Lt. Col. David Collins forms penal settlement
in Port Phillip Bay

EVENTS OF THE WEEK

NT: Darwin.
Military Tattoo.
Showgrounds.
6th to 8th Oct.

NSW: Wollongong.
The Travelling
Australian
Bicentennial
Exhibition opens.
8th to 11th Oct.

TAS: Launceston.
Royal Launceston
Show. Elphin
Showgrounds.
4th to 8th Oct.

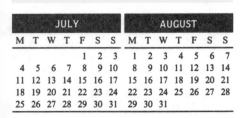

JULY							AUGUST						
M	T	W	T	F	S	S	M	T	W	T	F	S	S
				1	2	3	1	2	3	4	5	6	7
4	5	6	7	8	9	10	8	9	10	11	12	13	14
11	12	13	14	15	16	17	15	16	17	18	19	20	21
18	19	20	21	22	23	24	22	23	24	25	26	27	28
25	26	27	28	29	30	31	29	30	31				

SEPTEMBER							OCTOBER						
M	T	W	T	F	S	S	M	T	W	T	F	S	S
			1	2	3	4	31					1	2
5	6	7	8	9	10	11	3	4	5	6	7	8	9
12	13	14	15	16	17	18	10	11	12	13	14	15	16
19	20	21	22	23	24	25	17	18	19	20	21	22	23
26	27	28	29	30			24	25	26	27	28	29	30

NOVEMBER							DECEMBER						
M	T	W	T	F	S	S	M	T	W	T	F	S	S
1	2	3	4	5	6					1	2	3	4
7	8	9	10	11	12	13	5	6	7	8	9	10	11
14	15	16	17	18	19	20	12	13	14	15	16	17	18
21	22	23	24	25	26	27	19	20	21	22	23	24	25
28	29	30					26	27	28	29	30	31	

MONDAY **10** OCTOBER

On this day in 1803
John Silkhorne becomes first white man
to die in Victoria

9.00	
9.30	
10.00	
10.30	
11.00	
11.30	
12.00	
12.30	
1.00	
1.30	
2.00	
2.30	
3.00	
3.30	
4.00	
4.30	
5.00	
5.30	
6.00	

NOTES

" . . . public works as were in hand went on as usual; those employed on them in general barely exerted themselves beyond what was necessary to avoid immediate punishment for idleness."
Judge Advocate Collins

TUESDAY **11** OCTOBER

On this day in 1852
Australia's first university opens in Sydney

9.00	
9.30	
10.00	
10.30	
11.00	
11.30	
12.00	
12.30	
1.00	
1.30	
2.00	
2.30	
3.00	
3.30	
4.00	
4.30	
5.00	
5.30	
6.00	

NOTES

"I observe the natives revenge themselves on any they meet unarmed; it is not possible to punish them without punishing the innocent with the guilty, and our own people have been the agressors."
Captain Phillip

WEDNESDAY **12** OCTOBER

On this day in 1838
537 German Lutheran migrants
arrive in South Australia

9.00	
9.30	
10.00	
10.30	
11.00	
11.30	
12.00	
12.30	
1.00	
1.30	
2.00	
2.30	
3.00	
3.30	
4.00	
4.30	
5.00	
5.30	
6.00	

NOTES

"What I asked of officers is so very little, and so far from being what would degrade either the officer or the gentleman in our situation . . . it was all I asked but was continuously refused."
Captain Phillip

JANUARY							FEBRUARY						
M	T	W	T	F	S	S	M	T	W	T	F	S	S
				1	2	3	1	2	3	4	5	6	7
4	5	6	7	8	9	10	8	9	10	11	12	13	14
11	12	13	14	15	16	17	15	16	17	18	19	20	21
18	19	20	21	22	23	24	22	23	24	25	26	27	28
25	26	27	28	29	30	31	29						

MARCH							APRIL						
M	T	W	T	F	S	S	M	T	W	T	F	S	S
1	2	3	4	5	6						1	2	3
7	8	9	10	11	12	13	4	5	6	7	8	9	10
14	15	16	17	18	19	20	11	12	13	14	15	16	17
21	22	23	24	25	26	27	18	19	20	21	22	23	24
28	29	30	31				25	26	27	28	29	30	

MAY							JUNE						
M	T	W	T	F	S	S	M	T	W	T	F	S	S
30	31					1			1	2	3	4	5
2	3	4	5	6	7	8	6	7	8	9	10	11	12
9	10	11	12	13	14	15	13	14	15	16	17	18	19
16	17	18	19	20	21	22	20	21	22	23	24	25	26
23	24	25	26	27	28	29	27	28	29	30			

THURSDAY 13 OCTOBER

On this day in 1823
Francis Forbes appointed first Chief Justice
of Supreme Court of N.S.W.

9.00	
9.30	
10.00	
10.30	
11.00	
11.30	
12.00	
12.30	
1.00	
1.30	
2.00	
2.30	
3.00	
3.30	
4.00	
4.30	
5.00	
5.30	
6.00	

NOTES

"Officers that have been nominated to sit on a court martial have challenged my authority to issue warrants. On examination of my commission it was decided that no power . . . had been delegated by the Admiralty."

Captain Phillip

JULY							AUGUST						
M	T	W	T	F	S	S	M	T	W	T	F	S	S
				1	2	3	1	2	3	4	5	6	7
4	5	6	7	8	9	10	8	9	10	11	12	13	14
11	12	13	14	15	16	17	15	16	17	18	19	20	21
18	19	20	21	22	23	24	22	23	24	25	26	27	28
25	26	27	28	29	30	31	29	30	31				

FRIDAY 14 OCTOBER

On this day in 1958
Antarctic explorer, Douglas Mawson, dies

9.00	
9.30	
10.00	
10.30	
11.00	
11.30	
12.00	
12.30	
1.00	
1.30	
2.00	
2.30	
3.00	
3.30	
4.00	
4.30	
5.00	
5.30	
6.00	

NOTES

"Day by day the Governor sat in his office or walked around the infant town, he was constantly harrowed by pitiful complaints and appeals of all classes; but throughout he remains cheerful, hopeful and resourceful."

Judge Advocate Collins

SEPTEMBER							OCTOBER						
M	T	W	T	F	S	S	M	T	W	T	F	S	S
			1	2	3	4	31					1	2
5	6	7	8	9	10	11	3	4	5	6	7	8	9
12	13	14	15	16	17	18	10	11	12	13	14	15	16
19	20	21	22	23	24	25	17	18	19	20	21	22	23
26	27	28	29	30			24	25	26	27	28	29	30

SATURDAY 15 OCTOBER

On this day in 1970
Melbourne's Westgate Bridge collapses
during construction; 35 die

"I show favour to no man and will not even avail myself of private resources in this time of famine, but will share alike with the meanest of my colonists."

Captain Phillip

SUNDAY 16 OCTOBER

On this day in 1867
James Nash discovers gold at Gympie, Qld

EVENTS OF THE WEEK

NSW: Sydney. Captain Arthur Phillip R N Founding Governor Anniversary Ceremony. Botanic Gardens. 11th Oct.

QLD: Gold Coast. Commonwealth Bank Bicentennial Cycle Classic. 15th to 30th Oct.

NSW: Sydney. Australian Bicentennial Air Show. Richmond RAAF Base. 12th to 16th Oct.

NOVEMBER							DECEMBER						
M	T	W	T	F	S	S	M	T	W	T	F	S	S
	1	2	3	4	5	6				1	2	3	4
7	8	9	10	11	12	13	5	6	7	8	9	10	11
14	15	16	17	18	19	20	12	13	14	15	16	17	18
21	22	23	24	25	26	27	19	20	21	22	23	24	25
28	29	30					26	27	28	29	30	31	

MONDAY 17 OCTOBER

On this day in 1949
Snowy Mountains hydro-electric scheme
becomes operational

9.00	
9.30	
10.00	
10.30	
11.00	
11.30	
12.00	
12.30	
1.00	
1.30	
2.00	
2.30	
3.00	
3.30	
4.00	
4.30	
5.00	
5.30	
6.00	

NOTES

"The cellar has been completed
. . . all spirits on board the
FYSHBURN were landed; and she,
being cleared and discharged from
government employ, hove down and
prepared for her return to
England."

Judge Advocate Collins

TUESDAY 18 OCTOBER

On this day in 1948
TAA introduces pressurised Convairs on
Melbourne-Brisbane air service

9.00	
9.30	
10.00	
10.30	
11.00	
11.30	
12.00	
12.30	
1.00	
1.30	
2.00	
2.30	
3.00	
3.30	
4.00	
4.30	
5.00	
5.30	
6.00	

NOTES

" . . . the hours of labour were
shortened on account of the
weakness of the labourers through
want of food, the convicts were
bootless and almost naked, the
clothes of the marines were in
tatters."

Judge Advocate Collins

WEDNESDAY 19 OCTOBER

On this day in 1872
Largest known mass of gold discovered,
235,143 grams, at Hill End, N.S.W.

9.00	
9.30	
10.00	
10.30	
11.00	
11.30	
12.00	
12.30	
1.00	
1.30	
2.00	
2.30	
3.00	
3.30	
4.00	
4.30	
5.00	
5.30	
6.00	

NOTES

"The Governor never looses
faith in the people or the future of
the colony, which he regards with
something akin to the feeling of a
father for a child."

Judge Advocate Collins

JANUARY							FEBRUARY						
M	T	W	T	F	S	S	M	T	W	T	F	S	S
				1	2	3	1	2	3	4	5	6	7
4	5	6	7	8	9	10	8	9	10	11	12	13	14
11	12	13	14	15	16	17	15	16	17	18	19	20	21
18	19	20	21	22	23	24	22	23	24	25	26	27	28
25	26	27	28	29	30	31	29						

MARCH							APRIL						
M	T	W	T	F	S	S	M	T	W	T	F	S	S
	1	2	3	4	5	6					1	2	3
7	8	9	10	11	12	13	4	5	6	7	8	9	10
14	15	16	17	18	19	20	11	12	13	14	15	16	17
21	22	23	24	25	26	27	18	19	20	21	22	23	24
28	29	30	31				25	26	27	28	29	30	

MAY							JUNE						
M	T	W	T	F	S	S	M	T	W	T	F	S	S
30	31					1			1	2	3	4	5
2	3	4	5	6	7	8	6	7	8	9	10	11	12
9	10	11	12	13	14	15	13	14	15	16	17	18	19
16	17	18	19	20	21	22	20	21	22	23	24	25	26
23	24	25	26	27	28	29	27	28	29	30			

THURSDAY 20 OCTOBER

On this day in 1966
US President Lyndon Johnson visits Australia
for talks on Vietnam

9.00	
9.30	
10.00	
10.30	
11.00	
11.30	
12.00	
12.30	
1.00	
1.30	
2.00	
2.30	
3.00	
3.30	
4.00	
4.30	
5.00	
5.30	
6.00	

NOTES

"When my marines are
antagonistic, when my convicts are
calling for food, when my colony
seems to be on the verge of
disaster, I am truly in a position of
lonely and magnificent isolation."
Captain Phillip

FRIDAY 21 OCTOBER

On this day in 1890
Chief Justice proclaims Western
Australia's constitution

9.00	
9.30	
10.00	
10.30	
11.00	
11.30	
12.00	
12.30	
1.00	
1.30	
2.00	
2.30	
3.00	
3.30	
4.00	
4.30	
5.00	
5.30	
6.00	

NOTES

"The Governor having left the
choice of route to myself, I will sail
around the south of New Zealand
and Cape Horn, it will be a
dangerous passage among the ice,
fraught with storms."
Captain Hunter aboard the SIRIUS

SATURDAY 22 OCTOBER

On this day in 1846
Public meeting in Sydney to protest proposed
resumption of transportation

"It is only the iron will of the
Governor that keeps him at the
helm; I observe at Social gatherings,
and as on this visit of inspection, he
is frequently a silent sufferer of
intense pain."
Judge Advocate Collins

SUNDAY 23 OCTOBER

On this day in 1942
Australian 9th Division fights at El Alamein

EVENTS OF THE WEEK

ACT: Canberra.
The Travelling
Australian
Bicentennial
Exhibition opens.
17th to 21st Oct.

TAS: Hobart.
Royal Hobart Show.
Royal Showground,
Glenorchy.
19th to 22nd Oct.

NSW: Sydney.
Sydney Opera House
Open Day and
Forecourt Pageant.
Opera House tours.
23rd Oct.

JULY							AUGUST						
M	T	W	T	F	S	S	M	T	W	T	F	S	S
				1	2	3	1	2	3	4	5	6	7
4	5	6	7	8	9	10	8	9	10	11	12	13	14
11	12	13	14	15	16	17	15	16	17	18	19	20	21
18	19	20	21	22	23	24	22	23	24	25	26	27	28
25	26	27	28	29	30	31	29	30	31				

SEPTEMBER							OCTOBER						
M	T	W	T	F	S	S	M	T	W	T	F	S	S
			1	2	3	4	31					1	2
5	6	7	8	9	10	11	3	4	5	6	7	8	9
12	13	14	15	16	17	18	10	11	12	13	14	15	16
19	20	21	22	23	24	25	17	18	19	20	21	22	23
26	27	28	29	30			24	25	26	27	28	29	30

NOVEMBER							DECEMBER						
M	T	W	T	F	S	S	M	T	W	T	F	S	S
1	2	3	4	5	6					1	2	3	4
7	8	9	10	11	12	13	5	6	7	8	9	10	11
14	15	16	17	18	19	20	12	13	14	15	16	17	18
21	22	23	24	25	26	27	19	20	21	22	23	24	25
28	29	30					26	27	28	29	30	31	

On this day in 1856
South Australia forms first
government ministry

9.00	
9.30	
10.00	
10.30	
11.00	
11.30	
12.00	
12.30	
1.00	
1.30	
2.00	
2.30	
3.00	
3.30	
4.00	
4.30	
5.00	
5.30	
6.00	

NOTES

"It has now become absolutely necessary to compel the natives to keep at a greater distance from the settlement. We are having to fire upon them every time they approach as they are fully armed."
Captain Phillip

On this day in 1794
"Scottish Martyrs" (political prisoners)
arrive in Sydney

9.00	
9.30	
10.00	
10.30	
11.00	
11.30	
12.00	
12.30	
1.00	
1.30	
2.00	
2.30	
3.00	
3.30	
4.00	
4.30	
5.00	
5.30	
6.00	

NOTES

"In the establishment of the government the Governor maintains absolute control; no subject or no detail was too small to pass unnoticed under his watchful eye."
Judge Advocate Collins

On this day in 1835
First livestock landed at Williamstown,
Port Phillip

9.00	
9.30	
10.00	
10.30	
11.00	
11.30	
12.00	
12.30	
1.00	
1.30	
2.00	
2.30	
3.00	
3.30	
4.00	
4.30	
5.00	
5.30	
6.00	

NOTES

"Collins and myself drew up a form of land grant which will be maintained with slight modification so long as the first system of grants remain in vogue; and we have initiated the system of land leases by the Crown."
Captain Phillip

JANUARY

M	T	W	T	F	S	S
				1	2	3
4	5	6	7	8	9	10
11	12	13	14	15	16	17
18	19	20	21	22	23	24
25	26	27	28	29	30	31

FEBRUARY

M	T	W	T	F	S	S
1	2	3	4	5	6	7
8	9	10	11	12	13	14
15	16	17	18	19	20	21
22	23	24	25	26	27	28
29						

MARCH

M	T	W	T	F	S	S
1	2	3	4	5	6	
7	8	9	10	11	12	13
14	15	16	17	18	19	20
21	22	23	24	25	26	27
28	29	30	31			

APRIL

M	T	W	T	F	S	S
				1	2	3
4	5	6	7	8	9	10
11	12	13	14	15	16	17
18	19	20	21	22	23	24
25	26	27	28	29	30	

MAY

M	T	W	T	F	S	S
30	31					1
2	3	4	5	6	7	8
9	10	11	12	13	14	15
16	17	18	19	20	21	22
23	24	25	26	27	28	29

JUNE

M	T	W	T	F	S	S
		1	2	3	4	5
6	7	8	9	10	11	12
13	14	15	16	17	18	19
20	21	22	23	24	25	26
27	28	29	30			

THURSDAY 27 OCTOBER

On this day in 1927
Melbourne gangster "Squizzy" Taylor dies
in shootout with rival

9.00	
9.30	
10.00	
10.30	
11.00	
11.30	
12.00	
12.30	
1.00	
1.30	
2.00	
2.30	
3.00	
3.30	
4.00	
4.30	
5.00	
5.30	
6.00	

NOTES

"It is an unpleasant situation
for the detachment doing duty in
this country, that it is not within
my power to restore the harmony
which is so very requisite in our
situation, between Major Ross and
the Officers."

Captain Phillip

FRIDAY 28 OCTOBER

On this day in 1916
Conscription Referendum defeated;
Labor Party splits on issue

9.00	
9.30	
10.00	
10.30	
11.00	
11.30	
12.00	
12.30	
1.00	
1.30	
2.00	
2.30	
3.00	
3.30	
4.00	
4.30	
5.00	
5.30	
6.00	

NOTES

"As from today all daily orders
are to be issued by the Governor,
with the exception of the purely
battalion orders of Major Ross. He
also intends to control the criminal
and civil courts."

Judge Advocate Collins

SATURDAY 29 OCTOBER

On this day in 1880
Judge Barry sentences Ned Kelly to hanging

"The proceedings from criminal
and civil courts are carefully
considered and revised with regard
to the punishment ordered; in the
exercise of this jurisdiction the
Governors' actions always were
tempered with mercy."

Judge Advocate Collins

SUNDAY 30 OCTOBER

On this day in 1918
Turkey surrenders after
AIF attacks in Palestine

EVENTS OF THE WEEK

NT: Coburg
Peninsula.
Opening of the Port
Essington
Reservation.
27th Oct.

WA: Bridgetown.
Blackwood
Marathon Relay.
Blackwood River
Valley. 29th Oct.

VIC: Traralgon.
The Travelling
Australian
Bicentennial
Exhibition opens.
28th to 31st Oct.

JULY								AUGUST						
M	T	W	T	F	S	S	M	T	W	T	F	S	S
				1	2	3	1	2	3	4	5	6	7
4	5	6	7	8	9	10	8	9	10	11	12	13	14
11	12	13	14	15	16	17	15	16	17	18	19	20	21
18	19	20	21	22	23	24	22	23	24	25	26	27	28
25	26	27	28	29	30	31	29	30	31				

SEPTEMBER								OCTOBER						
M	T	W	T	F	S	S	M	T	W	T	F	S	S
			1	2	3	4	31					1	2
5	6	7	8	9	10	11	3	4	5	6	7	8	9
12	13	14	15	16	17	18	10	11	12	13	14	15	16
19	20	21	22	23	24	25	17	18	19	20	21	22	23
26	27	28	29	30			24	25	26	27	28	29	30

NOVEMBER								DECEMBER						
M	T	W	T	F	S	S	M	T	W	T	F	S	S
	1	2	3	4	5	6				1	2	3	4
7	8	9	10	11	12	13	5	6	7	8	9	10	11
14	15	16	17	18	19	20	12	13	14	15	16	17	18
21	22	23	24	25	26	27	19	20	21	22	23	24	25
28	29	30					26	27	28	29	30	31	

On this day in 1923
Police strike commences in Melbourne;
lasts five days

9.00	
9.30	
10.00	
10.30	
11.00	
11.30	
12.00	
12.30	
1.00	
1.30	
2.00	
2.30	
3.00	
3.30	
4.00	
4.30	
5.00	
5.30	
6.00	

NOTES

"We have discovered sand that contains a very large proportion of metal. We had it in a strong fire for twenty-four hours, but we could not get it to melt, I suppose it to be Blacklead."

Captain Phillip

On this day in 1838
James Raymond introduces pre-paid postage
to Australia; first in British Empire

9.00	
9.30	
10.00	
10.30	
11.00	
11.30	
12.00	
12.30	
1.00	
1.30	
2.00	
2.30	
3.00	
3.30	
4.00	
4.30	
5.00	
5.30	
6.00	

NOTES

"Moses Tucker and John Power were charged with stealing five boards from my yard. Thomas Young and the prisoners gave evidence. Both prisoners were found guilty and sentenced to 200 lashings in the usual manner. Power received his punishment but Tucker only part of his, being forgiven for the rest."

Judge Advocate Collins

On this day in 1942
Australians recapture Kokoda and
drive Japanese forces back

9.00	
9.30	
10.00	
10.30	
11.00	
11.30	
12.00	
12.30	
1.00	
1.30	
2.00	
2.30	
3.00	
3.30	
4.00	
4.30	
5.00	
5.30	
6.00	

NOTES

"A party, led by Lt. Johnston and accompanied by the Governor and Mr Alt went up the harbour to Rose Hill to establish the second settlement."

Private John Easty

JANUARY							FEBRUARY						
M	T	W	T	F	S	S	M	T	W	T	F	S	S
				1	2	3	1	2	3	4	5	6	7
4	5	6	7	8	9	10	8	9	10	11	12	13	14
11	12	13	14	15	16	17	15	16	17	18	19	20	21
18	19	20	21	22	23	24	22	23	24	25	26	27	28
25	26	27	28	29	30	31	29						

MARCH							APRIL						
M	T	W	T	F	S	S	M	T	W	T	F	S	S
1	2	3	4	5	6					1	2	3
7	8	9	10	11	12	13	4	5	6	7	8	9	10
14	15	16	17	18	19	20	11	12	13	14	15	16	17
21	22	23	24	25	26	27	18	19	20	21	22	23	24
28	29	30	31				25	26	27	28	29	30	

MAY							JUNE						
M	T	W	T	F	S	S	M	T	W	T	F	S	S
30	31				1				1	2	3	4	5
2	3	4	5	6	7	8	6	7	8	9	10	11	12
9	10	11	12	13	14	15	13	14	15	16	17	18	19
16	17	18	19	20	21	22	20	21	22	23	24	25	26
23	24	25	26	27	28	29	27	28	29	30			

On this day in 1824
First Australian trial by jury begins in Sydney

9.00	
9.30	
10.00	
10.30	
11.00	
11.30	
12.00	
12.30	
1.00	
1.30	
2.00	
2.30	
3.00	
3.30	
4.00	
4.30	
5.00	
5.30	
6.00	

NOTES

"The new settlement is sixteen miles inland, a small redoubt was thrown up, and a Captains detachment posted in it, to protect the convicts who were employed to cultivate the land."

Captain W. Tench

On this day in 1934
Kingsford-Smith makes first Brisbane-San Francisco air crossing

9.00	
9.30	
10.00	
10.30	
11.00	
11.30	
12.00	
12.30	
1.00	
1.30	
2.00	
2.30	
3.00	
3.30	
4.00	
4.30	
5.00	
5.30	
6.00	

NOTES

"The land at the new settlement and the surrounding country is as fine as any I have seen in England. Cultivation without heavy clearing of the land is rare . . . "

Captain Phillip

On this day in 1935
Charles Moses begins 30 year term as General Manager of ABC

"One or two small vessels of 30 or 40 tons would, likewise, be employed to great advantage in the colony, and which I beg leave to submit for their Lordships' consideration."

Captain Phillip in letter to Nepean

On this day in 1861
Electric telegraph links Brisbane with N.S.W., Vic. and S.A.

EVENTS OF THE WEEK

SA: Adelaide. Military Tattoo 31st Oct. to 3rd Nov.

VIC: Melbourne. The Travelling Australian Bicentennial Exhibition opens. 6th to 12th Nov.

VIC: Melbourne. Melbourne Cup. Flemington Racecourse. 1st Nov.

	JULY							AUGUST					
M	T	W	T	F	S	S	M	T	W	T	F	S	S
				1	2	3	1	2	3	4	5	6	7
4	5	6	7	8	9	10	8	9	10	11	12	13	14
11	12	13	14	15	16	17	15	16	17	18	19	20	21
18	19	20	21	22	23	24	22	23	24	25	26	27	28
25	26	27	28	29	30	31	29	30	31				

	SEPTEMBER							OCTOBER					
M	T	W	T	F	S	S	M	T	W	T	F	S	S
			1	2	3	4	31					1	2
5	6	7	8	9	10	11	3	4	5	6	7	8	9
12	13	14	15	16	17	18	10	11	12	13	14	15	16
19	20	21	22	23	24	25	17	18	19	20	21	22	23
26	27	28	29	30			24	25	26	27	28	29	30

	NOVEMBER							DECEMBER					
M	T	W	T	F	S	S	M	T	W	T	F	S	S
	1	2	3	4	5	6				1	2	3	4
7	8	9	10	11	12	13	5	6	7	8	9	10	11
14	15	16	17	18	19	20	12	13	14	15	16	17	18
21	22	23	24	25	26	27	19	20	21	22	23	24	25
28	29	30					26	27	28	29	30	31	

MONDAY 7 NOVEMBER

On this day in 1861
First Melbourne Cup run; "Archer" wins

9.00	
9.30	
10.00	
10.30	
11.00	
11.30	
12.00	
12.30	
1.00	
1.30	
2.00	
2.30	
3.00	
3.30	
4.00	
4.30	
5.00	
5.30	
6.00	

NOTES

"My Court of Criminal Jurisdiction tried John Thomas, who was indicted for, on October 30, *with force and arms*, one pound of castile soap, value of 1/6, of the goods and chattels of Mary Hill, feloniously did steal, take and carry away." (Thomas pleaded not guilty. Thomas was found guilty and sentenced to 500 lashes.)

Captain Phillip

TUESDAY 8 NOVEMBER

On this day in 1907
Judge H.B. Higgins introduces world's first basic wage concept

9.00	
9.30	
10.00	
10.30	
11.00	
11.30	
12.00	
12.30	
1.00	
1.30	
2.00	
2.30	
3.00	
3.30	
4.00	
4.30	
5.00	
5.30	
6.00	

NOTES

"We are now only a few days from Sydney Cove and have sighted what appears to be a dangerous reef on which the sea broke very high; the weather does not permit us to examine how far it extends to the northward . . . we are anxious to be back in the Cove."

David Blackburn aboard the *GOLDEN GROVE*

WEDNESDAY 9 NOVEMBER

On this day in 1914
HMAS "Sydney" destroys German cruiser "Emden" off Cocos Island

9.00	
9.30	
10.00	
10.30	
11.00	
11.30	
12.00	
12.30	
1.00	
1.30	
2.00	
2.30	
3.00	
3.30	
4.00	
4.30	
5.00	
5.30	
6.00	

NOTES

" . . . as for the distresses of the women they are past description as they are deprived of tea and other things . . . and as they unprovided with clothes, those who have young children are quite wretched."

Extract of letter from female convict

JANUARY							FEBRUARY						
M	T	W	T	F	S	S	M	T	W	T	F	S	S
				1	2	3	1	2	3	4	5	6	7
4	5	6	7	8	9	10	8	9	10	11	12	13	14
11	12	13	14	15	16	17	15	16	17	18	19	20	21
18	19	20	21	22	23	24	22	23	24	25	26	27	28
25	26	27	28	29	30	31	29						

MARCH							APRIL						
M	T	W	T	F	S	S	M	T	W	T	F	S	S
1	2	3	4	5	6					1	2	3
7	8	9	10	11	12	13	4	5	6	7	8	9	10
14	15	16	17	18	19	20	11	12	13	14	15	16	17
21	22	23	24	25	26	27	18	19	20	21	22	23	24
28	29	30	31				25	26	27	28	29	30	

MAY							JUNE						
M	T	W	T	F	S	S	M	T	W	T	F	S	S
30	31				1				1	2	3	4	5
2	3	4	5	6	7	8	6	7	8	9	10	11	12
9	10	11	12	13	14	15	13	14	15	16	17	18	19
16	17	18	19	20	21	22	20	21	22	23	24	25	26
23	24	25	26	27	28	29	27	28	29	30			

THURSDAY 10 NOVEMBER

On this day in 1791
Samuel Enderby begins whaling
industry in Australia

9.00	
9.30	
10.00	
10.30	
11.00	
11.30	
12.00	
12.30	
1.00	
1.30	
2.00	
2.30	
3.00	
3.30	
4.00	
4.30	
5.00	
5.30	
6.00	

NOTES

"The settlement was excited
when the *GOLDEN GROVE* hauled
into Sydney Cove on her return
from Norfolk Island . . . its safe
return augers well for the future."
Chief Surgeon White

FRIDAY 11 NOVEMBER

On this day in 1975
Sir John Kerr, Governor-General,
dismisses Whitlam government

9.00	
9.30	
10.00	
10.30	
11.00	
11.30	
12.00	
12.30	
1.00	
1.30	
2.00	
2.30	
3.00	
3.30	
4.00	
4.30	
5.00	
5.30	
6.00	

NOTES

"Fighting took its toll among
the marines . . . so small is our
number, and so necessary is every
individual who composes it, for one
purpose or another, that the loss of
even a single man may truly be
considered as an irreparable dis-
advantage!"
Chief Surgeon White

SATURDAY 12 NOVEMBER

On this day in 1961
Huge iron ore discoveries in
Pilbara region announced

"The accounts I have received
from Norfolk Island are most
favourable. Vegetables are in
abundance, corn they have sown
promises well, and pepper is found
in great plenty . . . the people are
very healthy."
Captain Phillip

SUNDAY 13 NOVEMBER

On this day in 1954
Australia's first automatic time telephone
service introduced

EVENTS OF THE WEEK

TAS: Hobart.
Military Tattoo.
Fifteen hundred
Australian and
international
military personnel
take part.
10th to 12th Nov.

ACT: Canberra.
ACT Model Speed
Boat Championships.

Radio-controlled
speed boats race.
Nerang Pool,
Commonwealth
Park.
12th and 13th Nov.

JULY								AUGUST						
M	T	W	T	F	S	S		M	T	W	T	F	S	S
				1	2	3		1	2	3	4	5	6	7
4	5	6	7	8	9	10		8	9	10	11	12	13	14
11	12	13	14	15	16	17		15	16	17	18	19	20	21
18	19	20	21	22	23	24		22	23	24	25	26	27	28
25	26	27	28	29	30	31		29	30	31				

SEPTEMBER								OCTOBER						
M	T	W	T	F	S	S		M	T	W	T	F	S	S
			1	2	3	4		31					1	2
5	6	7	8	9	10	11		3	4	5	6	7	8	9
12	13	14	15	16	17	18		10	11	12	13	14	15	16
19	20	21	22	23	24	25		17	18	19	20	21	22	23
26	27	28	29	30				24	25	26	27	28	29	30

NOVEMBER								DECEMBER						
M	T	W	T	F	S	S		M	T	W	T	F	S	S
	1	2	3	4	5	6					1	2	3	4
7	8	9	10	11	12	13		5	6	7	8	9	10	11
14	15	16	17	18	19	20		12	13	14	15	16	17	18
21	22	23	24	25	26	27		19	20	21	22	23	24	25
28	29	30						26	27	28	29	30	31	

On this day in 1868
Steele Rudd (A.H. Davis), writer
and journalist, born

9.00	
9.30	
10.00	
10.30	
11.00	
11.30	
12.00	
12.30	
1.00	
1.30	
2.00	
2.30	
3.00	
3.30	
4.00	
4.30	
5.00	
5.30	
6.00	

NOTES

"No Church is yet begun and is
scarcely thought of; other things
seem to be of greater notice &
concern & most would rather see a
Tavern, a Playhouse, a Brothel —
anything sooner than a place for
publick worship."

Rev. Richard Johnson

On this day in 1791
Colony's first grape vine planted
at Parramatta

9.00	
9.30	
10.00	
10.30	
11.00	
11.30	
12.00	
12.30	
1.00	
1.30	
2.00	
2.30	
3.00	
3.30	
4.00	
4.30	
5.00	
5.30	
6.00	

NOTES

"I should be glad of a fresh
supply of paper, send me
Blackstone's Reports, any author
that treats on costs, any Law
publications of note that has
appeared since my departure, with
whatever Acts of Parliament you
may think necessary."

Letter by Judge Advocate Collins

On this day in 1920
Hudson Fysh and P.J. McGinness found
QLD & NT Aerial Service (QANTAS)

9.00	
9.30	
10.00	
10.30	
11.00	
11.30	
12.00	
12.30	
1.00	
1.30	
2.00	
2.30	
3.00	
3.30	
4.00	
4.30	
5.00	
5.30	
6.00	

NOTES

"The two store-ships have each
lower yard and top-gallant masts
from Norfolk Island; I have ordered
them to deliver to Deptford Yard,
England to determine how far the
timber of that island may be
useful."

Captain Phillip

JANUARY							FEBRUARY						
M	T	W	T	F	S	S	M	T	W	T	F	S	S
				1	2	3	1	2	3	4	5	6	7
4	5	6	7	8	9	10	8	9	10	11	12	13	14
11	12	13	14	15	16	17	15	16	17	18	19	20	21
18	19	20	21	22	23	24	22	23	24	25	26	27	28
25	26	27	28	29	30	31	29						

MARCH							APRIL						
M	T	W	T	F	S	S	M	T	W	T	F	S	S
	1	2	3	4	5	6					1	2	3
7	8	9	10	11	12	13	4	5	6	7	8	9	10
14	15	16	17	18	19	20	11	12	13	14	15	16	17
21	22	23	24	25	26	27	18	19	20	21	22	23	24
28	29	30	31				25	26	27	28	29	30	

MAY							JUNE						
M	T	W	T	F	S	S	M	T	W	T	F	S	S
30	31			1					1	2	3	4	5
2	3	4	5	6	7	8	6	7	8	9	10	11	12
9	10	11	12	13	14	15	13	14	15	16	17	18	19
16	17	18	19	20	21	22	20	21	22	23	24	25	26
23	24	25	26	27	28	29	27	28	29	30			

THURSDAY **17** NOVEMBER

On this day in 1869
Suez Canal opens, shortening voyage
to and from Europe

9.00	
9.30	
10.00	
10.30	
11.00	
11.30	
12.00	
12.30	
1.00	
1.30	
2.00	
2.30	
3.00	
3.30	
4.00	
4.30	
5.00	
5.30	
6.00	

NOTES

"Issued a memorandum to the Commodores of all ships bound for New South Wales. Ships must bring a sufficient quantity of provisions to serve them whilst on the coast and for their return to Europe . . . such ships who have people on board who are to remain at the settlement are to be landed with two years provisions."

Captain Phillip

FRIDAY **18** NOVEMBER

On this day in 1834
Edward Henty forms settlement
at Portland, Vic.

9.00	
9.30	
10.00	
10.30	
11.00	
11.30	
12.00	
12.30	
1.00	
1.30	
2.00	
2.30	
3.00	
3.30	
4.00	
4.30	
5.00	
5.30	
6.00	

NOTES

"An elegant brick house is built for the Governor, and another of hewn stone for the Lieut. Govr. A hospital was begun on our arrival here, and is not yet half finished, nor fit to receive any objects."

A marine officer

SATURDAY **19** NOVEMBER

On this day in 1800
First copper coins arrive from England
for use as currency

"The *GOLDEN GROVE* and *FYSHBURN* have departed for England . . . only the tiny *SUPPLY* remained — one little seventy foot brig, 150 tons of timber transport — connecting the settlement to civilisation."

Judge Advocate Collins

SUNDAY **20** NOVEMBER

On this day in 1813
George Evans becomes first explorer
to cross Great Dividing Range

EVENTS OF THE WEEK

NSW: Orange. Australian National Field Days. Latest agricultural equipment and services. Borenore. 16th to 19th Nov.

VIC: Melbourne. Military Tattoo. 19th Nov. to 3rd Dec.

NSW: Sydney. Diabetes Federation Congress. Darling Harbour Convention Centre. 20th to 25th Nov.

On this day in 1791
Twenty convicts escape from Sydney and
attempt to reach China by land

9.00	
9.30	
10.00	
10.30	
11.00	
11.30	
12.00	
12.30	
1.00	
1.30	
2.00	
2.30	
3.00	
3.30	
4.00	
4.30	
5.00	
5.30	
6.00	

NOTES

"A further report from King
that some driftwood, a cocoanut,
and a small piece of wood like the
handle of a fly-flap having been
driven on shore at Norfolk Island,
gave suggestion to an idea that an
inhabited island is at no great
distance."

Captain Phillip

On this day in 1956
Melbourne hosts XVI Olympiad

9.00	
9.30	
10.00	
10.30	
11.00	
11.30	
12.00	
12.30	
1.00	
1.30	
2.00	
2.30	
3.00	
3.30	
4.00	
4.30	
5.00	
5.30	
6.00	

NOTES

"The Governor, who is our only
authority, has taken steps to ensure
the embelishment of good order and
propriety continues in the colony
and for erradicting villany and
idleness."

Judge Advocate Collins

On this day in 1923
Australia's first public wireless broadcast
begins; in Sydney

9.00	
9.30	
10.00	
10.30	
11.00	
11.30	
12.00	
12.30	
1.00	
1.30	
2.00	
2.30	
3.00	
3.30	
4.00	
4.30	
5.00	
5.30	
6.00	

NOTES

"Rose Hill is becoming
resourceful but Johnston reports
conflicts with the natives. I have
sent Captain Campbell to that place
with powers to govern, attended
with a reinforcement party of
sixteen marines."

Captain Phillip

JANUARY							FEBRUARY						
M	T	W	T	F	S	S	M	T	W	T	F	S	S
				1	2	3	1	2	3	4	5	6	7
4	5	6	7	8	9	10	8	9	10	11	12	13	14
11	12	13	14	15	16	17	15	16	17	18	19	20	21
18	19	20	21	22	23	24	22	23	24	25	26	27	28
25	26	27	28	29	30	31	29						

MARCH							APRIL						
M	T	W	T	F	S	S	M	T	W	T	F	S	S
	1	2	3	4	5	6					1	2	3
7	8	9	10	11	12	13	4	5	6	7	8	9	10
14	15	16	17	18	19	20	11	12	13	14	15	16	17
21	22	23	24	25	26	27	18	19	20	21	22	23	24
28	29	30	31				25	26	27	28	29	30	

MAY							JUNE						
M	T	W	T	F	S	S	M	T	W	T	F	S	S
30	31				1				1	2	3	4	5
2	3	4	5	6	7	8	6	7	8	9	10	11	12
9	10	11	12	13	14	15	13	14	15	16	17	18	19
16	17	18	19	20	21	22	20	21	22	23	24	25	26
23	24	25	26	27	28	29	27	28	29	30			

On this day in 1642
Abel Tasman makes first landfall
in Van Diemen's Land

9.00	
9.30	
10.00	
10.30	
11.00	
11.30	
12.00	
12.30	
1.00	
1.30	
2.00	
2.30	
3.00	
3.30	
4.00	
4.30	
5.00	
5.30	
6.00	

NOTES

"A hen sitting on eighteen eggs
brought forth sixteen chickens . . . it
has added greatly to our livestock-
starved settlement."

Farmer/marine Scott

On this day in 1789
Aborigine, "Bennelong", captured to provide
information on local areas and traditions

9.00	
9.30	
10.00	
10.30	
11.00	
11.30	
12.00	
12.30	
1.00	
1.30	
2.00	
2.30	
3.00	
3.30	
4.00	
4.30	
5.00	
5.30	
6.00	

NOTES

" . . . kingaroo rats are like
mutton . . . a kind of chickweed
tastes like spinach . . . ground ivy is
used for tea; but a scarcity of salt
and sugar makes our best meals
insipid."

Extract of letter from female convict

On this day in 1855
Van Diemen's Land officially named Tasmania

"I think I can say none have
given it a fairer trial than
myself . . . but with few exceptions
all are heartily sick of the
expedition, & wish themselves back
safe in old England."

Rev. Richard Johnson

On this day in 1872
Large sales of Queensland sugar
in Melbourne at £35 per ton

EVENTS OF THE WEEK

TAS: Launceston.
The Travelling
Australian
Bicentennial
Exhibition opens.
21st to 24th Nov.

NATIONAL Major
Cities.
Bicentennial
Women's Cricket

World Cup. Final at
Melbourne Cricket
Ground.
27th Nov. to 18th
Dec.

JULY								AUGUST						
M	T	W	T	F	S	S		M	T	W	T	F	S	S
				1	2	3		1	2	3	4	5	6	7
4	5	6	7	8	9	10		8	9	10	11	12	13	14
11	12	13	14	15	16	17		15	16	17	18	19	20	21
18	19	20	21	22	23	24		22	23	24	25	26	27	28
25	26	27	28	29	30	31		29	30	31				

SEPTEMBER								OCTOBER						
M	T	W	T	F	S	S		M	T	W	T	F	S	S
			1	2	3	4		31					1	2
5	6	7	8	9	10	11		3	4	5	6	7	8	9
12	13	14	15	16	17	18		10	11	12	13	14	15	16
19	20	21	22	23	24	25		17	18	19	20	21	22	23
26	27	28	29	30				24	25	26	27	28	29	30

NOVEMBER								DECEMBER						
M	T	W	T	F	S	S		M	T	W	T	F	S	S
	1	2	3	4	5	6					1	2	3	4
7	8	9	10	11	12	13		5	6	7	8	9	10	11
14	15	16	17	18	19	20		12	13	14	15	16	17	18
21	22	23	24	25	26	27		19	20	21	22	23	24	25
28	29	30						26	27	28	29	30	31	

MONDAY 28 NOVEMBER

On this day in 1855
Victoria forms first government ministry

9.00	
9.30	
10.00	
10.30	
11.00	
11.30	
12.00	
12.30	
1.00	
1.30	
2.00	
2.30	
3.00	
3.30	
4.00	
4.30	
5.00	
5.30	
6.00	

NOTES

"The practise of thieving is increasing, in order to prevent this, if possible, an order was given, any convict found guilty of theft will wear no other clothing save a canvas frock and trousers."
Judge Advocate Collins

TUESDAY 29 NOVEMBER

On this day in 1948
GM-H launches first mass-produced
Australian car; Holden 48/125

9.00	
9.30	
10.00	
10.30	
11.00	
11.30	
12.00	
12.30	
1.00	
1.30	
2.00	
2.30	
3.00	
3.30	
4.00	
4.30	
5.00	
5.30	
6.00	

NOTES

"James Davis found guilty of treating Mr Reed of the *SUPPLY* with disrespect had a notation put on his papers by Collins with my approval . . . of the sentence of 400 lashes you are to receive 50 on this day, and 50 on every Saturday following until you have received the above mentioned 400."
Captain Phillip

WEDNESDAY 30 NOVEMBER

On this day in 1854
Peter Lalor elected to lead diggers
at Eureka Stockade

9.00	
9.30	
10.00	
10.30	
11.00	
11.30	
12.00	
12.30	
1.00	
1.30	
2.00	
2.30	
3.00	
3.30	
4.00	
4.30	
5.00	
5.30	
6.00	

NOTES

"It is becoming difficult to make the convicts perform a day's labour . . . those that work — a full ration — those that don't — to receive two thirds only."
Captain Phillip

JANUARY								FEBRUARY						
M	T	W	T	F	S	S		M	T	W	T	F	S	S
				1	2	3		1	2	3	4	5	6	7
4	5	6	7	8	9	10		8	9	10	11	12	13	14
11	12	13	14	15	16	17		15	16	17	18	19	20	21
18	19	20	21	22	23	24		22	23	24	25	26	27	28
25	26	27	28	29	30	31		29						

MARCH								APRIL						
M	T	W	T	F	S	S		M	T	W	T	F	S	S
1	2	3	4	5	6							1	2	3
7	8	9	10	11	12	13		4	5	6	7	8	9	10
14	15	16	17	18	19	20		11	12	13	14	15	16	17
21	22	23	24	25	26	27		18	19	20	21	22	23	24
28	29	30	31					25	26	27	28	29	30	

MAY								JUNE						
M	T	W	T	F	S	S		M	T	W	T	F	S	S
30	31				1					1	2	3	4	5
2	3	4	5	6	7	8		6	7	8	9	10	11	12
9	10	11	12	13	14	15		13	14	15	16	17	18	19
16	17	18	19	20	21	22		20	21	22	23	24	25	26
23	24	25	26	27	28	29		27	28	29	30			

THURSDAY 1 DECEMBER

On this day in 1821
Major-General Sir Thomas Brisbane takes over
as sixth Governor of colony

9.00	
9.30	
10.00	
10.30	
11.00	
11.30	
12.00	
12.30	
1.00	
1.30	
2.00	
2.30	
3.00	
3.30	
4.00	
4.30	
5.00	
5.30	
6.00	

NOTES

" . . . fresh food, including fish, was essential for the hospital. I, as with others, volunteered for daily fishing duty which had become a necessity, rather than a pleasure."

Chief Surgeon White

FRIDAY 2 DECEMBER

On this day in 1911
Douglas Mawson begins Australasian
Antarctic Expedition; lasts three years

9.00	
9.30	
10.00	
10.30	
11.00	
11.30	
12.00	
12.30	
1.00	
1.30	
2.00	
2.30	
3.00	
3.30	
4.00	
4.30	
5.00	
5.30	
6.00	

NOTES

"The first settlers had now been on shore for more than ten months but still the convicts stole and so the Governor hanged another one."

Private John Easty

SATURDAY 3 DECEMBER

On this day in 1854
Eureka Stockade battle: 6 soldiers
and 22 miners die

" . . . a female convict who received stolen goods was made a public example of. She was clothed with a canvas frock on which was painted in large characters R.S.G. (Receiver of stolen goods)."

Judge Advocate Collins

SUNDAY 4 DECEMBER

On this day in 1871
James Smith discovers world's richest tin
deposits at Mt. Bischoff, Tasmania

EVENTS OF THE WEEK

TAS: Hobart.
The Travelling
Australian
Bicentennial
Exhibition opens.
30th Nov. to 3rd Dec.

NSW: Sydney.
1988 Bicentennial
Pacific School
Games.
3rd to 10th Dec.

NSW: Sydney.
Round Australia
Bicentennial Ocean
Yacht Race due back
in Sydney Harbour.
3rd Dec.

JULY							AUGUST						
M	T	W	T	F	S	S	M	T	W	T	F	S	S
				1	2	3	1	2	3	4	5	6	7
4	5	6	7	8	9	10	8	9	10	11	12	13	14
11	12	13	14	15	16	17	15	16	17	18	19	20	21
18	19	20	21	22	23	24	22	23	24	25	26	27	28
25	26	27	28	29	30	31	29	30	31				

SEPTEMBER							OCTOBER						
M	T	W	T	F	S	S	M	T	W	T	F	S	S
			1	2	3	4	31					1	2
5	6	7	8	9	10	11	3	4	5	6	7	8	9
12	13	14	15	16	17	18	10	11	12	13	14	15	16
19	20	21	22	23	24	25	17	18	19	20	21	22	23
26	27	28	29	30			24	25	26	27	28	29	30

NOVEMBER							DECEMBER						
M	T	W	T	F	S	S	M	T	W	T	F	S	S
	1	2	3	4	5	6				1	2	3	4
7	8	9	10	11	12	13	5	6	7	8	9	10	11
14	15	16	17	18	19	20	12	13	14	15	16	17	18
21	22	23	24	25	26	27	19	20	21	22	23	24	25
28	29	30					26	27	28	29	30	31	

MONDAY 5 DECEMBER

On this day in 1953
First Australian oil discovered at Exmouth,
Western Australia

9.00	
9.30	
10.00	
10.30	
11.00	
11.30	
12.00	
12.30	
1.00	
1.30	
2.00	
2.30	
3.00	
3.30	
4.00	
4.30	
5.00	
5.30	
6.00	

NOTES

"My Judge Advocate advised that he had heard a complaint brought by Deborah Herbert, who accused her husband of beating her without just cause. Both gave evidence and Collins sentenced Deborah Herbert to 'receive 25 lashes and return to her husband'."

Captain Phillip

TUESDAY 6 DECEMBER

On this day in 1784
Transportation of convicts to
New South Wales authorised

9.00	
9.30	
10.00	
10.30	
11.00	
11.30	
12.00	
12.30	
1.00	
1.30	
2.00	
2.30	
3.00	
3.30	
4.00	
4.30	
5.00	
5.30	
6.00	

NOTES

"The pressure of current circumstances did much to bring life to a dead level. The marines were not so differently placed from the convicts; they had the same food, the same labour, the same shelter or the lack of it."

Chief Surgeon White

WEDNESDAY 7 DECEMBER

On this day in 1927
Dock workers end nationwide strike
which tied up all shipping

9.00	
9.30	
10.00	
10.30	
11.00	
11.30	
12.00	
12.30	
1.00	
1.30	
2.00	
2.30	
3.00	
3.30	
4.00	
4.30	
5.00	
5.30	
6.00	

NOTES

"The governor, under strong pressures from the troops & officers for an increase in rations insisted in a quiet, steady manner that the stocks were for the equal benefit of all."

Judge Advocate Collins

JANUARY

M	T	W	T	F	S	S
				1	2	3
4	5	6	7	8	9	10
11	12	13	14	15	16	17
18	19	20	21	22	23	24
25	26	27	28	29	30	31

FEBRUARY

M	T	W	T	F	S	S
1	2	3	4	5	6	7
8	9	10	11	12	13	14
15	16	17	18	19	20	21
22	23	24	25	26	27	28
29						

MARCH

M	T	W	T	F	S	S
	1	2	3	4	5	6
7	8	9	10	11	12	13
14	15	16	17	18	19	20
21	22	23	24	25	26	27
28	29	30	31			

APRIL

M	T	W	T	F	S	S
				1	2	3
4	5	6	7	8	9	10
11	12	13	14	15	16	17
18	19	20	21	22	23	24
25	26	27	28	29	30	

MAY

M	T	W	T	F	S	S
30	31					1
2	3	4	5	6	7	8
9	10	11	12	13	14	15
16	17	18	19	20	21	22
23	24	25	26	27	28	29

JUNE

M	T	W	T	F	S	S
		1	2	3	4	5
6	7	8	9	10	11	12
13	14	15	16	17	18	19
20	21	22	23	24	25	26
27	28	29	30			

THURSDAY 8 DECEMBER

On this day in 1941
Australia declares war on Japan after
Pearl Harbour bombed

9.00	
9.30	
10.00	
10.30	
11.00	
11.30	
12.00	
12.30	
1.00	
1.30	
2.00	
2.30	
3.00	
3.30	
4.00	
4.30	
5.00	
5.30	
6.00	

NOTES

"The natives at this time are
giving us little trouble; and had they
never been ill treated by our people,
instead of hostility, it is more than
probable than an intercourse of
friendship would have subsisted."
Judge Advocate Collins

FRIDAY 9 DECEMBER

On this day in 1909
Colin Defries attempts first powered flight
in Australia; travels 115 yards

9.00	
9.30	
10.00	
10.30	
11.00	
11.30	
12.00	
12.30	
1.00	
1.30	
2.00	
2.30	
3.00	
3.30	
4.00	
4.30	
5.00	
5.30	
6.00	

NOTES

"Henry Dodd held in very high
esteem by the Governor and the
Officers has gained by infinate tact,
a large influence over the
convicts . . . he has been put in
charge of all the agricultural details
at Rose Hill, he is a natural
gardener."
Judge Advocate Collins

SATURDAY 10 DECEMBER

On this day in 1919
Ross and Keith Smith win first
Britain-Australia air race

"The lash has no effect in
curbing the tide on crime, so the
Governor was 'turning people off' at
the tree . . . there were nearly 300
crimes punishable by hanging."
Judge Advocate Collins

SUNDAY 11 DECEMBER

On this day in 1792
Governor Phillip, in poor health,
leaves colony for England

EVENTS OF THE WEEK

ACT: Canberra.
Bicentennial Around
Australia Relay.
Finish — Parliament
House.
6th Dec.

ACT: Canberra.
Military Tattoo.
Bruce Stadium.
8th to 10th Dec.

SA: Adelaide.
First International
Junior Wheelchair
Games.
8th to 18th Dec.

	JULY								AUGUST					
M	T	W	T	F	S	S	M	T	W	T	F	S	S
				1	2	3.	1	2	3	4	5	6	7
4	5	6	7	8	9	10	8	9	10	11	12	13	14
11	12	13	14	15	16	17	15	16	17	18	19	20	21
18	19	20	21	22	23	24	22	23	24	25	26	27	28
25	26	27	28	29	30	31	29	30	31				

	SEPTEMBER								OCTOBER					
M	T	W	T	F	S	S	M	T	W	T	F	S	S
			1	2	3	4	31					1	2
5	6	7	8	9	10	11	3	4	5	6	7	8	9
12	13	14	15	16	17	18	10	11	12	13	14	15	16
19	20	21	22	23	24	25	17	18	19	20	21	22	23
26	27	28	29	30			24	25	26	27	28	29	30

	NOVEMBER								DECEMBER					
M	T	W	T	F	S	S	M	T	W	T	F	S	S
	1	2	3	4	5	6				1	2	3	4
7	8	9	10	11	12	13	5	6	7	8	9	10	11
14	15	16	17	18	19	20	12	13	14	15	16	17	18
21	22	23	24	25	26	27	19	20	21	22	23	24	25
28	29	30					26	27	28	29	30	31	

On this day in 1815
James Kelly begins 49 day circumnavigation
of Van Diemen's Land

9.00	
9.30	
10.00	
10.30	
11.00	
11.30	
12.00	
12.30	
1.00	
1.30	
2.00	
2.30	
3.00	
3.30	
4.00	
4.30	
5.00	
5.30	
6.00	

NOTES

" . . . there is the Love, the Mercy and Compassion of God. They prefer their lusts before their souls: yea, most of them would sell their souls for a glass of grogg — so blind — so hardened — so foolish are they."

Rev. Richard Johnson

On this day in 1975
Federal election landslide victory to Malcolm
Fraser, record 55 seat majority

9.00	
9.30	
10.00	
10.30	
11.00	
11.30	
12.00	
12.30	
1.00	
1.30	
2.00	
2.30	
3.00	
3.30	
4.00	
4.30	
5.00	
5.30	
6.00	

NOTES

" . . . the natives were all armed with lances, shields and spears and appeared very hungry . . . as their curiosity made them troublesome when we were preparing our dinner, I made a circle round us."

Captain Phillip at Botany Bay

On this day in 1968
Tasmanian referendum approves
establishment of gambling casino

9.00	
9.30	
10.00	
10.30	
11.00	
11.30	
12.00	
12.30	
1.00	
1.30	
2.00	
2.30	
3.00	
3.30	
4.00	
4.30	
5.00	
5.30	
6.00	

NOTES

" . . . he had not for more than a week past eaten his allowance . . . he was accustomed to deny himself even what was absolutely necessary to his existence . . . selling his provisions for money . . . in order to purchase his passage to England when his time should expire."

Judge Advocate Collins

JANUARY							FEBRUARY						
M	T	W	T	F	S	S	M	T	W	T	F	S	S
				1	2	3	1	2	3	4	5	6	7
4	5	6	7	8	9	10	8	9	10	11	12	13	14
11	12	13	14	15	16	17	15	16	17	18	19	20	21
18	19	20	21	22	23	24	22	23	24	25	26	27	28
25	26	27	28	29	30	31	29						

MARCH							APRIL						
M	T	W	T	F	S	S	M	T	W	T	F	S	S
1	2	3	4	5	6						1	2	3
7	8	9	10	11	12	13	4	5	6	7	8	9	10
14	15	16	17	18	19	20	11	12	13	14	15	16	17
21	22	23	24	25	26	27	18	19	20	21	22	23	24
28	29	30	31				25	26	27	28	29	30	

MAY							JUNE						
M	T	W	T	F	S	S	M	T	W	T	F	S	S
30	31					1			1	2	3	4	5
2	3	4	5	6	7	8	6	7	8	9	10	11	12
9	10	11	12	13	14	15	13	14	15	16	17	18	19
16	17	18	19	20	21	22	20	21	22	23	24	25	26
23	24	25	26	27	28	29	27	28	29	30			

THURSDAY 15 DECEMBER

On this day in 1882
Tailoress's Union established;
first all-female union

9.00	
9.30	
10.00	
10.30	
11.00	
11.30	
12.00	
12.30	
1.00	
1.30	
2.00	
2.30	
3.00	
3.30	
4.00	
4.30	
5.00	
5.30	
6.00	

NOTES

"I admire the Governor's restraint as at times he comes near to losing his temper with the Major, who seems to miss no chance of harrassing the Governor in every possible way."

Judge Advocate Collins

FRIDAY 16 DECEMBER

On this day in 1903
Women vote for first time
in Federal elections

9.00	
9.30	
10.00	
10.30	
11.00	
11.30	
12.00	
12.30	
1.00	
1.30	
2.00	
2.30	
3.00	
3.30	
4.00	
4.30	
5.00	
5.30	
6.00	

NOTES

"After five days I am completely satisfied that no part of Botany Bay can be adapted to the purpose of settlement; this fully confirms reports from others and my own opinions."

Captain Phillip

SATURDAY 17 DECEMBER

On this day in 1967
Prime Minister Harold Holt disappears off
Portsea, Vic.

"We have labor'd incessantly since we arrived here to raise all sorts of vegetables, and even at this distant period we can barely supply our tables, His Excellency's not excepted."

Officer of the marines

SUNDAY 18 DECEMBER

On this day in 1825
Ralph Darling, 7th Governor of NSW
arrives in Sydney

EVENTS OF THE WEEK

NSW: Sydney. The Travelling Australian Bicentennial Exhibition opens. Grand finale of national tour by the 25 semi-trailers which are carrying this innovative exhibition 20,000 km around Australia. Parramatta Park. 12th to 18th Dec.

	JULY							AUGUST					
M	T	W	T	F	S	S	M	T	W	T	F	S	S
				1	2	3	1	2	3	4	5	6	7
4	5	6	7	8	9	10	8	9	10	11	12	13	14
11	12	13	14	15	16	17	15	16	17	18	19	20	21
18	19	20	21	22	23	24	22	23	24	25	26	27	28
25	26	27	28	29	30	31	29	30	31				

	SEPTEMBER							OCTOBER					
M	T	W	T	F	S	S	M	T	W	T	F	S	S
			1	2	3	4	31					1	2
5	6	7	8	9	10	11	3	4	5	6	7	8	9
12	13	14	15	16	17	18	10	11	12	13	14	15	16
19	20	21	22	23	24	25	17	18	19	20	21	22	23
26	27	28	29	30			24	25	26	27	28	29	30

	NOVEMBER							DECEMBER					
M	T	W	T	F	S	S	M	T	W	T	F	S	S
1	2	3	4	5	6					1	2	3	4
7	8	9	10	11	12	13	5	6	7	8	9	10	11
14	15	16	17	18	19	20	12	13	14	15	16	17	18
21	22	23	24	25	26	27	19	20	21	22	23	24	25
28	29	30					26	27	28	29	30	31	

MONDAY 19 DECEMBER

On this day in 1865
Sam Poo, the Chinese bushranger,
is hanged in Sydney

9.00	
9.30	
10.00	
10.30	
11.00	
11.30	
12.00	
12.30	
1.00	
1.30	
2.00	
2.30	
3.00	
3.30	
4.00	
4.30	
5.00	
5.30	
6.00	

NOTES

"I have ordered boats to be got ready, and every preparation made, to go out, capture some natives and if necessary retain them by force . . . I will attempt to possess their reasons for harassing and destroying our people."

Captain Phillip

TUESDAY 20 DECEMBER

On this day in 1915
Evacuation of Gallipoli completed

9.00	
9.30	
10.00	
10.30	
11.00	
11.30	
12.00	
12.30	
1.00	
1.30	
2.00	
2.30	
3.00	
3.30	
4.00	
4.30	
5.00	
5.30	
6.00	

NOTES

"Sir, their is only Beef and Pork for less than twenty months, Flour, Rice, Butter & Pease for less than eighteen months, I will compile a full provisions stocktake for early January."

Andrew Miller

WEDNESDAY 21 DECEMBER

On this day in 1894
S.A. Government grants female suffrage;
among first in world

9.00	
9.30	
10.00	
10.30	
11.00	
11.30	
12.00	
12.30	
1.00	
1.30	
2.00	
2.30	
3.00	
3.30	
4.00	
4.30	
5.00	
5.30	
6.00	

NOTES

"Thomas Brimage and myself were tryed by a courtmartial for leaving the camp without leave for which we were sentenced 50 lashes each but the cortt recommended us to the commanding officer for mercy and we were forgiven."

Private John Easty

JANUARY								FEBRUARY						
M	T	W	T	F	S	S		M	T	W	T	F	S	S
				1	2	3		1	2	3	4	5	6	7
4	5	6	7	8	9	10		8	9	10	11	12	13	14
11	12	13	14	15	16	17		15	16	17	18	19	20	21
18	19	20	21	22	23	24		22	23	24	25	26	27	28
25	26	27	28	29	30	31		29						

MARCH								APRIL						
M	T	W	T	F	S	S		M	T	W	T	F	S	S
1	2	3	4	5	6							1	2	3
7	8	9	10	11	12	13		4	5	6	7	8	9	10
14	15	16	17	18	19	20		11	12	13	14	15	16	17
21	22	23	24	25	26	27		18	19	20	21	22	23	24
28	29	30	31					25	26	27	28	29	30	

MAY								JUNE						
M	T	W	T	F	S	S		M	T	W	T	F	S	S
30	31				1					1	2	3	4	5
2	3	4	5	6	7	8		6	7	8	9	10	11	12
9	10	11	12	13	14	15		13	14	15	16	17	18	19
16	17	18	19	20	21	22		20	21	22	23	24	25	26
23	24	25	26	27	28	29		27	28	29	30			

THURSDAY 22 DECEMBER

On this day in 1888
Henry Lawson publishes his first short story
"His Father's Mate"

9.00	
9.30	
10.00	
10.30	
11.00	
11.30	
12.00	
12.30	
1.00	
1.30	
2.00	
2.30	
3.00	
3.30	
4.00	
4.30	
5.00	
5.30	
6.00	

NOTES

" . . . by the surgeons returns it appears that twenty have died from disorders of long standing, and which is more than probable would have carried them off sooner in England."

Captain Phillip

FRIDAY 23 DECEMBER

On this day in 1861
First metropolitan horse-drawn carriage service begins in Sydney

9.00	
9.30	
10.00	
10.30	
11.00	
11.30	
12.00	
12.30	
1.00	
1.30	
2.00	
2.30	
3.00	
3.30	
4.00	
4.30	
5.00	
5.30	
6.00	

NOTES

"Yultide is almost upon us and my hope is by no means exhausted despite the difficulties met with; given time, and additional force, together with proper people for cultivating the land . . . I know now that I can make a nation."

Captain Phillip

SATURDAY 24 DECEMBER

On this day in 1826
Edmund Lockyer arrives at King George Sound, W.A. to form penal settlement

" . . . as to myself I am satisfied to remain as long as my services are wanted, and my health is strong; I am serving my country and serving the course of humanity to the best of my ability."

Captain Phillip

SUNDAY 25 DECEMBER

On this day in 1974
Darwin devastated by cyclone Tracy

EVENTS OF THE WEEK

CHRISTMAS DAY
25th Dec.

JULY							AUGUST						
M	T	W	T	F	S	S	M	T	W	T	F	S	S
				1	2	3	1	2	3	4	5	6	7
4	5	6	7	8	9	10	8	9	10	11	12	13	14
11	12	13	14	15	16	17	15	16	17	18	19	20	21
18	19	20	21	22	23	24	22	23	24	25	26	27	28
25	26	27	28	29	30	31	29	30	31				

SEPTEMBER							OCTOBER						
M	T	W	T	F	S	S	M	T	W	T	F	S	S
			1	2	3	4	31					1	2
5	6	7	8	9	10	11	3	4	5	6	7	8	9
12	13	14	15	16	17	18	10	11	12	13	14	15	16
19	20	21	22	23	24	25	17	18	19	20	21	22	23
26	27	28	29	30			24	25	26	27	28	29	30

NOVEMBER							DECEMBER						
M	T	W	T	F	S	S	M	T	W	T	F	S	S
1	2	3	4	5	6					1	2	3	4
7	8	9	10	11	12	13	5	6	7	8	9	10	11
14	15	16	17	18	19	20	12	13	14	15	16	17	18
21	22	23	24	25	26	27	19	20	21	22	23	24	25
28	29	30					26	27	28	29	30	31	

MONDAY 26 DECEMBER

On this day in 1945
First Sydney-Hobart Yacht Race begins

9.00	
9.30	
10.00	
10.30	
11.00	
11.30	
12.00	
12.30	
1.00	
1.30	
2.00	
2.30	
3.00	
3.30	
4.00	
4.30	
5.00	
5.30	
6.00	

NOTES

"I have sent a letter attached to a box of flax from Norfolk Island to Under Secretary Nepean requesting the want of a person that understands the preparing and manufacture of flax. I believe if properly dressed it would be superior to any that grows in Europe."

Captain Phillip

TUESDAY 27 DECEMBER

On this day in 1803
Convict William Buckley escapes; at large for 32 years

9.00	
9.30	
10.00	
10.30	
11.00	
11.30	
12.00	
12.30	
1.00	
1.30	
2.00	
2.30	
3.00	
3.30	
4.00	
4.30	
5.00	
5.30	
6.00	

NOTES

"Mr. Reid, the carpenter of the *SUPPLY* commenced construction of a boathouse for the purpose of building, with the timber of this country, a launch and hoy capable of conveying provisions to Rose Hill."

Judge Advocate Collins

WEDNESDAY 28 DECEMBER

On this day in 1850
Henry Parkes founds the "Empire" newspaper

9.00	
9.30	
10.00	
10.30	
11.00	
11.30	
12.00	
12.30	
1.00	
1.30	
2.00	
2.30	
3.00	
3.30	
4.00	
4.30	
5.00	
5.30	
6.00	

NOTES

"The working convicts were employed on Saturdays, until 10 o'clock in the forenoon, in forming a landing place on the East side of the Cove. At the point on the West side, a magazine was marked out, to be constructed of stone, and large enough to contain fifty or sixty barrels of powder."

Judge Advocate Collins

JANUARY								FEBRUARY						
M	T	W	T	F	S	S		M	T	W	T	F	S	S
				1	2	3		1	2	3	4	5	6	7
4	5	6	7	8	9	10		8	9	10	11	12	13	14
11	12	13	14	15	16	17		15	16	17	18	19	20	21
18	19	20	21	22	23	24		22	23	24	25	26	27	28
25	26	27	28	29	30	31		29						

MARCH								APRIL						
M	T	W	T	F	S	S		M	T	W	T	F	S	S
1	2	3	4	5	6							1	2	3
7	8	9	10	11	12	13		4	5	6	7	8	9	10
14	15	16	17	18	19	20		11	12	13	14	15	16	17
21	22	23	24	25	26	27		18	19	20	21	22	23	24
28	29	30	31					25	26	27	28	29	30	

MAY								JUNE						
M	T	W	T	F	S	S		M	T	W	T	F	S	S
30	31					1				1	2	3	4	5
2	3	4	5	6	7	8		6	7	8	9	10	11	12
9	10	11	12	13	14	15		13	14	15	16	17	18	19
16	17	18	19	20	21	22		20	21	22	23	24	25	26
23	24	25	26	27	28	29		27	28	29	30			

THURSDAY 29 DECEMBER

On this day in 1920
Special court inquiry into 44-hour-week
for all trades

9.00	
9.30	
10.00	
10.30	
11.00	
11.30	
12.00	
12.30	
1.00	
1.30	
2.00	
2.30	
3.00	
3.30	
4.00	
4.30	
5.00	
5.30	
6.00	

NOTES

"I posed myself the question how to improve our relationship with the natives. There is still no verbal communication between them and us and in spite of all attempts there have been no voluntary move from them to remedy this situation."

Captain Phillip

FRIDAY 30 DECEMBER

On this day in 1857
Sydney Stock Exchange opens
for public business

9.00	
9.30	
10.00	
10.30	
11.00	
11.30	
12.00	
12.30	
1.00	
1.30	
2.00	
2.30	
3.00	
3.30	
4.00	
4.30	
5.00	
5.30	
6.00	

NOTES

"A native named MANLEY secured by soldiers at Manley Bay was clothed and I made him dine with me this day. He is secured with a rope and a man leades him abought. A house has been built for him and his keeper."

James Scott

SATURDAY 31 DECEMBER

On this day in 1958
N.S.W. Government legislates for
equal pay for women

"I will give a dinner for all the naval, marine and civil officers for to-morrow New Years Day, I intend to also invite "Manly" who I found out this day that his name is "Arabanoo". Nothing will give me greater pleasure than to see him at ease with the party."

Captain Phillip

SUNDAY 1 JANUARY

On this day in 1819
First orphan school for boys opens in Sydney

EVENTS OF THE WEEK

SA: Adelaide. Fifteenth Australian Scout Jamboree. Mt Lofty Ranges. 27th Dec. to 7th Jan.

NATIONAL PUBLIC HOLIDAY: All states except South Australia. 27th Dec.

BOXING DAY 26th Dec.

NSW: Sydney. AWA Sydney-Hobart Yacht Race. Sydney Harbour. 26th Dec.

JULY							AUGUST						
M	T	W	T	F	S	S	M	T	W	T	F	S	S
				1	2	3	1	2	3	4	5	6	7
4	5	6	7	8	9	10	8	9	10	11	12	13	14
11	12	13	14	15	16	17	15	16	17	18	19	20	21
18	19	20	21	22	23	24	22	23	24	25	26	27	28
25	26	27	28	29	30	31	29	30	31				

SEPTEMBER							OCTOBER						
M	T	W	T	F	S	S	M	T	W	T	F	S	S
		1	2	3	4	31						1	2
5	6	7	8	9	10	11	3	4	5	6	7	8	9
12	13	14	15	16	17	18	10	11	12	13	14	15	16
19	20	21	22	23	24	25	17	18	19	20	21	22	23
26	27	28	29	30			24	25	26	27	28	29	30

NOVEMBER							DECEMBER						
M	T	W	T	F	S	S	M	T	W	T	F	S	S
	1	2	3	4	5	6				1	2	3	4
7	8	9	10	11	12	13	5	6	7	8	9	10	11
14	15	16	17	18	19	20	12	13	14	15	16	17	18
21	22	23	24	25	26	27	19	20	21	22	23	24	25
28	29	30					26	27	28	29	30	31	

INFORMATION INDEX

HOLIDAYS

☐ AUSTRALIAN PUBLIC HOLIDAYS   ■ INTERNATIONAL HOLIDAYS

☐ AUSTRALIAN SCHOOL HOLIDAYS

JANUARY 1988

1 New Year's Day (Australia) (U.K.) (N.Z.) (U.S.A.) (Japan)
15 Coming of Age (Japan)
18 Martin Luther King Junior's Birthday (U.S.A.)
26 Australia Day
27 Northern Territory Term 1 begins
    Queensland Term 1 begins

FEBRUARY 1988

2 New South Wales Term 1 begins
    A.C.T. Term 1 begins
    South Australia Term 1 begins
4 Victoria Term 1 begins
    Western Australia Term 1 begins
6 Waitangi Day (N.Z.)
11 Foundation Day (Japan)
12 Abraham Lincoln's Birthday (U.S.A.)
15 George Washington's Birthday (U.S.A)
16 Tasmania Term 1 begins

MARCH 1988

7 Eight Hours Day (Tasmania)
    Labour Day (Western Australia)
14 Labour Day (Victoria)
17 Bank Holiday (Northern Ireland)
21 Spring Equinox Day (Japan)
31 Western Australia Term 1 ends
    A.C.T. Term 1 ends
    Victoria Term 1 ends
    Queensland Term 1 ends
    New South Wales Term 1 ends

APRIL 1988

1 Good Friday (Australia) (N.Z.) (U.K.)
2 Easter Saturday (Australia) (N.Z.)
4 Easter Monday (Australia) (N.Z.) (U.K.)
5 Easter Tuesday (Victoria and Tasmania only)
8 Northern Territory Term 1 ends
11 Queensland Term 2 begins
    New South Wales Term 2 begins
    Western Australia Term 2 begins
    A.C.T. Term 2 begins
    Victoria Term 2 begins
15 South Australia Term 1 ends
18 Northern Territory Term 2 begins
25 Anzac Day (Australia) (N.Z.)
26 South Australia Term 2 begins
29 Emperor's Birthday (Japan)

MAY 1988

2 Labour Day (Queensland)
    May Day (Northern Territory)
    Bank Holiday (U.K.)
3 Constitution Day (Japan)
5 Children's Day (Japan)
16 Adelaide Cup Day (South Australia)
26 Memorial Day (U.S.A.)
27 Tasmania Term 1 ends
30 Bank Holiday (Scotland and Northern Ireland)

JUNE 1988

6 Foundation Day (Western Australia)
    Queen's Birthday (N.Z.)
13 Queen's Birthday (Australia except Western Australia)
14 Tasmania Term 2 begins
24 Western Australia Term 2 ends
    Victoria Term 2 ends
    Queensland Term 2 ends

JULY 1988

1 Show Day (Alice Springs)
    Northern Territory Term 2 ends
    A.C.T. Term 2 ends
    New South Wales Term 2 ends
    South Australia Term 2 ends
4 Independence Day (U.S.A.)
11 Queensland Term 3 begins
    Victoria Term 3 begins
12 Bank Holiday (Northern Ireland)
13 Western Australia Term 3 begins
18 New South Wales Term 3 begins
    A.C.T. Term 3 begins
    South Australia Term 3 begins
22 Show Day (Darwin)

AUGUST 1988

1 Picnic Day (Northern Territory)
    Bank Holiday (Scotland)
    Bank Holiday (New South Wales)
2 Northern Territory Term 3 begins
17 Exhibition Day (Brisbane)
26 Tasmania Term 2 ends
29 Bank Holiday (U.K. except Scotland)

SEPTEMBER 1988

5 Labour Day (U.S.A.)
12 Tasmania Term 3 begins
15 Old People's Day (Japan)
16 Queensland Term 3 ends
    Victoria Term 3 ends
22 Show Day (Melbourne)
23 Autumn Equinox Day (Japan)
    Western Australia Term 3 ends
    South Australia Term 3 ends
    New South Wales Term 3 ends
    A.C.T. Term 3 ends
30 Northern Territory Term 3 ends

OCTOBER 1988

3 Victoria Term 4 begins
    Labour Day (New South Wales)
    Queensland Term 4 begins
10 Labour Day (South Australia)
    New South Wales Term 4 begins
    A.C.T. Term 4 begins
    Northern Territory Term 4 begins
    Western Australia Term 4 begins
    Columbus Day (U.S.A.)
    Sports Day (Japan)
11 South Australia Term 4 begins
24 Labour Day (N.Z.)

NOVEMBER 1988

1 Melbourne Cup Day (Melbourne)
3 Cultural Day (Japan)
7 Recreation Day (Northern Tasmania)
11 Veterans' Day (U.S.A.)
23 Labour Day (Japan)
24 Thanksgiving (U.S.A.)

DECEMBER 1988

9 Queensland Term 4 ends
    Northern Territory Term 4 ends
16 Western Australia Term 4 ends
    A.C.T. Term 4 ends
    South Australia Term 4 ends
    New South Wales Term 4 ends
21 Tasmania Term 3 ends
22 Victoria Term 4 ends
26 Christmas Day Holiday (Australia) (N.Z.) (U.K.) (U.S.A.)
27 Boxing Day Holiday (Australia — except South Australia) (N.Z.) (U.K.)
28 Proclamation Day (South Australia)

* Queensland School Holidays were correct at time of printing but subject to change.

1987

	JANUARY					FEBRUARY					MARCH			
S	4	11	18	25	1	8	15	22	1	8	15	22	29
M	5	12	19	26	2	9	16	23	2	9	16	23	30
Tu	6	13	20	27	3	10	17	24	3	10	17	24	31
W	7	14	21	28	4	11	18	25	4	11	18	25	
Th	1	8	15	22	29	5	12	19	26	5	12	19	26
F	2	9	16	23	30	6	13	20	27	6	13	20	27
S	3	10	17	24	31	7	14	21	28	7	14	21	28

	APRIL				MAY					JUNE			
S	5	12	19	26	3	10	17	24	31	7	14	21	28
M	6	13	20	27	4	11	18	25	1	8	15	22	29
Tu	7	14	21	28	5	12	19	26	2	9	16	23	30
W	1	8	15	22	29	6	13	20	27	3	10	17	24
Th	2	9	16	23	30	7	14	21	28	4	11	18	25
F	3	10	17	24	1	8	15	22	29	5	12	19	26
S	4	11	18	25	2	9	16	23	30	6	13	20	27

	JULY				AUGUST					SEPTEMBER			
S	5	12	19	26	2	9	16	23	30	6	13	20	27
M	6	13	20	27	3	10	17	24	31	7	14	21	28
Tu	7	14	21	28	4	11	18	25	1	8	15	22	29
W	1	8	15	22	29	5	12	19	26	2	9	16	23	30
Th	2	9	16	23	30	6	13	20	27	3	10	17	24
F	3	10	17	24	31	7	14	21	28	4	11	18	25
S	4	11	18	25	1	8	15	22	29	5	12	19	26

	OCTOBER				NOVEMBER					DECEMBER			
S	4	11	18	25	1	8	15	22	29	6	13	20	27
M	5	12	19	26	2	9	16	23	30	7	14	21	28
T	6	13	20	27	3	10	17	24	1	8	15	22	29
W	7	14	21	28	4	11	18	25	2	9	16	23	30
T	1	8	15	22	29	5	12	19	26	3	10	17	24	31
F	2	9	16	23	30	6	13	20	27	4	11	18	25
S	3	10	17	24	31	7	14	21	28	5	12	19	26

1988

	JANUARY					FEBRUARY				MARCH			
S	3	10	17	24	31	7	14	21	28	6	13	20	27
M	4	11	18	25	1	8	15	22	29	7	14	21	28
Tu	5	12	19	26	2	9	16	23	1	8	15	22	29
W	6	13	20	27	3	10	17	24	2	9	16	23	30
Th	7	14	21	28	4	11	18	25	3	10	17	24	31
F	1	8	15	22	29	5	12	19	26	4	11	18	25
S	2	9	16	23	30	6	13	20	27	5	12	19	26

	APRIL				MAY					JUNE			
S	3	10	17	24	1	8	15	22	29	5	12	19	26
M	4	11	18	25	2	9	16	23	30	6	13	20	27
Tu	5	12	19	26	3	10	17	24	31	7	14	21	28
W	6	13	20	27	4	11	18	25	1	8	15	22	29
Th	7	14	21	28	5	12	19	26	2	9	16	23	30
F	1	8	15	22	29	6	13	20	27	3	10	17	24
S	2	9	16	23	30	7	14	21	28	4	11	18	25

	JULY				AUGUST					SEPTEMBER			
S	3	10	17	24	31	7	14	21	28	4	11	18	25
M	4	11	18	25	1	8	15	22	29	5	12	19	26
Tu	5	12	19	26	2	9	16	23	30	6	13	20	27
W	6	13	20	27	3	10	17	24	31	7	14	21	28
Th	7	14	21	28	4	11	18	25	1	8	15	22	29
F	1	8	15	22	29	5	12	19	26	2	9	16	23	30
S	2	9	16	23	30	6	13	20	27	3	10	17	24

	OCTOBER				NOVEMBER					DECEMBER			
S	2	9	16	23	30	6	13	20	27	4	11	18	25
M	3	10	17	24	31	7	14	21	28	5	12	19	26
Tu	4	11	18	25	1	8	15	22	29	6	13	20	27
W	5	12	19	26	2	9	16	23	30	7	14	21	28
Th	6	13	20	27	3	10	17	24	1	8	15	22	29
F	7	14	21	28	4	11	18	25	2	9	16	23	30
S	1	8	15	22	29	5	12	19	26	3	10	17	24	31

1989

	JANUARY					FEBRUARY				MARCH			
S	1	8	15	22	29	5	12	19	26	5	12	19	26
M	2	9	16	23	30	6	13	20	27	6	13	20	27
Tu	3	10	17	24	31	7	14	21	28	7	14	21	28
W	4	11	18	25	1	8	15	22	1	8	15	22	29
Th	5	12	19	26	2	9	16	23	2	9	16	23	30
F	6	13	20	27	3	10	17	24	3	10	17	24	31
S	7	14	21	28	4	11	18	25	4	11	18	25	

	APRIL				MAY					JUNE			
S	2	9	16	23	30	7	14	21	28	4	11	18	25
M	3	10	17	24	1	8	15	22	29	5	12	19	26
Tu	4	11	18	25	2	9	16	23	30	6	13	20	27
W	5	12	19	26	3	10	17	24	31	7	14	21	28
Th	6	13	20	27	4	11	18	25	1	8	15	22	29
F	7	14	21	28	5	12	19	26	2	9	16	23	30
S	1	8	15	22	29	6	13	20	27	3	10	17	24

	JULY				AUGUST					SEPTEMBER			
S	2	9	16	23	30	6	13	20	27	3	10	17	24
M	3	10	17	24	31	7	14	21	28	4	11	18	25
Tu	4	11	18	25	1	8	15	22	29	5	12	19	26
W	5	12	19	26	2	9	16	23	30	6	13	20	27
Th	6	13	20	27	3	10	17	24	31	7	14	21	28
F	7	14	21	28	4	11	18	25	1	8	15	22	29
S	1	8	15	22	29	5	12	19	26	2	9	16	23	30

	OCTOBER				NOVEMBER					DECEMBER			
S	1	8	15	22	29	5	12	19	26	3	10	17	24	31
M	2	9	16	23	30	6	13	20	27	4	11	18	25
Tu	3	10	17	24	31	7	14	21	28	5	12	19	26
W	4	11	18	25	1	8	15	22	29	6	13	20	27
Th	5	12	19	26	2	9	16	23	30	7	14	21	28
F	6	13	20	27	3	10	17	24	1	8	15	22	29
S	7	14	21	28	4	11	18	25	2	9	16	23	30

TEMPERATURE

100°C	BOILING POINT OF WATER
40°C	HEAT WAVE CONDITIONS
35°C	
37°C	BODY TEMPERATURE
30°C	HOT
25°C	WARM
20°C	MILD
15°C	COOL
10°C	COLD TO VERY COLD
5°C	
0°C	FREEZING POINT OF WATER

LENGTH

80 μm	Approximately the thickness of a human hair
1 mm	Approximately the thickness of a five cent piece
2 mm	Approximately the thickness of a matchstick
1 cm	Approximately the width of an index fingernail
25 mm	Approximately one inch
10 cm	Approximately the width of a man's fist
1 m	A long stride
50 m	Length of an Olympic Swimming Pool
8 klm	Approximately five miles

VOLUME

1 ml	Approximately one eye dropper full
5 ml	One standard teaspoonful
200 ml	Approximately 7 fluid ounces
600 ml	A little more than 1 pint
1 litre	A familiar wine quantity
200 l	The capacity of a 44-gallon drum
1 m³	Approximately 1⅓ cubic yards

WEIGHT

1 g	Approximately the mass of three aspirin tablets
5 g	Approximately the mass of a two cent piece
50 g	Approximately the mass of a golf ball
500 g	A little more than one pound
1 kg	A little more than two pounds
20 kg	Luggage allowance for economy class air travel
70 kg	About 11 stone
1 t	A little less than one ton

VELOCITY

6 km/h	Average speed for swimming 100 m in one minute
24 km/h	Average speed for running a four-minute mile
36 km/h	Average speed for running 100 m in 10 seconds
60 km/h	Approximately 35 mph
100 km/h	Approximately 60 mph
800 km/h	Approximately 500 mph

METRIC MEASUREMENT

LENGTH

1000	picometres	= 1 nanometre
1000	nanometres	= 1 micrometre
1000	micrometres	= 1 millimetre
10	millimetres	= 1 centimetre
100	millimetres	= 1 decimetre
10	centimetres	= 1 decimetre
1000	millimetres	= 1 metre
100	centimetres	= 1 metre
10	decimetres	= 1 metre
1000	metres	= 1 kilometre
1852	metres	= 1 international nautical mile

PRESSURE AND STRESS

1000	micropascals	= 1 millipascal
1000	millipascals	= 1 pascal
100	pascals	= 1 millibar
1000	pascals	= 1 kilopascal
10	millibars	= 1 kilopascal
1000	kilopascals	= 1 megapascal
1000	megapascals	= 1 gigapascal

TIME

1000	nanoseconds	= 1 microsecond
1000	microseconds	= 1 millisecond
1000	milliseconds	= 1 second
1000	seconds	= 1 kilosecond
60	seconds	= 1 minute

FREQUENCY

1000	hertz	= 1 kilohertz
1000	kilohertz	= 1 megahertz
1000	megahertz	= 1 gigahertz
1000	gigahertz	= 1 terahertz

FORCE

1000	micronewtons	= 1 millinewton
1000	millinewtons	= 1 newton
1000	newtons	= 1 kilonewton
1000	kilonewtons	= 1 meganewton

VELOCITY

3.6 kilometres per hour	= 1 metre per second
3600 kilometres per hour	= 1 kilometre per second

VOLUME AND CAPACITY

1000	cu millimetres	= 1 cu centimetre
1000	cu centimetres	= 1 cu decimetre
1000	cu decimetres	= 1 cu metre
1	millilitre	= 1 cu centimetre
10	millilitres	= 1 centilitre
10	centilitres	= 1 decilitre
1000	millilitres	= 1 litre
100	centilitres	= 1 litre
100	litres	= 1 hectolitre
1000	litres	= 1 kilolitre
		= 1 cu metre
10	hectolitres	= 1 kilolitre

AREA

100	sq millimetres	= 1 sq centimetre
100	sq centimetres	= 1 sq decimetre
10 000	sq centimetres	= 1 sq metre
100	sq decimetres	= 1 sq metre
10 000	sq metres	= 1 hectare
100	hectares	= 1 sq kilometre

MASS

1000	micrograms	= 1 milligram
200	milligrams	= 1 metric carat
1000	milligrams	= 1 gram
5	metric carats	= 1 gram
1000	grams	= 1 kilogram
1000	kilograms	= 1 tonne

ENERGY (WORK & HEAT)

1000	millijoules	= 1 joule
1000	joules	= 1 kilojoule
1000	kilojoules	= 1 megajoule
3.6	megajoules	= 1 kilowatt hour
1000	megajoules	= 1 gigajoule
1000	gigajoules	= 1 terajoule

POWER

1000	microwatts	= 1 milliwatt
1000	milliwatts	= 1 watt
1000	watts	= 1 kilowatt
1000	kilowatts	= 1 megawatt
1000	megawatts	= 1 gigawatt
1000	gigawatts	= 1 terawatt

WORLD STANDARD TIMES

The following is the time in the cities listed when it is 12 noon Eastern Standard Time in Australia.

Athens	4.00 a.m.
Auckland	2.00 p.m.
Bangkok	9.00 a.m.
Beijing	10.00 a.m.
Berlin	3.00 a.m.
Bombay	7.30 a.m.
Brussels	3.00 a.m.
Budapest	3.00 a.m.
Buenos Aires	*11.00 p.m.
Cairo	4.00 a.m.
Calcutta	7.30 a.m.
Canton	10.00 a.m.
Cape Town	4.00 a.m.
Chicago	*8.00 p.m.
Copenhagen	3.00 a.m.
Delhi	7.30 a.m.
Detroit	*9.00 p.m.
Dublin	2.00 a.m.
Frankfurt	3.00 a.m.
Geneva	3.00 a.m.
Harare	4.00 a.m.
Helsinki	4.00 a.m.
Ho Chi Minh City	9.00 a.m.
Hong Kong	10.00 a.m.
Honolulu	*4.00 p.m.
Islamabad	7.00 a.m.
Istanbul	4.00 a.m.
Jakarta	9.00 a.m.
Jerusalem	4.00 a.m.
Johannesburg	4.00 a.m.
Karachi	7.00 a.m.
Kuala Lumpur	10.00 a.m.
Leningrad	5.00 a.m.
Lisbon	3.00 a.m.
London	2.00 a.m.
Los Angeles	*6.00 p.m.
Madras	7.30 a.m.
Madrid	3.00 a.m.
Manila	10.00 a.m.
Mexico City	*8.00 p.m.
Montevideo	*11.00 p.m.
Montreal	*9.00 p.m.
Moscow	5.00 a.m.
Nairobi	5.00 a.m.
New Orleans	*8.00 p.m.
New York	*9.00 p.m.
Oslo	3.00 a.m.
Ottawa	*9.00 p.m.
Panama	*9.00 p.m.
Paris	3.00 a.m.
Quebec	*9.00 p.m.
Rangoon	8.30 a.m.
Riyadh	5.00 a.m.
Rio de Janeiro	*11.00 p.m.
Rome	3.00 a.m.
Rotterdam	3.00 a.m.
San Francisco	*6.00 p.m.
Singapore	10.00 a.m.
Stockholm	3.00 a.m.
Suva	2.00 p.m.
Tehran	5.30 a.m.
Toronto	*9.00 p.m.
Tokyo	11.00 a.m.
Vancouver	*6.00 p.m.
Vienna	3.00 a.m.
Warsaw	3.00 a.m.
Washington D.C.	*9.00 p.m.
Wellington	2.00 p.m.
Winnipeg	*8.00 p.m.
Yokohama	11.00 a.m.

* Denotes previous day
(Adjust for local Summertime where applicable)

METRIC STANDARDS

A = ampere	kA = kiloampere	MC = megacoulomb	MV = megavolt
C = coulomb	kC = kilocoulomb	mg = milligram	mW = milliwatt
°C = Celsius	kg = kilogram	Mg = megagram	MW = megawatt
cL = centilitre	kHz = kilohertz	mH = millihenry	min = minute
cm = centimetre	kJ = kilojoule	MHz = megahertz	N = Newton
cm² = square centimetre	kL = kilolitre	mJ = millijoule	nA = nanoampere
cm³ = cubic centimetre	km = kilometre	MJ = megajoule	nC = nanocoulomb
CM = metric carat	km² = square kilometre	mL = millilitre	ng = nanogram
cP = centipoise	km³ = cubic kilometre	μm = micrometre	nH = nanohenry
cSt = centistokes	km/h = kilometre per hour	Mm = megametre	nm = nanometre
dB = decibel	km/s = kilometre per second	mm = millimetre	ns = nanosecond
dL = decilitre	kN = kilonewton	mm² = square millimetre	nT = nanotesla
dm = decimetre	kΩ = kilohm	mm²/	pA = picoampere
dm² = square decimetre	kPa = kilopascal	s = square millimetre per second	Pa = pascal
dm³ = cubic decimetre	ks = kilosecond		Pa.s = pascal second
EHz = exahertz	kS = kilosiemens	mm³ = cubic millimetre	pC = picocoulomb
F = farad	kV = kilovolt	ML = megalitre	pF = picofarad
g = gram	kW = kilowatt	mN = millinewton	pH = picohenry
GHz = gigahertz	kWh = kilowatt hour	MN = meganewton	PHz = petahertz
GJ = gigajoule	L = litre	mΩ = milliohm	pm = picometre
GΩ = gigohm	m = metre	MΩ = megohm	s = second
GPa = gigapascal	m/s = metre per second	mPa = millipascal	S = siemens
GW = gigawatt	m² = square metre	MPa = megapascal	t = tonne
h = hour	m²/s = square metre per second	mPa.s = millipascal second	T = tesla
H = henry		ms = millisecond	THz = terahertz
ha = hectare	m³ = cubic metre	m/s = metre per second	TJ = terajoule
hL = hectolitre	mA = milliampere	mS = millisiemens	TW = terawatt
Hz = hertz	mb = millibar	mT = millitesla	V = volt
J = joule	mC = millicoulomb	mV = millivolt	W = watt

CONVERSION FORMULAE

LENGTH
To convert — *Multiply by*
milli-inches into micrometres 25.4
inches into millimetres 25.4
inches into centimetres 2.54
inches into metres 0.0254
feet into millimetres 304.8
feet into centimetres 30.48
feet into metres 0.3048
yards into metres 0.9144
fathoms into metres 1.8288
chains into metres 20.1168
furlongs into metres 201.168
miles, statute into kilometres 1.609344
miles, nautical into kilometres 1.852

VOLUME & CAPACITY
To convert — *Multiply by*
cubic inches into cubic centimetres 16.387064
cubic inches into litres 0.016387
cubic feet into cubic metres 0.0283168
cubic feet into litres 28.316847
UK pints into litres 0.5682613
UK quarts into litres 1.1365225
cubic yards into cubic metres 0.7645549
UK gallons into litres 4.54609
UK gallons into cubic metres 0.0045461
UK fluid ounces into cubic centimetres 28.413063

AREA
To convert — *Multiply by*
square inches into square millimetres 645.16
square inches into square centimetres 6.4516
square feet into square centimetres 929.0304
square feet into square metres 0.092903
square yards into square metres 0.836127
square yards into ares 0.0083613
acres into square metres 4046.8564
acres into hectares 0.4046856
square miles into square kilometres 2.589988

MASS
To convert — *Multiply by*
grains into milligrams 64.79891
grains into metric carats 0.323995
grains into grams 0.064799
pennyweights into grams 1.555174
ounces into grams 28.349523
ounces troy into grams 31.103477
ounces into kilograms 0.0283495
pounds into kilograms 0.4535924
stones into kilograms 6.3502932
hundredweights into kilograms 50.802345
tons into kilograms 1016.0469
tons into metric tonnes 1.01605
taels into grams 37.799
kati into kilograms 0.60479

POWER
To convert — *Multiply by*
foot pounds-force per second into watts 1.35582
horsepower into watts 745.7
foot pounds-force per second into kilowatts 0.001356
horsepower into kilowatts 0.7457
horsepower into metric horsepower 1.01387

TEMPERATURE
°F to °C add 40 × by 5/9 subtract 40
°C to °F add 40 × by 9/5 subtract 40

VELOCITY

CONVERSION TABLE:
1ft/s = 0.3048 m/s (exact);
1 kn = 1.852 km/h (exact).
Approximate values:
1 mph = 1.609 km/h = 0.4470 m/s

CONVERSION TABLES

HOW TO USE THEM

The central figures can be read as either metric or imperial. Thus 1 foot equals 0.3048 metres or 1 metre equals 3.280840 feet.

When figures to be converted exceed 9, simply move the decimal point one place to the right for each zero. Thus 10 feet equals 3.048 metres.

Similarly when converting figures less than 1 move the decimal point one place to the left for each decimal point in the figure to be converted. For example, 0.1 of a foot equals 0.03048 metres.

When determining the conversion of a figure involving whole numbers and fractions add the two conversions.

For example, 1.2 feet equals 0.30480 metres (1 foot)
+ 0.06096 metres (0.2 feet)
= 0.36576 metres

Similarly 120 feet equals 30.480 metres (100 feet)
+ 6.096 metres (20 feet)
= 36.576 metres

Please note that the last decimal place is not always rounded accurately when calculating this way.

LENGTH

Inches			Millimetres
0.03937	· 1 ·		25.40
0.07874	· 2 ·		50.80
0.11811	· 3 ·		76.20
0.15748	· 4 ·		101.60
0.19685	· 5 ·		127.00
0.23622	· 6 ·		152.40
0.27559	· 7 ·		177.80
0.31496	· 8 ·		203.20
0.35433	· 9 ·		228.60

Inches			Centimetres
.393700	· 1 ·		2.54000
.787402	· 2 ·		5.08000
1.181102	· 3 ·		7.62000
1.574803	· 4 ·		10.16000
1.968504	· 5 ·		12.70000
2.362205	· 6 ·		15.24000
2.755906	· 7 ·		17.78000
3.149606	· 8 ·		20.32000
3.543307	· 9 ·		22.86000

Feet			Metres
3.280840	· 1 ·		0.3048
6.561680	· 2 ·		0.6096
9.842520	· 3 ·		0.9144
13.123359	· 4 ·		1.2192
16.404199	· 5 ·		1.5240
19.685038	· 6 ·		1.8288
22.965878	· 7 ·		2.1336
26.246718	· 8 ·		2.4384
29.527558	· 9 ·		2.7432

Yards			Metres
1.093613	· 1 ·		0.91440
2.187226	· 2 ·		1.82880
3.280839	· 3 ·		2.74320
4.374452	· 4 ·		3.65760
5.468065	· 5 ·		4.57200
6.561678	· 6 ·		5.48640
7.655291	· 7 ·		6.40080
8.748904	· 8 ·		7.31520
9.842517	· 9 ·		8.22960

Miles			Kilometres
0.621371	· 1 ·		1.60934
1.242742	· 2 ·		3.21869
1.864113	· 3 ·		4.82803
2.485484	· 4 ·		6.43738
3.106855	· 5 ·		8.04672
3.728226	· 6 ·		9.65606
4.349597	· 7 ·		11.26541
4.970968	· 8 ·		12.87475
5.592339	· 9 ·		14.48410

VOLUME & CAPACITY

Cu. Inches			Cu. Centimetres
0.061024	· 1 ·		16.38706
0.122048	· 2 ·		32.77413
0.183072	· 3 ·		49.16119
0.244096	· 4 ·		65.54826
0.305120	· 5 ·		81.93532
0.366144	· 6 ·		98.32238
0.427168	· 7 ·		114.70945
0.488192	· 8 ·		131.09651
0.549216	· 9 ·		147.48358

Fluid Ounces			Cu. Centimetres
0.03520	· 1 ·		28.4131
0.07039	· 2 ·		56.8261
0.10559	· 3 ·		85.2392
0.14078	· 4 ·		113.6522
0.17598	· 5 ·		142.0653
0.21117	· 6 ·		170.4784
0.24637	· 7 ·		198.8914
0.28156	· 8 ·		227.3045
0.31676	· 9 ·		255.7176

Cu. Feet			Litres
0.035315	· 1 ·		28.3168
0.070630	· 2 ·		56.6337
0.105940	· 3 ·		84.9505
0.140588	· 4 ·		113.2674
0.176574	· 5 ·		141.5842
0.211888	· 6 ·		169.9011
0.247203	· 7 ·		198.2179
0.282518	· 8 ·		226.5348
0.317832	· 9 ·		254.8516

Cu. Feet			Cu. Metres
35.31467	· 1 ·		0.02832
70.62934	· 2 ·		0.05664
105.94401	· 3 ·		0.08496
141.25868	· 4 ·		0.11328
176.57335	· 5 ·		0.14160
211.88802	· 6 ·		0.16992
247.20269	· 7 ·		0.19824
282.51736	· 8 ·		0.22656
317.83203	· 9 ·		0.25488

Cu. Yards			Cu. Metres
1.30795	· 1 ·		0.76455
2.61590	· 2 ·		1.52910
3.92385	· 3 ·		2.29365
5.23180	· 4 ·		3.05820
6.53975	· 5 ·		3.82275
7.84770	· 6 ·		4.58730
9.15565	· 7 ·		5.35185
10.46360	· 8 ·		6.11640
11.77155	· 9 ·		6.88095

VOLUME & CAPACITY

UK Pints			Litres
1.75976	· 1 ·		0.56826
3.51952	· 2 ·		1.13652
5.27928	· 3 ·		1.70478
7.03904	· 4 ·		2.27305
8.79880	· 5 ·		2.84131
10.55856	· 6 ·		3.40957
12.31832	· 7 ·		3.97783
14.07808	· 8 ·		4.54609
15.83784	· 9 ·		5.11435

UK Quarts			Litres
0.87988	· 1 ·		1.13652
1.75976	· 2 ·		2.27304
2.63964	· 3 ·		3.40956
3.51952	· 4 ·		4.54608
4.39940	· 5 ·		5.68260
5.27928	· 6 ·		6.81912
6.15916	· 7 ·		7.95564
7.03904	· 8 ·		9.09216
7.91892	· 9 ·		10.22868

UK Gallons			Litres
0.21997	· 1 ·		4.54609
0.43994	· 2 ·		9.09218
0.65991	· 3 ·		13.63827
0.87988	· 4 ·		18.18436
1.09985	· 5 ·		22.73045
1.31982	· 6 ·		27.27654
1.53979	· 7 ·		31.82263
1.75976	· 8 ·		36.36872
1.97973	· 9 ·		40.91481

POWER

Horsepower			Kilowatts
1.341022	· 1 ·		0.7457
2.682044	· 2 ·		1.4914
4.023066	· 3 ·		2.2371
5.364088	· 4 ·		2.9828
6.705110	· 5 ·		3.7285
8.046132	· 6 ·		4.4742
9.387154	· 7 ·		5.2199
10.728176	· 8 ·		5.9656
12.069198	· 9 ·		6.7113

MASS

Ounces			Grams
0.035274	· 1 ·		28.349523
0.070548	· 2 ·		56.699046
0.105812	· 3 ·		85.048569
0.141096	· 4 ·		113.398092
0.176370	· 5 ·		141.747615
0.211644	· 6 ·		170.097138
0.246918	· 7 ·		198.446661
0.282192	· 8 ·		226.796184
0.317466	· 9 ·		255.145707

Grains			Grams
15.4324	· 1 ·		0.06480
30.8648	· 2 ·		0.12960
46.2972	· 3 ·		0.19440
61.7296	· 4 ·		0.25920
77.1620	· 5 ·		0.32400
92.5944	· 6 ·		0.38880
108.0268	· 7 ·		0.45360
123.4592	· 8 ·		0.51840
138.8916	· 9 ·		0.58320

Pounds			Kilograms
2.204622	· 1 ·		0.453592
4.409244	· 2 ·		0.907184
6.613866	· 3 ·		1.360776
8.818488	· 4 ·		1.814368
11.023110	· 5 ·		2.267960
13.227732	· 6 ·		2.721552
15.432354	· 7 ·		3.175144
17.636976	· 8 ·		3.628736
19.841598	· 9 ·		4.082328

Cwt.			Kilograms
0.019684	· 1 ·		50.80234
0.039368	· 2 ·		101.60469
0.059052	· 3 ·		152.40704

0.078736	· 4 ·		203.20938
0.098420	· 5 ·		254.01173
0.118104	· 6 ·		304.81408
0.137788	· 7 ·		355.61642
0.157472	· 8 ·		406.41977
0.177156	· 9 ·		457.22112

Tons			Kilograms
0.000984	· 1 ·		1016.0469
0.001968	· 2 ·		2032.0938
0.002952	· 3 ·		3048.1407
0.003936	· 4 ·		4064.1876
0.004920	· 5 ·		5080.2345
0.005904	· 6 ·		6096.2814
0.006888	· 7 ·		7112.3283
0.007872	· 8 ·		8128.3752
0.008856	· 9 ·		9144.4221

AREA

Sq. Inches			Sq. Centimetres
0.15500	· 1 ·		6.45160
0.31000	· 2 ·		12.90320
0.46500	· 3 ·		19.35480
0.62000	· 4 ·		25.80640
0.77500	· 5 ·		32.25800
0.93000	· 6 ·		38.70960
1.08500	· 7 ·		45.16120
1.24000	· 8 ·		51.61280
1.39500	· 9 ·		58.06440

Sq. Feet			Sq. Metres
10.76391	· 1 ·		0.09290
21.52782	· 2 ·		0.18580
32.29173	· 3 ·		0.27870
43.05564	· 4 ·		0.37160
53.81955	· 5 ·		0.46450
64.58346	· 6 ·		0.55740
75.34737	· 7 ·		0.65030
86.11128	· 8 ·		0.74320
96.87519	· 9 ·		0.83610

Sq. Yards			Sq. Metres
1.19599	· 1 ·		0.83610
2.39198	· 2 ·		1.67226
3.58797	· 3 ·		2.50839
4.78396	· 4 ·		3.34453
5.97995	· 5 ·		4.18065
7.17594	· 6 ·		5.01678
8.37193	· 7 ·		5.85291
9.56792	· 8 ·		6.68904
10.76391	· 9 ·		7.52517

Acres			Hectares
2.47105	· 1 ·		0.40469
4.94210	· 2 ·		0.80938
7.41315	· 3 ·		1.21407
9.88420	· 4 ·		1.61876
12.35525	· 5 ·		2.02345
14.82630	· 6 ·		2.42814
17.29735	· 7 ·		2.83283
19.76840	· 8 ·		3.23752
22.23945	· 9 ·		3.64221

Sq. Miles			Sq. Kilometres
0.38610	· 1 ·		2.58999
0.77220	· 2 ·		5.17998
1.15830	· 3 ·		7.76997
1.54440	· 4 ·		10.35996
1.93050	· 5 ·		12.94995
2.31660	· 6 ·		15.53994
2.70270	· 7 ·		18.12993
3.08880	· 8 ·		20.71992
3.47490	· 9 ·		23.30991

HUMAN WEIGHTS — STONES/KILOS

Stones	Kilos	Stones	Kilos
0.5	3.1	8.0	50.8
1.0	6.3	10.0	63.5
1.5	9.5	12.0	76.2
3.0	19.0	14.0	88.9
4.0	25.4	16.0	101.6
5.5	34.9	18.0	114.3
6.0	38.1	20.0	127.0

COUNTRY PROFILES

COUNTRY	AUSTRALIA	USA	UNITED KINGDOM
Official Name	Australia	United States of America	United Kingdom
Major Languages	English	American English	English, Welsh
Major Ethnic Groups	European	European, Negro and Mulatto	English, Welsh, Scottish, European
Main Religions	Anglican, Roman Catholic, Uniting Church	Protestant, Roman Catholic, Jewish	Anglican, Roman Catholic
Area	7 682 300 sq km	9 363 123 sq km	244 046 sq km
Arable Land	4 871 000 sq km (1984)	4 191 175 sq km (1983)	187 200 sq km
Forest (inc. woodlands)	409 380 sq km (1985)	2 984 850 sq km	20 370 sq km
Population			
Total	15 750 thousand (1985)	239 280 thousand (est. 1985)	56 120 thousand (1985)
Growth	1.2%	1% (1970-82)	−0.1% (1980-84)
Capital	Canberra 265 thousand	Washington D.C. 3369 thousand (1983)	London 6696 thousand (1981)
Other Main Cities	Sydney, Melbourne, Adelaide, Brisbane, Perth	New York, Philadelphia, Chicago, Houston, Los Angeles	Manchester, Liverpool, Glasgow, Birmingham, Newcastle
Density	2.01 per sq km	25.3 per sq km	228 per sq km
Births, Deaths (per 1,000 people)	15.6 births; 9.1 deaths (1985)	15.7 births; 8.7 deaths (1984)	12.8 births; 11.8 deaths (1984)
National Income			
Total	$A186 410 million (1984)	$US3 211 000 million (1984)	£282 900 million (1984)
Average per Person	$A12 026	$US13 419 (1984)	£5041 (1984)
Telephones	6 188 thousand (1985)	181 891 thousand (1983)	23 600 thousand
Currency	Dollar of 100 cents	United States dollar of 100 cents	Pound Sterling of 100 new pence
Government	Federal system. Parliamentary democracy. Bicameral.	Presidential republic. Bicameral.	Parliamentary democratic monarchy. Bicameral.
Education	Compulsory ages 6-15 years	Generally compulsory age 6-16. Variations between states.	Compulsory ages 5-16
Agriculture			
Production of Main Crops	Wheat 18 635 thousand tonnes; sugar cane 25 448 thousand tonnes; barley 5559 thousand tonnes (1984-85)	Corn 48 200 thousand tonnes; wheat 15 900 thousand tonnes; soy beans 64 600 thousand tonnes (1982)	Wheat 10 880 thousand tonnes; barley 10 080 thousand tonnes; oats 465 thousand tonnes (1983)
Livestock Count	22 738 thousand cattle; 149 248 thousand sheep; 2 463 thousand pigs (1985)	116 000 thousand cattle; 42 000 thousand pigs; 10 400 thousand sheep; 1 550 thousand goats; 373 950 thousand chickens (1985)	13 213 thousand cattle; 34 802 thousand sheep; 7689 thousand pigs; 129 436 thousand poultry (1984)
Industrial Production			
General Index	1980 = 100; April 1986 = 104	1980 = 100; June 1986 = 114	1980 = 100; December 1985 = 105
Coal	138 960 thousand tonnes (1985)	242 135 thousand tonnes (Jan-April '86) 726 405 thousand tonnes (est. 1986)	74 910 thousand tonnes (Jan-May '86); 179 784 thousand tonnes (est. 1986)
Crude Oil	26 700 thousand tonnes (1985)	216 997 thousand tonnes (Jan-June '86) 433 994 thousand tonnes (est. 1986)	52 429 thousand tonnes (Jan-May '86); 125 830 thousand tonnes (est. 1986)
Pig Iron and Ferro-Alloys	5328 thousand tonnes (1985)	19 228 thousand tonnes (Jan-May '86) 46 148 thousand tonnes (est. 1986)	4210 thousand tonnes (Jan-June '86); 8420 thousand tonnes (est. 1986)
Crude Steel	5772 thousand tonnes (1985)	34 567 thousand tonnes (Jan-May '86) 82 961 thousand tonnes (est. 1986)	6255 thousand tonnes (Jan-May '86); 15 012 thousand tonnes (est. 1986)
Sulphuric Acid	1780 thousand tonnes (1985)	7 800 thousand tonnes (Jan-Mar '86) 31 200 thousand tonnes (est. 1986)	1023 thousand tonnes (Jan-June '86); 2046 thousand tonnes (est. 1986)
Electricity	41 550 million kW h (est. 1985)	794 059 million kW h (Jan-April '86) 2 382 177 million kW h (est. 1986)	135 040 million kW h (Jan-May '86) 324 096 million kW h (est. 1986)
Average per Person	2638 kW h (est. 1985)	9956 kW h (est. 1986)	5775 kW h (est. 1986)
Motor Vehicles	385 thousand (est. 1985)	1962 thousand (Jan-Feb '86) 11 772 thousand (est. 1986)	636 thousand (Jan-June 1986) 1 272 thousand (est. 1986)
Balance of Payments			
Balance of Trade (fob)	$1469 million deficit (Sept '86)	$US108 281 million deficit (1984)	£4101 million deficit (1984)
Invisible Balance (services, transfers: net)	$903 million (Sept '86)	$US11 412 million deficit (1984)	£5036 million (1984)
Balance on Capital Account	$2600 million (October 1986)	$US101 532 million deficit (1984)	£3291 million deficit (1984)
Prices (indices)			
Wholesale	1980 = 100; 1985 = 144	1970 = 105; 1984 = 340	Input prices 1972 = 100; 1982 = 548.9 (Basic materials and fuel used in all manufacturing industries)
Consumer	1980-81 = 100; 1985 = 141.1	1970 = 110; 1984 = 390	1974 = 100; 1985 = 373.2
Weights and Measures	Metric system	Imperial system	Converting to metric from imperial
Employment			
Working population	7481.4 thousand (Aug 1986)	113 200 thousand (1983)	26 360 thousand (June 1984)
% in agriculture	5.4	3 (1983)	1.2 (June 1984)
% in manufacturing	16	17 (1982)	21 (June 1984)
Unemployment	595.6 thousand (Aug 1986)	8539 thousand (1984)	3270 thousand (May 1986)
Unemployment (% rate)	8	7.5 (1984)	13.5 (May 1986)
Manufacturing employment	1 137 thousand (1985)	19 061 thousand (July 1986)	5506 thousand (1984)
External Trade			
Total imports	$A31 472 million (1985-86)	$US269 878 million (1983)	£84 790 million (1985)
From Australia	not applicable	$A3253.6 million (1985-86)	$A1151.2 million (1985-86)
Main Sources (% of total)	West Germany 8.7; Japan 26.3; U.S.A. 23; U.K. 8 (1985-86)	E.E.C. 17; Developing Countries 30.1 (1983)	E.F.T.A. 14.1; E.E.C. 46; U.S.A. 11 (1985)
Main Imports	Petroleum and related materials; textile yarns; organic chemicals; manufactures of metals	Minerals; fuels; machinery and transport equipment (1983)	Mineral fuels; lubricants and related materials; machinery and transport equipment; manufactured goods
Total Exports	$A30 083 million (1985-86)	$US200 485 million (1983) (Excluding military aid)	£78 331 million (1985)
To Australia	not applicable	$A7284.8 million (1985-86)	$A2516 million (1985-86)
Main Destinations (% of total)	Japan 31; U.S.A. 10.8; China P.R. 5; U.K. 3.8	E.E.C. 22.1; Developing Countries 27.9 (1983)	E.E.C. 46; U.S.A. 14; E.F.T.A. 9
Exports	Cereals; metalliferous ores; textile fibres; coal; non-ferrous metals	Machinery and transport equipment; food and live animals	Machinery; metal products; motor vehicles

EUROPE

AUSTRIA
VIENNA
Hilton International Wien
Telex 136799 Telephone 0222-75 26 52
Imperial
Telex 112630 Telephone 0222-65 17 65

BELGIUM
BRUSSELS
Hilton International — Brussels
Telex 22744 Telephone 02-513 88 77
Hyatt Regency Brussels
Telex 61871 Telephone 02-219 46 40
Brussels — Sheraton
Telex 846-2688
Telephone 800-334 84 81

CZECHOSLOVAKIA
PRAGUE
Inter-Continental Praha
Telex 121871 Telephone 02-231 1812
Interhotel Alcron
Telex 121814 Telephone 02-245 741/9
Interhotel Park
Telex 00878 Telephone 02-380 70

DENMARK
COPENHAGEN
d'Angleterre
Telex 15877 Telephone 01-12 00 95
Sheraton — Copenhagen
Telex 27450 Telephone 01-14 35 35
Royal
Telex 27155 Telephone 01-14 14 12

FINLAND
HELSINKI
Hesperia
Telex 122117 Telephone 90-431 01
Inter-Continental Helsinki
Telex 122159 Telephone 90-44 13 31

FRANCE
LYON
Sofitel Lyon
Telex 330225 Telephone 7-842 72 50
PARIS
Inter-Continental Paris
Telex 220114 Telephone 1-42 60 37 80
Prince de Galles
Telex 280627 Telephone 1-47 23 55 11
Hilton International Paris
Telex 200955 Telephone 1-42 73 92 00

GERMANY, WEST
BERLIN, WEST
Bristol Hotel Kempinski
Telex 0183553 Telephone 030-88 10 91
Steigenberger Berlin
Telex 181444 Telephone 030-210 80
COLOGNE
Dom Hotel Köln
Telex 8882919 Telephone 0221-23 37 51
Excelsior Hotel Ernst
Telex 8882645 Telephone 0221-27 01
DÜSSELDORF
Breidenbacher Hof
Telex 8582630 Telephone 0211-86 01
Hilton International Düsseldorf
Telex 8584376 Telephone 0211-43 49 63
Steigenberger Parkhotel
Telex 8582331 Telephone 0211-86 51
FRANKFURT
Frankfurt International
Telex 0413639 Telephone 069-23 05 61
Frankfurt Plaza
Telex 412573 Telephone 069-77 07 21
Steigenberger Hotel Frankfurter Hof
Telex 411806 Telephone 0611-20 12 51
HAMBURG
Inter-Continental Hamburg
Telex INCON D 2110
Telephone 040-41 41 50
Vier Jahreszeiten
Telex 211629 Telephone 040-34 94 1
MUNICH
Bayerischer Hof
Telex 0523409 Telephone 089-2 12 00
Sheraton — Munich Hotel & Towers
Telex 522391 Telephone 089-92 40 11
Vier Jahreszeiten
Telex 523859 Telephone 089-23 03 90

GREECE
ATHENS
Athenaeum Inter-Continental
Telex 221553 Telephone 01-902 36 66
Grande Bretagne
Telex 219615 Telephone 01-323 02 51
NJV-Meridien
Telex 210568 Telephone 01-325 53 01

IRELAND
DUBLIN
Jurys
Telex 25304 Telephone 01-60 50 00
Shelbourne
Telex 25184 Telephone 01-76 64 71

ITALY

MILAN
Hilton International Milano
Telex 330433 Telephone 02-69 83
Principe di Savoia
Telex 310052 Telephone 02-62 30
ROME
Excelsior
Telex 610232 Telephone 06-47 08
Hassler
Telex 610208 Telephone 06-679 26 51

LUXEMBOURG
LUXEMBOURG CITY
Aerogolf Sheraton
Telex 2662 Telephone 3 45 71
Le Grand Hotel Cravat
Telex 2846 Telephone 2 19 75
Holiday Inn
Telex 2751 Telephone 43 77 61

SWITZERLAND
GENEVA
Hilton International Genève
Telex 289704 Telephone 022-31 98 11
du Rhône
Telex 22213 Telephone 022-31 98 31
ZURICH
Baur au Lac
Telex 813567 Telephone 01-221 16 50
Zurich
Telex 56809 Telephone 01-363 63 63

UNITED KINGDOM
LONDON
Claridge's
Telex 21872 Telephone 01-629 88 60
Mayfair Inter-Continental London
Telex 262526 Telephone 01-629 77 77
Sheraton Park Tower
Telex 917222 Telephone 01-235 80 50

AMERICAS

BRAZIL
RIO DE JANEIRO
Meridien Copacabana
Telex 0212301
Telephone 021-275 99 22
Rio Othon Palace
Telex 0212265
Telephone 021-255 88 12
Rio Sheraton
Telex 02123485
Telephone 021-274 11 22

CANADA
MONTREAL
Le Chateau Champlain
Telex 05560048
Telephone 514-878 90 00
Les Quatre Saisons
Telex 0525142
Telephone 514-284 11 10
La Reine Elizabeth
Telex 05267584
Telephone 514-861 35 11
Ritz Carlton
Telex 0524322
Telephone 514-842 42 12
TORONTO
Four Seasons
Telex 0623131
Telephone 416-964 04 11
The King Edward
Telex 236233 Telephone 416-863 97 00
Royal York
Telex 06523918
Telephone 416-368 25 11
Toronto Harbour Castle Hilton
Telex 0622356
Telephone 416-869 16 00

MEXICO
MEXICO CITY
Alameda
Telex 01772416
Telephone 905-518 06 20
Camino Real
Telex 01773001
Telephone 905-203 21 21
Maria Isabel — Sheraton
Telex 1773936
Telephone 905-211 00 01
El Presidente Chapultepec
Telex 1776392
Telephone 905-250 77 00

UNITED STATES
CHICAGO
Park Hyatt on Water Tower Square
Telex 256216 Telephone 312-280 22 22
The Tremont
Telex 255157 Telephone 312-751 19 00
LOS ANGELES
Beverly Wilshire
Telex 698220 Telephone 213-275 42 82

NEW YORK
Grand Hyatt NY Park Ave at Grand Central
Telex 645616 Telephone 212-883 12 34
Inter-Continental New York
Telex 968677 Telephone 212-755 59 00
The Ritz Carlton
Telex 971534 Telephone 212-757 19 00
SAN FRANCISCO
Fairmont
Telex 910372600
Telephone 415-772 50 00
The Mark Hopkins Inter-Continental
Telex 340809 Telephone 415-392 34 34
The Westin St Francis
Telex 278584 Telephone 415-397 70 00
WASHINGTON D.C.
The Madison
Telex 64245 Telephone 202-862 16 00
The Sheraton-Carlton
Telex 440650 Telephone 202-638 26 26

MIDDLE EAST, ASIA AND PACIFIC

CHINA
BEIJING
Beijing Hotel
Telex 22426 Telephone 01-55 83 31
Jianguo
Telex 22439 Telephone 01-500 22 33

EGYPT
CAIRO
Meridien Le Caire
Telex 22325 Telephone 02- 84 54 44
Nile Hilton
Telex 92222 Telephone 02-74 07 77

HONG KONG
HONG KONG ISLAND
Hong Kong Hilton
Telex 73355 Telephone 5-23 31 11
The Mandarin
Telex 73653 Telephone 5-22 01 11
KOWLOON PENINSULA
The Peninsula
Telex 43821 Telephone 3-66 62 51
The Regent Hong Kong
Telex 37134 Telephone 3-721 12 11

INDIA
BOMBAY
Taj Mahal Inter-Continental
Telex 112442 Telephone 022-202 33 66

JAPAN
OSAKA
The Plaza
Telex 5245557 Telephone 06-453 11 11
Royal
Telex 63350 Telephone 06-448 11 21
TOKYO
The Century Hyatt Tokyo
Telex 29411 Telephone 03-349 01 11
Keio Plaza Inter-Continental
Telex 26874 Telephone 03-344 01 11
The New Otani
Telex 24719 Telephone 03-265 11 11

KOREA, SOUTH
SEOUL
Hyatt Regency Seoul
Telex 24136 Telephone 02-798 00 61/9
Lotte
Telex 28313 Telephone 02-771 10
Sheraton Walker Hill
Telex 28517 Telephone 02-444 82 11
Shilla
Telex 24160 Telephone 02-233 31 11

MALAYSIA
KUALA LUMPUR
Holiday Inn City Centre
Telex 30239 Telephone 03-248 10 66
Kuala Lumpur Hilton
Telex 30495 Telephone 03-42 21 22

NEW ZEALAND
AUCKLAND
Sheraton — Auckland
Telex 60231 Telephone 09-79 51 32
South Pacific
Telex 2231 Telephone 09-77 89 20
WELLINGTON
James Cook Hotel
Telex 3871 Telephone 04-72 58 65

SINGAPORE
SINGAPORE
Century Park Sheraton
Telex 21817 Telephone 732 12 22
Dynasty
Telex 36633 Telephone 734 99 00
Hilton International Singapore
Telex 21491 Telephone 737 22 33
The Mandarin Singapore
Telex 21528 Telephone 737 44 11

INTERNATIONAL DIRECT DIALLING CODES

	Dialling Out Code (Access)	Dialling In Code (Country)
Argentina	00	54
Australia	0011	61
Austria	00	43
Bahrain	00	973
Belgium	00	32
Bolivia	na	591
Brazil	00	55
Burma	na	95
Canada	011	1
Chile	na	56
China	na	8
Egypt	00	20
Fiji	na	679
Finland	990	358
France	19	33
Germany, East	06	37
Germany, West	00	49
Greece	00	30
Hong Kong	106	852
India	900	91
Indonesia	00	62
Iran	00	98
Iraq	00	964
Ireland	16	353
Israel	00	972
Italy	00	39
Japan	001	81
Kenya	na	254
Malaysia	00	60
Mexico	00	52
Netherlands	09	31
New Zealand	00	64
Norway	095	47
Pakistan	00	92
Panama	00	507
Philippines	00	63
Poland	00	48
Portugal	07	351
Saudi Arabia	00	966
Singapore	004 or 005	65
South Africa	091	27
Spain	07	34
Sweden	009	46
Switzerland	00	41
Thailand	na	66
Turkey	9~9	90
United Kingdom	010	44
United States	011	1
Uruguay	00	598
Zimbabwe	na	263

The list of figures on the left indicates the specified country's dial code to gain access to ISD. In the list on the right is that country's ISD code.
Example: to dial the United Kingdom from Australia 0011 44 (then area code and number).
Example: to dial the United States from the United Kingdom 010 1 (then area code and number).

TRADE

PRINCIPAL EMBASSIES, HIGH COMMISSIONS AND CONSULATES. (Trade information is available from these offices.)

ARGENTINA
Australian Embassy,
Avenida Santa Fe 846 Piso 8°,
(Swissair Building),
Buenos Aires.
Tel: (1) 312 6841/48.

AUSTRIA
Australian Embassy,
Mattiellistrasse 2-4,
A-1040 Vienna.
Tel: (222) 52 8580, 52 9710.

BELGIUM
Australian Embassy,
6-8 Rue Guinard,
1040 Brussels.
Tel: (2) 231 0500.

BRAZIL
Australian Embassy,
Shis Q1 9, Conj16, Casa 1,
Brasilia, D.F.
Tel: (61) 248 5569.

BRUNEI
Australian High Commission,
Teck Guan Plaza,
Jalan Sultan,
Bandar Seri Begawan,
Brunei.
Tel: 29435/6.

CANADA
Australian High Commission,
The National Building,
130 Slater Street,
Ottawa K1P 5H6.
Tel: (613) 236 0841.

Australian Consulate-General,
Suite 2324, Commerce Court West,
cnr. King and Bay Streets,
Toronto, Ontario M5L 1B9.
Tel: (416) 367 0783.

Australian Consulate-General,
800 Oceanic Plaza,
1066 West Hastings Street,
Vancouver B.C. V6E 3X1.
Tel: (604) 684 1177/8.

CHILE
Australian Embassy,
420 Gertrudis Echenique,
Las Condes,
Santiago de Chile.
Tel: (2) 228 5065.

CHINA, PEOPLE'S REPUBLIC OF
Australian Embassy,
15 Dongzhimenwai Street,
San Li Tun, Beijing.
Tel: (1) 52 2331/6.

DENMARK
Australian Embassy,
Kristianagade 21,
2100 Copenhagen.
Tel: (2) 26 2244.

EGYPT
Australian Embassy,
5th Floor, Cairo Plaza South,
Corniche el Nil, Boulac,
Cairo.
Tel: (2) 77 7900.

FIJI
Australian High Commission,
Dominion House,
Thomson Street, Suva.
Tel: 31 2844.

FRANCE
Australian Embassy,
4 Rue Jean Rey,
75724 Paris, Cedex 15.
Tel: (1) 4 575 6200.

GERMANY, FEDERAL REPUBLIC OF
Australian Embassy,
Godesberger Allee 107,
5300 Bonn 2.
Tel: (228) 8 1030.

GREECE
Australian Embassy,
15 Messogeion Street,
Ambelokipi,
11526 Athens.
Tel: (1) 775 7650/4.

HONG KONG
Australian Consulate-General,
Harbour Centre,
Wanchai,
25 Harbour Road,
Hong Kong.
Tel: (5) 73 1881.

HUNGARY
Australian Embassy,
Room 736, Forum Hotel,
Apaczai Csere JU 12-14,
Budapest V.
Tel: (1) 18 8346.

INDIA
Australian High Commission,
Australian Compound,
No. 1/50 — G Shantipath,
Chanakyapuri,
New Delhi 21.
Tel: (11) 60 1336/9.

Australian Consulate-General,
Makers Towers, E. Block,
Cuffe Parade, Colaba,
Bombay.
Tel: (22) 21 1071/2.

INDONESIA
Australian Embassy,
Jalan Thamrin 15,
Jakarta.
Tel: (21) 32 3109.

Australian Consulate,
Jalan Raya Sanur 146,
Tanjung Bungkak,
Bali.
Tel: 2 5997-8.

IRAQ
Australian Embassy,
Masbah 398/35,
Baghdad.
Tel: (1) 719 3435, 719 3430.

IRELAND
Australian Embassy,
Fitzwilton House,
Wilton Terrace,
Dublin 2.
Tel: (1) 76 1517/9.

ISRAEL
Australian Embassy,
185 Hayarkon Street,
Tel Aviv.
Tel: (3) 24 3152.

ITALY
Australian Embassy,
Via Alessandria 215,
Rome 00 198.
Tel: (6) 83 2721.

Australian Consulate-General,
Via Turati 40,
Milan 20121.
Tel: (2) 659 8728/9.

JAPAN
Australian Embassy,
1-14 Mita 2 Chome,
Minato-Ku,
Tokyo.
Tel: (3) 453 0251/9.

Australian Consulate-General,
Osaka International Building,
Azuchimachi 2 Chome, Higashi-Ku,
Osaka.
Tel: (6) 271 7071/6.

JORDAN
Australian Embassy,
Between 4th and 5th Circles,
Wadi Sir Road,
Jabel Amman.
Tel: (6) 61 3246/7.

KENYA
Australian High Commission,
Development House,
Moi Avenue,
Nairobi.
Tel: (2) 33 4666/7.

KOREA, REPUBLIC OF
Australian Embassy,
Kukdong-Shell Building,
58-1 Shinmoonro 1-Ka,
Chongro-Ku, Seoul.
Tel: (2) 720 6491/5.

KUWAIT
Australian Embassy,
Al-Rashed Building,
Fahd Al-Salem Street,
Kuwait.
Tel: 241 5844, 243 3560.

LAOS
Australian Embassy,
Rue J Nehru,
Quartier Phone Xay,
Vientiane.
Tel: 2477.

MALAYSIA
Australian High Commission,
6 Jalan Yap Kwan Seng,
Kuala Lumpur.
Tel: (3) 242 3122.

MALTA
Australian High Commission,
Airways House,
Gaiety Lane,
Sliema.
Tel: 3 8201.

MEXICO
Australian Embassy,
Plaza Polancoll,
Torre B, 10th Pisa,
Jaime Balmes,
Colonia Los Morales,
11510 Mexo D.F.
Tel: (5) 395 6265.

NETHERLANDS
Australian Embassy,
Koninginnegracht 23,
2514 AB, The Hague.
Tel: (70) 63 0983.

NEW CALEDONIA
Australian Consulate-General,
18 Rue de Marechal Foch,
Noumea.
Tel: 27 2414.

NEW ZEALAND
Australian High Commission,
72-78 Hobson Street,
Thorndon,
Wellington.
Tel: (4) 73 6411/2.

Australian Consulate-General,
7th and 8th Floors,
Union House,
32-38 Quay Street,
Auckland.
Tel: (9) 3 2429.

NIGERIA
Australian High Commission,
16 Adeola Hopewell Street,
Victoria Island,
Lagos.
Tel: (1) 61 8876.

PAKISTAN
Australian Embassy,
Plot 17,
Sector G4/4,
Diplomatic Enclave No. 2,
Islamabad.
Tel: (51) 82 2111/5.

PAPUA NEW GUINEA
Australian High Commission,
Waigani, Hohola,
Port Moresby.
Tel: 25 9333.

PERU
Australian Embassy,
Edificio Plaza,
6th Floor,
Natalio Sanchez 220,
Lima.
Tel: (14) 28 8313/5.

PHILIPPINES
Australian Embassy,
Bank of the Philippine Islands Building,
Ayala Avenue corner Paseo de Roxas,
Manilla.
Tel: (2) 817 7911.

POLAND
Australian Embassy,
Estonska 3/5,
Saska Kepa,
Warsaw.
Tel: (2) 17 6081.

PORTUGAL
Australian Embassy,
Avenida de Liberdade 244-4°,
Lisbon 1200.
Tel: (1) 52 3350, 52 3421.

SAUDI ARABIA
Australian Embassy,
Murabaa District,
(opposite Riyadh Palace Hotel),
Riyadh.
Tel: (1) 488 7788.

SINGAPORE
Australian High Commission,
25 Napier Road,
Singapore 10.
Tel: 737 9311.

SOLOMON ISLANDS
Australian High Commission,
Hong Kong and Shanghai Bank Building,
Mendana Avenue,
Honiara.
Tel: 2 1561.

SOUTH AFRICA
Australian Embassy,
4th Floor, Mutual and Federal Centre,
220 Vermeulen Street,
Pretoria.
Tel: (12) 325 4315.

Australian Consulate,
1001 Colonial Mutual Building,
106 Adderley Street,
Cape Town.
Tel: (21) 23 2160.

SPAIN
Australian Embassy,
Paseo de la Castellana 143,
Madrid 28046.
Tel: (1) 279 8504/3/2/1.

SWEDEN
Australian Embassy,
Sergels Torg 12,
Stockholm C.
Tel: (8) 24 4660.

SWITZERLAND
Australian Embassy,
29 Alpenstrasse,
Berne.
Tel: (31) 43 0143.

Australian Consulate,
56-58 Rue de Moillebeau,
Petit Saconnex,
1211 Geneva 19.
Tel: (22) 34 6200.

SYRIA
Australian Embassy,
128A Farabi Street,
Mezzeh,
Damascus.
Tel: (11) 66 4317.

THAILAND
Australian Embassy,
37 South Sathorn Road,
Bangkok 12.
Tel: (2) 286 0411.

TONGA
Australian High Commission,
Salote Road,
Nuku'alofa.
Tel: 2 1244/5.

TURKEY
Australian Embassy,
83 Nenehatun Caddesi,
Gazi Osman Pasa,
Ankara.
Tel: (41) 36 1240.

UNION OF SOVIET SOCIALIST REPUBLICS
Australian Embassy,
13 Kropotkinsky Pereulok,
Moscow.
Tel: (095) 246 5011/6.

UNITED KINGDOM
Australian High Commission,
Australia House,
The Strand,
London WC2 B4LA.
Tel: (1) 379 4334.

Australian Consulate,
Hobart House,
80 Hanover Street,
Edinburgh EH22D1.
Tel: (31) 226 6271.

Australian Consulate,
Chatsworth House,
Lever Street,
Manchester M1 2D1.
Tel: (61) 228 1344.

UNITED STATES OF AMERICA
Australian Embassy,
1601 Massachusetts Avenue,
Nw,
Washington DC 20036.
Tel: (202) 797 3000.

Australian Consulate-General,
Suite 1742, 3550 Wilshire Boulevard,
Los Angeles CA 90010.
Tel: (213) 380 0980/2.
(N.B. LOS ANGELES CONSULATE-GENERAL
WILL BE RELOCATING BUT NO NEW
ADDRESS IS AVAILABLE AT PRESENT).

Australian Consulate-General,
1 Illinois Centre, Suite 2212,
111 East Wacker Drive,
Chicago 60601.
Tel: (312) 329 1740.

Australian Consulate-General,
1000 Bishop Street,
Honolulu,
Hawaii 96813.
Tel: (808) 524 5050.

Australian Consulate-General,
1990 South Post Oak Boulevard,
Suite 800,
Houston, Texas. 77056-9998.
Tel: (713) 629 9131.

Australian Consulate-General,
International Building,
636 Fifth Avenue,
New York NY 10111.
Tel: (212) 245 4000.

Australian Consulate-General,
Qantas Building, 360 Post Street,
San Francisco 8.
Tel: (415) 362 6160.

VANUATU
Australian High Commission,
Melitco House,
Vila,
Tel: 2777.

VENEZUELA
Australian Embassy,
Centre Plaza, Torre C, Piso 20,
Primera Transversal,
Los Palos Grandes,
Caracas.
Tel: (2) 283 3487.

VIETNAM, SOCIALIST REPUBLIC OF
Australian Embassy,
66 Ly Thuong Kiet,
Hanoi.
Tel: 5 2736.

WESTERN SAMOA
Australian High Commission,
Fea Gai Ma Leata Building,
Beach Road,
Tamaligi, Apia.
Tel: 2 3411.

YUGOSLAVIA
Australian Embassy,
13 Cika Ljubina,
1100 Belgrade 6.
Tel: (11) 62 4655.

ZAMBIA
Australian High Commission,
Memaco House,
Sapele Road, (off South End, Cairo Road),
Lusaka.
Tel: (1) 21 9001/3.

ZIMBABWE
Australian High Commission,
Throgmorton House,
cnr Samora Machel Avenue and Julius
Nyerere Way,
Harare.
Tel: (0) 79 4591/4.

Information supplied by Department of Foreign Affairs.

RESTAURANTS

VICTORIA

CLAUDE FORELL — Writer for The Age Good Food Guide.

MELBOURNE

GLO GLO'S — *Toorak*.
Seductive, soignee and sophisticated. Modern French cuisine, beautifully presented. Expensive. Licensed.

MIETTA'S — *City*.
Grand old dining room upstairs. Exquisite food, marvellous wines. Distinguished club lounge downstairs. Always open. Expensive. Licensed.

JEAN JACQUES BY-THE-SEA — *St Kilda*.
Superb seafood in a tastefully-restored historic bathing pavilion. Licensed.

FLEURIE — *Toorak*.
Brilliantly creative French cuisine in a delightful setting. Fixed-price menus; expensive. B.Y.O.

TANSY'S — *North Carlton*.
Unassuming place, but young couple cook with rare skill, sensitivity and imagination. Fixed prices. B.Y.O.

LYNCH'S — *South Yarra*.
Stylish, convivial, with a touch of decadence. First-class French cuisine. Licensed.

FLOWER DRUM — *City*.
Gilbert Lau's consummate hostmanship and high culinary standards make this Melbourne's top Chinese restaurant. Licensed.

SLATTERY'S — *City*.
A cafe that has blossomed into a small but elegant restaurant, where the food is invariably distinguished. B.Y.O.

FRANCE-SOIR — *South Yarra*.
Very French bistro. Traditional food served in brightly modern setting with an insouciant sense of style. B.Y.O.

CENTRO CAFE — *South Melbourne*.
Modern cafe, Italian style: fresh, casual and relaxing. Food surpasses that of more fashionable rivals. B.Y.O.

SOUTH AUSTRALIA

MARGARET KIRKWOOD — Freelance food consultant in Adelaide, food writer, television presenter and radio personality.

ADELAIDE

DA LIBERO — *Kent Town*.
Relaxed and comfortable. Italian restaurant with outdoors atmosphere in air-conditioned courtyard area. Licensed.

DUTHY'S — *Malvern*.
Specialised in fresh regional foods with artistic flair. Licensed and B.Y.O.

ERICA'S BRASSERIE — *Norwood*.
Delicious, attractive, light meals. Courtyard at rear. Licensed.

MISTRESS AUGUSTINE'S RESTAURANT — *North Adelaide*.
Fresh local produce used with flair. Licensed.

PHEASANT FARM RESTAURANT — *Nuriootpa*.
Specialises in game and trout from the farm. Lakeside setting in Barossa Valley. Licensed and B.Y.O.

THE VINTNERS RESTAURANT — *Angaston*.
International cuisine in picturesque environment in Barossa Valley. Fully licensed.

GINLING — *Plympton*.
Cantonese cuisine. Banquet, take-away service. Fully licensed.

ALPHUTTE RESTAURANT — *City*.
International cuisine with Swiss influence. Licensed.

MEZES — *City*.
Greek cuisine. Boulevard seating. Licensed and B.Y.O

RAPPS GOURMET CAFE — *City*.
Casual atmosphere. Modern Australian cuisine. Seasonal menu which changes daily. B.Y.O.

TASMANIA

STUART DIWELL — Food and wine writer for The Adelaide Advertiser, Australian Gourmet, Choice Magazine and The Sunday Tasmanian.

HOBART

COONEYS
Tasmania's best restaurant. Top quality, innovative Creole dishes at excellent prices. One of the state's best wine lists. Licensed.

SISCO'S
The flavour of Spain. Highlight dishes include the paella and trout with almonds. Licensed.

DEAR FRIENDS
Premier silver service. Expensive but great food and service make it a real treat. Licensed.

SAKURA
Hobart's only Japanese restaurant. Best of Japan from sashima to sukiyaki. An excellent venue for groups. Licensed.

PROSPECT HOUSE
Near historic Richmond, one of Australia's most beautiful restaurants, specialising in game. Also top class accommodation. Licensed.

SALAMANCA TERRACE
In one of Hobart's most historic precincts. One of the best value eateries in town. Inventive courses, great salads and wine list. Ideal for lunch. Licensed.

THE ASTOR GRILL
Tasmania's best meat restaurant with brilliant steaks and grilled seafood. Booking essential. Licensed.

BEARDS
One of Hobart's most charming French restaurants renowned for its game and fish. Licensed.

THE ASIAN RESTAURANT — *Wrest Point Casino*.
The roulette may be a bit of a gamble but the food is not. It's consistently good. Licensed.

LAUNCESTON

THE ARISTOCRAT
The state's only Greek restaurant and the equal of any in Melbourne. Try their octopus or their mixed platters. Excellent value. Licensed.

QUEENSLAND

DAVID BRAY — Restaurant writer for The Courier-Mail and editor Brisbane Good Food Guide.

PORT DOUGLAS

NAUTILUS
Stunning setting, great cooking with some Asian influence, genuinely good service. Licensed.

BRISBANE

RAGS GARDEN RESTAURANT — *Petrie Terrace*.
Consistently in the top few licensed restaurants in Brisbane with great food, good wines and pleasant ambience. Licensed.

RESTAURANT BAGUETTE — *Ascot*.
Brilliant building, good wine list, usually fine food. Licensed.

CORONATION MOTEL RESTAURANT — *Milton*.
Probably the best seafood in Brisbane. Good wines, too. Lic.

KELVIN HOUSE — *Kelvin Grove*.
Lovely old Queensland building, nicely restored, with some of the most enterprising food in town. Licensed.

THE FOUNTAIN ROOM — *South Brisbane*.
Magnificent setting, more than adequate food and wine list. Licensed.

ORIENTAL — *Valley*.
Oldest-established Oriental place in town, and the best. Lic.

CLOAK AND DAGGER — *East Brisbane*.
The doyen of Brisbane bring-your-owns (liquor), and still probably the best.

CZARS — *City*.
Put yourself in the hands of Vladimir and find out what Russian cuisine is all about. Licensed.

COOLANGATTA

OSKAR'S — *on the beach*.
One of the world's great beach settings. Good food, big wine list and interesting customers. Licensed.

NEW SOUTH WALES

JERRY LACEY — Assistant editor of The Sydney Morning Herald and contributor to The Sydney Morning Herald Good Food Guide.

SYDNEY

SUNTORY — *City*.
Brilliant teppan, shabu shabu etc. in ryokan, a traditional Japanese inn with water garden. Licensed.

THAI ORCHID — *Surry Hills*.
Best value in town. Trad Thai cuisine plus special dishes for non-chilli eaters. Licensed.

BEROWRA WATERS INN — *Berowra Waters*.
Superb setting and sensational menu, the brainchild of Gay Bilson; French based. Open Friday–Sunday. Licensed.

MAYUR — *City*.
Joint venture of Indian Tea Board and Tourist Board; classic dishes from Northern India in high-class comfort. Licensed.

THE MIXING POT — *Glebe*.
Brilliant Italian menu — try to get outside to the charming garden in good weather. Best vitello tonnato in town. Licensed.

EJ's — *City*.
Neo-traditional cooking — the cold meat pies are a must. Lic.

DOYLE'S ON THE BEACH — *Watson's Bay*.
Incredible helpings of fish and chips to satisfy the biggest eaters. Beautiful people, superb harbour views. An institution. Licensed.

IMPERIAL PEKING HARBOURSIDE — *The Rocks*.
Views of the Harbour Bridge and Opera House and some of the best Chinese food you'll eat. Licensed.

THE BALKAN — *Darlinghurst*.
Cheapest way to fill stomachs; favourite with students. Balkan mixed grill a must. B.Y.O.

TWENTY-ONE EXPRESSO — *Double Bay*.
Snacks or full meals. Best hamburger in town. Licensed.

WESTERN AUSTRALIA

STEWART VAN RAALTE — Writer for The Western Mail and host of 'A Matter of Food' on Radio 6PR.

PERTH

THE OCEAN ROOM — *Scarborough*.
Outstanding haut cuisine restaurant. Pressed Duck Dish its speciality. Licensed.

THE SHALIMAR RESTAURANT — *Northbridge*.
Creamy textured curries, spiced and marinated chicken and the best pilau rice I've tasted. All of the style of India's north. B.Y.O.

STEPHENIES RESTAURANT — *Nedlands*.
River views beaten only by the modern, French cuisine and Perth's best wine list. Licensed.

THE JADE COURT — *Cottesloe*.
Jack Lau is a Chinese cook of outstanding talent, his skills are on display at the Jade Court. Licensed.

JESSICA'S SEAFOOD RESTAURANT — *City*.
City's finest house of seafood. Licensed.

HILLCREST RESTAURANT — *South Perth*.
Outstanding French/Swiss cuisine at very affordable prices. Licensed.

MAMMA MARIA'S RESTAURANT — *Northbridge*.
A bistro, one that can boast the finest grilled chicken in town, in addition the pasta is a favourite. Licensed.

PRIDEAU'S RESTAURANT — *Nedlands*.
A very beautiful restaurant, beautiful ambience, beautiful food and wonderful people. Licensed.

THE SHIMA RESTAURANT — *City*.
Japanese cuisine Teppanyaki style delightfully performed around the hot grill, delicious results with ultra fresh food. Licensed.

CORZINO'S RESTAURANT — *Highgate*.
Italian cuisine with all the elegance and professional colour this great food deserves. There is no menu — Joe Corzino himself is the walking-talking menu. Licensed.

NORTHERN TERRITORY

GARY SHIPWAY — Editor Sunday Territorian.

DARWIN

FLINDERS RESTAURANT, SHERATON HOTEL — *City*.
Silver service. First class international cuisine and service. Licensed.

SIGGIS RESTAURANT, BEAUFORT HOTEL — *City*.
Silver service. Specialising in superb European cuisine. Lavish decor complements intimate booth style eating. Licensed.

LA CHAUMIERE — *City*.
In the heart of the city. Favourite in Darwin for many years. Specialises in French cuisine. They may not be French but curry prawns are a must. Licensed.

CHARLIE'S OLYMPIC — *City*.
Good old fashioned Italian cooking. The simplistic decor matches the no-fuss down to earth atmosphere. Excellent range of "mother country" wines. Licensed.

TAI HUNG TOL RESTAURANT — *Parap*.
Darwin's top Chinese Restaurant for many years. Extensive menus catering for Sichuan and Cantonese style food. Comfortable friendly atmosphere. Licensed.

PRICKLES — *Parap*.
Mexican cuisine. A no-frills restaurant, but the food is hot, spicy and tasty. A B.Y.O., it provides an extremely cheap night out.

ALICE SPRINGS

MR PICKWICK'S
An old converted house it is full of charm with a pleasant intimate atmosphere. Innovative a la carte menu. Extensive wine list and 25 international beers. Licensed.

THE TERRACE RESTAURANT, ELKIRA HOTEL
Creative cuisine. A la carte menu. Large wine list. Pleasant atmosphere. Licensed.

STUART AUTO RESTAURANT
Popular family restaurant with grill room. Creole style cuisine. Extensive choice of Barossa and Hunter Valley wines. Lic.

KATHERINE

ALEXANDERS RESTAURANT
B.Y.O. restaurant and coffee lounge. Innovative a la carte menu. Comfortable surrounds, service good.

A.C.T.

MICHAEL FOSTER — Wine and food writer for the Canberra Times.

CANBERRA

GARDEN TERRACE — *Near city*.
Classical food. Superb sauces. Expensive. Licensed.

CHEZ MOUSTACHE — *Narrabundah*.
Belgian. Place to enjoy hearty provincial food with flavour and style. Friendly, efficient service. Very fairly priced. B.Y.O. and Licensed.

FRINGE BENEFITS — *City*.
Modern. Some delightful innovative dishes, especially desserts. Bright, airy atmosphere. Licensed.

TANG DYNASTY — *Kingston*.
Elegant decor. Some great dishes (beggars chicken a must). Not cheap. Licensed.

RUBY — *Dickson*.
Hong Kong barbecue their speciality with an extensive menu. Food and service belie extent of restaurant. Licensed.

THAI ORCHID — *Phillip*.
Elegantly balanced food with restrained, delicate use of spices. Decor matches. Licensed.

HONEYDEW WHOLEMEAL — *City*.
Gourmet vegetarian. No pretend-meat. Wholesome, delicious, interesting. Fair prices. B.Y.O.

OLIVE BRANCH — *City*.
Specially grown lamb, kid. Ask for selected platters. Big Greek flavours and helpings. Licensed.

VIETNAM VILLAGE — *Page*.
Early Vietnamese in Canberra. Simple, clean. Balanced menu of now-accepted delights. Inexpensive. B.Y.O.

BYRNE'S MILL — *Queanbeyan*.
International. Lovely nooks, crannies. Interesting wine list complements interesting dishes, lovely sauces. Very fair prices. Licensed.

MAJOR GALLERIES

NEW SOUTH WALES

Art Gallery of N.S.W.
Art Gallery Rd, The Domain, 2000. Ph (02) 225 1700.

S. H. Ervin Art Gallery
National Trust Centre, Observatory Hill, Sydney 2000.
Ph (02) 27 5374.

Newcastle Region Art Gallery
Laman St, Newcastle 2300. Ph (049) 23 263.

Wollongong City Gallery
Cnr Keira & Burelli Sts, Wollongong 2500.
Ph (042) 29 9111.

VICTORIA

National Gallery of Victoria
180 St Kilda Rd, Melbourne 3004. Ph (03) 618 0222.

University Gallery
University of Melbourne, Parkville 3052.
Ph (03) 344 5148.

The McClelland Art Gallery & Cultural Centre
Studio Park, Boundary Rd, Langwarrin 3910.
Ph (03) 789 1671.

Geelong Art Gallery
Little Malop St, Geelong 3220. Ph (052) 93 645.

Ballaarat Fine Art Gallery
40 Lydiard St Nth, Ballarat 3350. Ph (053) 31 5622.

City of Hamilton Art Gallery
Brown St, Hamilton 3300. Ph (055) 73 0460.

City of Mildura Arts Centre
199 Cureton Ave, Mildura 3500. Ph (050) 23 3733.

SOUTH AUSTRALIA

Art Gallery of South Australia
North Terrace, Adelaide 5000. Ph (08) 223 7200.

The Centre Gallery
Education Centre, 31 Flinders St, Adelaide 5000.
Ph (08) 227 4469.

Hahndorf Academy Gallery and Museum
68 Main St, Hahndorf 5245. Ph (08) 388 7250.

QUEENSLAND

Queensland Art Gallery
Qld Cultural Centre, South Bank, Sth Brisbane 4101.
Ph (07) 240 7333.

Brisbane Civic Art Gallery
City Hall, King George Square, Brisbane 4000.
Ph (07) 225 4355.

The Centre Gallery
135 Bundall Rd, Surfers Paradise 4217.
Ph (075) 31 9521.

Perc. Tucker Regional Gallery
Flinders St, Townsville 4810. Ph (077) 72 2560.

Rockhampton City Council Art Gallery
Victoria Parade, Rockhampton 4700. Ph (079) 27 7129.

WESTERN AUSTRALIA

Art Gallery of Western Australia
Perth Cultural Centre, Perth 6000. Ph (09) 328 7233.

Fremantle Art Gallery
6 Short St, Fremantle 6160. Ph (09) 335 5855.

Geraldton Art Gallery
Town Hall, Chapman Rd, Geraldton 6530.
Ph (099) 21 6811.

NORTHERN TERRITORY

The Museums and Art Gallery of the Northern Territory
Conagher St, Darwin 5790. Ph (089) 4211.

TASMANIA

National Trust of Australia (Tasmania)
'Runnymede', 61 Bay Rd, New Town 7008.
Ph (002) 28 1269.

Queen Victoria Museum and Art Gallery
Wellington St, Launceston 7250. Ph (003) 31 6777.

A.C.T.

Australian War Memorial
Anzac Parade, Campbell 2601. Ph (062) 43 4211.

Australian National Gallery
Parkes Place, Parkes 2600. Ph (062) 71 2411.

MAJOR THEATRES

SYDNEY

Seymour Theatre Centre
Cnr Cleveland St and City Rd, Haymarket 2000.
Ph (02) 692 3511.

Sydney Opera House Drama Theatre
The Sydney Opera House, Bennelong Pt, Sydney 2000.
Ph (02) 250 7111.

New Theatre
542 King St, Newtown 2042. Ph (02) 519 3403.

Theatre Royal
M.L.C. Centre, King St, Sydney 2000. Ph (02) 231 6111.

Her Majesty's Theatre
Railway Square, 107 Quay St, Sydney 2000.
Ph (02) 212 1066.

The Regent Theatre
487 George St, Sydney 2000. Ph (02) 264 2487.

MELBOURNE

Her Majesty's Theatre
219 Exhibition St, Melbourne 3000. Ph (03) 663 3211.

Universal Theatre
19 Victoria St, Fitzroy 3065. Ph (03) 419 3777.

Athenaeum Theatre
188 Collins St, Melbourne. Ph (03) 63 3831.

Princess Theatre
163 Spring St, Melbourne 3000. Ph (03) 662 2911.

National Theatre
Cnr Carlisle St & Barkly St, St Kilda 3182.
Ph (03) 534 0221.

Palais Theatre
Lower Esplanade, St Kilda 3182. Ph (03) 534 0651.

Sidney Myer Music Bowl
Kings Domain, Alexandra Ave, Melbourne 3000.
Ph (03) 617 8332.

Comedy Theatre
240 Exhibition St, Melbourne 3000. Ph (03) 662 3233.

ADELAIDE

Adelaide Festival Theatre
King William Rd, Adelaide 5000. Ph (08) 213 4788.

Royalty Theatre
65 Angas St, Adelaide 5000. Ph (08) 223 5765.

Sheridan Theatre
50 MacKinnon Parade, Nth Adelaide 5006.
Ph (08) 267 3751.

BRISBANE

Twelfth Night Theatre
4 Cintra Rd, Bowen Hills, Brisbane 4006.
Ph (07) 52 7622.

Suncorp Theatre
Turbot St, Brisbane 4000. Ph (07) 221 5177.

Arts Theatre
210 Petrie Terrace, Brisbane 4000. Ph (07) 369 2344.

Cement Box Theatre
University of Qld, St Lucia 4067. Ph (07) 371 6734.

Cremorne Theatre
Performing Arts Complex, South Bank, South Brisbane
4101. Ph (07) 240 7444.

Brisbane Repertory Theatre — La Boite
57 Hale St, Brisbane 4000. Ph (07) 379 1622.

New Edward Street Theatre
Brisbane Arts Community Centre, 109 Edward St,
Brisbane 4000. Ph (07) 221 1527.

PERTH

Regal Theatre
474 Hay St, Subiaco 6008. Ph (09) 381 1557.

His Majesty's Theatre
825 Hay St, Perth 6000. Ph (09) 321 6288.

Premier Theatre
293 Stirling St, Perth 6000. Ph (09) 328 7437.

HOBART

The Playhouse
106 Bathurst St, Hobart 7000. Ph (002) 34 1536.

The Theatre Royal
29 Campbell St, Hobart 7000. Ph (002) 34 6266.

CANBERRA

Canberra Theatre Centre
Civic Square, Canberra City 2601. Ph (062) 57 1077.

Theatre 3
Ellery Circuit, Acton 2601. Ph (062) 47 4222.

DARWIN

Darwin Performing Arts Centre
93 Mitchell St, Darwin 5790. Ph (089) 81 9022.

OPERA THEATRES

Opera House, Concert Hall, Music Room,
Opera Theatre and Drama Theatre
Sydney Opera House, Bennelong Pt, Sydney 2000.
Ph (02) 250 7111.

The Opera Theatre
58 Grote St, Adelaide 5000. Ph (08) 212 6833.

Lyric Theatre
Performing Arts Complex, South Bank, Sth Brisbane
4101. Ph (07) 240 7444.

MAJOR HOTELS IN EACH STATE

QUEENSLAND

BRISBANE CITY
Hilton International Brisbane
190 Elizabeth Street 4000. Telephone (07) 231 3131
Mayfair Crest International
Cnr Ann & Roma Streets 4000. Telephone (07) 229 9111
Sheraton-Brisbane Hotel & Towers
249 Turbot Street 4000. Telephone (07) 835 3535

GOLD COAST
Conrad International Hotel & Jupiters Casino
Broadbeach Island 4218. Telephone (075) 92 1133
Ramada Hotel
Paradise Centre 4217. Telephone (075) 59 3499

TOWNSVILLE
Sheraton Breakwater Casino — Hotel
Sir Leslie Thiess Drive 4810. Telephone (077) 72 4066

CAIRNS
Hilton International Cairns
Wharf Road 4870. Telephone (070) 52 1599

NEW SOUTH WALES

SYDNEY, CITY
Hilton International Sydney
259 Pitt Street 2000. Telephone (02) 266 0610
Holiday Inn Menzies
14 Carrington Street 2000. Telephone (02) 2 0232
Hotel Inter-Continental Sydney
117 Macquarie Street 2000. Telephone (02) 230 0200
Hyatt Kingsgate
William Street 2011. Telephone (02) 357 2233
Sheraton Wentworth
61 Phillip Street 2000. Telephone (02) 230 0700
The Regent of Sydney
199 George Street 2000. Telephone (02) 238 0000
The Sydney Boulevard Hotel
90 William Street 2000. Telephone (02) 357 2277

SYDNEY, SUBURBAN
Hilton International Sydney Airport
20 Levy Street, Arncliffe 2205. Telephone (02) 597 0122

VICTORIA

MELBOURNE, CITY
Menzies at Rialto
495 Collins Street 3000. Telephone (03) 62 0111
Hyatt on Collins
123 Collins Street, Melbourne. Telephone (03) 657 1234
The Regent of Melbourne
25 Collins Street 3000. Telephone (03) 653 0000
Rockmans Regency
Cnr Lonsdale & Exhibition Streets 3000. Telephone (03)
662 3900
Southern Cross Hotel
131 Exhibition Street 3000. Telephone (03) 653 0221

MELBOURNE, SUBURBAN
Hilton International Melbourne
192 Wellington Parade, East Melbourne 3002. Telephone
(03) 419 3311

SOUTH AUSTRALIA

ADELAIDE, CITY
Hilton International Adelaide
233 Victoria Square 5000. Telephone (08) 217 0711

WESTERN AUSTRALIA

PERTH, CITY
Ansett International
10 Irwin Street 6000. Telephone (09) 325 0481
Merlin Hotel
99 Adelaide Terrace 6000. Telephone (09) 323 0121
Hilton International Perth – The Parmelia
Mill Street 6000. Telephone (09) 322 3622
Sheraton Perth
207 Adelaide Terrace 6000. Telephone (09) 325 0501

TASMANIA

LAUNCESTON
Launceston Federal Country Club Hotel-Casino
Country Club Avenue 7250. Telephone (003) 44 8855

HOBART
Wrest Point Federal Casino
410 Sandy Bay Road 7005. Telephone (002) 25 0112.

A.C.T.

Noahs Lakeside International
London Circuit, Canberra 2600. Telephone (062) 47 6244

MAJOR INFORMATION CENTRES THROUGHOUT AUSTRALIA

VICTORIA

WESTCOAST TOURISM LTD
83 Ryrie Street, Geelong 3220
Telephone (052) 9 7220

SOUTH EAST COAST TOURISM LTD
240 Main Street, Bairnsdale 3875
Telephone (051) 52 3234 or (051) 52 3444

MURRAY TOURISM LTD
60 Deakin Avenue, Mildura 3500
Telephone (050) 23 4853 or (050) 23 3619

NORTH EAST TOURISM LTD
Western Sector
143 High Street, Nagambie 3608
Telephone (057) 94 2647

Eastern Sector
Tone Road, Wangaratta 3677
Telephone (057) 21 5711 or (057) 21 5454

GOLD CENTRE TOURISM
202 Lydiard Street North, Ballarat 3350
Telephone (053) 32 2694

WIMMERA TOURISM LTD
20 O'Callaghan's Parade, Horsham 3400
Telephone (053) 82 3778

MELBOURNE TOURISM AUTHORITY
Nauru House
80 Collins Street, Melbourne
Telephone (03) 654 2288

TASMANIA

TASMANIAN TOURIST BUREAU
80 Elizabeth Street, Hobart 7000
Telephone (002) 30 0211

TASMANIAN TOURIST BUREAU
Paterson Street, Launceston 7250
Telephone (003) 32 2101

TASMANIAN TOURIST BUREAU
18 Rooke Street, Devonport 7310
Telephone (004) 24 1526

TASMANIAN TOURIST BUREAU
48 Cattley Street, Burnie 7320
Telephone (004) 30 2224

TASMANIAN TOURIST BUREAU
39–41 Orr Street, Queenstown 7467
Telephone (004) 71 1099

WESTERN AUSTRALIA

HOLIDAY WA CENTRE
772 Hay Street, Perth 6000
Telephone (09) 322 2999

HOLIDAY WA CENTRE
41 High Street, Fremantle 6160
Telephone (09) 430 5555

HOLIDAY WA
142 Stirling Terrace, Albany 6330
Telephone (098) 41 4088

HOLIDAY WA
Papuana Street, Kununurra 6743
Telephone (091) 68 1044

HOLIDAY WA
Australia House, Maritana Street,
Kalgoorlie 6430
Telephone (090) 21 3378

HOLIDAY WA
South West Tourism Directorate
2nd Floor, Crown Law Building
65 Wittenoom Street, Bunbury 6230
Telephone (097) 22 0500

HOLIDAY WA
Suncorp Building, Welcome Road,
Karratha 6714
Telephone (091) 85 0122

HOLIDAY WA
30 Robinson Street, Carnarvon 6701
Telephone (099) 41 2406

ROCKINGHAM TOURIST AND INFORMATION
CENTRE
33 Rockingham Road, Rockingham 6168
Telephone (095) 27 3656

GERALDTON TOURIST BUREAU (Inc.)
Chapman Road, Geraldton 6530
Telephone (099) 21 3999

QUEENSLAND

BRISBANE VISITORS & CONVENTION
BUREAU
Ground Floor, City Hall, King George Square,
Brisbane 4000
Telephone (07) 221 8411

BUNDABERG DISTRICT DEVELOPMENT
BOARD LTD
Cnr Bourbong & Mulgrave Streets,
Bundaberg 4670
Telephone (071) 72 2406 or (071) 72 2333

CAPRICORN TOURISM & DEVELOPMENT
ORGANISATION
Curtis Park, Gladstone Road,
Rockhampton 4700
Telephone (079) 27 2055 or (079) 22 4773

DARLING DOWNS/SOUTHERN BORDER
TOURIST REGION
61 Marsh Street, Stanthorpe 4380
Telephone (076) 81 1799

FAR NORTH QLD PROMOTION BUREAU LTD
Cnr Sheridan & Aplin Streets, Cairns 4870
Telephone (070) 51 3588

GLADSTONE PROMOTION & DEVELOPMENT
LTD
Shop 6, City Centre, 100 Goondoon Street,
Gladstone 4680
Telephone (079) 72 4000

GOLD COAST VISITORS & CONVENTION
BUREAU
Suite 12, Pacific Fair, Regent Street,
Broadbeach 4217
Telephone (075) 38 4688

GREATER BRISBANE REGIONAL TOURIST
ASSOCIATION
1st Floor, Suncorp Building, Herschel Street,
Brisbane 4000
Telephone (07) 221 1562

GULF SAVANNAH TOURIST ORGANISATION
Suite 3, 79 Abbott Street, Cairns 4870
Telephone (070) 51 1420

MACKAY HOLIDAY REGION COUNCIL
Tourist Information Centre, Nebo Road,
Mackay 4740
Telephone (079) 52 2677

NORTH QUEENSLAND VISITORS BUREAU
301 Flinders Mall, Townsville 4810
Telephone (077) 71 2724

NORTH WEST QUEENSLAND TOURISM &
DEVELOPMENT BOARD
Centenary Park, Marian Street, Mt Isa 4825
Telephone (077) 43 4611 (Development) or
(077) 43 7966 (Tourism)

OUTBACK QUEENSLAND REGIONAL TOURIST
ASSOCIATION
Shire Council Offices, Blackall 4472
Telephone (074) 57 4255

SUGAR COAST-BURNETT REGIONAL TOURISM
BOARD LTD
Keers Commercial Centre
Cnr Alice & Bazaar Streets,
Maryborough 4650
Telephone (071) 22 3444

SUNSHINE COAST TOURISM & DEVELOPMENT
BOARD LTD
1st Floor, Noel Burns House, Nicklin Way,
Buddina 4575
Telephone (071) 44 5655

TOOWOOMBA AND GOLDEN WEST REGIONAL
TOURIST ASSOCIATION
541 Ruthven Street, Toowoomba 4350
Telephone (076) 32 1988

WHITSUNDAY TOURISM ASSOCIATION INC
45 Shute Harbour Road, Airlie Beach 4802
Telephone (079) 46 6673

A.C.T.

CANBERRA TOURIST BUREAU
Jolimont Centre, Northbourne Avenue
Canberra City 2601
Telephone (062) 45 6564

CANBERRA VISITOR & CONVENTION BUREAU
Northbourne Avenue, Canberra City 2601
Telephone (062) 47 4730

NEW SOUTH WALES

MACARTHUR COUNTRY TOURIST
ASSOCIATION
"Macaria" 37 John Street, Camden 2570
Telephone (046) 66 6370

TOURIST INFORMATION CENTRE
200 Mann Street, Gosford 2250
Telephone (043) 25 2835

BLUE MOUNTAINS TOURIST INFORMATION
CENTRE
Echo Point Road, Katoomba 2780
Telephone (047) 82 1833

PENRITH DISTRICT INFORMATION
ASSOCIATION
Kendell Street, Penrith 2750
Telephone (047) 32 2422 or AH (047) 32 2663

HAWKESBURY MUSEUM & TOURIST
INFORMATION CENTRE
Thompson Square, Windsor 2750
Telephone (045) 77 2310

LEISURE COAST TOURIST ASSOCIATION
90 Crown Street, Wollongong 2500
Telephone (042) 28 0300

SHOALHAVEN TOURIST INFORMATION
CENTRE
Princes Highway, Bomaderry 2541
Telephone (044) 21 0778

BEGA TOURIST INFORMATION CENTRE
91 Gipps Street, Bega 2550
Telephone (0649) 2 2045

COOMA VISITORS CENTRE
119 Sharp Street, Cooma 2630
Telephone (0648) 2 1108

TOURISM COMMISSION OF NSW
158 Sharp Street, Cooma 2630
Telephone (0648) 2 1519

TOURIST INFORMATION CENTRE
2 Montague Street, Goulburn 2580
Telephone (048) 21 5343

QUEANBEYAN TOURIST & INFORMATION
CENTRE
Farrer Place, Queanbeyan 2620
Telephone (062) 98 0241

HUNTER AND LOWER NORTH COAST
TOURIST AUTHORITY
187 King Street, Newcastle 2300
Telephone (049) 26 2522

MANNING VALLEY TOURIST ASSOCIATION
Pacific Highway, Chatham, Taree 2430
Telephone (065) 52 1801

SINGLETON TOURIST INFORMATION CENTRE
Townhead Park, Singleton 2330
Telephone (065) 72 3973

BALLINA TOURIST INFORMATION CENTRE
Norton Street, Ballina 2478
Telephone (066) 86 3484

COFFS HARBOUR TOURIST INFORMATION
CENTRE
Castle Street, Coffs Harbour 2450
Telephone (066) 52 1522

CHESHIRE TOTAL SERVICE STATION
94 Church Street, Glen Innes 2370
Telephone (067) 32 2808

INVERELL INFORMATION CENTRE
Cnr Captain Cook Drive and Campbell Street,
Inverell 2360
Telephone (067) 22 1693, Ext. 242

TOURIST INFORMATION CENTRE
Pacific Highway, Murwillumbah
Telephone (066) 72 1340

NORTH WEST TOURIST ASSOCIATION
South Street, Gunnedah 2380
Telephone (067) 42 1564

MOREE TOURIST INFORMATION CENTRE
Jellicoe Park, Alice Street, Moree 2400
Telephone (067) 52 9599

TAMWORTH VISITOR'S CENTRE
CWA Park, Kable Avenue, Tamworth 2340
Telephone (067) 66 3641

TOURISM COMMISSION OF NSW
140 Phillip Street, Sydney 2000
Telephone (02) 231 7100

TRAVEL CENTRE OF NSW
Pitt Street (Cnr Spring Street), Sydney 2000
Telephone (02) 231 4444

TOURIST INFORMATION CENTRE
254 Argent Street, Broken Hill 2880
Telephone (070) 6077

NORTHERN TERRITORY

NORTHERN TERRITORY GOVERNMENT
TOURIST BUREAU
31 Smith Street Mall, Darwin 5790
Telephone (089) 81 6611

NORTHERN TERRITORY GOVERNMENT
TOURIST BUREAU
Ford Plaza, Cnr Todd Mall & Parson Street,
Alice Springs 5751
Telephone (089) 52 1299

TENNANT CREEK VISITOR INFORMATION
CENTRE
Patterson Street, Tennant Creek 5760

KATHERINE VISITOR INFORMATION CENTRE
Katherine Terrace, Katherine 5780

SOUTH AUSTRALIA

BARMERA TRAVEL CENTRE
Barwell Avenue, Barmera 5345
Telephone (085) 88 2289

BERRI TOURIST AND TRAVEL CENTRE
24 Vaughan Terrace, Berri 5343
Telephone (085) 82 1655

BORDERTOWN TOURIST OFFICE
Council Chambers, 43 Woolshed Street,
Bordertown 5268
Telephone (087) 52 1044

BURRA & DISTRICT TOURIST INFORMATION
CENTRE
2 Market Square, Burra 5417
Telephone (088) 92 2154

CEDUNA TOURIST OFFICE
O'Laughlin Terrace, Ceduna 5690
Telephone (086) 78 2702

THE BAYWORLD MUSEUM, AQUARIA &
TOURIST INFORMATION CENTRE
Foreshore, Glenelg 5045
Telephone (08) 294 5833

GOOLWA REAL ESTATE &
TRAVEL PTY LTD
1 Cadell Street, Goolwa 5214
Telephone (085) 55 2122

YORKE PENINSULA TOURIST
DEVELOPMENT ASSOCIATION
Graves Street, Kadina 5554
Telephone (088) 21 2093

KANGAROO ISLAND TOURIST OFFICE
Dauncey Street, Kingscote 5223
Telephone (0848) 22 540

LOXTON TOURIST & TRAVEL CENTRE
East Terrace, Loxton 5333
Telephone (085) 84 7919

LYNDOCH TOURIST & INFORMATION
CENTRE
c/- Mrs D. Charles, 34 Barossa Valley
Highway, Lyndoch 5351
Telephone (085) 24 4069

MENINGIE TOURIST INFORMATION CENTRE
Melaleuca Crafts and Activity Centre
Princes Highway, Meningie 5264
Telephone (085) 75 1259

NATIONAL TRUST TOURIST OFFICE
Admella Gallery, 1 Mount Gambier Road,
Millicent 5280
Telephone (087) 33 3205

TOURIST INFORMATION CENTRE
Jubilee Highway East, Mount Gambier 5290
Telephone (087) 24 1730

BAROSSA VALLEY TOURIST ASSOCIATION
INCORPORATED
66 Murray Street, Nuriootpa 5355
Telephone (085) 62 1309

TOURIST INFORMATION CENTRE
27 Arthur Street, Penola 5277
Telephone (087) 37 2855

HOMESTEAD PARK TOURIST INFORMATION
CENTRE
Elsie Street, Port Augusta 5700
Telephone (086) 42 2035

NARACOORTE & DISTRICT TOURIST
ASSOCIATION
c/- The Sheep's Back, MacDonnell Street,
Naracoorte 5271
Telephone (087) 62 1518

RENMARK TOURIST CENTRE
Murray Avenue, Renmark 5341
Telephone (085) 86 6704

ROBE TOURIST INFORMATION CENTRE
c/- District Council of Robe, Royal Circus,
Robe 5276
Telephone (087) 68 2003

WAIKERIE TRAVEL CENTRE
20 McCoy Street, Waikerie 5330
Telephone (085) 41 2295

PORT LINCOLN TOURIST OFFICE
Civic Building, Tasman Terrace, Port
Lincoln 5606
Telephone (086) 82 3255

CORPORATION OF THE CITY OF PORT PIRIE
TOURIST INFORMATION CENTRE
115 Ellen Street, Port Pirie 5540
Telephone (086) 32 1222

VICTOR TRAVEL & TOURIST SERVICE
2 Stuart Street, Victor Harbour 5211
Telephone (085) 52 1200

TOURIST & INFORMATION CENTRE
3 Patterson Street, Whyalla 5600
Telephone (086) 45 7428

1988 YEAR PLANNER

JANUARY	FEBRUARY	MARCH	APRIL	MAY	JUNE	JULY	AUGUST	SEPTEMBER	OCTOBER	NOVEMBER	DECEMBER
1 F	1 M	1 T	1 F	1 S	1 W	1 F	1 M	1 T	1 S	1 T	1 T
2 S	2 T	2 W	2 S	2 M	2 T	2 S	2 T	2 F	2 S	2 W	2 F
3 S	3 W	3 T	3 S	3 T	3 F	3 S	3 W	3 S	3 M	3 T	3 S
4 M	4 T	4 F	4 M	4 W	4 S	4 M	4 T	4 S	4 T	4 F	4 S
5 T	5 F	5 S	5 T	5 T	5 S	5 T	5 F	5 M	5 W	5 S	5 M
6 W	6 S	6 S	6 W	6 F	6 M	6 W	6 S	6 T	6 T	6 S	6 T
7 T	7 S	7 M	7 T	7 S	7 T	7 T	7 S	7 W	7 F	7 M	7 W
8 F	8 M	8 T	8 F	8 S	8 W	8 F	8 M	8 T	8 S	8 T	8 T
9 S	9 T	9 W	9 S	9 M	9 T	9 S	9 T	9 F	9 S	9 W	9 F
10 S	10 W	10 T	10 S	10 T	10 F	10 S	10 W	10 S	10 M	10 T	10 S
11 M	11 T	11 F	11 M	11 W	11 S	11 M	11 T	11 S	11 T	11 F	11 S
12 T	12 F	12 S	12 T	12 T	12 S	12 T	12 F	12 M	12 W	12 S	12 M
13 W	13 S	13 S	13 W	13 F	13 M	13 W	13 S	13 T	13 T	13 S	13 T
14 T	14 S	14 M	14 T	14 S	14 T	14 T	14 S	14 W	14 F	14 M	14 W
15 F	15 M	15 T	15 F	15 S	15 W	15 F	15 M	15 T	15 S	15 T	15 T
16 S	16 T	16 W	16 S	16 M	16 T	16 S	16 T	16 F	16 S	16 W	16 F
17 S	17 W	17 T	17 S	17 T	17 F	17 S	17 W	17 S	17 M	17 T	17 S
18 M	18 T	18 F	18 M	18 W	18 S	18 M	18 T	18 S	18 T	18 F	18 S
19 T	19 F	19 S	19 T	19 T	19 S	19 T	19 F	19 M	19 W	19 S	19 M
20 W	20 S	20 S	20 W	20 F	20 M	20 W	20 S	20 T	20 T	20 S	20 T
21 T	21 S	21 M	21 T	21 S	21 T	21 T	21 S	21 W	21 F	21 M	21 F
22 F	22 M	22 T	22 F	22 S	22 W	22 F	22 M	22 T	22 S	22 T	22 S
23 S	23 T	23 W	23 S	23 M	23 T	23 S	23 T	23 F	23 S	23 W	23 F
24 S	24 W	24 T	24 S	24 T	24 F	24 S	24 W	24 S	24 M	24 T	24 S
25 M	25 T	25 F	25 M	25 W	25 S	25 M	25 T	25 S	25 T	25 F	25 S
26 T	26 F	26 S	26 T	26 T	26 S	26 T	26 F	26 M	26 W	26 S	26 M
27 W	27 S	27 S	27 W	27 F	27 M	27 W	27 S	27 T	27 T	27 S	27 T
28 T	28 S	28 M	28 T	28 S	28 T	28 T	28 S	28 W	28 F	28 M	28 W
29 F	29 M	29 T	29 F	29 S	29 W	29 F	29 M	29 T	29 S	29 T	29 T
30 S		30 W	30 S	30 M	30 T	30 S	30 T	30 F	30 S	30 W	30 F
31 S		31 T		31 T		31 S	31 W		31 M		31 S

1988 STAFF LEAVE

NAME	JANUARY	FEBRUARY	MARCH	APRIL	MAY	JUNE	JULY	AUGUST	SEPTEMBER	OCTOBER	NOVEMBER	DECEMBER

1988 FLOW CHART

AN AUSTRALIAN MOSAIC

by

HARRY GORDON

THE ESSAYS

PREFACE

Some nations have had an **assertive** relationship with history. They have tended to make it happen. Some of these, like Britain, Russia, France and Japan, are older countries. Others, like the United States, are comparatively young.

At one time or another, countries in this category have flexed their muscles. They have been the power-houses which have driven events, and occasionally they have been companions to violence. Some such countries have explored, invaded, conquered; some have incubated revolutions; some have taken on the role of international policemen; some have achieved positions of economic dominance which have enabled them to influence world affairs.

With a number of other nations, the role has been more passive. History has happened **to** them. They have reacted to events rather than caused them. They have gone to other people's wars. Their past has been shaped, to some degree at least, by people from other lands. They have been afflicted by depressions and recessions which began somewhere else, like distant bushfires.

Australia is such a country. It is an ancient country, a youthful nation: a place which has had much of its history inflicted on it. It is a country where the exploration and conquest have been domestic, much related to the taming of a harsh, ungenerous land.

Even Australia's foundation was in a sense inflicted on it. Americans take pride in a **positive** beginning: the founders of their country were independent souls who made a choice. They sailed away from a harsh mother country to forge a new civilisation, free of corruption and persecution. No such noble myth offers itself to Australians. The founders, for the most part, did not make a choice. They were dumped against their will by a British government. They were outcasts, rejects.

In some parts of the world the neighbourhood has become aggressively congested, and this has affected the course of history. Bullies have moved in, sometimes bringing with them strange cultures, different languages. They have been resisted, and the result has been at best a smouldering, enduring resentment, at worst an ugly, uneven rhythm of border battles and civil wars.

Australia's neighbourhood has been the sea, and the very isolation of the place has done much to shape its history. The only attempt at invasion since the British arrived in 1788 took place in 1942, and it ended before the invaders had even reached the doorstep. It does not require a great sweep of logic to relate the dearth of battlefields in Australia to the distant loneliness of the continent.

CHAPTER ONE

A DISTANT LONELINESS

It was the loneliness, of course, which enabled Australia to slumber for so many centuries, while much aggressive history was being forged elsewhere, while great adventures were being undertaken in the cause of religion and sometimes just plain greed, while civilisations were progressively being nourished, prospering and declining.

During all that time and through millennia more, the occupiers of the unknown continent were the Aboriginals. They had arrived, in at least two waves but probably more, at least 40,000 years ago, maybe even 70,000 years ago.

Where they came from has long been the subject of archaeological detective work and argument; various theories about different waves of Aboriginal migration have nominated parts of Africa, south China, northern Japan, southern India, a group of islands in the Bay of Bengal and New Caledonia as possible starting points for the journeys.

None has achieved general acceptance — mainly because the Aboriginals have been here so long and achieved such separateness that no hypothesis can be proved by genetic or other scientific study — but there is less doubt about the final phase of their trek.

The historian **Geoffrey Blainey** has argued persuasively that the first discoverers arrived by way of south-east Asia, island-hopping their route south and east in times when the seas above Australia occupied far less space than

they do today, and when the continent stretched, without the intervention of a Torres or a Bass strait, from the top of New Guinea to the bottom of Tasmania.

The second discovery was preceded by a good deal of prodding around the coast by Dutch, Spanish, Portuguese and English explorers. Even before that, in the **1420's**, the Chinese eunuch **Zheng He**, who commanded trading fleets of 300 ships and 27,000 men, and did a little exploring and pillaging on the side, may have visited Australia. It has been written in China that **Zheng He**, a man of massive girth, once landed on a great southern land where he walked for weeks into central deserts, accompanied by a party of astronomers, seeking to make a clear reading of the stars.

The notion that a large continent did exist in the southern hemisphere, somehow managing to balance the land masses known to be in the north, surfaced first among Greek cartographers nearly 2000 years ago. Australia then was just a theory, but it at least had a name. Terra Australis Incognita, or Unknown Southern Land. The theory lapsed in Europe in medieval times, as did most interest in geography, and it was not until **Marco Polo** told of his voyages to China in the 13th century that any kind of desire to learn more about the rest of the world began to pulse even faintly in Europe.

The great land in the south remained little more than concept with a question mark until the brave push of the sixteenth century, when the Portuguese sea-captain **Magellan** discovered the Pacific Ocean, and Spanish explorers began to unlock it. These were times of intense rivalry between the explorers of Spain, Portugal, Holland and England, as Europe ventured from the confines of medieval geography and thought. They were also arrogantly uncomplicated times, when any part of the world whose inhabitants could not defeat the Europeans in battle was considered European soil.

△ *Early Aboriginal rock carvings in Northern Australia. Difficulty in accurate dating has led to much archaeological discussion.*

◀ *When the Aboriginals migrated to Australia the ocean level was much lower. Torres Strait and Bass Strait did not exist. Bali was not an island and Java was part of Asia.*

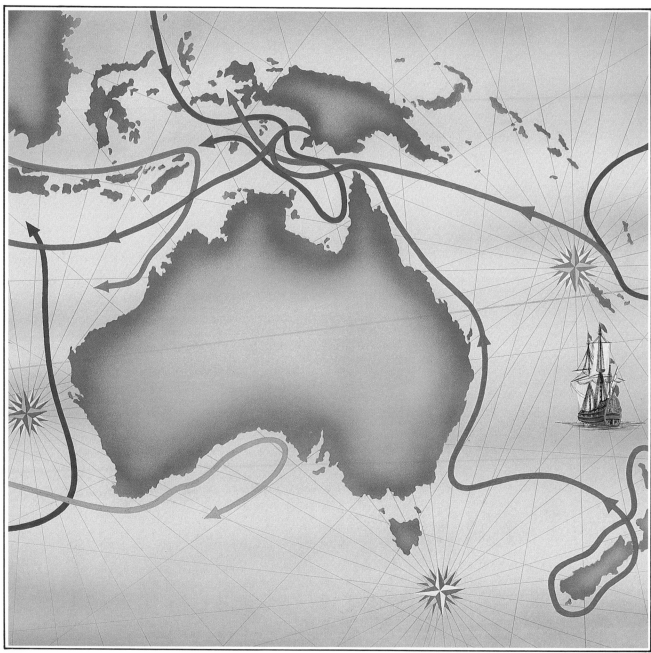

It was a greedy, adventurous age, when enthusiastic sailors were able to make a landing, run up a flag and proclaim that the land on which they were standing now belonged to their monarch.

The Spanish explorer **Quiros** convinced himself in **1606** that he had found Terra Australis Incognita, and promptly claimed for his king "this Bay . . . and all of the lands which I sighted and am going to sight, and of all this region of the South as far as the Pole, which from this time shall be called Austriala del Espiritu Santo, with all its dependencies and belongings". It was a grand, ringing proclamation. Sadly though for **Quiros**, not to mention **King Phillip III**, he had the wrong place. He had found not the missing continent, but an island in the group which **Captain James Cook** would later call the New Hebrides.

Soon afterwards **Quiros** headed for home, abandoning the second ship in his expedition, under the command of his companion **Torres**, and headed back to civilisation. **Torres** continued exploring, and he was rather more successful; he found the strait which bears his name, and sailed along the narrow gap it created between New Guinea and the Australian mainland. In doing so, he came closer to discovering Terra Australis than any of the European sea captains who had set out to find the place.

It was the Dutch explorers and traders, making their way to the Spice Islands of the East Indies and the Malay Archipelago, who made most of the earliest physical contact with Australia. Some were justifiably inquisitive to learn more about the great land mass which had been sighted by Portuguese seamen as early as the 16th century.

Some just bumped into the place accidentally. They found themselves swept onto the rugged, inhospitable west coast as they scudded northward toward the Indies before the lusty south-east trade winds.

What so many navigators were doing when they found themselves blown onto rocks on that treacherous side of the continent was taking a fashionable short-cut. The old Portuguese and Dutch seaway to India and the Indies involved skirting the Cape of Good Hope, sailing north to Madagascar, passing the Seychelles and the Maldive Islands, then heading south past Sumatra to Java. The exercise amounted to a kind of reverse U-turn. **Captain Hendrik Brouwer** experimented with a quicker passage in **1611**, using the prevailing westerlies to race due east from Cape Town across the bottom of the Indian Ocean, then pick up the trade winds for a swift run north.

This route — which really meant sprinting three thousand miles from the Cape before the Roaring Forties, then taking a hard left — was adopted five years later by the Dutch East India Company as the official route to the spices. The trouble was that, when they plotted this course, the Dutch had no knowledge of the outline of Australia's west coast, and the ships had no precise means of calculating longitude at sea before making their run north.

Consider the case of the **Gulden Seepaard**, or **Golden Seahorse**, in 1627:

Courtesy West Australian Museum

it failed to make the hard left turn in time and was blown clean below Australia, into the Great Australian Bight. It sailed for another thousand miles along the underbelly of the unknown continent until it reached a group of islands at the eastern extremity of the Bight. So accident and exuberant winds led to discovery; the archipelago still bears the name of **Nuijts** (or **Nuyts**), after **Pieter Nuijts**, a member of the Council of the Indies, who was on board the **Golden Seahorse** at the time of its involuntary expedition. The ship passed not far from the site of the city that is now called Adelaide.

Paradoxically, the Great Southern Land, which had excited so much curiosity over the centuries, offered no great enticement once it had finally been located. Most sailors who made landfall on its northern and western coastlines were utterly unimpressed.

The first Dutch ship to collide with the coast was the **Duyfken**, or **Little Dove**, under the command of **Willem Jansz**; he skirted the west, vertical side of the Cape York Peninsula and made two landings. **Jansz** found a barren coast, no worthwhile vegetation and a collection of belligerent natives, who responded to an attempt to make contact with a spear assault in which one Dutch sailor was killed. He called the country New Holland, but gave a report to the East India Company which amounted to a maritime, 17th century version of the thumbs-down. "No good to be done here," says a cryptic note in the company's books.

THE SAVAGE COAST

The earliest recorded shipwreck in Australian waters was that of the English galleon *Tryal*, which sank with 138 people aboard.

It was the first of a large number of British and Dutch ships which ran foul of the West Australian coastline en route to the Indies.

The *Tryal* foundered near Barrow Island in 1622, and was recovered off the Monte Bello Islands in 1969.

◁ Seven years later the Dutch ship *Batavia*, carrying a rich cargo of jewels and currency, was wrecked on the Abrolhos Islands near what is now Geraldton.

It was carrying 316 passengers and crew. While the captain, *Francis Pelsart* and a small group sailed to Java in a small boat to summon a rescue ship, a number of the Dutch crew mutinied, seizing the cargo and killing about 15 of the shipwrecked people.

In 1656 the *Ver gulde Draeck* (known as the *Gilded Dragon*) was wrecked near Ledge Point, 110 km north of Fremantle.

Over 118 people were drowned, and of the survivors, only seven managed to reach Batavia.

Courtesy National Library.

WILLIAM DAMPIER
Born in 1652, the son of a Somerset farmer, Dampier was left an orphan at 16, took to the sea, made a voyage to Newfoundland, served on an East Indiaman bound for Java.

He worked as assistant manager of a plantation in Jamaica, and later as a trader and logwood cutter, before becoming a member of a buccaneering gang which roamed the Spanish Main, sacking, plundering and burning.

He first visited Australia in 1688 aboard the pirate ship Cygnet *and later returned as a Royal Navy captain in charge of HMS Roebuck.*

His book, A New Voyage Round the World, *published in 1697, was a big success, running into four editions in two years.*

He published three more books on his voyages, and died in 1715.

That kind of impression was echoed often, by men who stood on sandy hills and rocky vantage points, and peered around for any kind of evidence which might suggest that the land possessed some kind of value. The journal of **Jan Carstensz**, *from* **1623**, *records that he saw no fruit-bearing trees "nor anything that man could make use of . . . The Inhabitants, too, are the most wretched and poorest creatures that I have ever seen."*

The East India Company was content enough with this situation, since it wanted no competition in the trading field. In **1645** *the directors of the company offered this rather selfish observation on Australia: "It were to be wished that the said land continued still unknown and never explored, so as to tell foreigners the way to the Company's overthrow."*

The East India Company need not have worried. The problem for Australia at the time was that it had no visible means of support. In an age when the Indian and Pacific Oceans, from Africa to America, were developing a marvellous market-place for the sale and exchange of precious stones, pepper, nutmeg and all kinds of rare spices, tea, calicos, silks, breadfruit and other fruits and vegetables, grain, fish and shellfish, Australia had nothing to offer.

A lucrative network of sea routes and exotic trading posts existed all around in the seventeenth and eighteenth centuries, but even the most visionary merchant or entrepreneur would have been pushed to find potential in Australia. It possessed no fruit that could be found, or grain, or vegetables, or precious stones. The country beyond the bays and beaches was distinctly inhospitable . . . dry, rocky, offering little prospect of fresh water. The vegetation was mysterious, often stunted. The natives, withdrawn and unhelpful, were not fishermen and showed no inclination to involve themselves in any kind of trading.

The sailors who sampled the country were not to know that it did possess wealth, that from some of the distant cliffs and forests and mountains they could see would one day be extracted all kinds of minerals, gold, silver, bauxite, uranium, iron ore and copper. They did not know, because they were searching for marketable goods that were easily visible. Hidden minerals had no meaning, no use, in those times. The rejection of the continent, as either a

provider of wealth or even of a worthwhile port of call, was understandable, and justifiable.

One of the bleakest early assessments of Australia came from **William Dampier**, a complex but highly confident adventurer who visited the South Seas as both a rogue pirate and a fairly incompetent Royal Navy commander, doubling up as a colourful travel writer and an amateur naturalist.

Dampier was on the pirate ship **Cygnet** when it made a carousing sort of journey, via the Mexican coast, the Philippines, the China and Java Seas and Timor, to a small corner on the northwest coast of Australia. It was England's first tenuous toehold on the continent, and it seems to have been as unappetising a lump of land as ever repelled an explorer.

The **Cygnet** came to anchor and was careened in January **1688** in a lonely, unknown inlet — believed to be somewhere near the present Cygnet Bay in King Sound. The ship was beached for six weeks, and **Dampier** spent most of the time roaming around, making notes.

"The land is dry, rocky and barren," he reported in his book, New Voyage Around the World, which be-came something of a best-seller. "There is no water unless you make wells for it, and inland, as far as man can see, is just stony, empty desert."

Dampier squinted across the wastelands towards the morning sun, and he saw "neither herb, root pulse nor any sort of grain . . . nor any sort of bird or beast".

The natives were "the miserablest wretches in the world . . . the Hodmandods of Monomatapa, though a nasty people, are gentlemen to these". He felt they differed "but little from brutes". The flies annoyed him immensely. They were so bad, he wrote with some feeling, "that no fanning would keep them from coming to one's face; and without the assistance of both hands to keep them off, they will creep into one's nostrils, and mouth too, if the lips are not shut very close".

Flying over the north-west region nearly 300 years after **Dampier** made those observations, the visitor finds it hard to blame the man for not wanting to probe a little deeper.

△ *Even today visitors to this part of Australia go to great lengths to protect themselves from the flies.*

◁ *A part of north-west Australia as Dampier would have seen it.*
"The land is dry, rocky and barren."

The vast stretches of pre-Cambrian rock, which have been here for perhaps a billion years, have an endless, empty, almost lunar look — relieved only by white-trunked ghost gum, sprouting precariously from the red-and-purple face of some great rock that has no name.

*The plane banks, and the pilot points down vaguely. "Iron ore, it's everywhere," he says. The visitor looks again, trying to absorb the knowledge that this is one of the world's really wealthy pieces of raw real estate. Soon the plane is closing in on a runway, preparing to land at the iron ore port that bears the name of **Dampier**.*

Until the early 1960s, not a soul lived in Dampier; it was just a space on the map, part of the massive blank of north-west Australia. With the discovery of the world's richest deposit in the gorges of the Hamersley Range, the port became something of an instant town, with an air-conditioned invasion of factories, houses, supermarkets, banks, bars and beauty shops.

These days, in its bay, great fat ore carriers from Yokohama often squat ... sumo wrestlers of ships, with huge empty bellies waiting to be filled. The heat and pink iron-ore dust that swirls through the streets make this a thirsty town. At night the sound of electric guitars throbs from beer gardens to the beaches of a coastline which used to trap Dutch explorers.

This is the edge of Australia's last frontier, a place of iron and irony.

One of the first parts of Australia to be discovered, it has been one of the last to be exploited.

Three centuries later, the East India Company's harsh assessment is finally due for revision: some good can be done here.

◁ *Part of Dampier today. "Until the 1960's it was just a space on the map."*

◁ *An explosion rips the ore from the inhospitable land at Mt. Tom Price.*

◁ *An army of wheeled goliaths carry the ore to waiting trains.*

◁ *Mt. Tom Price from the air. The immense wealth, once hidden from the early visitors, laid bare.*

JAMES COOK *Born October 27, 1728 in a Yorkshire village, the second of nine children whose father was a farm worker.*

Cook spent some time as a teenage assistant in a grocery/haberdashery store, went to sea as an apprentice on a collier at the age of 18, and joined the Royal Navy in 1755.

Two years later he was given his own vessel, on which he charted the St Lawrence River in Canada.

In 1768 he was given command of HMS Endeavour, which was to go to Tahiti to observe the transit of Venus, and then to search for the Great South Land.

He made three great sweeping expeditions, and was killed in Hawaii in February 1779 while trying to settle a dispute between his crew and islanders.

Mark Twain, *who was 60 when he visited Australia for three and a half months in* **1895,** *summed up Australian history wryly. He wrote: "(It) . . . is almost always picturesque; indeed, it is so curious and strange, that it is itself the chiefest novelty the country has to offer, and so it pushes the other novelties into second and third place. It does not read like history, but like the most beautiful lies. And all of a fresh new sort, no mouldy old stale ones. It is full of surprises, and adventures, and incongruities, and incredibilities; but they are all true, they all happened."*

Captain James Cook, *who explored the east coast of Australia in the* **Endeavour** *in* **1770** *and claimed it for Great Britain, made his own distinctive contribution to the surprises and incongruities. He was a magnificent seaman, the* **Bradman** *of navigation; he became the first explorer who could ascertain his exact position at sea, and the positions of coasts, reefs and harbours; he was first to use a chronometer, which enabled him to establish correct longitude in the most arduous extremes of climate; he had great success in alleviating the disease of scurvy, by carrying with him supplies of sauerkraut, lemon juice and malt; he shrank oceans and caused atlases to be re-drawn. But as the first architect of English settlement in Australia, the forward scout of the great invasion, he produced some stunning misconceptions. With his chief naturalist,* **Joseph Banks,** *he shared an*

unfounded optimism that Botany Bay represented a lush paradise; they saw the place in an uncharacteristic week, when streams were flowing swiftly and grass was growing as in an English meadow, and concluded wrongly that this was a typical condition. As **Geoffrey Blainey** *has written, the mistake was crucial in Australian history.*

If they had realised that this week following 18 April **1770** *was an unusually wet time, if they had understood the infertile soil and the extreme summer heat, their report would have rejected Botany Bay . . . and no British settlement of the Australian continent would have taken place in* **1788.** *The name* **Cook** *gave to the land embodied the error. He seems to have seen Botany Bay as an echo of a verdant, special part of England. He gave it the most unlikely name of New South Wales.*

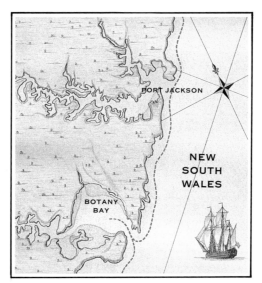

Cook also rejected what was probably the finest harbour in the world, Port Jackson, in favour of Botany Bay, about nine miles to the south. **Banks** *had been entranced by the hundreds of unknown trees — eucalypts, acacia, grevillea and banksia — around Botany Bay, and* **Cook** *was later to refer to the "lawns" and "the good grass", "as fine meadows as ever seen", and "a deep black soil capable of producing any kind of grain."*

Having left Botany Bay as best surveyed harbour of the newly charted continent, he passed the entrance to what is now Sydney Harbour, baptised it as Port Jackson in honour of one of the secretaries of the Admiralty, and noted that it might prove a safe anchorage.

He did not enter it.

The author Judith Wright has attributed to Cook a couple more miscalculations which she believes were of considerable later consequence to Aboriginals. He wrote that the natives had no "fix'd habitation," but "moved about from place to place like wild Beasts in search of food" — implying, in her view, that they had no claim on the land or title to it through cultivation, management or habitation.

Geoffrey Blainey has argued that the Aboriginals managed the land extremely well, in fact "reigned over the continent, and displayed a surprising mastery of its resources." Certainly they achieved an intimate relationship with the land unattainable by later Australians.

Cook's other error, says Judith Wright, was his assessment that the Aboriginals of the eastern coasts were few.

No figures are of course available, but the view of anthropologist A. R. Radcliffe-Brown — that Australia held an Aboriginal population of 250,000 to 300,000 at the time of the white man's arrival — is accepted by many historians.

Whether or not he chose the right place, whether or not some of his judgments added up to delusion, Captain James Cook provided the great incentive for the foundation of Australia. More than that, his discoveries inspired the two men who argued most convincingly for the settlement that came in 1788.

▷

The entrance to Port Jackson. . . . largely unchanged since Cook passed by.

Courtesy National Library.

JOSEPH BANKS *Born 1743.*

Son of a Lincolnshire medical man who became sheriff of his county and an MP, Banks *was a Lincolnshire landowner and immensely wealthy.*

An Old Boy of both Eton and Harrow and a graduate of Oxford, he was a Fellow of the Royal Society, not yet 25 years old, when he sailed with Captain James Cook *in the* Endeavour *in 1768.*

He took with him a suite of seven persons — the Swedish botanist Dr Carl Solander, *landscape artist* Alexander Buchan, *pictorial artist* Sydney Parkinson *and four servants, two of whom were negroes — and a goat.*

Later knighted, he became president of the Royal Society for almost half a century.

The Rainbow Lorikeet, ▷ *one of the few live species of fauna taken back to England by Banks.*

Courtesy of A.N.T. Photolibrary: *Photography by D & M Trouson*

These strong advocates were both veterans of **Cook's** expedition to Botany Bay in the **Endeavour** in **1770**: the botanist **Joseph Banks** and an American midshipman **James Mario Matra**.

They were good friends, they both saw New South Wales as the solution to problems created by the American War of Independence, and yet they had different visions for the new land. The loss of the American colonies had deprived Britain of a place to send its convicts; the jails and prison hulks were crammed full, and a new place of banishment was needed.

Banks told a House of Commons committee in **1779** that Australia was just the right place.

Matra, the son of a prosperous New York doctor, argued in **1783** in a proposal to the government that New South Wales should be settled by loyal British subjects who had been expelled from rebel colonies following America's declaration of independence.

By the time the government decided, in August **1786**, to establish a penal colony in New South Wales, the two had joined forces and had given strong, mutually supporting evidence to the Committee of Enquiry into transportation.

Banks' place in Australian history has long been recognised. While **Cook** was discovering the east coast, **Banks** was exploring the marvellous assembly of plants, birds, amphibians, mammals and reptiles, so abundant in the virgin continent.

It was his prodigious work, with **Dr Daniel Solander**, that caused **Cook** to rename the place he had first called Stingray Bay as Botany Bay.

It was his team which brought back to London the first samples from the Ark that was Australia: a magnificent rainbow lorikeet, alive; hides belonging to the wallaby, the rat kangaroo, the flying fox; altogether, more than a thousand species of dried plants, five hundred fish preserved in alcohol, five hundred bird skins, all kinds of minerals, innumerable insects.

It was he who attracted far more publicity than **Cook** after their triumphal return to England, he who (with **Solander**) had a long conference with the monarch about his discoveries, he who delighted the Royal Society.

Australian schoolchildren learn about him at an early age, and his name is tied to one of the most dramatic bush trees, the Banksia.

Matra has not fared so well.

His proposal for settling Australia, creatively argued and spelled out in nine pages of immaculate copperplate writing, amounted to some sort of blueprint for foundation.

He saw Australia as a source of flax and hemp to make sailcloth and ships' ropes; he saw it as a place to harvest tropical products like sugar-cane, tea, coffee, tobacco and cotton; he envisaged the exploitation of trees from New Zealand for the British fleets in India, and he felt the place had all kinds of possibilities as a trading base, even a war-time base against Spain or Holland.

All these notions provided secondary objectives (to the housing of prisoners) in the new land.

But **Matra** received little recognition for his inspiration.

A modest Sydney suburb which sits beside Botany Bay, surrounded by an oil refinery, a cemetery, a quarantine hospital and the Long Bay Jail — carries his name. But it is doubtful whether many who live or work in Matraville, or simply pass through the place, have ever been given much cause to think about the young American who had a vision for Australia.

JAMES MATRA (1745–1806), an American midshipman on Cook's Endeavour when it found Botany Bay, was the son of a wealthy New York doctor.

He held various consular posts with the British Foreign Service in Taenerife and Constantinople, and made a forceful proposal to the British government in 1783 for establishing a settlement in New South Wales.

The Sydney suburb of Matraville was named after him.

◁

The Banksia, the uniquely Australian plant that carries Sir Joseph Banks' name.

OUT OF THE MAZE

In some parts of Australia it is possible to stand where one of the earliest discoverers stood, and look down at a view which is substantially unchanged with the centuries.

Such a view exists from the peak of the hill on Lizard Island, at the top of the Great Barrier Reef.

From that point *Captain James Cook* scanned the waters eastward, looking for a gap which might allow him to regain the open sea and escape from the confinement of the reef which had kept him close to the coast for some 750 miles.

To reach the peak involves a climb along the scrubby spine, past great stones entwined with wild passionfruit and native, orange-dappled orchids.

From the top, the waters of the reef are daubed in different shades of blue . . . from near-black through grades of azure and aquamarine to the clear, deep sky-colour of the lagoons.

Chunks and blobs of land punctuate these waters: drowned mountains that are now islands, great ribbons of beaches, lofty palm trees like exclamation marks with umbrellas.

On the day he stood here in *1770, Cook* felt trapped and a little desperate.

Having sailed up the east coast of Australia after scrutinising Botany Bay, his ship *Endeavour* had foundered in the treacherous waters of the reef.

Either in moonshine or sunshine, his men had been dazzled by the gentle shimmer of the sea surface, and had no way of seeing the sharp reefs that thrust up from the ocean bed.

Cook had a man in the chains, swinging the fathoming lead, sounding the bottom, throughout those 750 miles; it was, as he wrote, "a circumstance that I dare say never happened to any ship before, and yet it was here absolutely necessary."

He had navigated the maze with infinite care, but in the middle of the night of June 11, the ship hit a reef and stuck fast.

It had to be beached and repaired on the mainland at Endeavour River, the site of Cooktown.

It was after this enforced stay on the mainland, for a month's work by carpenters and smiths, that *Cook* came to Lizard Island.

He named the island for the monster lizards which abounded on it, some of which the naturalist *Joseph Banks* captured.

He could see the outer edge of the Barrier Reef, and gaps were visible in it.

He found one and sailed through to the open ocean.

That should have ended his problems — but he quickly found himself being blown back towards "a wall of Coral Rock rising almost perpendicular out of the unfathomable ocean."

He dropped anchor to try to hold the ship, but could find no bottom even within 50 metres of the reef.

Somehow, carried with astonishing rapidity by a swell, the *Endeavour* just managed to escape "being thrown upon this Reef where the Ship must be dashed to pieces in a Moment."

Courtesy National Library of Australia.

THE CAT THAT WASN'T

Australia's earliest explorers had great trouble explaining what a kangaroo looked like. Francis Pelsart, *a commodore of the East India Company, was on the* Batavia *when it hit a coral reef in the Abrolhos group off what is now Geraldton, Western Australia. He called it a cat.*

William Dampier, in 1699, referred to it as a racoon. He noted the short forelegs and mentioned the jumping.

Captain James Cook described the animal as "something less than a greyhound, of a mouse colour, very slender made and swift of foot."

Joseph Banks was puzzled: "What to liken him to I could not tell, nothing certainly that I have seen at all resembles him." It was Pelsart *who left the first description of the kangaroo:* "On these islands there are large numbers of Cats, which are creatures of miraculous form, as big as a hare; the Head is similar to that of a Civet cat, the fore-paws are very short, about a finger long.

"Whereon there are five small Nails, or small fingers, as an ape's fore-paw, and the 2 hind legs are at least half an ell (c.32 centimetres) long, they run on the flat of the joint of the leg, so that they are not quick in running.

"The tail is very long, the same as a Meerkat; if they are going to eat they sit on their hind legs and take the food with their fore-paws and eat exactly the same as the Squirrels or apes do.

"Their generation or procreation is Very Miraculous, Yes, worthy to note; under the belly the females have a pouch into which one can put a hand, and in that she has her nipples, where have discovered that in there the Young Grow with the nipple in mouth, and have found lying in it some which were only as large as a bean, but found the limbs of the small beast to be entirely in proportion, so that it is certain that they grow there at the nipple of the mammal and draw the food out of it until they are big and can run.

"Even though when they are very big they still creep into the pouch when chased and the mother runs off with the . . ."

Courtesy Weldon Trannies/Reg Morrison.

CHAPTER TWO

PRISONERS ALL

Sydney Cove
1788

ARTHUR PHILLIP *was born on October 11, 1738 in the heart of the City of London.*

His father Jacob *was a native of Frankfurt who had settled in England as a language teacher.*

He began his sea career as an apprentice with the merchant navy but transferred to the Royal Navy during the Seven Years War.

He was 48 when given command of the fleet which made the first settlement in Australia.

On arrival he dismissed Botany Bay as a site, and located the settlement in Sydney Cove.

He was a gentle leader who did his utmost to establish and maintain good relations with the Aboriginals.

After five years, Phillip's health broke and he returned to London.

He died in 1814.

▷

It was a depressing outlook for prisoners during their gruelling eight month voyage to another hell in New South Wales.

A new land. A different, inhospitable-looking land. A terrifying land, in so many ways.

It is tempting to surmise the mood which existed among the great congestion of convicts and their mixed bag of attendants — marines and their wives and children, sailors of the Royal Navy, merchant seamen and officials — as they looked across the water from where their ships lay at anchor in Botany Bay on 20 January **1788**. They were presumably glad the journey was over; they had just completed eight months of sailing, with 48 deaths along the way, and they had covered 15,000 miles. For the convicts themselves, after all that time in cages between decks, with 16 inches of bed space across for each of them, the end of the journey meant space, some freedom to move.

It would have been hard not to

be excited as they waited to be landed on these strange shores so far across the world. Apprehensive, too. But for many the mood would have been one of sheer, bleak resignation ... even animal-like passivity. They had suffered in jails and on prison hulks in Britain, they had suffered in irons among rats, cockroaches and other diverse vermin as their little ships heaved their way west

across the South Atlantic to Rio de Janiero, then to the Cape of Good Hope, then to Australia; they were about to suffer some more, after being dumped in this place about which they knew nothing.

They were all prisoners, really, even those who were not being punished by the British system of justice. They were prisoners of distance. History might see them as a beachhead to a nation. But it would have been unreasonable then not to feel some sense of abandonment, with 3000 miles between them and the nearest white man.

Their preoccupation then was more with the business of survival than with any sense of occasion. Indeed, when the first anniversary of Foundation Day came around on 16 January **1789**, not one of the many diaries and journals being kept even

made a single remark about it. By that time many had died, food supplies were dangerously short, and optimism was on the ebb.

All the way from England, until the last leg from Cape Town, the 11 ships of the convict armada had sailed in close convoy. They separated for the first time when the commander, **Captain Arthur Phillip**, decided to sprint ahead in the **Supply** with the three fastest ships of the fleet, to make preparations for landing. Even so, they entered Botany Bay within two days of one another in January **1788**.

With them they brought 568 male and 191 female convicts. At Cape Town the first fleet had taken on a deck menagerie (poultry, rabbits, two bulls, seven cows, seven horses, 46 sheep, three goats and 28 pigs) plus a forest of fruit trees (oranges, lemons, quinces, apples, bananas, pears and figs).

THE TROUBLED MARINES

The 213 marines who accompanied the First Fleet to Australia, under the command of *Major Robert Ross*, had a troubled three and a half years in the new-born colony.

Within two months of their arrival, they had gone on strike.

They had been set to construction work alongside the convicts, and didn't like it.

Private John Easty, whose diary has been preserved, recorded on March 19 1788 that "the Battalion of marines Turned out and Said that they could not work any longer without being paid for it."

Captain Phillip agreed to pay them.

Almost exactly a year later, on March 18 1789, it was found that seven marines had been robbing the public stores of flour, meat, spirits, tobacco and many articles . . . this at a time when the colony was starving.

One of them, *Joseph Hunt*, gave evidence for the Crown.

The other six were found guilty, sentenced to death, and quickly executed.

Captain Watkin Tench wrote sadly in his diary: "An awful and terrible example of justice took place . . . which I record with regret, but it would be disengenuous to suppress, as the six marines, the flower of our battalion, were hanged by the public execution, on the sentence of a criminal court, composed entirely of their own officers."

Easty wrote that all six blamed *Hunt*, as he had devised the robbery scheme . . . "there was hardly a marine Present but what shed Tears officers and men."

The marine commander, *Major Ross*, was a disaster.

He resigned, refused to do guard duty, demanded luxuries, requested a ship home, and once promoted his nine-year old son to officer rank.

One convict who swore at him was given 600 lashes and put in irons for six months.

▷

From Botany Bay, Phillip set out to find a more suitable site and, about 9 miles to the north, headed into Port Jackson.

As soon as he arrived, it was obvious to **Phillip** that **Captain Cook's** Botany Bay was not the right place for a settlement. The anchorage **Cook** had chosen was exposed to the prevailing south-east winds, which were capable of fashioning a dangerous swell. The waters of the bay were too shallow to allow any kind of protection, which meant that most ships would have to anchor in the entrance, exposed to the open sea. Too much of the ground was low and boggy, the supply of fresh water was scarce.

Phillip quickly took off to explore the coast for a better site for settlement than Botany Bay offered, and soon was nosing between two rugged, protective headlands into the waters of Port Jackson. Before him stretched what he

later described in a letter to **Lord Sydney**, the Secretary of State for the Home Office, as "the finest harbour in the world, in which a thousand sail of the line may ride in the most perfect security". **Sydney's** Home Affairs portfolio gave him responsibility for prisons, and it was he who had presented the proposal for a penal colony in New South Wales to Cabinet.

Phillip, who decided to "honour" the new cove with **Sydney's** name, wrote that he was "fully persuaded that we should never have succeeded" if he had not taken the decision to move from Botany Bay to Port Jackson. He believed Sydney Cove had "the best spring of water", and "it was absolutely necessary to be certain of a sufficient quantity of Fresh Water." "Apart from that, the ships can Anchor so close to the Shore, that at a very small expense, Quays can be made at which the largest may unload."

By January 26 all ships of the fleet were anchored inside Port Jackson, off the cove. Enough ground was cleared to make way for an encampment for a guard party and the first group of convicts ashore. The British flag went up, possession was taken for **King George**, a feu de joie salute was fired by a party of marines, and plenty of healths were drunk . . . to the King, the Queen, the Prince of Wales and the colony.

Courtesy Horizon/Mark Burns.

The day after **Phillip's** fleet reached Sydney Cove was a Sunday — but it was not a day of rest; it was a time of almost fast-forward activity as work-parties stepped from longboats into what were literally woods. Some groups set about cutting down trees, others scouring for water, others netting fish; some unloaded stores, some set up the blacksmith's forge; tents went up, and the lines for **Phillip's** portable house and a hospital were marked.

Of the convicts put to work on these jobs, some had been in confinement afloat for months before the voyage began; they were standing on land for the first time in more than a year. Within two days all the male convicts and the marines had been unloaded, along with the collection of pioneer livestock, whose numbers had been depleted on the crossing from the Cape.

On the night of February 6 the convict women were landed, after extra rum rations had been handed out and just before the cove was struck by a violent electrical storm which split a great tree down the middle, and killed sheep, pigs and lambs. It was suffocatingly hot, and there was about the discordant, primitive combination of elements an almost surrealistic quality; events seemed almost orchestrated to

yield a low-life carnival, a drunken drenching orgy. The women, at least a third of whom were prostitutes, advanced on the tents for what surgeon **Arthur Smyth** was to describe as a "Scene of Debauchery and Riot".

Smyth wrote: "The Sailors in our Ship requested to have some Grog to make merry with upon the Women quitting the Ship . . . and about the time they began to be elevated, the Tempest came on. The scene which presented itself at this time and during the greater part of the night, beggars every description, some swearing, others quarrelling, others singing, not in the least regarding the Tempest . . ." London at its seamiest had arrived in Botany Bay.

△ *Phillip chose this site for his settlement. 200 years later, Joern Utzon's Sydney Opera House juts majestically beside the cove which became Circular Quay.*

NO FIXED RESIDENCE

After one of the earliest meetings with a party of natives, *John Hunter*, the captain of the *Sirius* and second-in-command of the first settlement gave the first documented description of the Aboriginals.

He wrote on January 31 1788: "The men in general are from five feet six inches to five feet nine inches high; are thin, but very straight and clean made; walk very erect, and are active.

"The women are not so tall, or so thin, but are generally well made; their colour is a rusty kind of black, something like that of soot, but I have seen many of the women almost as light as mulatto.

"We have seen a few of both sexes with tolerably good features, but in general they have broad noses, large wide mouths, and thick lips, and their countenance altogether not very prepossessing . . .

"The men wear their beards, which are short and curly, like the hair of the head.

"Men, women and children go entirely naked, as described by *Captain Cook*; they seem to have no fixed place of residence, but take their rest wherever night overtakes them: they generally shelter themselves in such cavities or hollows in the rocks upon the seashore, as may be capable of defending them from the rain, and, in order to make their apartment as comfortable as possible, they commonly make a good fire in it before they lie down to rest; by which means, the rock all around them is so heated as to retain its warmth like an oven for a considerable time . . ."

Hunter concluded: "In the different opportunities I have had of getting a little acquainted with the natives, who reside in and about this port, I am, I confess, disposed to think, that it will be no difficult matter, in due time, to conciliate their friendship and confidence . . . Whenever we have laid aside our arms, and have made signs of friendship, they have always advanced unarmed, with spirit . . . They will soon discover that we are not their enemies; a light they no doubt considered us on our arrival."

Phillip's reaction to the explosive outbreak of licentiousness which took place after the convict women landed was to assert his authority quickly. He assembled around him all the convicts and their children, 211 marines, with 27 wives and 14 children and all the seamen and officials he could muster, and proclaimed the official beginning of the colony. He became Captain-General and Governor-in-Chief of the territory of New South Wales and its dependencies; British Government was established, and he was formally at the head of the power structure, with authority that might have been interpreted as dictatorial.

To the badly hung-over men and women before him, after soldiers had marched in circle round them to the thumping of kettle-drums and thin piping of fifes, **Phillip** handed out a stinging lecture on the evils of promiscuity, the virtue of sobriety and the desirability of marriage as a fit and proper state for human beings; more specifically, he then warned that men found in women's tents at night would be shot at, and that anyone who stole food would be hanged.

That night **Phillip** treated his officers to a cold spread, a "collation", in a large tent. The wine flowed, but it was no gourmet meal. "The mutton was full of maggots," one of the guests summed up sadly. "Nothing will keep 24 hours in this country."

In the weeks that followed, tentative contact was made with the Aboriginals (to whom most of the soldiers and officers referred as Indians), food and wine were stolen, doomed escapes were made, and the first punishment handed out; 200 lashes on the bare back for a prisoner who gave a back-hander to a convict girl who refused to share some time under a tree in the woods.

Soon women, too, were being flogged. **Thomas Barrett**, an enterprising rogue who had even tried to organise a counterfeit coin scam while below decks in Rio en route to Australia, became the first man hanged . . . on February 27, the 34th day of settlement; he had stolen some bread and pork. **James Freeman** accepted the post as the colony's first hangman, in exchange for

Reference Courtesy National Library.

a free pardon. He did this with some reluctance, which was strange in the circumstances, since he was himself under the gallows ladder, with a rope around his neck and about to be executed for having stolen flour, when the bargain was struck.

One ironic form of punishment was exile to an uninhabited place . . . a kind of banishment of the banished. Fourteen weddings took place in the second week, and a stowaway free settler, **James Smith**, whose presence with the First Fleet was undetected until it reached Cape Town, was told by **Phillip** that he could stay in Botany Bay as a superintendent of convicts.

The Aboriginals viewed the intrusion of the white man on the continent with surprising equanimity. **Cook** remarked, on the day of his first landing, on the total lack of interest shown by the natives; an old woman gathering sticks, followed by her three children, "often looked at the ship but expressed neither surprise nor concern". **Phillip** appeared to be genuinely concerned for them, anxious to establish a friendly relationship. "The Natives, tho very friendly, appear to be numerous," he reported in his first (May 1788) dispatch home.

He was determined never to shoot at them, and was able to report that they "very readily returned the confidence I placed in them by going to them alone and unarmed". The women, he noted, were "not treated with any very great tenderness" but seemed in fact to be regarded as "inferior".

In July, in a second letter to **Lord Sydney**, he confirmed that the "Natives have been treated with the greatest Humanity and Attention, and every Precaution that was possible, has been taken to prevent their receiving any Insults". He planned to "reconcile them to live amongst us" so he could teach them "the Advantages they will reap from cultivating the Land". The natives were extremely wary with soldiers wearing red coats; they were intrigued with the white men's clothes, particularly hats, and **Captain Watkin Tench**, of the marines, recorded that they took a West Indian negro convict — of whom there were a number with the **First Fleet** — to be one of their own.

Relations between the races deteriorated over the months, as food supplies dwindled, grain and vegetables refused to flourish in the broken soil, and the colony began to starve. The natives had been distrustful of muskets since they had been fired on by a French expedition (led by **Captain Jean La Perouse**), and were less inclined to co-exist easily as the realisation dawned that the white man had come to stay, and were in fact daily plundering numbers of large fish from their larder in the bay. They were revolted at some of the floggings which took place in the colony, and at times had even tried to interfere with the punishment. They began to steal food, knives, shovels, livestock, spears were thrown, muskets fired, and before long the first murders occurred.

Tench recorded on May 30: "On first setting foot in this country, we were inclined to hold the spears of the natives very cheap. Fatal experience has, however, convinced us, that the wound inflicted by this weapon is not a trivial one; and that the skill of the Indians in throwing it, is far from despicable. Two convicts who were employed as rush cutters up the harbour were (from what cause we are yet ignorant) most dreadfully mangled and butchered by the natives. A spear had passed entirely through the thickest part of the body of one of them, though a very robust man, and the skull of the other was beaten in."

Then **Phillip**, the guardian of the Aboriginals, was himself attacked, receiving a spear wound in the shoulder. The injury was not serious, the aggressor was punished by other natives, and **Phillip** let the matter rest.

From the earliest days of
settlement, huge sharks
were seen cruising close to
the shore of the shanty
town that was rising on
Sydney Cove.

On March 23, 1788, less
than two months after the
landing, Lieutenant James
Bradley reported: "A shark
was caught this day 13 feet
long and after his jaws were
taken out they passed over
the largest man in the ship
without touching; the liver
gave us 26 gallons of oil, he
had four hooks within him
besides that which caught
him."

Again on May 9 Bradley
wrote that a shark had
attacked his fishing boat.
First it grabbed an oar,
then it went for the rudder
... "and did not quit it
until it was struck with the
Tiller".

The first recorded shark
attack was reported this
way in a broadside, or news
sheet, on January 1 1807:
"The presence of voracious
and monstrous sharks
cruising in the waters of
Port Jackson should be
only too well-known to the
parents of thoughtless
children and those who
indulge in aquatic pursuits
to require further warning;
but such is the case.

"Yesterday, a man
swimming in Cockle Bay
was attacked by a shark,
which severely wounded
him in the wrist.

"His account of the
circumstances states his
having seen the voracious
animal advancing towards
him, but was unfortunately
too far beyond his depth to
enable him to avoid the
danger — the very
consideration of being
exposed to which almost
deprived him of all power
of avoiding it.

"The shark quickly
gained upon him, and an
immediate painful death
seemed unavoidable.

"He soon found himself
in the pursuer's grasp, but
when siezed upon, he gave
a hideous roar, excited
equally by pain and terror;
when the shark foresaking
his hold for a moment,
afforded him an instant's
respite, which brought him
within the reach of safety."

△

*Nolfolk's Quality Row.
Previously Military Road,
with a view and "a little
distance" between the
military and hardened
criminals.*

Phillip *wasted no time in
sending a party to set up a sub-colony on
Norfolk Island, a thousand miles across
the Pacific, and a potential source of
flax and timber, as well as maybe a
more fertile place. Only 20 days after
the foundation of Sydney Cove,* **Philip
Gidley King** *sailed in the* **Supply** *to settle
on Norfolk, taking with him a petty
officer, surgeon's mate, two marines,
two men who understood the cultivation
of flax, with nine men and six women
convicts.*

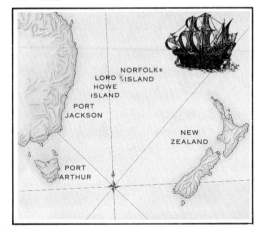

In March **1790**, *as isolation and
starvation were making conditions
desperate on the mainland, nearly a
third of the population, 281 persons,
were shipped to Norfolk Island. The
island was to fail as a supplier of naval
stores and as a base, mainly because of
its lack of a safe harbour, and from*
1813 *to* **1825** *it would be abandoned
with a few wandering pigs and goats as
the only evidence of its colonisation. In*
1825, *though, it was to be revived as a
most fearsome place of punishment; five
years later in Van Diemen's Land,
another awful penal colony would be
established at Port Arthur.*

In the later months of **1788** *the
accent was on survival rather than
expansion. The soil was poor, the fruit
trees would not yield, livestock and
poultry failed to do well, sheep were
killed by dogs, cattle got lost in the bush
and much seed turned out to be a host of
weevils.*

*Many of the inhabitants fell sick
with scurvy, food was rationed severely,
and many convicts risked the death
penalty to steal food and kill livestock.
In June the* **Supply** *was sent across to
Lord Howe Island to collect turtles, but
there were none. Until it could grow its
own food, the colony was dependent on
food ships from England ... and they
did not come.*

The **Sirius** *made an emergency
dash to Cape Town, where* **Captain John
Hunter** *took on wheat, barley, medical
supplies and enough provisions to feed
the colony for four months. He brought
them back, along with the news that still
no relief ships had left England. A ship
was finally dispatched — the* **Guardian**
— but it sank along the way.

*A flagstaff was erected at South
Head so that the arrival of English
supply ships could be signalled to the
Governor; and parties made repeated
trips to Botany Bay, just in case the
ships came to the wrong place. And still
they waited. Executions continued, and
people died of illness, but the small
decrease in the population in no way
helped the food to go farther.*

Tench *summed up the general
mood of depression in January* **1790**:
*"Our impatience of news from Europe
strongly marked the commencement of the
year. We had now been two years in the
country, and thirty-months from England,*

in which long period no supplies, except what had been procured at the Cape of Good Hope by the Sirius, had reached us. From intelligence of our friends and connections we had been entirely cut off, no communication whatever having passed with our native country since the 13th May 1787, the day of our departure from Portsmouth. Famine besides was approaching with gigantic strides, and gloom and dejection overspread every countenance."

On June 3 **1790**, a large ship carrying English colours was seen moving through the heads into the harbour. A small boat carrying the Governor went towards her; **Phillip** ascertained what she was, then returned to Sydney Cove. **Tench** went all the way to meet her, and soon the word LONDON could be made out on her stern. "Pull away, my lads! She is from Old England!', the crew shouted. "A few strokes more, and we shall be aboard! Hurrah for a bellyfull, and news from our friends."

News there was . . . and not just in the personal letters whose envelopes were torn apart quickly. They learned of that momentous event, the French Revolution, and of the fate of the **Guardian**. A bellyfull there was not. The big ship, the **Lady Juliana**, was carrying 225 female convicts rather than supplies of fresh food. They had been on their passage for 11 months, many of them were in a bad way physically, and they too needed to be fed.

The **Lady Juliana** was in fact the first ship of the Second Fleet. The later four ships brought with them enough food to enable the colony to survive, but it also brought more than 500 sick and dying convicts. It was something of a disaster for a colony which, even though it was slowly starving, had less than 50 people sick when the Second Fleet arrived.

Within 12 months a Third Fleet arrived with more convicts, fortunately in better condition, as well as essential provisions. **Phillip** went home at the end of **1791**, having led a fleet to Australia, made the first impact of civilisation, established a viable settlement and earned the mantle "**Father of Australia**". He became an admiral, and died in **1814**.

CAPTAIN
ARTHUR PHILLIP

FATHER
OF
AUSTRALIA

In the days of transportation, it was acknowledged that female convicts on board the transport ships did not always live virtuous lives.

But there was some surprise when the ship *Janus* arrived in May 1820 with 104 female convicts from England and Ireland, due to be distributed among the respectable married settlers or placed in the Government factory at Parramatta.

Most of the women were pregnant, and two of them lodged formal complaints that they had lived with the captain and the first mate during the long voyage.

At the request of the Governor, a full bench of magistrates investigated the claim.

A Roman Catholic priest, *Father Philip Connolly*, gave evidence that two or three women were constantly in the cabin of the captain, *Thomas J. Mowatt*.

"They were in the sleeping births, both day and night," he said.

Another priest, *Father Joseph Therry*, told the court that there was general and constant intercourse between all the sailors and the female convicts throughout the trip.

A prisoner, *Mary Long*, said: "When I have not been confined in the prison during the night, I have passed my time in the captain's cabin.

"I believe I am at this time in a pregnant condition.

"I charge *Captain Mowatt* with the cause of my being in this condition."

Lydia Eden testified that she was pregnant to the chief mate, *John Hedges*, and added: "I passed much of my time in his cabin.

"The surgeon knew of my going up and down, and of the other women too, and did not peremptorily order us to our prison, but only to be more circumspect . . . He said he would have a woman in his cabin, if it were not for the priests."

The magistrates found that prostitution did prevail to a great degree on the *Janus*, and that charges against *Mowatt* and his officers were true.

After 200 years and seven generations . . . a special pride. John Martin and his son William, of Caloundra, Queensland (pictured) are direct descendents of two Negro convicts who arrived in Sydney Cove with the First Fleet. In 1812 John Martin, from Africa, married the daughter of John Randall, from the West Indies, who had travelled with him in the transport ship "Alexander"

CHAPTER THREE

A DISTINCTIVE PEOPLE

THE EDITOR FROM THE WEST INDIES

Australia's first newspaper editor, the man who became known as "the father of the Australian press" was a West Indian, a Creole who had been born in St. Kitts. His name was *George Howe*.

He was educated in the West Indies and learned the rudiments of the printing trade from his father and his brother, who were employed in the government press of the West Indies. He determined to become a printer in London, and emigrated to England. He worked for several newspapers there, including finally The Times.

In April 1799, aged 30, under the name of *George Happy*, alias *Happy George*, he was convicted of having taken part in a robbery and sentenced to death. The following month his sentence was commuted to transportation for the term of his natural life, and he arrived in Sydney in *1800* aboard the convict ship *Royal Admiral*.

In 1802 he applied for, and obtained, the vacant position of Government Printer, and the following year he successfully sought permission from *Governor King* to start Australia's first newspaper, The Sydney Gazette and New South Wales Advertiser. On June 4 1806 he received a full pardon.

George Howe used to hustle round the ill-made streets of the harsh little stockade town that was Sydney, covering court cases, meeting ships, witnessing hangings.

Not only did he write the news, he bought his own paper, procured and often made his own ink, set the news in worn-out type, worked the primitive hand-press and finally delivered his own product.

When subscribers failed to pay their accounts, he doubled up as debt collector. When he ran out of white paper, he used any colour he could find.

The first recorded death in Sydney Cove was that of a Negro, a cook of the good ship **Prince of Wales**. He drowned in the harbour less than three weeks after **Captain Phillip's** First Fleet arrived in January **1788**, when a couple of skylarking cabin boys shook him from the hawser rope on which he was inching his way from the ship to a clump of rocks ashore. A few sailors on the **Prince of Wales** jumped overboard to try to save him, but he sank quickly and disappeared.

The nation's first bushranger was another Negro, one of a small group of black convicts who came out with **Phillip** and who managed at times to confuse the Aboriginals.

One of the first escapees from the convict colony was a Frenchman, known as **Peter Paris**, who talked his way aboard a ship of **La Perouse's** French fleet, which happened to be visiting Botany Bay at the time of **Phillip's** arrival; it was a doomed piece of desertion, because **La Perouse's** ships were wrecked a few weeks later in the Pacific, with all survivors either lost in a longboat or eaten by cannibals on the island of Vanitkoro.

The first adult victim of smallpox in the colony was a North American seaman on **Supply**, the ship which led the fleet into Sydney Cove. He was either an Indian or a Negro, and he contracted the disease and died after visiting a group of children afflicted by it.

The first newspaper editor, the man who became known as the father of the Australian press, was a West Indian Creole who was sentenced to death (later commuted to transportation) for having taken part in a robbery.

The polyglot nature of the earliest Australian settlers is not much appreciated. The founding cargo of prisoners included people from 11 nations, including a couple of lonely souls from France and Italy. As transportation continued to New South Wales and Van Diemen's Land over the next few decades, the convict population became more cosmopolitan. Apart from English, Scottish, Welsh and Irish felons, there were prisoners who had been born in Austria, Canada, the Cape

1 ENGLAND	6 CANAD
2 SCOTLAND	7 GIBRAI
3 WALES	8 GREEC
4 IRELAND	9 HOLLA
5 AUSTRIA	10 HUNGA

of Good Hope, Denmark, Egypt, France, Germany, Gibraltar, Greece, Holland, Hungary, India, Italy, Latvia, Madagascar, Mauritius, the Persian Gulf, Poland, Portugal, Russia, Sweden, the United States and the West Indies.

The arrival of this sad diversity of individuals represented the earliest seeding of the multicultural nation which exists today, and of the series of cultural collisions around which much of our history would be fashioned. To name an early few ... settlers versus Aboriginals, convicts versus soldiers and marines, white convicts versus black, Irish convicts versus the administration, Protestants versus Catholics, 'currency lads' — native-born colonials — versus the aristocracy, squatters versus merchants, emancipists (time-expired convicts) versus exclusivists, abstainers versus drinkers, Chinese versus Europeans.

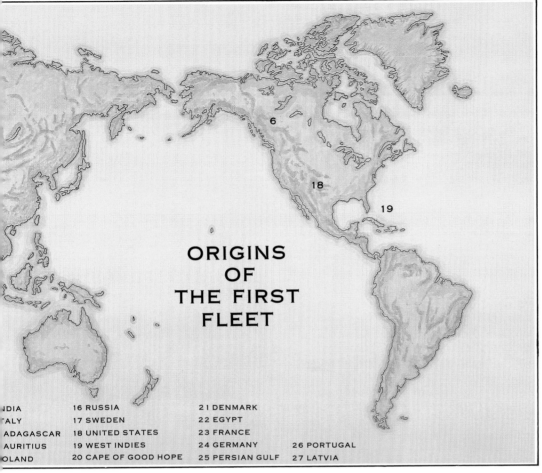

ORIGINS
OF
THE FIRST
FLEET

NDIA	16 RUSSIA	21 DENMARK
TALY	17 SWEDEN	22 EGYPT
ADAGASCAR	18 UNITED STATES	23 FRANCE
AURITIUS	19 WEST INDIES	24 GERMANY
OLAND	20 CAPE OF GOOD HOPE	25 PERSIAN GULF

26 PORTUGAL
27 LATVIA

Courtesy Dixson Galleries

PRIDE OF THE COLONIES
The first generation of native-born Australians, the sons and daughters of convicts (sketched here by the Spaniard *Juan Ravenet*), referred to themselves proudly as Currency Lads and Currency Lasses.

The term was to distinguish them from the 'sterling' of the British-born immigrants, for whom they had no special affection. They resented the airs affected by some of the immigrants, and the better treatment they sometimes received from the administration.

The first native-born white Australians did not have an easy time. A proportion of them were illegitimate, the product of unions with mistresses or prostitutes. Only a sixth of them went to school; many of them were earning wages by the time they were 10 years old. But they were, generally speaking, self-reliant, moral, law-abiding and industrious.

As pride in colonial birth increased, that first generation affected a certain style, and spoke of themselves often as 'the Natives'. They loved sport, and saw it as a means of distinguishing themselves. A sports magazine called The Currency Lad circulated among them, and there was a cricket club called the Currency Lads.

All of the interaction, between classes and philosophies and nationalities, was formative. Essentially, the history of Australia amounts to the gradual emergence, through all kinds of confrontations and compromises, of a distinctive people: a people whose character has been moulded by cultural tensions and ferment.

Courtesy National Library

△ *A latter day "currency lad" contrasts to a more soberly dressed Sydney couple.*

The Currency Lad.

Vol. I.]   SATURDAY AFTERNOON, AUGUST 25, 1832.   [Number 1.

Courtesy Steve Parish

Kakadu National Park ... scenes such as this remind visitors of the dreamtime. ▷

▽ *The flora in Kakadu; colourful and exotic.*

Courtesy Steve Parish

Three major waves of immigration have contributed to Australia's long history. The first comprised the Aboriginals, who are believed to have come in at least two major groups, separated by many thousands of years. The second, which began in Sydney Cove, was dominated by people and ships from the British Isles ... and by 1850 the British people would have outnumbered Aboriginals. The third wave had its beginnings in the late 1940s, and it marked the end of Australia's dependence on British migrants, capital, markets, technology and defence; it was polyglot and cosmopolitan, and it yielded a cultural diversity which had massive effects on Australian society.

The first Australians themselves comprised a multicultural society, in which hundreds of tribes had their own distinctive languages, traditions, customs, crafts and implements. Cautious counts have suggested that there were more than 250 Aboriginal languages, with even people living on the two facing shores of Sydney Harbour speaking separate languages. Tasmania had five different languages, and a journey along the coast from Sydney to Brisbane would have taken the traveller through 15 or 16 language or dialect zones. Archaeological finds continue to be made, and with them comes new evidence about the modes of living of the first immigrants.

One of the most spectacular of these discoveries, a camp-site which was occupied at least 22,000 years ago, is near the Oenpelli Mission on the East Alligator River in the Kakadu National Park. It has shown that the ancient inhabitants ate tortoises, possums and bandicoots, and that they used stone implements: axes, pounders and grinders. The separateness of the Aboriginal people has been cited by some historians as a reason why they were unable to offer any kind of cohesive resistance to the white invaders, why they were unable to negotiate any kind of treaty.

Among the most significant aspects of the second, largely Anglo-Saxon, wave of immigration was the faithful reproduction of British values and attitudes in a country so huge, so very different and so far away. It happened in the first place because the 163,000 convicts who came to Australia were in fact the subjects of selective migration, admittedly of a dubious kind: the vast bulk of them came from the British Isles, by way of jails and prison hulks. Other factors contributed, though. Britain's authority on the seas served to shut out other potential European colonisers, like the French and Dutch, in the decades which followed 1788; Australian territory was never disputed by colonists from other lands, as were Canada, South Africa and the United States. After the convict

phase ended, the British government subsidised immigration to Australia, with the intention of building up its new colony and at the same time relieving overcrowding and the social problems that accompanied it in England. Understandably, migrants from the British Isles were favoured.

Of the 1788 arrivals, the black convicts have attracted surprisingly little attention in the history books. They were all arrested in England, but they came from Africa and the West Indies. Like the odd Negro seaman in the First Fleet, some could have escaped a life of slavery in North America. Whatever their origin, they seemed to share a capacity for work and a fatalistic kind of independence; it was as if they felt it was worth taking awful risks, because nothing worse could happen to them. Some suffered a kind of double banishment; shipped to Australia in the most brutal kind of forced exile, they were sentenced for further crimes in Sydney Cove to be cast out to other places: a remote piece of bushland; the slave-camp prison for incorrigibles, Norfolk Island; Garden Island in Sydney Harbour, to work in chains; a rock in the harbour.

Two of the toughest of these convicts were Black Caesar who had been a 22-year-old servant called John Caesar when he was found guilty in 1786 of stealing £12 and fourpence, and Daniel Gordon (also known as Black Jemmey). Caesar, who became the first bushranger, was described by the Judge Advocate, David Collins this way: "Reputed to be the hardest working convict in the country, his frame was muscular and well calculated for hard labour ... He could in one day devour the full ration for two days. To gratify this appetite he was compelled to steal from others, and all his thefts were directed towards that purpose. He was such a wretch, and so indifferent about meeting death, that he declared while in confinement, that if he should be hanged, he would create a laugh before he was turned off, by playing off some trick upon the executioner." Because there seemed no point in making an example of him on the gallows, Black Caesar was sentenced to transportation for life to Norfolk Island (twice) and to work in irons on Garden Island. His escapades were those of a black Errol Flynn: he escaped from Garden Island, stole a getaway canoe, a musket and arms, terrorised the settlement with violent raids in which he stole food, wine and clothing, fought against Aboriginals and was wounded by them, surrendered and managed to extract a pardon from the Governor. He escaped twice more, and was finally shot dead — after a price of five gallons of spirit was put on his head — by an Aboriginal tracker named Wimbour.

The Negro Gordon was sentenced to death with another black youth, John Williams, for stealing wine; both were pardoned, and Gordon banished "to some other place", which turned out to be an island rock. After a time, he was brought back in company with some other desperadoes and pardoned again as an act of clemency to celebrate the birthday of King George III. In trouble a few months later, he received 500 lashes and the sentence of another exile-from-exile, transportation for life to Norfolk Island. On trial yet again for having stolen food and clothing, he took a gamble by pretending to have gone crazy, and it worked; he was judged unfit for the trial to proceed.

THE YEARS OF TRANSPORTATION

The convict transportation system, which began in 1788, died out over a period of 28 years.

Transportation to New South Wales was abolished in 1840, to Tasmania in 1853 and to Norfolk Island in 1855.

Courtesy Positive Image/J. North

The Moreton Bay 'secondary' penal settlement, established as a prison for runaway convicts in 1824, (above) ceased to exist in 1842.

The last state to see the end of the convict era was Western Australia, (below) in 1868. It had accepted convicts from 1850 to help overcome a serious labour shortage.

Courtesy Positive Image/Rick Altman

By the time the last group had arrived, 163,000 convicts had been transported. Most were aged between 15 and 29. The youngest transported convict was 10, the oldest 74.

THE FLOGGING PARSON

Samuel Marsden (1765–1838) came to Australia in 1794 as assistant chaplain of the colony, and went on to become the chief Anglican clergyman in New South Wales. He was one of the major figures of the earliest history of Australia, and one of the least admirable.

He acquired land, bred sheep, became a magistrate at Parramatta, and dispensed the kind of brutal judgment which earned for him the nickname of 'The Flogging Parson'. In particular he hated the Irish Catholics, and was forever convinced that they were plotting "some wild scheme of revenge".

Not only was he despised by the convicts for the harshness of his sentences . . . but he was often in conflict with a number of the Governors of New South Wales. Lachlan Macquarie refused to meet Marsden socially, except when it was absolutely necessary in the course of his duties.

Marsden made seven voyages to New Zealand, and supervised the establishment of the first European settlement at the Bay of Islands there.

That first little beachhead, of which **Caesar**, **Daniel Gordon** and their black comrades formed such an unlikely part, began the era in which Australia developed into something of a vast, sunburnt, Antipodean echo of the British Isles. Through the 19th and a good part of the 20th century, most trade was exchanged with Britain, and the cargoes were transported in British ships. The religions were transplanted from Britain, as were architectural and painting styles. The news came from British newspapers — carried at first by steamships which were met in Australian ports by Australian newsmen, and later by British undersea telegraph cables. Fashions were largely English, and most of the books on sale in Australian shops were printed in Britain. Australian schoolchildren grew up on a diet of comics and novelty papers which reflected English trends, English humour.

The governors, the bishops, the university professors came from England. Britain ran Australia's foreign policy, supervised its defence, gave it its laws, its social customs, its sports, its songs. Once, in the infant Sydney Cove, when a small potted primrose was shipped out, the nostalgia it evoked among settlers was so great that it became the subject of a painting by **Edward Hopley**.

The loyalty, the sense of being utterly tied to Britain, asserted itself in times of British crisis. Australia sent troops and ships to England's wars . . . to the Maori wars in New Zealand in **1863**, to the Sudan in **1885**, to the Boer War in **1900–02**, to the Boxer Rebellion in **1900**, and to two world wars. The rallying cry was "King and Country". The king was England's, the country of course Australia.

Courtesy National Library

The first large party of free immigrants, including a family of six, reached Sydney in **1793** in the **Bellona**, which also carried 17 female convicts. The imbalance between the sexes in those early decades of Australian society was striking. The pattern had been set in the First Fleet, with 568 male convicts and 191 females. Between **1797** and **1815**, three times as many males (5546) as females (1799) were transported; between **1817** and **1834**, 55,243 males and 7790 females arrived. Of the more than 160,000 convicts shipped out by the time transportation ended, only 16 per cent were women. This one-sided ratio undoubtedly led to various forms of licentiousness and sexual exploitation, but as the population grew and colonial cities developed a more stable family life emerged, and with it, more conventional attitudes to sexual morality.

Courtesy Mitchell Library

△
The Edward Hopley painting of "the small potted primrose" and "the nostalgia it evoked".

◁
Van Diemen's Land looking more like England than England, almost.

△
5 shillings; the cost of one acre of prime farmland.

From the middle of the **1820s**, free settlers outnumbered convicts still serving time, and the fabric of the society which was transplanting English civilisation in Australia was varied. The free settlers included people who had simply immigrated, mainly with the promise of being sold good, cheap land (initially, five shillings an acre); by **1830**, 14,000 of these people had arrived. Then there were former officers who asked for land grants at the end of their periods of service, and were automatically granted them; **John Macarthur**, who had arrived with the Second Fleet as a member of the New South Wales Corps, was such a person. He received a grant of some of the best land at Parramatta, and became one of a powerful elite known as the 'exclusives'. A third and most significant segment of the free-settler population comprised the emancipists, convicts who had served their sentences and received comparatively small land grants. Finally there were the ticket-of-leave men, who lived in a kind of twilight zone ... they were tenuously free, living in a state of some uncertainty.

Courtesy National Library

▷
Elizabeth Farm. Named after Macarthur's wife.

The ticket-of-leave system had been introduced by **Governor Phillip**, to enable convicts whose behaviour had been good to find work and receive wages. They could not own land, and the ticket lasted only a year; it had to be renewed annually, and it could be revoked at any time. Initially the tickets-of-leave were given to convicts who had served four years with good conduct of a seven-year sentence. Some were granted for convicts who performed special services, like giving information on the whereabouts of escaped prisoners who had turned bandits. Some tickets-of-leave were handed out on arrival in Sydney Harbour to gentlemen convicts, or those who were seen to have special talents.

An editorial in Sydney's first newspaper, the Sydney Gazette, once summed up the status of the ticket-of-leave document appropriately. "A ticket-of-leave," it said, "is the most tender kind of liberty that can be conceived, it is liberty in one sense, and non-liberty in another ... Under the present system, a ticket-of-leave exempts a man from the service of one master, while upon the other he becomes the slave of thousands of others. From the Magistrate, down to the meanest constable in the district, a ticket-of-leave holder is continually kept the subject of apprehension." This fragile state of freedom could be lost if a ticket-holder was deemed "by any officer, soldier or Constable" to be idle, insolent, or of charging too much for his services.

△
Camden Park, the Macarthur family's final home west of Sydney.

◁
A "ticket-of-leave" a convict's first step to freedom.

Courtesy Mitchell Library

EXPLORER, ADVOCATE, PUBLISHER

William Charles Wentworth (1793–1872) **was born on Norfolk Island, the son of D'Arcy Wentworth, who was assistant surgeon to the Second Fleet and later superintendent of convicts at Norfolk Island.**

In 1813, in company with *Gregory Blaxland* and *William Lawson*, he made the first crossing of the Blue Mountains and opened the way for pastoral expansion on the western plains.

After studying law in Britain, he returned to Australia, where he emerged as a supporter of the rights of emancipists — freed convicts — and an advocate of representative government and trial by jury.

His sympathy for the emancipists — he was obviously not one himself — had been explained by an episode in England. He once saw his father described in print as an emancipist, considered this to be a slur, and demanded an apology. On later investigation he learned that, while his father had not been a convict, he had in fact stood trial twice for highway robbery ... and had been strongly advised that his future lay in New South Wales.

Wentworth **published the *Australian* newspaper with another lawyer, *Robert Wardell*. They campaigned together for political reform, clashed often with *John Macarthur* and the 'exclusives' who followed him, and fought a running war with *Governor Sir Ralph Darling*.**

◁

John Macarthur.

Courtesy Mitchell Library

A clear social division existed between the two most important groups in the colony, the exclusives and the emancipists. It was really the basis for Australia's first long-simmering political conflict, one that continued as the colony moved from the status of a penal colony whose main function it was to house, punish and rehabilitate convicts, to that of a producer of raw material in the form of wool. The exclusives, led by **John Macarthur**, *were wealthy land-owners who saw themselves as almost instant aristocrats, better able to run the new country than anyone else, even the governors; their idea was that Australia should operate on a plantation style, with convicts and ex-convicts constituting a cheap labour force which would contribute to the efficient production of wool. The emancipists, led by* **William Charles Wentworth**, *resented the power and the attitudes of the exclusives, and demanded a say for ex-convicts in the running of the colony.*

An early ally of the emancipists was **Governor Lachlan Macquarie**, *who arrived at the end of* **1809**, *at a time when the colony had an adult population of 19,000 ... all but 2804 of whom had been transported as convicts. At that time 59,000 hectares of land were owned by just a few exclusives, while a very large number of emancipists owned smaller plots totalling 77,000 hectares.*

Macquarie *saw the ex-convicts as people who had much to contribute, and tried to unite them with other free settlers at social functions; such attempts were usually resented by the exclusives.* **Macquarie** *wrote: "Once a convict has become a free man, he should in all respects be considered on a footing with every other man in the colony, according to his rank in life and his character." Where he could, he encouraged emancipists. He used the skills of the convict architect* **Francis Greenway**, *commissioning him to design buildings in Sydney and elsewhere, and his personal physician was* **William Redfern**, *a doctor who had been transported for his part in* **1801** *in a Royal Navy mutiny.*

Courtesy Mitchell Library

DESIGNING CONVICT

The convict architect *Francis Greenway*, whose patron was *Governor Lachlan Macquarie*, was a poor businessman. Practising in Bristol, he went bankrupt and forged a contract. For this he was sentenced to death and the sentence commuted to 14 years' transportation.

Beginning in *1816, Macquarie* put him in charge of the design and building of all government works in New South Wales. His main assignments were convict barracks: the Female Factory in Parramatta (*1819*) and the Hyde Park Barracks for men in Sydney (*1819*).

Three major *Greenway* buildings survive in their intended form: St. Matthew's Church in Windsor, the Hyde Park Barracks and St. James' Church in Sydney.

When *Macquarie* (who had succeeded *Governor William Bligh*) returned to England in *1821, Greenway* lost his official post as the colony's civil architect. He was dismissed for having demanded an architect's fee in addition to his salary.

In *1838*, Australia's finest Georgian architect died a pauper, and was buried in an unmarked grave.

▷

Governor Lachlan Macquarie.

Courtesy National Library

DISASTERS ON THE WAY

One of the great hazards for early immigrants to Australia was shipwreck. In August 1845 the barque *Cataraqui* bound for Melbourne from Liverpool with 375 migrant passengers and a crew of 38, struck a reef in Bass Strait. Only nine survived. It was Australia's worst maritime disaster.

In January 1854, 297 were drowned when the iron sailing ship *Tayleur*, on her maiden voyage from Liverpool to Australia, struck rocks off Lambay Island, near Dublin.

When the *Dunbar* sank near South Head, Sydney, in August 1857, 120 people were lost. There was one survivor.

Only two survived when the iron clipper *Loch Ard*, carrying a complement of 54, struck rocks near Cape Otway, Victoria, in January 1878. Both survivors were 18 years old ... an apprentice called *Tom Pearce* and a passenger, *Eva Carmichael.*

The early decades of the 19th century saw the beginnings of substantial immigration from places other than the British Isles. English values dominated the community, and ties with Britain remained intense ... but Europeans started to arrive — from Italy, Greece, Germany, Malta and Scandinavia. They came from big cities and remote villages, sometimes to get away from poverty, famine, political and religious persecution; occasionally state governments paid their fares. They came to work on goldfields, sugar-cane farms, vineyards, railroads, wheatfields, and they formed small, isolated pockets ... Germans in rural villages in South Australia, the Victorian Wimmera and Queensland's Darling Downs, the Greeks in and around Melbourne (which was to become, in the late 20th century, third in Greek population to Athens), the Italians in scattered communities all the way around Australia, from Perth (which had a score of Italian organ-grinders) to the canefields of North Queenland.

Courtesy National Library

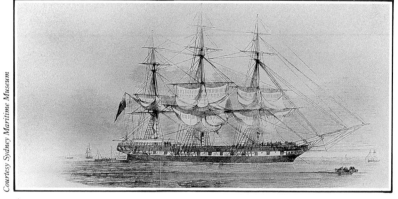

Courtesy Sydney Maritime Museum

△
The Dunbar, only one survived.

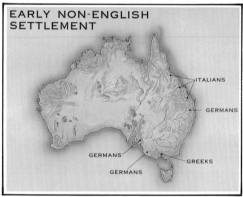

EARLY NON-ENGLISH SETTLEMENT

ITALIANS

GERMANS

GERMANS

GREEKS

GERMANS

Courtesy Stella & Ray Graetz

Victoria Regina

1841
No. 6

An Act for the Naturalization of certain Persons Natives of Germany.

Whereas certain persons natives of Germany whose names are hereinafter mentioned having applied by Petition to the Governor to be admitted to the rights and privileges of British Subjects: And for the encouragement of Agriculture and in consequence of their good conduct and observance of the Laws during their residence in this Province an Act for their Naturalization was passed by the Governor in Council on the 11th day of February 1840: And whereas the said Act being informal without the previous sanction of the Crown Her Majesty has been pleased to authorise the re-enactment of the same.

George Grey Esquire, Governor and Commander-in-Chief

Courtesy National Library

△
"Free settlers" prepare to leave for their new life in New South Wales.

◁
Berthed in Sydney Cove; the gateway to New South Wales.

"AUSTRALIA'S ONE SAINT . . ."

Caroline Chisholm, whose face adorns the five-dollar note, has been called Australia's greatest woman pioneer. She was known in Sydney Cove as 'the immigrant's friend', and she laboured hard among newly arrived settlers, particulary young women.

From 1840 to 1846, she met every migrant ship that landed in Sydney Harbour, finding jobs for women passengers, setting up an immigrants' home in Sydney where girls could live until jobs and accommodation could be found for them. Sometimes she escorted 'new chums' into the bush on her white horse, Captain.

In six years Mrs. Chisholm settled 11,000 people as servants or farmers in New South Wales, relieving congestion and distress in the city of Sydney as she introduced individuals and families to country districts.

On a visit to Britain in 1846 she promoted migration to Australia by obtaining firm employment contracts for single women and by causing conditions on migrant ships to be improved. She had a powerful ally in the writer Charles Dickens. Her Family Colonisation Loan Society advanced passage money to families to enable them to migrate as entire units.

The French historian Michelet called this astonishing, spirited woman "Australia's one saint". London Punch called her "a second Moses, in bonnet and shawl". She died in 1877.

◁
Caroline Chisholm

Courtesy National Library

THE ARCHITECT OF ADELAIDE

The man who chose the site of the city of Adelaide, surveyed it and planned it, was *Colonel William Light*. He was 50 years old when he arrived in South Australia, charged with the task of finding the right place for the new settlement.

Light decided that the entrance to the Adelaide River, with its surrounding fertile plains and mountain ranges, was ideal. He sketched his plan in a hot week over Christmas, and it had its critics. He clashed with the colonial administration when he was urged to adopt quicker and less accurate surveying methods.

Light later wrote "I leave it to posterity . . . to decide whether I am entitled to blame or praise."

Light learned his mapping skills in both the English navy and the army, serving under the *Duke of Wellington*. Apart from siting and planning Adelaide, *Light* divided the rest of the country into sections, selected areas for secondary towns and mapped 2500 kilometres of coastline.

Bethany, an early German village in the Barossa. ▷

The Germans made a significant contribution to the settlement of Australia. They came in bulk first in the **1830s**, to escape a life of religious persecution after Lutherans had been offended by a forced union between their Church and the Reformed or Calvinist Church. By **1861** there were about 27,000 Germans in Australia and by the **1890s** more than 40,000. By this time the Germans were the largest non-British minority in Australia.

From the earliest days, talented individuals from the German states forced their way into Australian history. German scientists and German seamen had sailed on **Cook's** voyages. A German who had served in the British Army, **Augustus Theodore Henry Alt**, laid out the first settlements at Sydney and Parramatta, and became Surveyor-General of New South Wales. Another German soldier, **Philip Schaffer**, developed one of Australia's first vineyards on land granted to him at Parramatta in **1791**. Another German, **Christian Carl Ludwig Ruemker** was Australian Government Astronomer from **1827**, and during his nine years in the colony he discovered a number of comets. The strangely obsessed wanderer **Ludwig Leichhardt**, who perished on an expedition to the inland in **1848**, came to Australia from Berlin in **1842**. The explorer and botanist **Baron Sir Ferdinand Jakob Heinrich von Mueller**, son of a Prussian army officer,

immigrated at the age of 22 in **1847**; he was founding Government Botanist in Victoria in **1853**, and later director of Melbourne's Botanical Gardens, considered to be the finest and best-planned in Australia. Another prominent early botanist was **Amalie Dietrich**, from Saxony, whose name is carried by a number of Australian botanical and entomological species. In **1900** the editor of the influential Melbourne newspaper the Age was a German, **Gottlieb Schueler**.

The German settlements in South Australia, which began when a Lutheran pastor, **Augustus Kavel**, brought a shipload of his flock to swamplands near Port Adelaide in **1838**, were essentially communal in nature. By **1841** there were 1800 Germans among the 14,000 people in the last Australian colony to be established . . . the one which hosted no convicts. Joined by their faith, their common language and culture, they

△
*An example of their faith
. . . a German Lutheran
church in the Barossa.*

◁
The Barossa today.

cropped vegetables and milked cows;
church bells tolled each day to signal the
start of work, prayer time, breaks for
meals, the coming of dusk. The bells
also tolled in times of danger. The
community spread through the valley
that **Colonel William Light** called
Barossa; in towns with names like
Klemzig, Hahndorf and Langmeil,
children received educations that were
essentially, exclusively German,
German architecture was reproduced
and ultimately marvellous vineyards
were born.

The Germans made their
biggest Australian imprint on the
Barossa Valley, but they speared out to
other important areas in Australia.
About 6000 of them worked on the
goldfields at Ballarat, Bendigo and
Castlemaine, and one of the leaders of
the Eureka Stockade uprising was a
Hanoverian called **Frederick Vern**.
Three Germans died in the fighting,
including a Prussian called **Thomen**
who was a lieutenant to the rebellion's
leader, **Peter Lalor**. The Germans were
pioneers in the Wimmera, in the Mallee
wheatfields, in vineyards around
Bendigo, Geelong and Rutherglen, in
NSW towns like Holbrook (which was
once called Germantown), around
Grafton, Armidale, the Darling Downs,
Bundaberg, Maryborough and Mackay.
The Queensland government offered
free and assisted passage to German
settlers, and by **1891** there were 15,000
of them in the state.

△
*The cooper plies his trade
today just as he did decades
before.*

◁
The old way; 1986

The **1891** census of the Australian population recorded 3890 Italian-born and 482 Greek-born residents in Australia. One settlement near Woodburn, NSW, became known as 'Little Italy'; its members supplied timber, grew fruit and vegetables, worked sugar farms. Many Italians who accepted the offer of assisted passages from the Queensland government to work as cane-cutters in the far north went on to acquire their own farms. By **1981** there were 275,883 Italian-born residents of Australia, and more than half a million Australians of Italian background.

Around **1830** a group of Greeks from the Ionian Islands were given free passages to work in the vineyards of the **Macarthur** family at Camden, NSW. Seamen who jumped ship were among the Greeks who joined the gold rushes of the **1850**s. In Queensland the Diamantina River and the town of Roma were named after the first wife of the first Governor, **Diamantina Roma**, who came from the island of Ithaca and was active in the colony's social life. By **1921**, 3654 Greeks were living in Australia, and by **1981** Australia's Greek-born residents totalled 146,625.

The third migratory wave, which began after the **1939–45** war, not only signalled the end of Australia's British era, it transformed the country hugely in an astonishingly short time, by forging a society which was more culturally varied, more vigorous, more tolerant. It also helped to double the population, with people from more than 120 countries. It was by any standards a massive episode in migration, one of the most successful in the history of the world.

It happened — it was designed — because of a number of factors. Australia had a huge shortage of houses, apartments, schools and hospitals. Transport services were run down, coal and steel production had declined, industries were faced with closure, primary producers were having trouble in obtaining essential supplies. The country was war-weary. What it needed most of all was a workforce. In

the ground, in rock faces, underneath the ocean, were all kinds of exciting minerals and energy forces, but to exploit them required people. The slump in the birthrate of the Depression years, when for the first time the rate of natural increase fell below one per cent of the population, was beginning to be felt. Also, in **1945–46**, as the government of **Ben Chifley** was beginning to grapple with all these problems, the number of people leaving Australia exceeded arrivals by 9763; the following year the loss was 6443.

Courtesy National Library

The **Chifley** Labour Government's most significant contribution to Australia's future was its immigration policy. For years politicians had preached that Australia's vast spaces offered an invitation to invasion, and that threat had become reality with the Japanese thrust; but in the Labour movement there had long been another fear ... that foreigners would deprive Australian trade unionists of jobs by working for low wages. Certainly, if Australia wanted to take the gamble and increase its population dramatically, potential migrants would not be hard to find. There had probably never been a time in New World history when so many people were looking for new homelands. After the downfall of Germany and a series of Communist takeovers in eastern Europe, masses of displaced persons and refugees were in the market.

Courtesy Herald & Weekly Times Limited

In fact both sides of politics embraced the idea of mass migration as the way ahead for Australia. **Arthur Calwell**, *who as Immigration Minister showed some unexpected qualities of statesmanship, put it bluntly: "We may have only the next 25 years to make the best possible use of our second chance to survive . . . Our first requirement is additional population. We need it for defence and for the fullest expansion of our economy." The then Leader of the Opposition,* **R. G. (later Sir Robert) Menzies**, *said: "I believe that upon the possibility of our securing a substantial migration to Australia during the next 30 years will depend, not only the preservation of Australian independence, but also the true prospects of advancement of social benefits in Australia." When he took government in* **1949**, **Menzies** *continued to give immigration the highest priority.*

△
Whilst bitter political enemies, Arthur Calwell (left) and Sir Robert Menzies (right) agreed on the importance of an aggressive immigration policy.

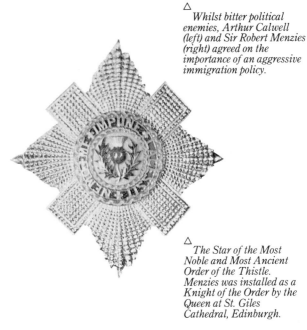

△
The Star of the Most Noble and Most Ancient Order of the Thistle. Menzies was installed as a Knight of the Order by the Queen at St. Giles Cathedral, Edinburgh.

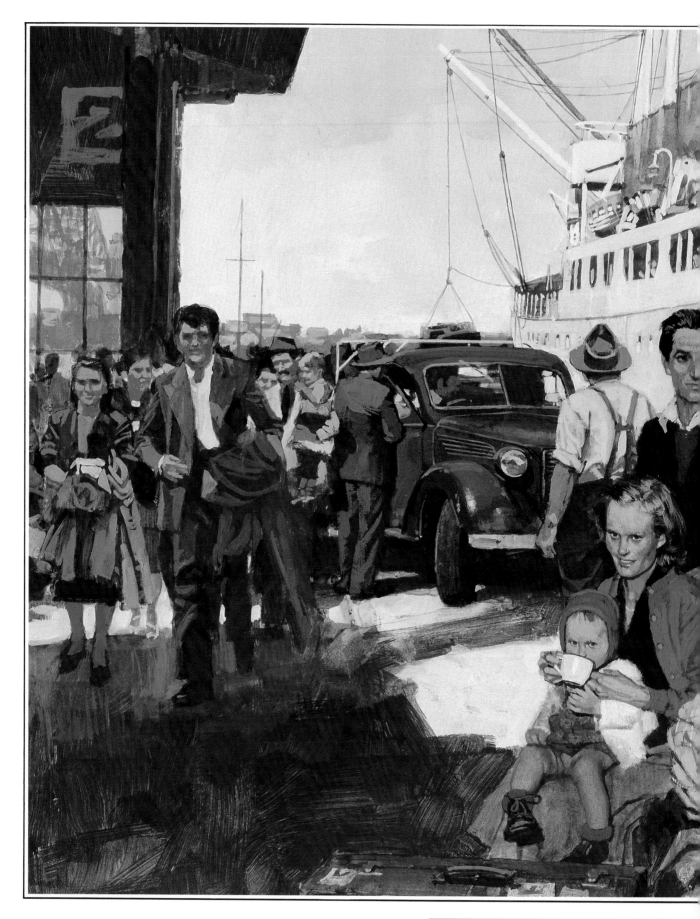

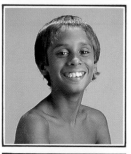

A cosmopolitan nation . . . here a happy luncheon with people from many different ethnic backgrounds. ▷

*Between **1950** and **1970**, some 2½ million migrants arrived, and more than half of them were non-British. In those 20 years a self-consciously British community accommodated 337,000 Italians, 192,000 Greeks, 145,000 Dutch, 120,000 Yugoslavs, 115,000 Germans, 50,000 Poles. About 60 per cent of Australia's post-World War II migrants received passage assistance. Since **1945**, migration and births to immigrant settlers have contributed about half of Australia's population increases. A significant development was the relaxation in **1966** of the previous very restrictive entry policy towards people of non-European descent.*

*From January **1959** to June **1970**, 24,000 migrants arrived from the United States. In many ways this was an extension of the 'Go west, young man' policy which had caused so many Americans, armed with dreams, hopes, ambitions, to move across their country to the Californian coast. Certainly it was the biggest influx of American settlers since the gold rush days of more than a century before.*

*An important aspect of Australia's post-war immigration policy (which has seen intakes of as many as 185,000 settlers in one year . . . **1969–70**) has been the nation's willingness to accept people who have been fleeing some kind of oppression. Since the **1939–45** war, 430,000*

refugees and displaced persons have settled in Australia — from Europe, Asia, the Middle East, Central and South America and more recently, Africa. They have often come equipped with not much more than hope combined with a sense of escape, but they have contributed a good deal to Australia's economic, social and cultural progress. They have included:

*• 170,000 from Europe, including 63,400 from Poland, 34,700 from Estonia, Latvia and Lithuania, and 23,500 from Yugoslavia. These came between **1947** and **1954**; they were all displaced by the war, and Australia's contribution to resettlement was second only to that of the United States, which accepted 282,000.*

*• 14,100 Hungarians, following the **1956** uprising in Hungary. Some of the settlers were Olympic athletes, visiting Melbourne for the **1956** Games at the time.*

*• 5700 Czechoslovakians, after similar events in their country in **1968**.*

• 13,300 White Russians from China, sponsored by the World Council of Churches.

• *95,300 Indo-Chinese between April 1975, when the Vietnam war ended, and June 1985. As a proportion of Australia's population, this was the highest intake of such refugees by any country.*

• *22,800 East Europeans since 1978 — particularly from 1980 to 1983 as a result of martial law in Poland.*

• *Other refugee groups to settle in Australia have included 18,100 Lebanese, 2500 others from the Middle East, 6300 Timorese, 4800 Soviet Jews, 2800 Latin Americans and 250 Africans.*

What this has all added up to has been an exciting blend of cultures, with four out of every 10 residents of Australia having either been born overseas or having at least one overseas-born parent. Of the 21 per cent of the population born overseas, more than half have come from non-English speaking countries. More than 300 languages, including 200 Aboriginal dialects, are spoken in Australia, and more than a third of Australia's overseas-born residents regularly use a language other than English.

And what of the Aboriginals, the first of the nation's immigrants, the people who lived in such harmony with the land through the millennia before the Europeans came? Today they number 160,000, including an estimated 40,000 of full Aboriginal descent and 15,200 Torres Strait Islanders. In their presence, a cosmopolitan beachhead has grown into a cosmopolitan nation.

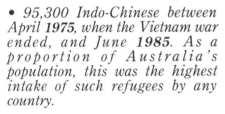

◁

A Greek Australian proud of being "Oz".

Courtesy Lea Danlea, Broadbeach Waters, Qld

SO DIFFERENT

At first blink, it is hard to discern much similarity between the Irish and the Chinese. They do not indulge in much mutual traffic, physically or culturally. Nor do they have reason to . . . in any kind of racial or geographical line-up, they would tend to occupy utterly different zones.

The truth is, though, that in one sense they have a good deal in common. Australian history is the denominator, the place where they shared — admittedly five or six decades apart — some remarkably similar experiences. In colonial Australia, a strange unity was born.

For a start, both groups managed to qualify as oppressed minorities. They did this because, for reasons which in cool and comfortable hindsight turn out to be so very alike, they were seen to be dangerous. Mostly they were different from the rest, and in the climate of suspicion which existed in early Australia, that very fact was seen to pose a threat.

*The Irish, although they constituted part of **Phillip**'s Sydney Cove beachhead, were always a group apart. They worshipped differently, they spoke Gaelic to each other, they brought with them a whole rag-bag of strange customs and superstitions. They held wakes for the dead, where people sang and danced and even drank themselves into a very boozy condition. They dressed distinctively, wore funny hats, smoked clay pipes. They kept at times to themselves, maybe drawn together by the oppression that surrounded them in the early days. They had different values, and the colonial establishment looked down upon them as inferior beings, people who were refugees from poverty. They indulged in 'chain' migration, tending to establish a base and bring out other members of their families. They were also rebellious and resentful, in the words of **Governor Hunter** in **1798** "lawless and turbulent".*

The Queenslander, 1904, John Oxley Library, Brisbane

. . . SO ALIKE

And the Chinese? They too were a group apart. They too spoke a language no one else could understand, and they too worshipped differently . . . talking to effigies of gods, burning incense before them, offering them real food and wine. They too dressed in different attire, and saluted their dead in a most unusual fashion, even wanting to retain their bones for burial elsewhere. Like the Irish, they brought with them strange customs; they smoked opium and gambled at games the whites could not comprehend. They erected joss houses, and ate parts of animals that other people threw to the dogs. They stayed together, like the Irish, and they were also seen to be inferior because they had fled poverty. They too indulged in a form of 'chain' migration, bringing out people from their own villages. Their biggest fault, though, was that they worked harder than anyone else, for less money.

The truth was that neither the Irish nor the Chinese conformed, and that aroused suspicion. In many ways they were markedly different from each other — the Chinese, unlike the Irish, were never violent (except in cases of extreme provocation), and they were never accused of insubordination or sedition but they both incurred hostility. It was a hostility based on fear.

▽
Wherever the Chinese settled, temples (joss houses) such as this one appeared.

Courtesy La Trobe Collection, State Library of Victoria

Courtesy Trades Union Congress, London

THE MEN OF TOLPUDDLE

Probably the best-known of the political prisoners transported to Australia were the six 'Tolpuddle martyrs' . . . Dorsetshire villagers who had been sentenced in 1834 to seven years' penal servitude for having formed an early trade union.

The villagers, faced with a wage cut from seven to six shillings a week, well below subsistence level, met to form a Friendly Society of Agricultural Labourers. They were charged under an anti-sedition Act of 1797 with "administering unlawful oaths".

Their sentences and their subsequent exile caused a public furore in Britain, which led ultimately to pardons for all six. The leader, George Loveless, a lay preacher as well as a farm labourer, had been sent to Van Diemen's Land; the others to New South Wales. All returned to England between 1837 and 1839.

They all had a difficult time. James Brine, one of the martyrs, was assigned to a magistrate named Robert Scott at Glindon on the Hunter River. Scott set him to digging postholes, even though his bare feet were so lacerated that he could not push them onto the spade. Brine wrapped a piece of iron hoop around a foot, to put his weight on the spade.

The similarities do not end there. Both races were involved in two of the ugliest, bloodiest battles of the 19th century . . . the Irish at Castle Hill, the Chinese at Lambing Flat. In those conflicts, both were the sufferers in one-sided combat. Both nationalities migrated during the same century in large numbers to one other part of the world: the United States. And a final, ironic link: because of one small, pathetic incident, the Irish were ridiculed for years by the aristocracy as foolish people who thought they could desert the convict colony and somehow walk to (of all places) China.

Of the 163,000 prisoners who began the voyage from the British Isles during the convict years, nearly 40,000 (29,466 males, 9104 females) were sent direct from Ireland. Of the convicts sent from England, about 8000 were Irish-born and about the same number were of Irish descent. Overall, the Irish element accounted for about a quarter of all the convicts transported. Many of these were women: of all the female prisoners shipped out between 1815 and 1821, some 55 per cent were from Ireland.

The first convicts sent direct from Ireland arrived from Cork in the **Queen** on November 26 **1791**. In that shipload were 133 males and 22 females . . . the youngest 11-year-old **David Fay**, of Dublin, the oldest **Patrick Fitzgerald**, 64. The last of the Irish prisoners landed in Western Australia in January **1868** in the **Hougoumont**: 63 Fenian rebels who carried with them a pride, an arrogance really, which separated them utterly from the wretched thieves and prostitutes who were dumped with the earliest cargos. The Fenians were political rebels, educated and articulate, and they were treated as confined gentlemen rather than prisoners during their voyage of transportation.

They even produced their own handwritten newspaper aboard ship. They did not like common criminals, and they did not like what they saw of Australia. One of them, **John Casey**, put his disgust into words in an article for the Irish journal, the Irishman:

"The population of Western Australia

Courtesy State Library of Victoria

The 4

A WEEKLY JOURNAL OF

No. 1.]   MELBOURNE, THU

Banks.

PROVINCIAL and SUBURBAN BANK,
LIMITED,
FOR ASSISTING MANUFACTURERS,
TRADERS, MECHANICS, AND OTHERS,
ON THE CO-OPERATIVE PRINCIPLE.

CAPITAL, £100,000,
(With power to increase,)
IN 20,000 SHARES OF £5 EACH.

The Bank will be Incorporated under the "Companies' Statute, 1864," Limiting the Liability of Shareholders.

PROVISIONAL COMMITTEE:

Jas. F. Born, Esq., 22 Nicholson-street, gentleman.
Wm. H. Barlow, Esq., Packington-street, Kew, gentleman.
Thos. Bligh, Esq., Flinders-lane, merchant.
Hermann Buttner, Esq., Melbourne, merchant.
Robert Cumming, Esq., Mulgrave, farmer.
R. Dehnert, Esq., Simpson's-road, manufacturer.
Joel Eade, Esq., ex-Mayor of Collingwood, Hoddle-street.
Thos. A. Ewing, Esq., Brunswick-street, chemist.
Jas. Forbes, Esq., Asphalte Works, South Yarra.
Isaac R. Fawcett, Esq., Gertrude-street, Fitzroy, merchant.
Thos. Greenwood, Esq., Victoria Parade, contractor.
Richmond Henty, Esq., South Yarra, commission agent.
Geo. Irish, Esq., Brunswick-street, produce merchant.
W. F. King, Esq., newspaper proprietor, Melbourne.
J. Lively, Esq., Gertrude-street, merchant.
David Mitchell, Esq., Walsh-street, West Melbourne, gentleman.
John Martin, Esq., Buckingham Terrace, Rathdowne-street.
William Ryan, Esq., Hotham, Councillor.
Albert L. Tucker, Esq., J.P., Mayor of Fitzroy, gentleman.
Alex. Jamieson, Esq., Lorne Cottage.
With power to add to their number.

TRUSTEES:
The Hon. Francis Robertson.
The Hon. Robert Walsh, late Attorney-General.

SOLICITORS:

Banks.

The Savings' Banks also receive lar yearly to their deposits, which are pl Government in the present Banks again employed, to the exclusion of th and mechanical classes.

The system of co-operative busir well understood throughout the varic Europe, and has been productive o results in the United States of Americ France, Belgium, and the Swiss Co People's Banks are now in successfu and from small beginnings, have bec importance in each State.

In Victoria, the co-operative syster scarcely tried (except in mining pursi in so far as the experiment has been proved successful. The beneficial eff tual Assurance and Building Societi the Victorian Permanent Building So deposits over £100,000, Langlands' Fo pany, and the eminently prosperous Mutual Provident Assurance Society, lished reports may well convince all fits arising from societies established a worked on the co-operative or mutu it is considered that a Bank, formed ev on the co-operative basis, when pr ported by its shareholders, need not of business from the general public, interests are, to a certain extent, cen the success of the Company.

It is therefore proposed to establ under the designation of "THE PROV SUBURBAN BANK, LIMITED," to be upon a sound system, and the correc of a People's Bank, governed by a B rectors, chosen from the shareholde consist of a president and four dire general manager. The qualification will be the holding of fifty shares. T intelligence, integrity, and administ city, are to be found amongst our tra mechanics, as evidenced by the success ment of our numerous Building an Societies, and several Insurance Com

The Bank will conduct a general mate banking business, discount bills advances upon the security of deposi grant cash credits on the true Scottis which is carried into works of an ex public character, as well as small un Interest only charged on the daily D if in credit, the general rate on curre allowed. The projector has been over connected with Scotch Banking, and c

may be divided into two classes — those actually in prison, and those who richly deserve to be there . . . all are equally dishonest. What more can be expected from a nation of felons . . . More real depravity, more shocking wickedness, more undisguised vice and immorality is to be witnessed at midday in the most public thoroughfares of Perth, with its population of 1500, than in any other city of 50 times its population, either in Europe or America."

A good number of the Irish convicts were transported for political offences — for protest and rebellion against poverty and oppression — but not nearly as many as romantic legend

, NEWS, LITERATURE, &c.

NOVEMBER, 1872. [PRICE SIXPENCE.

Banks.

under proper regulations, afford sub-
nefit also to the farmer and vigneron,
ustrial classes and producers requiring
advances who have hitherto been sub-
expenses of mortgages, &c., which
ided by transacting business with the
ank. It is also believed that a Bank
the above principles will acquire a
mand of funds, when generally sup-
the people. It will be enabled to take
al loans and grant advances to sub-
orations, either by purchasing or re-
heir debentures. Deposit· may be
om Friendly Societies, who no doubt
hise with the objects of the proposed
romote industry and savings among
de, and to enable them to utilise their
ons in their respective works and em-
affording thereby the best security to
ader and depositor for the stability of
nd its success.
r is set forth in this prospectus, as to
les and operations of the proposed
be fully mirrored to, nnd is embodied
cles of Association, a draft of which
bmitted to the shareholders for their
, the usual manner.

ORM OF APPLICATION.

Provisional Committee,
L AND SUBURBAN BANK, LIMITED.
en,—Herewith I hand you the sum of
Being a deposit of Ten Shillings per
Shares of £5 each in the
pany, which I request you will allot to
hereby agree to accept the same or any
r that may be allotted, and to pay all
may be made, and to hold such Shares
ne provisions of the Memorandum and
Association constituting the Company.
remain, Gentlemen,
Your obedient Servant,
Name in full......................
Occupation ....
Residence ....
Date ....

Trade Addresses.

nd Station Owners, Landed Proprietors, Farmers and others,
MEN—After a residence of many
n the Western District, and during the

Trade Addresses.

WILLIAM IEVERS and SON, 101 Cardigan
street, Carlton, HOUSE, LAND, and
COMMISSION AGENTS (Official Valuators).
Let and Sell all descriptions of House and Land
Property, collect rents, and negotiate loans at
lowest rates. Agents to the Victoria Fire and
Life Insurance Company and Savings' Institute.
Loan Brokers.

COACH FACTORY,
Brunswick-street, Fitzroy.
JOHN HACKETT, proprietor, builds to order
every description of English and American style
of Carriages at the lowest remunerating prices.

NEILS HANSON, COACH BUILDER, 4 and 6
Therry-street, Melbourne, next Stork Hotel.
All repairs executed with the utmost despatch,
and on most moderate terms.

T. HICKEY, Bookseller and Stationer, 243
Elizabeth-street, Melbourne.
Country orders promptly attended to.
Cheap account books and stationery always on
sale.

Public Notices.

V. J. M.
A GRAND BAZAAR,
Under the Patronage of his Lordship the Right
Rev. Dr. Goold, Lord Bishop of Melbourne,
IN AID OF
The Magdalen Asylum,
(125 inmates) and
The Industrial Reformatory, and
Preservation Classes,
(190 inmates, total 315) ; in care of the
NUNS OF THE GOOD SHEPHERD,
ABBOTSFORD, will be held in the
TOWN HALL, CITY OF MELBOURNE.

TUESDAY, WEDNESDAY, THURSDAY,
FRIDAY, SATURDAY, 3RD, 4TH, 5TH, AND
6TH DECEMBER, 1872.

STALLS:
No. 1 Stall—Mrs. P. J. Martin, Mrs. Quirk,
Mrs. and Miss Dunne, Mrs. and Miss Feehan,
Mrs. Norton, Mrs. Harney, the Misses Hayes,

△ *A permanent reminder of the Reverend Samuel Marsden is the plaque on an old chapel near Cobbitty, NSW*

◁ *The picturesque and historic cottage adjacent to Heber Chapel.*

Courtesy Victoria Police, P R Division

The **Reverend Samuel Marsden**, *the Anglican chaplain who deservedly acquired the nickname '*the Flogging Parson*', summed up the view of many when he wrote:*

> *"The number of catholic convicts is very great in the settlement; and these in general composed of the lowest class of the Irish nation, who are the most wild, ignorant and savage race ... men that have been familiar with robberies murders and every horrid crime from their infancy ... governed entirely by the impulse of passion and always alive to rebellion and mischief they are very dangerous members of society ... They are extremely superstitious artful and treacherous ... They have no true concern whatever for any religion nor fear of the Supreme Being; but are fond of riot drunkenness and cabals ..."*

The desire of the Irish prisoners to escape manifested itself first in the form of a bizarre attempt by some of the first direct cargo, to walk to China. They had been set down, after an immensely long journey, in a hostile environment on the other side of the world. China was also on the other side of the world, and it represented, in their unencumbered imagination, an exotic goal, maybe a haven. The path to China amounted to a symbol, a simple dream, a way out. But the attempt was seen as evidence of essential Irishness ... stupidity blended with conspiracy and a refusal to accept things as they were.

has suggested. As with the English convicts, about three-quarters of them were thieves; only about one-fifth of the Irish could fairly be described as social or political rebels.

The first image of the Irish was of a people who were wild, dangerous, restless, seditious and a little crazy. "Nearly as wild themselves as the cattle," was the description applied by the Judge Advocate, **Colonel David Collins**. *For their part, the Irish saw themselves as a doubly subjugated people. Even at home many of them yearned for freedom. In Australia, where they found themselves subjected to tougher punishment and greater vigilance than other convicts, the desire to be free was even stronger.*

Ned Kelly to his gang as police advanced at Glenrowan: "Come out, boys, and we'll whip the lot of them."

Ned Kelly, after being shot in the legs at Glenrowan: "I am done. I am done."

Ned Kelly to Mr. Justice Sir Redmond Barry at his trial for murder: "I do not fear death, and I am the last man in the world to take a man's life away."

Ned Kelly to Judge Barry: "I dare say the day will come when we shall all have to go to a bigger court than this."

Ned Kelly to Judge Barry after being sentenced to death: "I will meet you there."

Ned Kelly in jail, awaiting execution: "For my own part, I do not care a straw about my life ... I fear it (dying) as little as to drink a cup of tea."

Ned Kelly's mother to him, in the condemned cell: "Mind you die like a Kelly, Ned."

Ned Kelly on the gallows: "Ah well, I suppose it has come to this! ... Such is life!"

△ The Irish march on Sydney. "Death or Liberty" was their cry.

For years the early rulers of the colony feared an uprising by the Irish. The garrison was small enough, and reputation of the Irish convicts as a seditious, dangerous, foolhardy mob continued to grow. Finally, in **1804**, rebellion did break out at Castle Hill, on the outskirts of Sydney. A couple of Irishmen, **Philip Cunningham** and **William Johnston**, led a march on Sydney by 266 Irish prisoners who had been working in labour gangs; they made their stand on a knoll which later became known as Vinegar Hill, and they were quickly subdued. **Cunningham** was badly wounded, then executed, and **Johnston** and other leaders hanged in chains, which was a special badge of disgrace. The insurgents had killed nobody, but had shouted for 'Death or Liberty', and had demanded ships to take them home. The uprising was ended swiftly, in bloody disorder; it was the only real mutiny of convicts to take place on the Australian mainland.

The Irish leaders at Vinegar Hill were men of experience, responsibility, even education. **Cunningham** was a skilled workman who acted as a supervisor of stonemasons; like other leaders, he had his own house. Why did they embark on an exercise which could never have been anything more than a brave gesture? The historian **Patrick O'Farrell** has seen the rebellion as ''not (one) of crushed desperation, but of sentiment and hope, forlorn maybe; an affirmation of spirit that, in less spectacular forms, continued to echo down the lower corridors of Australian history ... What drove the Irish was not only ideologies and dreams, but frustrations, sickness of heart, and impulses of affront: in a word pride, which in the circumstances of convictism ... expressed itself in grim determination not to be broken.''

"STAND AND DELIVER"

The convict system spawned the earliest bushrangers. They were mainly prisoners in Van Diemen's Land who had been provided with guns to hunt kangaroos and who decided to escape, form gangs and take their chances in the bush.

One of the most conspicuous of them was *Michael Howe*, who led a gang of 28 which cut a swathe of terror through Tasmania from *1812* to *1818*, stealing sheep, burning crops and houses.

He had a mountain hide-out, acquired a devoted Aboriginal 'wife', *Black Mary*, and fancied himself as a *Dick Turpin* who robbed from the rich and helped the poor. He was shot and beheaded by bounty hunters in *1818*.

Matthew Brady led a gang which shot its way out of countless police ambushes. He was finally captured by the settler *John Batman*, the future founder of Melbourne, and hanged in *1826*.

Alexander Pearce, who tended to eat his companions when he was very hungry on the run, was executed and also beheaded. *Martin Cash*, an Irishman who became the last romantic Tasmanian bushranger, absconded four times from Port Arthur and lived to the age of 67 as a farmer.

The gold rushes of the 1850s produced an outbreak of bushranging in Victoria, with most of the offenders still escapees from Van Diemen's Land. A resurgence occurred in New South Wales in the 1860s, and by this time the marauding bands were not only made up of ex-convicts. There were also 'wild colonial boys' . . . native-born Australians like *Frank Gardiner, Ben Hall* and *John Gilbert*.

Bold Jack Donahoe, celebrated in ballad as the wild colonial boy, was in fact an Irishman who had been sentenced to transportation for life in Dublin in *1823*. He was killed by a squad of mounted police in September *1830*.

Of all the bushrangers, the one most celebrated in myth was virtually the last . . . *Ned Kelly*. The *Kelly* gang — his brother *Dan, Steve Hart* and *Joe Byrne* — began its career in March 1878 when *Ned* wounded a constable who was attempting to arrest *Dan* for cattle thieving. In October the *Kellys* shot three policemen dead.

After they had committed audacious bank robberies in Euroa and Jerilderie, the governments of Victoria and New South Wales put a price of £8000 on the heads of the gang. This was enough to tempt *Aaron Sherritt*, one of their early associates and a former school mate of *Joe Byrne*, to turn informer. The gang promptly executed him.

The *Kelly* gang was

destroyed in a final shoot-out at Glenrowan on June 28 1880. The sole survivor was *Ned*, who was badly wounded. He was hanged in Melbourne in November 1880.

The young Steve Hart

Courtesy RHSV

Courtesy Rex Nan Kivell Collection

SPIDER LADY WITH A HORSE WHIP

Lola Montes, an exotic dancer who was born in Ireland as *Maria Gilbert*, travelled the goldfields of California and later Victoria, entrancing diggers with her daring "spider dance". They sometimes threw gold nuggets onto the stage to express their appreciation.

In Europe she had well-publicised affairs with such notables as *Franz Liszt* and *Alexandre Dumas*, but her visit to Australia in 1856 was mainly notable for her horse-whipping of the editor of the Ballarat Times, *Harry Seekamp*.

Seekamp had criticised her dance as immoral. *Lola Montes* set about him with a whip in the bar of the United States Hotel. He just happened to have his own whip with him, and used it on Miss *Montes*.

They exchanged many blows, and after they lost control of their whips they seized each other's hair. The crowd stopped the fight, and *Seekamp* retired to another bar.

The *1828* census of New South Wales, when the entire population amounted to less than 40,000, demonstrates the degree to which the Irish had invaded Australian society . . . and, in a sense, triumphed against ungenerous odds. Irish-born Catholics numbered about 8000, and another 2000 were colonial-born of Irish parentage. Of the 8000 Irish-born, 5000 were free, and only one in 10 had come to Australia as free settlers. That meant that 4500 were emancipated convicts, and they were doing fairly well. A quarter of the free Irishmen in the colony held land, livestock or both. A good number of the others were doing well in commerce, moving upstream in colonial society, establishing themselves as people of substance.

It was the gold rushes which accounted for one of the most formidable assaults on Australia by Irish immigrants. In one decade, between *1851* and *1860*, 101,000 of them came. Indeed, it has been argued that the Irish who migrated to Australia were more motivated — by the promise of gold, of land, of adventure, of some kind of prosperity — than those who headed for the United States. Certainly they had more reason to be committed: the distance involved, which suggested little hope of return, and the expense of the trip, made emigration to Australia a major decision. The Irish went to America comparatively late, largely as a result of the famine of *1845–50*, and they gravitated to cities where the power structure was already established. The Irish immigrants were in Australia at the beginning, as convicts; they took opportunities on the land, and they shared, however modestly at first, in the building of a society and an economy.

Along the way they gave the country heroes . . . all kinds of individuals who made diverse contributions to the nation's tensions, its cultures, its conflicts, and ultimately its history. People like the bushrangers, so celebrated in pub ballads, **Bold Jack Donahoe** and the **Wild Colonial Boy** ('Jack Duggan *or maybe* Doolan *was his name*'); like **Captain Moonlight, Matthew Brady** and the man who inspired one of the most laudatory phrases in the Australian language . . . 'as game as **Ned Kelly**'. People like **Robert O'Hara Burke**, who made his great contribution to history by perishing, lost and brave, while trying to slice his way across the heart of the continent with a carnival of camels. Like the prizefighters **Les Darcy** and **Larry Foley**, the political leaders **Scullin** and **Lang**, the Eureka Stockade rebellion leader **Peter Lalor**, the reformist judge and architect of industrial arbitration **Henry Higgins**. Like **Daniel Mannix**, the Roman Catholic Archbishop of Melbourne who was at the core of many great Australian controversies, but none more bitter or significant than the brawl with Prime Minister **Billy Hughes** during World War One over conscription.

Courtesy National Library

Like the Irish, the Chinese flooded into Australia during the gold rush years. They had arrived first in large numbers in the **1840**s as an alternative source of cheap labour to convicts ... at a time when the transportation system was being dismantled. About 2000 coolies came from Amoy, Hong Kong and Singapore at that time, mainly to work as shepherds. The squatters who employed them treated them badly, sending them thousands of kilometres inland, giving them shorter food rations than white workers, paying them about a quarter the normal wage. When news of the gold rush came, the Chinese labourers had no compunction about deserting their flocks and heading for the goldfields.

The gold rush began with the discovery of the precious metal near Bathurst in New South Wales in **1851**, but it accelerated to a frantic degree with discoveries in Victoria, in the same month that the colony was formally separated from NSW. Work on farms stopped; businesses closed in the cities; arriving ships were left unloaded. The fortune seekers came from the United States, the British Isles, continental Europe, all parts of Australia ... and China.

The Californian gold rush of **1849** had attracted 35,000 Chinese, and by June **1854** there were 2000 Chinese on the Victorian goldfields. Fifteen months later there were 17,000. By **1859** 40,000 Chinese were at work in Victoria, and a year or so later another 10,000 in NSW; mostly they worked over rejected mullock heaps in abandoned fields, seeking gold that white miners had missed in their urge to move to fresher, richer finds. Sometimes, when things were bad, the white miners returned to fields they had left; when they found the Chinese in possession, in tented camps, they became violent. The Chinese wore their national costumes, carried their belongings on eight-foot poles stretched from shoulder to shoulder, smoked opium, wore pigtails, set up joss houses, worshipped effigies and were accused of wasting water. Mostly, though, they offended the whites because they reaped rewards by fossicking where others had

△ The lure of gold; Chinese arrive at Cooktown, Queensland.

▽ Two Chinese coins dating from the 17th century found on the goldfields of the Palmer River, Queensland.

Courtesy Stan Greaves, Cairns, Qld

Illustrated Sydney News, 4 September, 1880

△ *A plaque at Robe commemorating the landings of Chinese diggers.*

△ *Lambing Flat today. Nothing but memories and ghosts.*

failed, and they were content with minimum income for maximum labour. Racially, culturally, economically, they were despised . . . and also feared.

The Victorian government, alarmed at the inflow of Chinese and the fear that most of the gold they were finding was being sent back to China, imposed a tax of £10 a head on every Chinese landing at a Victorian port. The Chinese had a fine communication system; the next shipment of immigrants from China simply landed at Port Adelaide, and marched across the Victorian border. Then the Chinese learned about another little port at Robe, much nearer the Victorian border. During 1856 and 1857 some 15,000 Chinese landed there, some of them jumping off ships and swimming ashore. From there they took off, following white guides and carrying about 80 kilograms apiece on their shoulder poles, for the goldfields.

Silhouetted across the sky in their bamboo hats and their single-file crocodile lines, they offered a strange dusk sight to shepherds on plains in western Victoria.

On July 4 1857, a mob of 120 European miners used pick handles and wooden clubs to attack a Chinese camp of 2400 in the Buckland River valley, driving them from the diggings; they burnt 500 tents and a new temple, stole thousands of dollars worth of gold and bashed the Chinese. Dozens of similar riots occurred, with the Chinese offering little resistance.

The pigtail was imposed on the Chinese people by Manchu conquerors in 1644 as a symbol of shame and disgrace, but over the next two centuries it became something of a symbol of pride. It was said that a man without one would have no peace after death.

The Chinese on the Australian goldfields generally wore pigtails, but were sometimes forced to lose them. In one jail, the superintendent ordered that all inmates should have their hair cropped short every month; this meant that Chinese prisoners had to have their pigtails cut.

The family of one such convict, *Ping Shang*, wrote to the authorities from Hong Kong, pointing out that if he was to lose his pigtail his sentence might as well be increased heavily from 12 months. They said that if he returned home, he would be unemployable without a pigtail, and would in fact have to be hidden for years until he grew a new one. The plea succeeded; he was allowed to keep his pigtail.

Later Chinese arrivals on the goldfields coiled their pigtails, because these were seen by some miners as an invitation to violence. In the savage assault on Chinese miners at Lambing Flat in 1861, many Europeans set out to hack off as many pigtails as they could.

At Lambing Flat, near the NSW town of Young, between 2000 and 3000 white diggers attacked a Chinese tent town in July **1861**, rounding up the coolie miners with whips, knives and bludgeons as if they were cattle. They cut off pigtails and hoisted them on sticks as flags. A Sydney Morning Herald reporter wrote that pigtails were torn off "with the scalp attached". One miner returned to a Victorian goldfield with 27 pigtails attached to his belt, like so many trophies. Chinese who attempted to hide in their shafts were said to have been buried as white rioters filled them in.

The pattern of confrontation continued in Queensland in the **1860s** and **1870s** as miners invaded goldfields on the Fitzroy, Mary and Palmer Rivers. Up to 18,000 Chinese worked on the Palmer and its tributaries, outnumbering their European counterparts heavily. Notices appeared beside creeks: "Any Chinaman found past this point will be shot." The Chinese were regularly raided, both by white miners and by Aboriginals, who felt they were a threat to fishing grounds. One historian, **Hector Holthouse**, has written of a belief by cannibal Aboriginals that the Chinese tasted better than whites.

△
The rallying flag used by European diggers at Lambing Flat.

As published in The Truth, 27 March 1960

WHY WE MUST KEEP AUSTRALIA

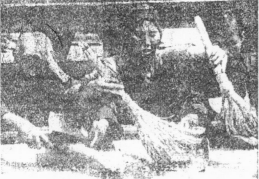

● It's a great day for the poverty-stricken Chinese when a rice truck makes a delivery ... After unloading, there's always the chance of a few sweepings to eke out a starvation diet.

WHITE

BY SPECIAL REP. DAVID PYNT ...

● I HAVE just returned from a tour of the Far East convinced beyond all doubt we MUST retain our "White Australia" policy.

Life, like labor, is so cheap in the Far East that any move to relax the strict laws on Asian immigration would mean the disappearance overnight of Australia's high standard of living.

The majority of people in these terribly over-crowded areas don't live—they just exist.

There are millions who have never heard of hygiene, schools, a home of their own—or even a day free from work.

They have never heard of the 40-hour week, unions, or holidays.

Judged on Australia's standard of living—a standard regarded as among the highest in the world—these people are un-civilised.

The greatest tragedy is that little can be done to help them.

The population is growing too fast (over a million a year in Chinese areas like Hongkong) and not enough schools, homes and hospitals can be built to accommodate them.

Any Australian seeing Hongkong for the first time would be appalled at the living standards.

People — even babies and youngsters — sleep in shifts. There is not enough time in a day for all to find even a floor to rest on.

Mothers, sometimes with two or three children, find a reasonably quiet street—if that is possible—and a piece of pavement is their home.

Many homeless Chinese move into the business section of Hongkong when workers finish for the day.

In one street a woman for the past few months has been placing her six-month-old baby in a cardboard box to sleep on the footpath at the entrance to a large business house. Her two-year-old child sleeps beside the box.

Inside the building, workers on the first floor can't use the toilet after 5 p.m.

A Chinese family takes over at that time, using the tiny space to sleep and eat.

A mile-long stretch in a Chinese area is said to be the most densely populated area in the world.

It is impossible to estimate how many live or exist there. Tens of thousands of men, women and children are herded together like sheep.

Refugees from Red China are flowing into Hongkong at a tremendous rate.

They have taken over huge sleep hills, which have mushroomed overnight into areas dotted with thousands of hastily built huts and canvas shelters.

The thought of being buried alive under landslides when the wet season starts in a few months hasn't even occurred to them. All that interests them is the present—and the fact they have a tiny piece of land to call their home.

Children, even as young as three and four, are working.

They rush to open car doors, helping out the occupants and whispering "careful" in the hope they will receive a few cents as a reward.

There is an army of shoe-shine boys, mostly under the age of 10, whose only possessions are boxes containing tins of polish and a few rags.

Every 10 or 15 yards you can find beggars—even women with babies on their backs—seeking a few pence to buy food.

The position in Communist China is no better. If you are too old to work you don't eat.

That is why the tens of thousands in Red China who have ended their working days have to rely on their children, relatives or friends in Hongkong to send money for food.

It is estimated that about £80,000 is sent from Hongkong to Red China each month for the aged to buy food and clothing.

The average Chinese man and woman knows only one thing: Work.

The tensions of the goldfields were aggravated as the output from the diggings declined. Victoria, Queensland, South Australia and New South Wales all took various actions to restrict Chinese immigration. The prejudice, based mainly on fear that it would be impossible for Australian labour to compete with harder-working, less-demanding Chinese workers, persisted through the late decades of the 19th century and culminated in 1901 in the passing of the Immigration Restriction Act, which was the vehicle for the White Australia policy. This policy had the effect of excluding non-European settlers.

About 3600 Pacific Islanders were repatriated, and 2500 allowed to stay in Australia, mainly in Queensland. Some 32,000 Chinese, already resident in Australia, remained, as did small communities of Afghans, Indians and Japanese.

That restrictive policy remained in force for more than 50 years; it was relaxed in the late 1940s, around the time Australia's great surge of post-war immigrants began. Further watering-down occurred in the 1950s and 1960s, and the policy was finally abolished in 1973.

Punch, 2 June 1888, National Library

"OUTSIDE, SIR! OUTSIDE!"

A cartoon from the late 19th century depicting Australia's fear of Asian immigration is echoed some seventy years later by this newspaper article.

Courtesy G. Dean

A SPECIAL BRAND OF INNOCENCE

Courtesy N.S.W. Public Library

△ "Our Don", every boy's hero of heroes.

△ Dame Nellie Melba, a glittering star.

To be a schoolchild in Australia in the late 1930s and at the beginning of the 1940s was to live in an endearingly innocent place at what seemed to be an uncomplicated time in history.

It could not of course be known then that Australia was close to the end of what might be called its Anglo-Saxon era. The atlas, opened at a double-page spread for the map of the world, looked to be positively daubed in reassuring red ... the red of Empire. Great chunks of lumpy Africa wore red, as did the inverted triangle of India, with the blob of (then) Ceylon below it, and the whole wide swathe of Canada slashed across the top of the North American continent. All kinds of imperial islands and archipelagoes cluttered the oceans, and to the north the Malayan peninsula and Singapore looked such impressive bastions, clad in the colour of the neighbourhood letter-box.

It was a confident enough time, a time before cynicism. Australia had sent off its young men to two world wars and endured a depression, and yet it remained so untouched by bitterness, maybe even by worldliness. It revered a quality called mateship, loved **Bradman**, **Melba** and **Opperman**, still lamented the untimely losses of **Phar Lap** and **Les Darcy**.

It played or watched sport on Saturdays, ate roast dinners on Sundays, and hung out the washing, propped on lines strung across backyards, on Mondays. It rolled its own. Its business was mostly primary produce, wool and wheat. On Friday nights it ate fish and chips, but adventurous souls sampled Chinese food, sometimes even with chopsticks. A new food arrived, and people watched it sizzle with onions on grills in the windows of shops run by men called **Bill** and **Bert**; the hamburger, like the chocolate malted and the Saturday matinee, had come to town. A decade or two later, the kind of people who watched minced beef cook would be looking at television sets in shop windows, and they would be even more fascinated.

For most people, it was possible then to move from one side of Melbourne or Sydney to the other, across all the inner suburbs, and not hear a word spoken of any language other than English. A thick coating of bland, comfortable homogeneity spread right across the nation. One country town looked much like another; there was always a Railway or a Royal Hotel, and a Greek steak 'n eggs cafe on the main street. The suburban greengrocers were mainly Italian, but in those car-less days there was another way to buy fruit and vegetables: to listen for the clip-clop that signalled the arrival nearby of the Chinese vendor. He came straight from his market garden, wearing a black cap and tunic and usually a wide grin, with a horse, a black-canopied wagon and a set of scales to weigh out his tomatoes, onions and potatoes. The corner-store grocer scooped servings of flour and sugar out of great sacks on his counter, and sometimes he handed out broken biscuits to small boys, from large rectangular tins with swallows and cockatoos on them.

Schoolchildren would assemble on Monday mornings around a flagpole, and they would recite: "I love God and my country, I will honour the flag, I will serve the King, I will cheerfully obey my parents, teachers and the laws." Thus pledged, they would march around the bitumen playground to the thick beat of a bass drum, the tinny rattle of kettledrums and the piping of flutes.

Occasionally it **was** possible to listen to other languages ... and not just the brogues that seemed to become trapped in some Scots and Irish families for generations after immigration. At one primary school in Elwood, Melbourne, a small boy used to carry the bass drum while his best friend, a Greek, thumped it with a cushion-headed stick. They climbed peppercorn trees, stole quinces and nectarines over back-lane fences, kicked rolled-up paper footballs, shared a very Australian boyhood ... with one essential difference.

The Greek boy went to Greek school on Saturday mornings, attended the Greek Orthodox church, wore Greek national costume — with a short bobbed skirt, and pompoms on the shoes — on special occasions. He and his brother and sisters spoke Greek at home, because their mother knew little English. In her kitchen, the Australian boy learned to speak some basic Greek, and he was told about the awful behaviour of conquering Turks. Beside the sink, he learned that another culture existed. It had been transplanted from a lost village in Greece to a suburb of Melbourne, and it flourished in that kitchen.

On May 24 the primary schools would celebrate Empire Day. Little cardboard Union Jacks would be handed out, for pinning on shirts and blouses, and under the flagpole there would be speeches about the red parts on the map, and then much marching to the drums and flutes. Afterwards the children would be taken in buses and trams to Luna Park, where the Union Jack pinned to their breast entitled them to free rides. They would snigger at their own grotesque trick-mirror images in the Giggle Palace, hurtle along the fearful Big Dipper route, skid down the Jack and Jill slide, and try to scare each other with strange whoops in the darkened River Caves. Exciting stuff, and sometimes afterwards they were a little sick from all the rides and gluttonous serves of sticky fairy floss. Thus they made their once-a-year salute to the British Empire.

△ "... another culture existed."

Courtesy Horizon/Serge Golikov

△ Luna Park: behind the grotesque face fairy floss and thrills.

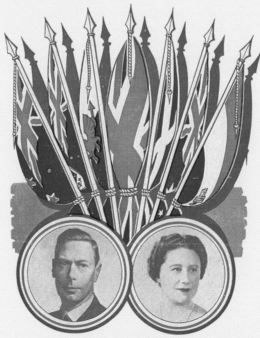

◁ Australia's innocence and Britain's Empire — the 30s and 40s saw their end.

Courtesy Australian War Memorial

△ *U.S. and Australian troops march down Elizabeth St. Sydney — a common foe but sometimes angry enemies.*

△ *Refugees in Europe — "reffos" in Australia.*

As the forties began, new kids arrived at some of the bigger high schools. They had strange names, wore jackets trimmed across the pockets with leather, carried satchels that buckled and looked positively out-of-place beside the Gladstone bags carried by Australian boys, and they came from places like Breslau, Warsaw, Budapest, Krakow, Leipzig, Prague and Bremen. They were good students, reserved and serious of manner, little addicted to the playing of games. Their eyes were often dark, and sometimes they seemed to smoulder; they were mainly Jews whose families had fled from ghettos, from religious and political oppression, even from labour camps. They gave a fresh dimension to the newspaper headlines about **Hitler** and **Mussolini**. They were **victims**. Behind their backs, though, people called them 'reffos'. In St. Kilda some of them opened bakeries, and crammed shop windows with exotic cakes, biscuits and confections ... not far down the road from those other dispensers of fashionable new food, **Hamburger Bert** and **Hamburger Bill**.

The public mood of those days remained fairly xenophobic. The new arrivals from Europe, the Greek cafe proprietors, the Italian greengrocers and the Chinese market gardeners were tolerated well enough, but they were expected not to exert their difference too much. On a bus or a tram, when two Europeans were talking animatedly in their own tongue, interruptions would come from middle-aged passengers who could tolerate this situation no longer: "You're in Australia now, mate. Why don't you speak English like the rest of us?" Was it suspicion? Inferiority complex? Maybe a little of both, and somehow inherent, a product of generations of distant sameness. Vaguely such incidents recalled another time in Australia ... in **1800**, when a whole crew of Irishmen who had been talking in Gaelic were brought to trial on that basis alone; it had been assumed to uncomprehending eavesdroppers that they must have been plotting, planning seditious acts.

The beginning of the end of the British era coincided with the intrusion of an outside culture on Australia. It was not planned; it was just the way the cards of history happened to fall. The war into which Australia had entered so bravely in **1939** was going badly; by late **1941** the most notable feature of the nation was its sheer vincibility. Those fine bastions to the north, Singapore and the Malayan peninsula, had capitulated quickly to the invading Japanese. The capital ships **HMS Repulse** and **HMS Prince of Wales** had just been sunk, and the Royal Navy, our traditional protector since the days of **Governor Phillip**, was clean out of Pacific muscle. With the fall of Singapore, Australia lost an entire army division, and its three other fighting divisions were all occupied with the Germans and Italians in the Middle East.

Courtesy Australian War Memorial

△
General Douglas MacArthur and Curtin; for Australia an historic partnership.

At this desperate moment in the nation's history the Prime Minister was **John Curtin**, a self-effacing man who wore a battered felt hat and suffered from defective eyesight; he used to be a journalist before he graduated to the less frenzied craft of politics. **Curtin** argued heatedly with the British leader, **Winston Churchill**, for the withdrawal of Australian troops from the Middle East to defend their homeland.

On December 17 **1941**, after an angry exchange of telegrams with **Churchill** and 10 days after the Japanese attacked Pearl Harbour, **Curtin** wrote a very frank article for the Melbourne Herald. In it he said:

"Without any inhibitions of any kind, I make it quite clear that Australia looks to America, free of any pangs as to our traditional links of kinship with the United Kingdom."

It was one of the most memorable statements ever made by an Australian leader, and it is interesting that it was written for a newspaper article, not uttered in some stirring speech. In such measured language, and so very sparely — in just 31 words — **Curtin** signalled a change in the navigation of Australia's foreign policy, and its history.

Even though **Curtin's** forthright statement will always be seen as a courageous break with the past and a visionary piece of military judgment, the truth is that the man had no choice. Saviours were in short supply in the Pacific in **1941**. No matter, though. What emerged was an incongruous partnership between the shy **Curtin** and the flamboyant, salad-chested **General Douglas MacArthur**. Theirs became one of the most significant double acts in Australian history.

A major cultural collision arrived, as the Australia of the early forties, that distant, simple place of seven million people, was engulfed over three years by more than a million American servicemen, who would take home with them 12,000 brides. Generally, the Australians liked the American invaders, although there were problems with their Australian counterparts, mainly (and predictably) over girls and disparate rates of pay.

At that traumatic time, Australia became aware of its aloneness, its vulnerability. The emotional rope which linked it to Britain had become frayed, and could never really be repaired. Sometime in the forties, between **Curtin's** announcement and the decision by a later government to pump in as many immigrants as possible from Europe, Australia's special brand of innocence departed. It could never return.

▽
A Melbourne girl with her American boyfriend . . . was she one of the 12,000 war brides?

Courtesy Herald & Weekly Times

Courtesy Horizon/Terreen Dawes

CHAPTER FOUR

OUT THERE

△ *Charles Darwin in 1840.*

THE PIONEER MERINOS

Sheep had come to Australia with the First Fleet, but it was the arrival in *1797* of the first Spanish merino sheep that offered the real cradle for an infant industry which would grow massively, until Australia became the world's number one supplier.

It happened because *King Charles IV of Spain* had given two merino rams and four ewes to the Dutch government, and these had in turn been sent to a *Colonel Gordon,* commander of the forces of the Dutch East India Company at the Cape of Good Hope; the intention was to allow him to establish a breeding stock.

In *1797* two British naval vessels called at Cape Town to take on supplies during a journey to New South Wales. *Colonel Gordon* had recently died, and his widow did not want to raise sheep.

She offered the two visiting captains 26 merinos at four guineas apiece. They pooled their money and bought the lot.

A number of the sheep perished on the voyage, but the survivors, owned by *Captain H. Waterhouse,* constituted Australia's pioneer merino flock.

An early observer of the Australian scene was the 26-year-old scientist **Charles Darwin**, *who was later to publish his theories on the evolution of living things in the most controversial book of the 19th century, Origin of Species. His impressions on the evolution of Australia, based on two months' observation in* **1836**, *were generally incisive — if not always enthusiastic.*

"Nothing but sharp necessity would compel me to emigrate," he wrote after looking hard in New South Wales at "a whole community ... rancorously divided into parties on almost every subject ... (and where) ... there is much jealousy between the children of the rich emancipist and the free settlers." And when his ship, **HMS Beagle**, *sailed he made it clear that he left Australia's shores "without sorrow or regret".*

Some of his perceptions, though, managed to scratch at the very essence of Australia. He quickly came to the conclusion that much of the colony's early prosperity could be attributed to the government's power, by use of forced labour, to open good roads. In fact the fine, 20-feet wide Great Western Highway, which cut through the peaks, cliffs and chasms of the Blue Mountains that had hemmed in the colony, was hewn by convicts promised a free pardon by **Governor Macquarie** *for a job finished on time. This became the largest, most important road of the continent, the pathway to Bathurst and beyond. Hundreds of convicts, working in gangs and sometimes in chains, created the three roads — the Great Western, the Great Northern and the Great Southern — which speared inland from the sea.*

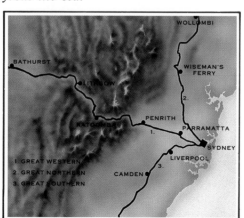

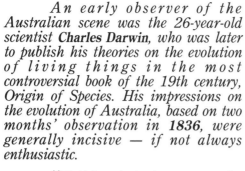

Courtesy Horizon/Australian Museum

Darwin *obviously found himself bored at dinner parties by the twin preoccupation of the locals with money and sheep. "The whole population," he wrote, "are bent on acquiring wealth. Amongst the higher orders wool and sheep-grazing form the constant subject of conversation." He noted the unending push by settlers in search of fresh pastures, and stressed the potential for making fortunes: "The capital of a person, without any trouble on his part, produces him treble interest to what it will in England, and with care he is sure to grow rich."*

These observations were perceptive. **Darwin** *was visiting New South Wales at a significant moment in its history, when the colony was feeling its muscles. The story of Australia in the early and middle decades of the 19th century was one of a community seeking to become richer, driven to push far, and then farther again. There existed a compulsion to strain against confinement, to unlock the land, to reach new frontiers which promised hope, opportunity and ultimately wealth. It was the notion of unlocking the land which motivated the squatters, miners, pastoralists and selectors, inspired the explorers, offered scope to the bushrangers and spurred the discovery of better communications, like the overland telegraph.*

Australia's history amounts largely to a study of isolation and the need to cope with it. The people about whom **Darwin** *wrote in the* **1830s** *were not only a long way from their parent country; they were busy creating a new kind of isolation, a loneliness which few*

Courtesy La Trobe Library

◁ *Far left — the plains around Bathurst today.*

◁ *Near left — the convicts pushing the road through the mountains that would open up this area.*

▽ *Fred Lowry*

"TELL 'EM I DIED GAME"

of them had known before. They were intent on moving into the vast empty spaces they knew were out there, towards the centre of this great continent.

The pressure to expand came first from settlers who felt wedged in by geography; their livestock were breeding, outgrowing the acres they had either bought or been granted; the pastures had been halted by the spine of low mountains that ranged north-south, roughly parallel to the east coast. At the time **Darwin** *was watching, Australia was going through a period of transition . . . turning itself into a place of commerce, with an economy based on wool and whaling, casting off its role as a huge penitentiary for England's unwanted.*

Whaling and sealing had been the major export industries in the early years, and even as late as **1833** *whaling remained the dominant form of trade. But the sheep were taking over; out beyond that rim of mountains was a great beckoning pasture, an expanse of grassland that was believed to be just about limitless. Of the livestock which would feed on it, sheep represented the way ahead. This was an age long before refrigeration, when beef would become a commodity for shipping away in bulk. The wool off the sheep's back replaced itself and was not perishable; most important of all, there existed a large and growing market for it in the mill towns of Yorkshire and the textile centres of Europe. It was a market offering prices which could justify the high cost of sending wool long distances overland, and then by sea to the other side of the world.*

The advances of the shepherds began after **Gregory Blaxland**, *a prosperous free settler from Kent, led two companions,* **William Lawson** *and* **William Charles Wentworth**, *on an expedition which found a way to cross that seemingly impassable barrier, the Blue Mountains.* **Blaxland** *was characteristic of the breed of settler referred to by* **Charles Darwin** *. . . obsessed with the potential for wool, hungry for more land and more wealth, unable to contain his steadily growing flock, even though he had been granted 4800 acres of rich pasture-land near Sydney. The crossing was made in* **1813**; *by* **1819** *24 flocks of sheep and 1400 cattle were grazing west of the mountains, and further west, some 150 miles from the coast, the little village of Bathurst was coming alive. The sheep continued to ooze steadily through the mountains, and by* **1825** *one third of the colony's sheep had made the crossing.*

The advance, and the economic promise that accompanied it, posed a problem for successive governors. Their prime task was the efficient, orderly running of a colony that was still, in those early decades of the century, an open prison with a vastly outnumbered army and constabulary. A concentrated settlement was much easier to supervise; a population which stretched itself thinly around the continent offered all kinds of invitation to bushrangers and other rogues. Efforts were made by the authorities to contain the spread, to impose 'limits of occupation' which were sanctioned areas of settlement within defined distances, and which themselves continued to grow larger around Sydney — but it was an impossible task. The advance developed into an unruly, leapfrog kind of invasion, as frantic in its way as the gold rush.

"Tell 'em I died game."
That was the sentiment of so many bushrangers, who saw themselves as defiant heroes, conforming to romantic ballads of the trade.
Often they did die game. They were young, too, as this sad table shows . . .

Black Caesar
shot dead, 32
Alexander Pearce
hanged, 34
Bold Jack Donahoe
shot dead, 24
Ben Hall
shot dead, 27
Johnny Dunn
hanged, 19
Matthew Brady
hanged, 27
Ned Kelly
hanged, 25
Johnny Gilbert
shot dead, 25
Steve Hart
shot dead, 22
Joe Byrne
shot dead, 23
Frederick Ward
(Captain Thunderbolt)
shot dead, 34
Andrew Scott
(Captain Moonlight)
hanged, 37
Dan Morgan
shot dead, 35
Michael Howe
shot dead, 33
Fred Lowry
shot dead, 27
Johnny Piesley
hanged, 28

△
*"The Swaggie" — a
romantic illustration.*

Courtesy La Trobe Library

△
*As the squatters
prospered, the grandeur and
opulence of their homes
became staggering.* ▷

To the land-grabbers who took
part in this headlong race towards open
space, occupation meant ownership. The
rush involved all kinds: scoundrels who
established themselves by stealing
someone else's animals, and reputable
people who already owned land
legitimately but felt disposed to take a lot
more. What they did to signal
possession was to erect shepherds' huts
and sheepyards. Usually, because it
suited the mood of the time, they took
more land than they needed; a man
whose flock warranted 5000 acres
might annexe 100,000 acres. They were
known as 'squatters', because the name
signified exactly what they were doing,
and the term was applied derisively at
first; but nobody took away the land they
grabbed and, over the years, as their
possession came to be legitimised, the
word lost any sense of stigma and even
came to denote a certain brand of
aristocracy.

"Up rode a squatter, mounted on
his thoroughbred," say the words of
Australia's essential song, Waltzing
Matilda, "Down came the troopers, one,
two, three . . .". They capture the sense of
squiredom, legality and even style that
the term came to embody. Many of the
squatters became land barons,
gentlemen with huge mansions, social

Illustrated Australian News 12 July 1875

△
"The Swaggie" — the reality was not romantic at all.

△
Thomas Henty . . . his family's illegal squatting near Portland Bay turned him into one of the richest pastoralists in Victoria.

*pretensions and political influence. They were tested over the years by droughts, floods, bushfires, disease and at times the wrath of Aboriginals, and many of them failed. But they seized millions of hectares of land, within the official borders of settlement and outside them, and by the end of the **1840**s the sheep lands of Australia stretched in a huge arc sweeping from South Australia to the semi-tropical Queensland coast; it was some 2200 kilometres long in its inner curve, and 650 kilometres across at its broadest. By that time Australia's sheep population numbered 18 million.*

*Some of the bolder squatting episodes were the more bountiful. In **1834** the **Henty** family, originally farmers from Sussex, sailed from Launceston with their own ark — a 57-ton schooner called **Thistle**. When they landed at Portland Bay after a punishing trip in wild seas, they had lost six working bullocks, two cows, two calves and 12 heifers. They settled illegally on the rich plains of the western district of what is now Victoria, a father, his wife and seven sons. When, in **1836**, the NSW Surveyor-General, **Thomas Mitchell**, took an expedition on behalf of the government to explore what was believed to be virgin land between the Murray River and the Bass Strait coast, he was astonished to find the audacious **Hentys** well established in control of a huge and flourishing pastoral enterprise. A thousand miles to the north, a 24-year-old Scot, **Patrick Leslie**, led 2100 sheep and 22 convicts to incredibly lush pastures in the Darling Downs.*

△
John Batman; from his land purchases sprang a colony.

▽
Batman's 600,000 acre purchase.

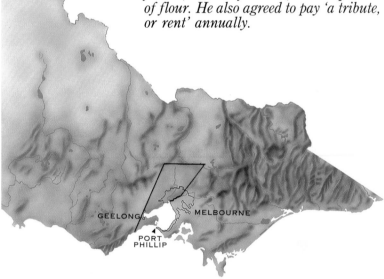

GEELONG   MELBOURNE

PORT PHILLIP

Courtesy La Trobe Library Collection

△
In just 50 years from Batman's purchase of land, the Melbourne Cup had become a grand event.

Not long after the **Henty** *expedition, other settlers and businessmen in Launceston and Hobart were speculating on the prospects of settlement at Port Phillip, which had been visited by* **Hamilton Hume** *and* **William Hovell** *in a bumbling sort of expedition in* **1824**. *A private 'Port Phillip Association' was formed by graziers in Van Diemen's Land, and in* **1835** *their representative,* **John Batman**, *35-year-old son of a convict, sailed into Port Phillip Bay. He solemnly purchased 600,000 acres of land — "as rich land as I ever saw in my life" — from the Aboriginals in residence. The payment: 20 pairs of blankets, 30 knives, 12 tomahawks, 10 looking-glasses, 12 pairs of scissors, 50 handkerchiefs, 12 red shirts, 4 flannel jackets, 4 suits of clothes, and 50 pounds of flour. He also agreed to pay 'a tribute, or rent' annually.*

The government in Sydney ruled that all private occupation of the district was illegal, but by the time it could make any attempt to enforce the order Melbourne and Geelong were already substantial and growing towns. The government was forced to accommodate the illegal settlements, *and by* **1839** *to declare Port Phillip a separate district with its own superintendent. By* **1840** *there were 10,291 people in the district, and before too long most of them were pushing for separation from New South Wales, giving seed to a rivalry which would be lasting and sometimes bitter.*

Inevitably, the spread of the squatters encompassed South Australia, whose rich soil and abundant pastures had delighted the explorer **Charles Sturt** *when he first saw it in* **1830**. *The new colony had been founded in* **1836** *in a warm glow of idealism by a private firm, the South Australian Company, and settled first on Kangaroo Island by British immigrants. The earliest aspirations were high, even a little pious: South Australia's growth would be planned and orderly (unlike that of New South Wales); its agricultural and economic development would be systematic, with a fixed uniform price for land; it would foster religious liberty; its immigrants, screened and chosen in England, would be sober, young married or marriageable people of both sexes, chosen in about equal numbers to avoid the social problems which occurred in New South Wales; no convicts would be transported to the colony; the Aboriginals would be assisted into voluntary embrace of the Christian religion; when the population reached 50,000, self-government would be introduced.*

Things did not of course work out that way. Before too long some of the fine principles were sinking. Speculators tried to cash in, religious arguments broke out, high officials quarrelled about the site (and the name) of the capital, governors were recalled, immigration was suspended, there was trouble with the natives, the colony went bankrupt. Immigrants from the 'pickpocket' colonies of New South Wales and Van Diemen's Land arrived, among them time-expired and pardoned convicts, mixed with a number of runaways. One ex-convict named **Magee** *achieved the distinction of becoming the first criminal tried, convicted and executed in the ambitious new colony; he fired a pistol at a lawman during a break-in, and was strung up from a gum tree in North Adelaide.*

The advance of the squatters from New South Wales was certainly not part of the grand development plan, but it signalled a welcome reversal in economic fortune. Further prosperity came to South Australia from other events unenvisaged by the planners: The discovery and subsequent mining of copper at Kapunda and on the Burra Burra Creek, and the invention by **John Ridley**, Australia's first miller, of a reaping machine which reduced the number of workers needed for harvest. After the success of the sheep squatters and copper miners, markets for wheat were found in Adelaide, then other parts of Australia and later Singapore; by the mid-1840s, after a faulty start, South Australia was beginning to fulfil the founding dream of becoming one of the first agricultural colonies in the world. The success of the **Ridley** stripper was to be followed by a positive explosion of technological innovation in South Australia ... the first in the colonies. Inventions in agricultural machinery included the "stump jump" plough, the "mulleniser" (a log roller which cleared difficult scrub in the Mallee country) and later a complete harvester, which stripped, winnowed and bagged in one process. Australia's first agricultural college would be established in South Australia in **1884**.

The Swan River colony in Western Australia had also been established (in **1829**) amid high hopes and a desire to keep out convicts. The idea was that land should be granted to settlers in proportion to the capital they invested in the colony. The land turned out to be miserable and unyielding, and labour resources were few. Some settlers headed back to England, and others to the convict colonies in the east. In **1846**, six years after the transportation system to New South Wales had been abandoned, the despairing West Australian settlers begged the British Government to turn the place into a penal colony. In **1850** it obliged, and the shipments continued until **1868**. Finally there was a source of labour to build bridges and roads ... and particularly to the port of Fremantle, 12 miles from the site of the new capital.

By mid-century, the unlocking process had resulted in the opening up (and closure after 11 years) of a settlement at the extreme north-central tip of the continent, called Port Essington. The island of Van Diemen's Land, second oldest of the colonies, had no worthwhile land 'out there', but the settlers were making the best use of what they had. The colony grazed sheep, grew wheat, possessed flour mills, breweries and tanneries; Hobart was an important port for wool, whaling, rope and sail making and shipbuilding. In the Port Phillip District, along the southern coast of New South Wales, the main port serving the squatters was Geelong — but Melbourne was growing fast as a town of merchants and dealers. The spread in Queensland had been led by the squatting rush to the Darling Downs, but now the settlers were soaking further west and north.

Subsidised immigration, which of course involved a selection process, was beginning gently to correct the early imbalance of the sexes. By **1850**, only 20 years after a time when males outnumbered females by three to one, Australia had only 143 males to every 100 females, although the disparity was greater in the adult population. By **1900** there would be only 110 males for every 100 females, and by **1916** females in Australia would be as numerous as males.

△ A stump-jump plough; the 1840s modern technology.

△ Fremantle today; a far cry from the hardships of the early settlement.

Courtesy Horizon/Margaret Olah

△ Van Diemen's Land or Tasmania; sheep are still of major importance.

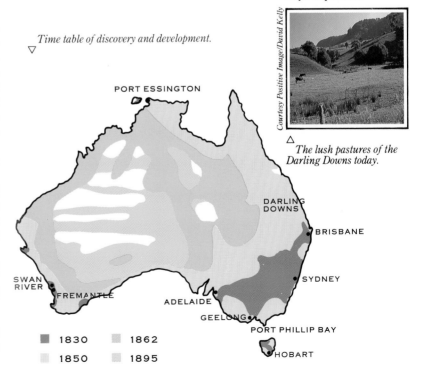

△ The lush pastures of the Darling Downs today.

Courtesy Positive Image/David Kelly

Time table of discovery and development. ▽

PORT ESSINGTON

SWAN RIVER

FREMANTLE

ADELAIDE

DARLING DOWNS

BRISBANE

SYDNEY

GEELONG

PORT PHILLIP BAY

HOBART

1830	1862
1850	1895

Courtesy National Library

△
Ernest Giles

Courtesy National Library

△
Charles Sturt

Courtesy Mitchell Library

△
Edward John Eyre

Courtesy Mitchell Library

△
Edmund Kennedy

The forward scouts of the great pastoral invasion were the explorers. Australia's great phase of inland exploration lasted from the crossing of the Blue Mountains in 1813 until the final desert journey in 1876 of Ernest Giles, who described himself as "the last of the Australian explorers". By the time it began the whole coastline had been reasonably defined; now there was a desire to fill in the massive blanks between the oceans. All kinds of botanical and geological wonders awaited discovery, but the motivation for early exploration was less concerned with a quest for knowledge than a simple desire to expand the farm.

What kind of people were the explorers? About many of them there was a nobility of purpose, a sense of splendid mission. Some, like Leichhardt, possessed a certain heroic madness. Some, like O'Hara Burke, were gloriously vulnerable, sadly bereft of bushmanship. Others, like Eyre and Sturt and Stuart, were orderly, efficient, disciplined and utterly tenacious. All of them, whether egotistical or jealous of their rivals or just plain curious, were essentially adventurous souls who between them solved the abiding mysteries: what was out there, beyond the dry horizons?; how big were the deserts, the jungles, the bushlands?; did an inland sea really exist?; why did the rivers flow inland instead of emptying into broad oceans?

For one explorer, Charles Sturt, the notion of a vast inland sea became almost an obsession. Such a body of water was one of the great geographical myths of early Australia: it began as something of a hunch by William Dampier, and was speculated on by such respected discoverers as Matthew Flinders. Sturt, who arrived in Sydney in 1827 in charge of an army detachment on a convict ship, made two significant river expeditions, the second of which followed the Murray all the way and led to the foundation of Adelaide. Then, in 1844, he marched off optimistically from Adelaide with 15 men and a whaleboat to seek his inland sea . . . and finally, after six agonising months in which his party was punished by drought and scurvy, he gave up. His dream died in the Simpson Desert.

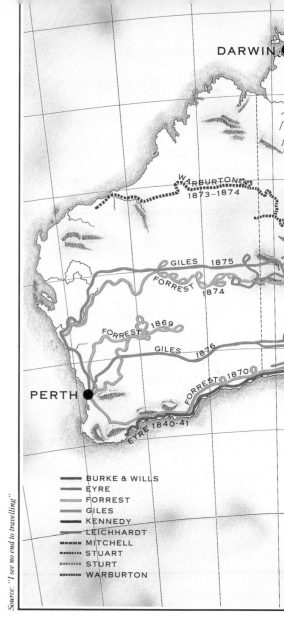

Source: "I see no end to travelling"

There were others who sought a great river, a kind of northern Nile, or maybe a western Mississippi. Edward John Eyre, at the age of 25, was convinced he must find one as he trudged 1000 miles from Adelaide to Albany in Western Australia, seeking an overland stock route. He did not once see running water, and came close to perishing in hot winds and stinging sands after Aboriginal guides murdered his companion, John Baxter, and fled with his food supplies and firearms. His was an incredible journey, the first such east-west crossing, and one which showed pastoralists where stock could not be taken. Thomas Mitchell and George Grey searched in vain for a northern river, and the myth remained until Ernest Giles finally demolished it with his crossings of the continent from east to west in 1875 and west to east in 1876. Between them Giles, Peter Warburton and John Forrest established

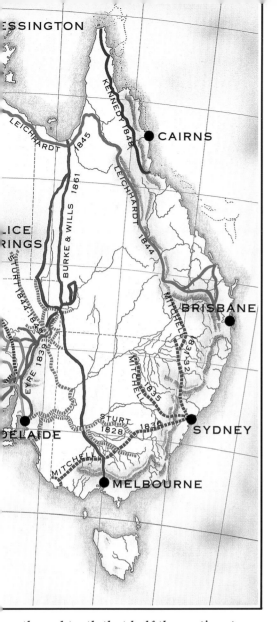

△
Ludwig Leichhardt

△
Peter Warburton

△
John Forrest

the sad truth that half the continent was virtually desert.

For the explorers, the hazards came from the elements, starvation, illness in the form of scrub typhus and scurvy, native attacks and the pure occupational risk of getting lost. Brave young **Edmund Kennedy**, seeking to conquer North Queensland jungles, was speared to death by natives; his party of 13 was tracked by day and night by hostile Aboriginals, and only three survived. The ornithologist **John Gilbert**, a member of **John Gould**'s bird-collecting team, was speared to death during **Ludwig Leichhardt**'s first mission, from Brisbane to Port Essington. So was the botanist **Richard Cunningham**, in **Thomas Mitchell**'s party, near the present town of Narromine.

Leichhardt received a triumphant welcome when he returned

by sea to Sydney from his first expedition. "No king could have been received with greater joy or affection," he wrote. He made one more foray, heading out into the Central Australian deserts to be lost forever. It has never been known whether he and his party were killed by Aboriginals or died of starvation. The mystery has intrigued generations of Australians, and inspired one great novel, **Patrick White**'s *Voss*. Search parties led by other explorers, like **A. C. Gregory** and **John Forrest**, found no traces as they crisscrossed great tracts of the north, but still managed to contribute to geographical knowledge.

Of all the exploring tragedies, though, none has so entrenched itself in the national psyche as the fate of the Irish mounted trooper **Robert O'Hara Burke** and his younger companion **William Wills**. **Burke**, a brave man but with no experience in bushcraft, organisation or exploration, set out from Melbourne in August **1860** to slice his way vertically across the heart of the continent. It was an expedition conceived in some haste by the wealthy colony of Victoria, jealous of the exploratory achievements of South Australia and anxious to sponsor a north-south crossing before one was made by the dour, gritty Scot, **John McDouall Stuart**. **Burke** in fact did manage to lunge to the Gulf of Carpentaria, but, through bumbling and bad liaison, he and **Wills** perished on their return trip. Their fate inspired fine literature and art, but the truth was that the journey achieved little for science, exploration or pastoral settlement.

Stuart, much more careful and methodical than **Burke**, made one thrust after another, until he was able first to plant a Union Jack in the centre of the continent, and later make a wholly successful north-south crossing. His achievements are seen by many as the most significant in Australia in land exploration. One unlikely legacy of his crossing of the continent was ... a string of telegraph poles. The Overland Telegraph Line, which opened in **1872**, linking Australia with the telegraphic systems of the world, followed **Stuart**'s route through the centre.

Courtesy Mitchell Library

"MORE WONDERFUL EVERY TIME..."

In 1873, as he travelled with camels through the spinifex country of the central desert, the explorer W. C. Gosse saw before him a granite hump. He climbed a hill, and looked upon the rock that would become one of Australia's greatest tourist attractions.

"What was my astonishment," he wrote, "to find it was one immense rock rising abruptly from the plain." He called it Ayers Rock, after *Sir Henry Ayers*, who was then premier of South Australia. Its ancient Aboriginal name was Uluru.

On July 20 1873 Gosse and an Afghan companion tried to climb the sheer sides of the great monolith. He battled for a long time, finally reached the summit, and later walked all around the base.

"This rock," he wrote a week later, "appears more wonderful every time I look at it."

Courtesy Reg Morrison/Weldon Trannies

Courtesy South Australian Archives

Courtesy Steve Parish

Courtesy Mitchell Library

AFGHANS, CAMELS AND THE INLAND

Several hundred Afghans who immigrated in the second half of the 19th century played an important part in the opening up of Australia's harsh, arid interior.

These people, who worked as camel drivers and were known generally as Ghans, were not in fact all from Afghanistan. They came also from Rajastan, Baluchistan, West Pakistan, Egypt, Iran and Turkey.

Common to all the ethnic groups embraced as Ghans was their Muslim religion and their familiarity with the Pushtu language.

Although camels were brought to Australia as early as 1840, it was not until the expedition of *Burke* and *Wills* in 1860–61 that they were seriously considered for use in the interior. With the Afghans as drivers and breeders, they carried supplies and mail to remote settlements, including cattle stations and goldfields in Western Australia. They proved able to cross areas inaccessible to horses and bullocks.

Afghans and their camels supported the construction of such projects as the Overland Telegraph Line, from Port Augusta in the south to Darwin in the north, the Central Australia Railway and the water pipeline to the West Australian goldfields; they were involved in the surveys for the building of the Trans-Australian Railway.

By 1900, there were about 6000 camels and more than 390 drivers throughout Australia. Most of the Afghans remained, with government approval, after the introduction of 'White Australia' immigration legislation in 1901.

Courtesy National Library

THE SCOT WHO REACHED THE CENTRE

Edward J. Eyre set out from Adelaide in 1840 carrying a silken flag which he hoped to plant in the centre of Australia. *Sturt, Mitchell, Leichhardt, Gregory* and *Tolmer* were other explorers who tried to reach the very centre . . . and failed.

On April 21 1860, 72 years after *Governor Phillip* landed at Botany Bay and less than 24 years after the first white settlers arrived in South Australia, three men did reach the centre. They were 1200 miles from Adelaide and 100 miles north of the Tropic of Capricorn.

Their leader, *John McDouall Stuart*, a Scot who stood 5ft. 6in., wrote a note which he put in a bottle, then covered with a cone of stones. The note, found and made public 11 years later, said:

◁ John McDouall Stuart and party, consisting of two men and himself, arrived here from Adelaide on Saturday evening, the twentyfirst day of April 1860, and have built this cairn of stone and raised the flag to commemorate the event at the top of Mount Sturt. The centre is about two miles south-south-west at a small gum creek, where there is a tree facing south.
John McDouall Stuart
William Darton Kekwick
Benjamin Head
21st of April 1860
Centre of Australia.

Stuart called the place after his old expedition commander, *Charles Sturt*. The name was later changed to Central Mount Stuart.

"I MAY LIVE FOR FOUR OR FIVE DAYS . . ."

William Wills, second-in-command to *Robert O'Hara Burke* in the fateful expedition from Melbourne to the Gulf of Carpentaria, was 27 when he died at Cooper Creek in 1861. He was the son of a surgeon who had a practice in Ballarat.

Wills was the only member of the party to keep a proper record of events. He accompanied *Burke* on the sprint from Cooper Creek to the Gulf, and again through the desperate journey back . . . during which their companion *Charlie Gray* died, and they lost four of their six camels and their only horse.

Burke, Wills and *John King* staggered back to Cooper Creek, weak and exhausted, just seven hours after the base party had abandoned the camp. The party had waited four months; *Burke* had taken only enough supplies for three months on the trek north.

By the end of June 1861, both *Burke* and *Wills* were dead. An extract from *Wills*'s final diary entry, dated June 26:

"Nothing now but the greatest good luck can save us; and as for myself I may live four or five days if the weather continues warm. My pulse is at forty-eight, and very weak, and my legs and arms are nearly skin and bone. I can only look out like *Mr. Micawber* for 'something to turn up'; but starvation on nardoo is by no means unpleasant . . ."

Courtesy Julian Ashton Art School

△ "The Prospector" by
Julian Ashton.

For a while Melbourne and Geelong looked like ghost towns. The newly appointed Governor, **Charles La Trobe**, reported to London that gold fever in Victoria had become so frenzied that military reinforcements were needed. Of Melbourne, he wrote: "In some of the suburbs not a man is left."

The procession of events had begun in February **1851** when **Edward Hammond Hargraves**, a veteran of the Californian gold rush of '49, found gold near Bathurst. The news was withheld for a few months, but by May a rush had begun, and with it a drift of settlers from the new colony of Victoria. This was such a serious development that leading citizens formed a Gold Discovery Committee, offering rewards for discoveries within 200 miles of Port Phillip. By July the first Victorian find was made at Clunes by another veteran of California, and this was swiftly followed by others at Bendigo, Ballarat and Castlemaine. Suddenly the action was all on the Victorian diggings. By December of the same year there were 20,000 diggers spread out in camps in the midlands, and by the end of **1852** the Victorian population had swollen from 77,000 to nearly 170,000 in 18 months.

After the first frantic rush subsided, some sort of normalcy returned to Melbourne. A number of the citizens who had fled the city came to the conclusion that life on the goldfields was too primitive, that the making of fortunes was risky, that the diggings were places for brawny adventurers rather than clerks and shopkeepers. By January of **1852** enough men had returned from the goldfields to handle the season's shearing, and by March there were enough to bring in the harvest. The diggers' money was being spent largely in Melbourne, and it was circulating through the population. Saloonkeepers, tradesmen, landlords and property speculators did well, but the new prosperity asserted itself in the building of factories, roads, railways and all kinds of homes, from grand mansions to timber and canvas bungalows . . . as well as in the wearing by some of fancy waistcoats and bonnets, and rich silk dresses. Melbourne became the fastest-growing city in the world.

The gold rush, which began just after Victoria had separated officially from New South Wales, gave a bizarre new dimension to the growth pattern of Australia. In Melbourne ships were left unloaded, which often didn't cause great concern . . . because their crews had set off for the diggings, sometimes accompanied by their captains. Businesses closed, wives and cottages were deserted, shepherds left their flocks, often followed by their bosses.

On the diggings, conditions were nourishing a spirit of independence, equality and mateship. Towns like Ballarat were filled with optimistic armies of gold-seekers in brightly coloured shirts and moleskin vests, and honkytonk music bounced out from primitive swing-door saloons. There were Englishmen of all grades, from peasant labourers to noblemen with a past, Irish and continental refugees and rebels, ex-convicts and ex-soldiers, Californian 'fortyniners', Texans, New Englanders and Chinese ... great hordes of Chinese, whose very difference caused fear and ultimately discrimination. For the Europeans, though, the mining work was a great leveller. A man's background didn't matter; what counted was how hard he was prepared to work, and whether he was willing to help another in trouble. The shared hardship in this very equal society fostered a resentment of authority. The diggers felt they were being discriminated against by decisions of the New South Wales and Victorian governments to impose licence fees of thirty shillings a month on all people working on the diggings. They believed, with some justification, that the tax-collectors were often brutal, corrupt bullies, and that many of the troopers who took in charge diggers without licences were callous thugs.

All kinds of grievances and injustices culminated in the only armed rebellion by free citizens in Australia's history, the Eureka Stockade clash. The conflict occurred before dawn on December 3 1854, the morning after the miners met at Bakery Hill, Ballarat, and pledged loyalty to their leader, Peter Lalor. They flew a blue flag adorned with a Southern Cross, and around the flagpole they erected a flimsy wooden barricade of pushed-together dray and pit props. About 150 miners slept in the stockade overnight, and infantrymen, cavalrymen and troopers advanced on them. Some Californians on duty saw the troops and fired a volley, killing one private. Next came a furious charge by police and troopers, shooting and bayoneting, and in 20 minutes it was all over. Six men on the government side died, 34 miners were killed, and 114 were taken to jail in chains. The leaders, included Lalor, the Italian exile

Raffaello Carboni, the Hanoverian Frederick Vern and an American, James McGill. A jury later acquitted thirteen men of treason.

The rebellion led to the replacement of the hated monthly licence by a 'miner's right', costing only £1 a year. More than that, though, the uprising came to symbolise aggressive democracy ... a refusal to accept tyranny, and a preparedness if necessary to die for political rights.

The discovery of gold was one of the most significant events in Australian history. It forced the development of the country, propelling it from a vast collection of sheep runs into a modern nation. The ferment of the goldfields, and particularly Eureka, hastened the passage of civil liberties and democracy. The gold rush accelerated improvements in transport, communications and education, and it had a permanent effect on the progress of various colonies, either because they possessed gold or because they did not: Victoria prospered, Tasmania failed to do so. Melbourne, which had been a pastoral hamlet, became for a time the biggest city in Australia. By the end of the gold rush decade, there were 540,000 people in Victoria, more than half as many again as in New South Wales.

Courtesy National Library of Australia

Peter Lalor

"... If democracy means opposition to a tyrannical press, a tyrannical people, or a tyrannical government, then I have ever been, I am still, and will ever remain a democrat."

Letter to the Ballarat Star

Courtesy Queensland Newspapers

J. B. Chifley

"Eureka was more than an incident or a passing phase. It was greater in significance than the short-lived result against tyrannical authority would suggest. The permanency of Eureka in its impact on our development was that it was the first real affirmation of our determination to be the master of our own political destiny."

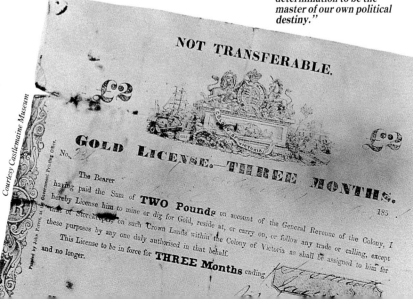

Courtesy Castlemaine Museum

NOT TRANSFERABLE.

GOLD LICENSE.— THREE MONTHS.

The Bearer having paid the Sum of **TWO Pounds** on account of the General Revenue of the Colony, I hereby License him to mine or dig for Gold, reside at, or carry on, or follow any trade or calling, except that of Storekeeper, on such Crown Lands within the Colony of Victoria as shall be assigned to him for these purposes by any one duly authorised in that behalf.

This License to be in force for **THREE Months** ending

and no longer.

185

CHAPTER FIVE

TILES IN THE MOSAIC

In the mosaic of Australia's past, some tiles stand out. They represent special moments, episodes, people, places. Some are associated with high achievement, or national glory. Some celebrate heroism, and Australia is a place which offers a certain brand of veneration to its heroes and heroines. Some tiles mark events which have moved with the passage of time into a zone called folklore. Some mark disasters, swift and savage, like floods and cyclones, or stealthy and self-inflicted, like the rabbit plague. Some are pathetic, bizarre, tragic, even funny. Once in a while just one event, like the assault on Broken Hill by two men with an ice-cream cart and a Turkish flag, manages to combine all of these components. Together they contribute, so very diversely, to our national story. Here are some of them.

FROM SIX COLONIES ... ONE NATION

For a large part of the 19th century there existed on the Australian continent six distinct colonies, buffered from each other by large tracts of fairly uninhabited country. They had been founded separately, and that was how they lived, each dependent on its capital city, each, in a sense, more directly linked with London than with each other. Enmities flourished, particularly between Melbourne and Sydney.

The arguments in favour of turning the colonies into one nation were compelling, and had been raised (and rejected) as early as **1847**. They had after all been settled by immigrants who brought with them the language of England, its laws, its values, its cultures, its traditions, its religious faiths. Gradually, among all the settlers and the early generations of native-born colonials, a spirit of sturdy independence was developing, blending well enough with a pride in English, Scottish and Irish origins. Traditional British attitudes were being refashioned a little in the new environment, and it was an environment that was generally uniform, in whichever colony the process was occurring. The settlers had a great deal in common, no matter how far away from each other they lived, and over the years they began to see themselves as Australians, rather than just as

Queenslanders or Victorians or New South Welshmen. So it happened that, in the minds of many men and women, the feeling of an Australian togetherness was evolving, long before the nation formally came together.

Apart from any sense of identity, a number of practical reasons combined to offer a strong case for federating the colonies. Defence was a factor. Ever since the Crimean War **(1853–56)**, there was a consciousness of vulnerability to sudden attack. Australians were suspicious of the Russians, the French, the Germans, the Japanese and the Chinese. No single colony could hope to operate an effective defence force. If there was to be a navy, if there was to be some concerted attempt at vigilance over the Australian coastline, it could occur only through a single, national government. The last British garrison soldier left Sydney in **1870**.

Then there was the matter of trade. The customs duties levied by each colony on the others' goods served increasingly as a nuisance, at a time when Sydney, Melbourne, Brisbane and Adelaide were linked by telegraph (in the **1860s**) and by railroad (in the **1880s**), and when all the colonies were keen to develop markets. One politician summed up a certain mood of self-interest about the project: "We shall create a glorious nation and meat will be cheaper."

There was no doubt that immigration policies needed a federal approach, as did foreign relations generally, and the supervision of postal and telegraphic communications. In **1889**, in the little town of Tenterfield near the Queensland border, the NSW Premier, **Sir Henry Parkes**, then 74 years old with a beard that flowed like a great white napkin, made a speech which stressed the need to federate. It has been suggested often that **Parkes** had slightly cynical motives ... that he had run out of policies and needed to establish a new political base. No matter. His speech touched a national nerve at just the right moment, so effectively that **Parkes** became known as 'the Father of Federation', even though he was to die five years before the great moment came.

In **1890** the governments of all the colonies sent representatives to Melbourne to discuss means of achieving federation, and the following year a National Australasian Convention met in Sydney. They talked for 38 days, under the leadership (following an injury to **Parkes** in a horse-cab accident) of **Sir Samuel Griffith**, 46, a Welsh-born barrister who became Queensland's first Premier and would be Australia's first Chief Justice. First they decided to found a Commonwealth of Australia; the next move, they agreed, would be to draft a constitution. Much haggling followed, between the larger and the smaller colonies, the protectionists and the free traders, the archrivals Sydney and Melbourne and the various political parties.

A problem which tested the framers of the constitution was the need to reconcile the democratic principle of 'one vote, one value' with the desire to give each state equal rights. The smaller states wanted no part of a great central government, in which their representatives would be vastly outnumbered. At the time New South Wales and Victoria contained about twice as many people as all the other four colonies; Tasmania's population was less than one-eighth that of New South Wales. What finally emerged was a plan for a federal system of government, rather like that in the United States. There would be two houses of parliament ... one elected on the basis of population alone, the other (the upper) on the basis of equal representation for each state.

Finally, in **1898**, steered to a large degree by New South Wales's **Edmund Barton**, who was to become Australia's first Prime Minister, representatives of all the colonies agreed on a constitution. It was **Barton** who coined the slogan "a nation for a continent and a continent for a nation".

Two referendums were held to allow all electors in the colonies to pass judgment on the constitution that meant federation. In June **1898** voters in Victoria, South Australia and Tasmania voted overwhelmingly to accept it, but in New South Wales the

Courtesy Weldon Trannies

IN CELEBRATION OF THE OPENING

PARLIAMENT of the COMMONWEAL of AUSTRALIA

To meet Their Royal Highnesses
The DUKE and DUCHESS of CORNWALL & YORK

His Majesty's
MINISTERS of STATE for AUSTRALIA
have the honor to invite

Mr. Colton M.L.A. & Mrs. Colton

to an Evening Reception at the
Exhibition Building MELBOURNE,
on the 9TH of May 1901, at 8 o'clock.

Courtesy Mitchell Library

Courtesy Weldon Trannies

vote was 71,595 in favour and 66,228 against; the NSW government had insisted that a vote of 80,000 affirmative votes would be needed for the referendum to be passed. Western Australia and Queensland had chosen to stay out. Advised of the decision to reject federation, the author **Rudyard Kipling**

wrote: "If you want to hurry up federation, you ought to make a syndicate to hire a few German cruisers to bombard Sydney, Melbourne and Brisbane for 20 minutes; there'd be a federated Australia in 24 hours."

Before the next referendum in June *1899*, NSW received an assurance that the national capital would be located in that state, but not within 100 miles of Sydney. This time Queensland joined in, and a majority in five states voted Yes. Western Australia, which had taken a 'don't know' position through most of the federation debate, decided at the last moment to join the others, mainly because of pressure from goldfields communities.

◁
*Edmund Barton,
Australia's first Prime
Minister.*

◁
*Sir Henry Parkes, "The
Father of Federation".*

Courtesy National Library of Australia

Courtesy National Library of Australia

So it happened that on the first day of the 20th century, Australia became a nation. The Commonwealth of Australia was proclaimed on January 1, **1901**, and more than half a million people thronged into Sydney — the place that **Captain Phillip** had chosen as a penal colony 113 years before — to celebrate. There had been rain, thunder and lightning through New Year's Eve, and the thousands of flags in the city were heavy and sodden, but the day itself was brilliant; Sydney was decorated as never before, the brass bands were out early, and a great uniformed procession stretched for two miles through the streets. Dragoons, Lancers, Lifeguards, Hussars, Maoris, Gurkhas, Sikhs, all marched below banners which proclaimed such slogans as 'the United States Welcomes United Australia' and 'One People, One Destiny'.

Queen Victoria died that same month, on January 22. When she took the throne in **1837**, Australia had consisted of four colonies: New South Wales, South Australia, Western Australia and Van Diemen's Land. The continent was largely unexplored, and the population was less than 160,000. Now, in the month she died, Australia was a federation of six sovereign states, with 3.8 million inhabitants and a new spirit of national consciousness.

▽ Four months and eight days after Federation the first federal parliament is declared open by the Duke of Cornwall and York.

▷ A quarter of a million people saw the swearing-in of Australia's first Governor General in this elaborate pavilion in Sydney's Centennial Park on the 1st of January 1901.

Courtesy Mitchell Library

THE FIRST PARLIAMENT

Four months after the proclamation of the Commonwealth of Australia in Sydney, the first parliament met in Melbourne ... and the southern capital attempted to outdo Sydney in the splendour of its celebrations. There was a grand parade for the Duke and Duchess of York, with 200 mounted stockmen in the lead, cracking whips, followed by 14,000 troops from every state and a number of overseas countries.

The Exhibition Building, site of the opening ceremony, was lit with 10,000 electric lights, and buildings throughout the city fairly bristled with electricity after dark. The first Governor-General, Lord Hopetoun, whose habit of powdering his hair had caused some interest during his term as Governor of Victoria in the 1890s, met the royal couple and later escorted them to a grand ceremonial concert.

The music hall singer Nellie Stewart, fresh from triumphs at Drury Lane in London, sang an ode to Australia. In all the excitement, the newly appointed cabinet ministers forgot to bow as they passed the Duke and Duchess. Lord Tennyson, the Governor of South Australia, made note of this awful blunder in his diary.

Victoria's Parliament House was the temporary home of federal parliament, while the location of a national capital was decided. In fact, the Commonwealth politicians continued to meet in Melbourne for 26 years, until another Duke of York opened Canberra's Parliament House in 1927.

CANBERRA'S CREATOR

The man who planned the city of Canberra in the Australian Capital Territory was Walter Burley Griffin, Chicago architect who had been much influenced by Frank Lloyd Wright. Griffin, born in 1876, submitted the winning design with his wife, Marion Mahoney, for the Australian government's international competition for a national capital.

He came to Australia in 1913 to design Canberra, but after 1920 he established a private practice in Melbourne and Sydney. He sought always to merge his structures, in content and design, with the environment. In Melbourne he designed Newman College at the University of Melbourne, the Capitol Theatre, an estate in the suburb of Eaglemont and a number of innovative houses in other suburbs.

He planned the New South Wales towns of Griffith and Leeton, but his designs were not put into effect. In 1924 he began to create the residential community of Castlecrag in Sydney, and later designed a number of municipal incinerators.

Griffin left Australia in 1935 to design a library for the University of Lucknow in India, and died in that city in 1937. Canberra's Lake Burley Griffin is named in his honour.

△
First of January 1901 and the procession to celebrate Federation threads its way through half a million Sydneysiders.

▷
Ten thousand lights adorn Melbourne's Exhibition Building to celebrate the first federal parliament.

Courtesy Herald & Weekly Times

NEW NATION, OLD WAR

When the Australian states federated in 1901, they were already at war. The Boer War had broken out in October 1899 between Britain and the Boer citizens of two republics, the Transvaal and the Orange Free State, and the Australian colonies had already committed themselves separately to support Britain.

Even before that, Australians had gone to war in support of Britain. In 1885, after news was received that *General Gordon of Khartoum* had been killed in the Sudan, the NSW Cabinet decided to send troops to help English troops against the Saracens. The contingent comprised 532 infantrymen, two batteries of field artillery and an ambulance unit. The conflict was in its last stages when the Australians arrived, and they saw little combat ... although seven died of illness and three were wounded.

For the Boer War, Australia sent about 16,500 troops, first as colonials and later as a Commonwealth contingent. The bushmen cavalry brigades earned a fine reputation as brave horsemen able to cope with a difficult environment. The Australians suffered about 500 casualties, half of them killed in action.

The new nation was busy militarily. While the Boer War was raging, news reached Australia of a terrible uprising in China against foreigners. The Chinese 'Boxers' had attacked the British, French, Russian, American, German and Japanese embassies in the imperial capital of Peking.

As with the Boer War, the Australian government felt compelled to offer help. A contingent of 451 men, comprising detachments from New South Wales and Victoria, sailed to China in the *Salamis* in August 1900. They were later joined by the South Australian gunboat *Protector*.

Courtesy Australian War Memorial

△
Trooper Ronald Easther of the 5th South Australian Contingent, the fully equipped bushman guerilla.

The Australians saw little action, but they received commendations from the British commander in the China Field Force, and returned to a heroes' welcome on May 3 1901 in Sydney.

AWAKENING A VISION

Courtesy The Bulletin

One of the most significant contributions to Australian writing — prose and verse — was made between 1880 and the early decades of the 20th century by a Sydney magazine, the Bulletin. Founded by John Feltham Archibald (after whom the Archibald Prize for portraiture and Sydney's Archibald Fountain were named) and John Haynes, this weekly journal established itself as the chief organ of Australian nationalism. As such, it inspired writers to seek Australian subjects, often with a bush emphasis, rather than cater for a transplanted English audience.

The journal supported nationalism, as well as republicanism, non-sectarian education and White Australia. It offered scope to such people as Henry Lawson, 'Banjo' Paterson, Norman Lindsay, Joseph Furphy, Steele Rudd, Victor Daley, Shaw Nielson and Adam Lindsay Gordon.

In the 20th century the vision of Australian writing, awakened by the Bulletin, spread wider. Novelists such as Miles Franklin, Katherine Susannah Prichard, Ethel 'Henry Handel' Richardson, Xavier Herbert, Eleanor Dark and Christina Stead emerged, as did poets like C.J. Dennis, Mary Gilmore, Bernard O'Dowd, Christopher Brennan, Kenneth Slessor, Robert D. Fitzgerald, Hugh McCrae, A.D. Hope, David Campbell and James McCauley.

Australian writing began to attract world attention in the years after World War II, as writers like Patrick White, Thomas Keneally, David Malouf and Shirley Hazzard forged international reputations.

Of them all, Patrick White (born 1912) has been the most successful. A former jackaroo and Cambridge graduate, he wrote such novels as The Tree of Man (1955) and Voss (1957), the latter based on the doomed explorer Ludwig Leichhardt. He has published collections of short stories, a screenplay, plays and an autobiography (Flaws in the Glass, 1980).

In 1973 White was awarded the Nobel Prize for literature, and he used the prize-money to set up an award for distinguished Australian writers.

Courtesy West Australian Newspapers Ltd

A FOLK-SONG SPECIALIST

Percy Grainger, one of the world's great authorities on folk music, was born in Brighton, Victoria, in 1882, but spent most of his life abroad. He claimed to have been influenced in his compositions by his Australian experience, even though his most popular works were arrangements of folk melodies from Ireland, the United Kingdom and Scandinavia.

He studied at the Hoch Conservatorium in Frankfurt, Germany, from 1895, and toured internationally as a concert pianist from 1901. He served in the United States Army as a band leader in the First World War, and became an American citizen in 1918. He died in 1961.

Other eminent Australian composers have included Malcolm Williamson, Donald Banks, Peter Sculthorpe and Richard Meale.

FOR VALOUR

Ninety-six Australians have won the Victoria Cross — the supreme award for acts of valour by members of Commonwealth forces — in wars spanning seven decades of this century. Of them, 91 have served in the Australian forces; the other five, with the British services and (in one case) the South African Constabulary.

The VC was introduced to reward conspicuous acts of gallantry in the Crimean War. All VCs presented have been made from gun metal taken from Russian artillery during that war. Colonial forces were originally not eligible to win the award, but this barrier was lifted in 1867 ... so that a New Zealander, *Charles Heaphy*, could be given a VC for valour in the Maori Wars. He died in Brisbane in 1881, and was buried in Toowong cemetery.

Soldiers dominate the Australian awards. Of them, 93 have gone to army men, and the remaining three to members of air force units. Seven VCs were awarded for actions in the trenches at Lone Pine, Gallipoli. Four were awarded to soldiers who fought with the Australian Army Training Team in Vietnam.

One VC winner who was not an Australian, the Irishman *Timothy O'Hea*, became involved in Australian history. After retirement from the British Army he arrived in Sydney in 1874 in time to join a search party for a supposed survivor of *Ludwig Leichhardt's* doomed 1848 expedition. O'Hea perished with *Andrew Hume* in south-west Queensland, in something of a repetition of the *Burke* and *Wills* tragedy.

The first award to a member of the Australian forces was to *Captain Neville Howse*, for bravery on July 24 1900 during the Boer War. The most recent was to *Warrant Officer II Keith Payne* for his actions on a patrol on May 14 1969 in Vietnam.

Courtesy Australian War Memorial

DESERTER WINS A VC

An Australian army deserter who was using an assumed name was awarded the Victoria Cross — the supreme decoration for gallantry in battle by members of the British Commonwealth forces — in France shortly before the end of World War I. He was *Maurice Buckley*, whose VC award was gazetted under the false name of *Gerald Sexton*.

Buckley, who was born in Melbourne in 1891, enlisted in the AIF in December 1914 and embarked for Egypt as a reinforcement for the Light Horse. He was shipped back to Australia and posted to Langwarrin Camp in September 1915. He deserted in January 1916 and was struck off the strength of the AIF the following March.

In May 1916 Buckley re-enlisted in the AIF under the alias of *Gerald Sexton. Gerald* was the name of his brother who had been killed six months previously, and *Sexton* was his mother's maiden name. He joined the 13th Battalion on the Somme in January 1917. In August he won the Distinguished Conduct Medal for an action in which he fired his Lewis gun from the hip to put a hidden enemy gun out of action.

The following month, on September 18, he again attacked with a Lewis gun to rush six machine-gun posts, capture a field gun and take nearly 100 German prisoners. His award of a VC for this action was gazetted under the name of *Sexton;* but he was invested under his proper name by *King George V* at Buckingham Palace.

A BOTCHED LANDING, AND A LEGEND IS BORN

Australia embraced the First World War with innocent eagerness. A few days before war was declared, as the crisis in Europe worsened, the Labor leader Andrew Fisher pledged Australia's support for Britain "to our last man and our last shilling". Constitutionally, Australia had no decision to make about entering the war; membership of the British Empire ensured that Australia was automatically involved the moment Britain entered hostilities. Fervently, the Australian people wanted to be part of that war. The government changed hands a month after the declaration in August 1914, with Labor taking office, but leaders of both sides of politics were united in their commitment of a contingent of 20,000 soldiers to any destination required by the British War Office.

Courtesy Victoria Barracks Museum & Historical Society

In the streets crowds sang traditional songs like 'Rule Britannia' and 'Soldiers of the King', and a new song was written ... 'Australia will be There'. The contingent of soldiers was called the Australian Imperial Force (AIF), and, although only the biggest and healthiest were chosen, the ranks of the 20,000 volunteers were filled within three weeks. Men came from all over Australia to join, some of them riding hundreds of miles on horseback to enlistment depots in the capital cities. One Queensland grazier rode 460 miles to the nearest railway station to offer himself in Adelaide for the Light Horse; when he found the quota filled, he sailed to Hobart, to find that again there were no vacancies; then he took another boat to Sydney, where he was able to join the army as a private, after a journey of 2000 miles.

They were paid five shillings a day (with another shilling after they left Australia), their training was makeshift, and it was agreed from the start that Australian brigades would not be incorporated into British divisions, as had been suggested by the British. They would have their own infantry division, a brigade of Light Horse, an Australian commander (Maj. Gen. W.T. Bridges) and their own code of discipline.

The first contingent left Australia in 26 troop-ships in late October, and by the end of 1914 another 30,000 had enlisted. This convoy was joined by 10 New Zealand ships to comprise the largest military expedition ever to have sailed across the world. Even before they left there had been action close to home: a shot across the bows stopped a German merchant vessel which tried to escape from Port Phillip Bay a few hours after war was declared, and Australian forces captured German New Guinea. In the Indian Ocean, the HMAS Sydney, escorting the troop convoy, broke off to "intercept and sink the German destroyer Emden".

The colonial troops were landed in Egypt, where they waited for months and achieved a reputation for insolence, independence of spirit and at times plain larrikinism. They were joined in the desert by a second contingent and formed into two divisions, one all-Australian and one made up of Australians and New Zealanders. A staff officer coined the name Anzacs for those raw, unruly soldiers who made up the Australian and New Zealand Army Corps. Wearied of training marches over hot sand, many of the Australians involved themselves in drunken brawls, the worst of which was 'the battle of the Wozzer' in the brothel district of Cairo. "I think we have to admit that our force contains more bad hats than others," the war correspondent C.E.W. Bean noted sadly in his diary.

On May 8 1915 Australians learned, from a dispatch published in Australian newspapers by an English war correspondent, that the Australians had distinguished themselves in the landing on the Gallipoli Peninsula. "There has been no finer feat in this war than this sudden landing in the dark and storming the heights," reported the correspondent, Ernest Ashmead-Bartlett. The Anzacs landed on the eastern side as part of a larger operation involving 75,000 troops — but something went horribly wrong. Instead of landing close to open plain, as planned, they were disembarked a mile to the north, confronted with steeply rising ridges and gorges. Instead of surprising the enemy in the half-light of early dawn, they found themselves under intense and withering fire from the Turkish defenders. Two thousand of the 16,000 Anzacs were killed or wounded on the first day. They charged the Turks with bayonets and rifles, drove them from their first line of trenches, and scaled a high ridge ... then were outflanked, caught in crossfire from Turkish reinforcements and forced to retreat.

Back on the beach, they could not be re-embarked without presenting a defenceless target to the Turks. They dug in, and began a series of incredible attempts to break out of the beach-heads. The Turks counter-attacked, and both sides consolidated their defences in a series of trenches. The Turks matched the willingness of the Australians to engage in frontal assaults. At one stage the British general in command, Sir Ian Hamilton, ordered the Anzacs to advance across two miles of open ground to attack a strongly prepared Turkish position which

British and French troops had failed to take. The Australian commander, *Colonel James McCay, protested against the stupidity of the order, without any success ...* and the result was carnage.

At home in the early days there was massive pride, and not much knowledge of the sheer awfulness of the warfare. The Melbourne Argus announced that Australia had "in one moment stepped into the world-wide arena in the full stature of great manhood". This "brave, bloody adventure," said the paper, had given Australia "a place among the nationals". As the massive casualty lists continued to be published, the national mood became less strident and braggart,

the rhetoric more sober.

In the battle of Lone Pine on Gallipoli, where close-quarter, even hand-to-hand, fighting took place without ceasing for four days and four nights, the Australians won seven Victoria Crosses, lost 80 officers and 2197 men, and killed 5000 Turks. *"The dead lay so thick",* wrote the correspondent *Bean,* "that the only respect which could be paid to them was to avoid treading on their faces."

It was because of the intervention of another Australian war correspondent, the young *Keith Murdoch, that the Gallipoli campaign was ended, and Allied forces evacuated. Murdoch visited Gallipoli for four days on his way to*

△ *The storming of Lone Pine on Gallipoli by the 1st Brigade. Seven VCs were awarded.*

London, and was appalled at what he saw. He talked with troops and other correspondents, and rightly became convinced that the campaign had been bungled from the start. He carried away a letter from the British correspondent *Ashmead-Bartlett* to the British Prime Minister, and wrote in strong terms to his own Prime Minister, *Andrew Fisher.* A secret Royal Commission followed, *Sir Ian Hamilton* was recalled, and Gallipoli was evacuated in a much more orderly fashion than it had been invaded. The Australians had lost 7600 killed and 19,500 had been wounded in the campaign.

THE BEST OF THEM ALL

"BILLY" P.M.

Prime Minister *Billy Hughes,* **arguing for** conscription in 1916:

"Germany has long coveted this grand and rich continent, and if she wins she will certainly claim it as an important part of her spoils. If Britain fails, in Australia there will not be warfare, but massacre. We will be like sheep before the Butcher."

These are some views on Sir John Monash, the Jewish engineer and militiaman who became commander of the Australian Army Corps in World War I ...

Sir Basil Liddel Hart, *widely recognised as the outstanding military commentator and historian of his generation:* "He had

probably the greatest capacity for command in modern war among all who held command."

British Prime Minister Lloyd George: "Monash was, according to the testimony of those who knew well his genius for war and what he accomplished by it, the most resourceful General in the whole of the British Army."

Maj. General Sir Kingsley Norris: "Monash ... was considered in 1918 for the post of Generalissimo of the Allied Forces in France, a command which fell to Foch."

The historian A.J.P. Taylor: ". . . the only general of creative originality produced by the First World War."

Anthony Eden (Viscount Avon): ". . . the ablest soldier of the war."

Viscount Montgomery of Alamein: "I would name Sir John Monash as the best general on the Western Front in Europe . . . the war might well have been over sooner, and certainly with fewer casualties, had Haig been relieved of his command and Monash appointed to command the British Armies in his place."

Courtesy Herald & Weekly Times

From there most of the First AIF went to the western front in France, where another 52,000 young Australians were to die. On Gallipoli was fashioned a special legend which had much to do with courage and sacrifice. Somehow that awful experience contributed to the shaping of the Australian character in rather the way the diggings did during the gold rush. Now the diggers had become Diggers. They shared again a spirit of independence and mateship, a contempt for high authority and an equality which had nothing to do with class or financial background.

The Australians were able to avenge themselves to some degree in the Western Desert on the Turks by attacking through Sinai, Palestine and Syria. While the infantrymen from Gallipoli went to France, the cavalrymen of the Light Horse regrouped in the desert and over a period of two years routed the Turkish army and the Germans who fought beside it. In one battle near the Suez Canal they killed or took prisoner 13,000 Turks for the loss of 200 Australians killed and 900 wounded.

On the Western Front, the squander of human life assumed new, appalling dimensions as the Australians were pumped into massive, doomed assaults on the heavily fortified German lines that twisted down from Belgium through France to Switzerland. General Douglas 'Butcher' Haig ordered some of the most costly advances in the history of warfare on the Somme river and at Passchendaele. On the first day of the Somme attack, British casualties amounted to 60,000 killed and wounded. The six Australian battalions involved at Fromelles suffered 5133 casualties within 16 hours, with another 400 taken prisoner. In the 60th Battalion, only 107 men survived from nearly 900. At Bullecourt the Australian Fourth Brigade was ordered to advance across snow in mass formation through uncut barbed wire, on the insistence of British general staff and against the objections of Australian commanders: of 3000 men, 2339 were killed. At the village of Pozieres, on the Somme, Australians who had been set the

△
Mates on Gallipoli. The legend begins.

task of winning a few hundred yards of ground lost 6842 killed and 17,513 wounded or gassed. At some point this slaughter of young life becomes hard to comprehend, even now ... but it just continued. At Messines and Ypres, another 7000 Australians were killed or wounded; at Passchendaele, the Anzacs and Canadians won seven miles of territory in a side-by-side advance ... at the cost of another 38,000 casualties.

Lieutenant John Alexander Raws, former reporter on the Melbourne Argus, wrote about Pozieres just before he died in 1916:

"We are lousy, stinking, ragged, unshaven, sleepless. I have one puttee, a dead man's helmet, another dead man's gas protector, a dead man's bayonet. My tunic is rotten with other men's blood, and partly splattered with a comrade's brains. It is horrible, but why should you people at home not know? Several of my friends are raving mad. I met three officers out in No Man's Land the other night, all rambling and mad."

Against this background of bloodshed on an unprecedented scale, the battle for conscription was fought in Australia. The war had imposed an intolerable strain on *Andrew Fisher*, the man who had promised every last man and

shilling, and he was replaced as Prime Minister after 15 months by *William Morris Hughes*, wizened, Welsh, irascible and 53. During a visit he made to London, Britain adopted military conscription, and *Hughes* became convinced that Australia needed to do the same. By this time more than 150,000 Australians were serving on the Western Front, and the recruitment rate had slowed by July 1916 to 6000 a month ... not enough by far to replace casualties.

With politicians, and particularly the Labor Party, split on conscription, Hughes decided to take the issue direct to the people. He campaigned for it passionately, but the vote was lost. Men in the armed forces voted 72,399 to 58,894 in favour of conscription, but people at home voted 1,160,033 to 1,087,557 against it. Re-elected in 1917, *Hughes* held another referendum, and gave a public undertaking that he would resign the prime ministership if this was defeated. It was lost again, more convincingly. *Hughes* resigned, but accepted re-appointment immediately. Conscription was one of the most bitter issues in Australian political history. What the votes showed was that large numbers of Australians, even those at the front, believed that nobody should be forced to fight for a cause in which they did not believe. At the war's end, the AIF was unlike any other army: it had suffered the highest proportion of casualties to population of all, and it had remained entirely composed of volunteers.

In some of the last great actions of the Western Front in 1918, the Australians defended *Amiens* against confident, advancing Germans. They stopped the enemy at Villers-Bretonneux and Dernancourt, and later handed over the defence of Villers-Bretonneux to the British. The Germans immediately counter-attacked and retook the town; the Australians, brought forward on Anzac Day, moved in again and turned the Germans back — at a cost of another 15,000 casualties. In the closing months, an Australian general, *John Monash*, was given command of the AIF divisions.

Senior British officers had some misgivings about such a high command going to a Jewish colonial militiaman, but the Australians felt more comfortable with their own general separating them from the British. His divisions formed the spearhead of the last great attack on the Hindenberg Line, one which ended with the demoralised Germans seeking a truce. In their final 40-mile advance, the Australians had taken 30,000 prisoners and helped very forcibly to end the war.

The cost of that war in Australian lives was twice as great as that which would occur in the next World War, 21 years later. Of a population of less than five million, more than 330,000 had volunteered and gone to the other side of the world to fight. Of those who went into the field, almost one in two was wounded and one in five was killed. King and Empire had been defended, and an entire generation had been mutilated.

OUR GERMANS ARE PUNISHED

The upsurge of anti-German feeling which occurred in Australia during the First World War led to the internment of thousands of German settlers, whose roots in Australia were very deep and who had contributed to industry, commerce, culture and the professions. Anti-German Leagues emerged, and people like the great painter **Hans Heysen** *were subjected to persecution.*

In South Australia alone, under the Nomenclature Act of 1917, 69 German place-names were changed to English or Aboriginal names. In the Barossa Valley, Klemzig became Gaza, after an Australian victory in Palestine; Handorf became Yantaringa. The township of Hamburg was called Haig, after the general who was sending vast numbers of troops to slaughter in the trenches on the Western Front.

In New South Wales, Germantown became Holbrook, in honour of a submarine commander called **Douglas Holbrook***. In Victoria, Mount Bismarck was renamed Mt. Kitchener.*

The ice-cream cart used in the ambush at ◁ *Broken Hill.*

Courtesy Mr R.H.B. Kearns MBE

THE TURKS WHO TOOK ON BROKEN HILL

On January 1 **1915**, some four months after the outbreak of the First World War, two men launched an attack on Australia from an ice-cream cart above which was fluttering a Turkish flag. They fired on the crowded, open carriages of a picnic train which was carrying 1200 men, women and children from Broken Hill to nearby Silverton.

The women picnickers wore bonnets and many of them were shielding themselves with umbrellas from the midsummer sun. The hampers and rugs were packed below temporary wooden benches which had been placed in 40 ore trucks.

Along the way the picnickers saw the ice-cream cart tethered to a tired old horse and carrying an unfamiliar flag ... a white crescent and star on a red background. Beside it were crouched two men who were known to many of the passengers. People waved at the ice-cream men before they realised that they were carrying rifles. As the train chugged slowly past, the pair began firing a barrage of bullets.

This crude, ridiculous ambush had been planned by **Mulla Abdulla**, camel-driver and butcher, and **Gool Mahomed**, drifter, who used to smoke Indian hemp together. In the cart that usually carried ice-cream, they had hidden Snider and Martini-Henry rifles, bandoliers of cartridges, and knives. Neither was in fact a Turk ... one was an Afghan Afridi

and the other a native of north-west India. Both were Mohammedans, and recognised the **Sultan of Turkey** as head of their Church.

Six people died in the Battle of Broken Hill, including both ice-cream men, who fled in their turbans and robes from the scene of the ambush and were shot down soon afterwards by police. As a result of the attack, feeling flared against foreigners in Broken Hill. That night the German club was burnt to the ground, mobs attacked an Afghan camel camp, and a couple of days later the Barrier Daily Truth published an editorial, headed 'The Terrible Turk', which insisted wrongly that the attackers were Turks.

Why did it happen? Nobody ever knew for certain. **Gool Mahomed** had a pleasant manner, and was generally considered to be a 'good Afghan'. **Mulla Abdulla**, an older man, was inclined to moodiness, and had recently been convicted of having killed meat off licensed premises. He had been unable to pay the fine.

One theory was that **Gool**, fired with fundamental Islamic patriotism, inflamed the resentment of the older man, whose limping walk made him the butt of cruel jokes from local children. Another was that the pair simply used the war as their excuse to even the score for the intolerance of townspeople towards the 'Afghan' group camped outside the town.

Courtesy National Gallery of Victoria

Courtesy National Gallery of Victoria

THE ARTISTS OF HEIDELBERG

When the young Australian artist **Tom Roberts** *returned in* **1885** *from a visit to England and Europe, he set up a number of camps in the countryside outside Melbourne devoted to open-air painting. With him went* **Frederick McCubbin**, *once his fellow-student, and they devoted themselves to an Australian version of Impressionism: capturing each subject as it appeared to the artist, recording it according to the light encompassing it.*

They lived simply, and slept on hessian bags slung between saplings, painting fast and constantly throughout their waking hours. They showed the 'impressions' painted on their first camp near Box Hill to a couple of other young painters, **Arthur Streeton** *and* **Charles Conder**. *They were strongly influenced, and other camps were set up at Heidelberg. Much work was done while the painters were based in a large, deserted farmhouse at Eaglemont, above Heidelberg.*

Then, in **1889**, **Roberts**, **McCubbin**, **Streeton** *and* **Conder** *put on an exhibition in company with some other artists whose effect on Australian art was far less profound. This was the '9 x 5' show, now almost legendary in Australian art. It took its name from the fact that the 183 paintings in it were all small, and many of them were done on cigar-box lids (9 x 5 inches).*

The camp disbanded after the exhibition, but its distinctive form of Impressionism represented a landmark in Australian art. It produced some of Australia's best-known paintings ... like **Roberts'** *Shearing the Rams and Bailed Up,* **McCubbin's** *The Wallaby Track and Down on his Luck, and* **Conder's** *Departure of the SS Orient — Circular Quay and Holiday at Mentone.*

Roberts *in particular celebrated the virtues of mateship, courage, hard work and resourcefulness. In a way, his paintings paralleled the prose of* **Henry Lawson** *and* **Joseph Furphy**. *And the Heidelberg School coincided with the beginning of a strong tradition in Australia for black-and-white art.*

The Bulletin, with its distinctly nationalistic philosophies, offered a bold, encouraging medium for such black-and-white artists as **Phil May**, *and later* **Norman Lindsay**, **David Low** *and* **Will Dyson**.

△
Frederick McCubbin's triptych "The Pioneer".

ESSENCE OF A PAINTING

When he was at work on 'Shearing the Rams' in 1890, Tom Roberts wrote to his close friend Arthur Streeton, who had shared a farmhouse with him and Charles Conder at Eaglemont, near Heidelberg. Theirs had been a painting commune, the heart of the Heidelberg School.

In his letter, Roberts explained the essence of the subject he wanted to portray: "Noble enough and worthy enough if I could express the meaning and the spirit — of strong masculine labour, the patience of the animals whose year's growth is being stripped away from them for men's use, and the great human interest of the whole scene."

△
"Shearing the Rams" by Tom Roberts.

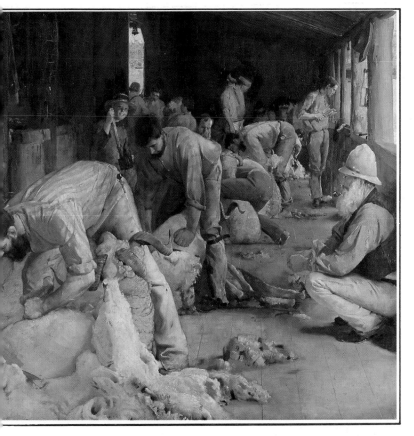

TWO PIONEERS CALLED SMITH

On December 10 **1919** the brothers **Smith** — **Ross** and **Keith** — landed their twin-engined Vickers Vimy biplane on Darwin's airfield to win the £10,000 offered by the Australian government for the first flight between Britain and Australia.

Ross, the pilot, was a 27-year-old South Australian who had served with the Australian Flying Corps in the Middle East during the First World War. **Keith**, 29 and a veteran of Britain's Royal Flying Corps, was the navigator. With them were two mechanics: Sergeants **Jim Bennett** and **Wally Shiers**.

A condition of the prize was that the journey had to be completed in 30 days. Once, during take-off from Calcutta, the plane was struck by two hawks, and **Ross Smith** had to battle to clear some treetops. At Surabaya they became bogged, and finally were able to leave after persuading locals to lay a take-off track of bamboo mats.

The last leg was from Atamboea, on Timor, to Darwin. They crossed the Arafura Sea, 760 kilometres, and landed at Fanny Bay after 27 days and 20 hours. Both the Smiths were knighted, and Prime Minister **Billy Hughes** presented them with their cheque in Melbourne. In 1922 **Sir Ross Smith** and Jim Bennett perished in a flying accident.

During the 1914–18 war Ross Smith won a Military Cross and bar, a Distinguished Flying Cross and two bars, and an Air Force Cross. He was the most decorated Australian airman of the war.

THE SPORT THAT BECAME A PLAGUE

The rabbit came to Australia with the First Fleet ... in company with a number of convicts whose crime in England had been to poach rabbits. The first consignment of livestock in 1788 listed five rabbits, along with an odd (and surprisingly small) assortment of bulls, sheep, goats, hogs, turkeys, geese, ducks and chickens. They were domestic rabbits, and they did not survive long in the savage environment, where there existed all kinds of predators, including native cats, tiger cats, goannas, wedge-tailed eagles, hawks and dingoes.

The man who achieved the doubtful distinction of nurturing Australia's rabbit population explosion was Thomas Austin, of Barwon Park, Winchelsea, near Geelong. He was a tenant farmer who became wealthy, and he aspired to be a member of the gentry. What he wanted most was to be a sporting squire, to take his guests at his grand house on hunting expeditions. In 1859 he had shipped out to him from Liverpool, in the clipper Lightning, 72 partridges, five hares and 24 wild rabbits. The Geelong Chronicle reported in May 1862 that Austin's venture was a great success: his partridges were amazing, his pheasants were laying, his rabbits numbered thousands. It did add that the rabbits were destroying trees and shrubs which had really been intended for pheasants and partridges. In 1865 Austin announced triumphantly that he had killed 20,000 rabbits on his property alone.

Within three years rabbits were over-running properties, causing the value of farmland in western Victoria to drop by half. The Times in London reported that the rabbit was threatening to starve the sheep off their runs. Over the next 20 years the great invasion moved across the Murray River and into South Australia. In the waterless Mallee country of Victoria, they learned to live off the sap of mallee roots. In another 20 years they were thriving even in the sand-hills near thirsty Birdsville. They adapted themselves marvellously. They could live in snow country and in the sub-tropics, everywhere in Australia below the Tropic of Capricorn. As the grey blanket spread across the country, as they bred in thousands of millions, they devastated crops and pastures and destroyed land which was already being damaged by overstocking.

Bounty hunters were used against them. W.E. Abbott, president of the NSW Central Stock Board of Advice, proposed a scheme by which 100 cats would be unleashed on every 10,000 rabbits.

When the NSW government offered a £25,000 reward for a final solution to the rabbit problem, the great Louis Pasteur claimed it with a plan for infecting rabbits with fowl cholera. It didn't work.

What did work best was a manipulated disease called myxomatosis, imported from Brazil and pushed by the Australian physician Dr. Jean Macnamara, whose childhood farm had been wiped out by rabbits. For a time the rabbit was nearly wiped out ... but the battle is not finished. The author Eric Rolls, historian of the rabbit and other imported pests, has written: "The eradication of the rabbit is vital to the soil, to the growth of the soil, and to the human and animal dwellers on it."

Courtesy News Limited

Courtesy MCC

△
Bert Oldfield felled by Larwood; Third Test, Adelaide.

◁
Bradman leads Australia against England for the last time; 1948.

BRADMAN: THE ULTIMATE HERO

Don Bradman *looms, well clear of any other figure, as the most outstanding Australian cricketer of all time. Many, including the selection panel of Australia's sporting Hall of Fame, have voted him the greatest Australian* **sportsman** *of all. And there are large numbers who would argue that he touched the lives of fellow Australians more than any other person.*

In a nation which worships sport, he became the ultimate hero. And not only in Australia. With **Dr. W.G. Grace**, *he ranks as the most influential player the game has known, revered in every country where cricket is played. Long after his retirement as a batsman, captain, selector and administrator, his reputation endures. He was to cricket everything that* **Babe Ruth** *was to baseball. That, and maybe something more. He was* **Ruth** *without the profanity, the beer, the tub shape.*

His impact on Australian society was somehow strengthened by the times in which he played. He came onto the international scene during the Depression and again immediately after the most horrifying war in history. In gloomy times, his

incomparable performances offered hope and pride to people who needed it. When so much was bad, he was simply the best. His impact on the game of cricket can be assessed, at one level anyway, by the knowledge that the ugly and dangerous tactic of Bodyline was devised expressly to stop him.

Others have since scored more runs and more centuries playing more matches in recent years, but still nobody has managed to score a century at an average of every third time out to bat. He made 117 first-class centuries, including one all-time record 452 not out, six innings of over 300 and 37 over 200. He top-scored in 24 of his 52 Tests.

Bradman *was a cricketing phenomenon, an innocent country boy from Bowral who attacked the fiercest bowlers in the world with zest, and gave massive enjoyment to great crowds. As a small boy he used to play for hours, hitting a golf ball against the brick base of a large water tank.*

At his first appearance for the Bowral School at the age of 12, he scored an unbeaten 115 of a total of 156 against Mittagong High School.

In country cricket he made some prodigious scores, and hit a magnificent 234 for Bowral against the Wingello team, whose bowling mainstay was a rising star called **Bill O'Reilly**. *He made a century in his first game of first-grade cricket (with St. George, in Sydney) and another century in his first Sheffield Shield match.*

His Test career spanned 20 years, from **1928** *to* **1948**. *Throughout his first-class career, which ended in the Australian summer of* **1948–49**, *Bradman amassed 28,067 runs. Many consider his 334 at Leeds, in* **1930**, *to be his finest Test innings, but Bradman's view was always that his 254 in the previous Test at Lord's was the most technically perfect he played.*

During that **1930** *tour of England,* **Bradman** *scored 974 runs with four centuries at an average of 139.14. Newspaper editors printed banners and posters which stated simply: 'Bradman versus England'.*

In **1949** *he became the only Australian ever to be knighted for services to cricket.*

"ONE TEAM IS TRYING TO PLAY CRICKET…"

The England Test team's tour of Australia in the summer of *1932–33* was the most bitterly controversial in the history of cricket. It was the Bodyline tour, and Bodyline was the word used to describe a form of bowling planned by the English captain, **Douglas Jardine**, with the express intention of curbing the phenomenal Australian batsman **Don Bradman**.

The spearhead of the Bodyline attack was a slightly built ex-miner, **Harold Larwood**, who — with back-up from two other bowlers, **Bill Bowes** and **Bill Voce** — exploited the technique of bowling very fast, short-pitched deliveries on the leg side, to a packed leg field.

The essence of Bodyline was that it forced the batsman to defend himself as well as his wicket. The ball flew high and fast around the head and shoulders of the batsman; usually his alternatives were to duck, or to risk being caught by the crowded field on the leg side.

Bradman later wrote of this form of bowling: "Neither defence nor attack could overcome it for long — unless the batsman was particularly lucky. Playing the good length balls and dodging the others may seem all right in theory, but it did not work in practice. The batsman doing this must of necessity be hit. In fact no Australian batsman of any note failed to be hit — some on many occasions."

Many of those hits to the body occurred during the Third Test in Adelaide, a game described by Wisden as "probably the most unpleasant ever played … altogether the whole atmosphere was a disgrace to cricket". **Bill Ponsford** took an awful beating, sustaining bruises all over his body, and at the other end the Australian captain, **Bill Woodfull**, was hit a tremendous blow over the heart by a ball from **Larwood**.

Woodfull batted on gamely for a while, ashen and groggy, but was out at 22. Afterwards the English manager **Pelham Warner** went to the Australian dressing room, where **Woodfull** was receiving treatment for his bruises, one a very livid mark above the heart. **Warner** said he had come to say how sorry he was, and to offer sympathy.

"I don't want to see you, Mr. Warner," said **Woodfull**. "There are two teams out there. One is trying to play cricket and the other is not. The game is too good to be spoilt. It is time some people got out of it."

Later, after the Australian, **Bert Oldfield**, had been hit sickeningly on the head by a ball from **Larwood**, and sustained a skull fracture, the Australian Cricket Board of Control sent an angry cable to the Marylebone Cricket Club in London, demanding that Bodyline be banned. It condemned the practice as "unsportsmanlike" and said that it threatened to upset "friendly relations existing between Australia and England".

The MCC sent back an equally belligerent cable, deploring the notion that there had been unsportsmanlike play and defending **Jardine** and his bowlers. The England team went on to win the Ashes, the Bodyline row was buried, and **Larwood** never again entered a Test arena. He dismissed **Bradman** four times in the Test series, and **Bradman** had missed the first Test through illness.

THE NATION MOURNS TWO GREAT CHAMPIONS

Courtesy Mitchell Library

Two of Australia's most legendary sporting heroes, a prizefighter and a racehorse, both died suddenly in the United States. The tragedies tested the abiding fondness which Australians generally had felt for America ever since the visit of the Great White Fleet in *1908*. The victims were both idolised in a nation which felt deeply about sport, and one illogical expression of common grief was to blame the Americans.

The boxer was **Les Darcy**, who had enlisted in Brisbane in *1916* for active service in the Great War. His mother had insisted on his discharge as a minor. Meantime, an urgent demand arrived for **Darcy** to fight in the U.S. To him, that meant the chance to become the first Australian to hold an undisputed world title. He went, and received a spectacular reception from **Tex Rickard**, who would soon be promoting the first million-dollar-gate fights.

Soon after **Darcy** arrived, a number of U.S. newspapers launched a campaign against him, accusing him of dodging service in the armed forces. He was banned from the prizering and forced to join a travelling vaudeville troupe. The ban was later lifted, and **Darcy** cleared of all charges; he took out U.S. nationalisation papers, and joined the Flying Corps. **Darcy** became ill suddenly, after trouble with an infected tooth, and died on May 24 **1917**. Australian newspapers said he had 'died of a broken heart'.

The horse was **Phar Lap**, and again a whole nation grieved for him. He was a giant of a horse, with a heart almost twice the size of an ordinary horse's, and he won an amazing 37 times out of 51 starts. After he won the **1930** Melbourne Cup before 72,800 people, with **Jimmy Pike** on his back, his owner decided to take him to the Agua Caliente Handicap in Tijuana, Mexico, then the richest horse-race in the world.

Phar Lap won the big race and was then taken to a stable outside San Francisco, while a contract was being negotiated with Metro-Goldwyn-Mayer for a series of short films in which the horse would star. Suddenly he went off his food, developed a high temperature, began to shiver violently. He died quickly on April 5 **1932**.

Colic had been diagnosed, but veterinary surgeons said later that death had been caused by an irritant poison.

When the news reached Australia, flags flew at half mast around the nation. Newspaper placards said simply: 'He's dead'. Newspapers demanded to know: 'Who killed **Phar Lap**?' — but it was never established whether the poisoning was accidental or intentional.

Courtesy Weldon Trannies

A NEW KIND OF HERO

The world really discovered flying after the First World War. Aviators, many of whom had learned to fly for combat in the war, became the new explorers ... Magellans in open cockpits, Leichhardts with goggles and helmets and fur collars.

It was a new time for a new kind of hero. There were first crossings of oceans to be made; marathon journeys between continents; solo flights to test a man's concentration and alertness as much as his capacity to fly; mail runs and air services to be pioneered. There were loops to be looped, and history to be made, in primitive flying contraptions made basically of wood and fabric.

Two of Australia's heroes of the air were Charles Kingsford Smith and Bert Hinkler. One of the heroines of that age was Amy Johnson. They all died in flying accidents.

Courtesy John Oxley Library

THE BOY FROM BUNDABERG

Bert Hinkler, the boy from Bundaberg, Queensland, grew up with one burning ambition: to fly planes. He built gliders as a teenager, and worked his way to Europe in a German freighter in 1912 with the idea of learning to fly. In London he became a mechanic with the Sopwith aviation company.

When war broke out he was 22. He joined the Royal Naval Air Service and was soon flying in combat as an observer. He won the Distinguished Service Medal, gained a commission, and later joined the Royal Flying Corps.

On demobilisation he bought an Avro Baby plane, took it to Australia, assembled it and in April 1921 established a world record for the longest non-stop solo flight by covering 850 miles from Sydney to Bundaberg. After he landed he taxied down the street

and parked the plane at his mother's gate.

On February 7 1928 he set off on a solo flight to Australia, determined to beat the time of 28 days set by Ross and Keith Smith in 1919. He arrived at Darwin on February 22, less than 16 days out from London. The Australian government gave him £2000, plus the Air Force Cross and the honorary rank of squadron-leader in the RAAF. He was idolised. Songs were written about him, and flappers wore close-fitting hats modelled on his helmet.

On a foggy night in January 1933 Hinkler took off in a Puss Moth from an English airfield, planning to reach Australia in eight days. In a terrible snowstorm over the Italian Alps, he flew into the side of a mountain. His body was found four months later, and he was buried in Florence.

Courtesy John Oxley Library

ACROSS THE PACIFIC

Charles Kingsford Smith, known as 'Smithy', was one of the great folk heroes of Australian history. His most famous flight was the first crossing of the Pacific Ocean, in company with C.T.P. Ulm as his second pilot and two Americans, **Harry Lyon** and James Warner.

Kingsford Smith, born in **1897,** learned to fly with the Australian Flying Corps in the Great War, and won the Military Cross for service with a fighter squadron. Before he began flying, he served in the Gallipoli campaign. After the war he spent about a year with flying circuses in California, sometimes working as a stunt man in movies, then returned to Australia and a job with the nation's first airline, **Norman**

Brearley's *Western Australian Airways.*

The Pacific flight was made from east to west in a three-engined Fokker called the **Southern Cross.** There were three hops ... from San Francisco to Honolulu, to Fiji and to Brisbane. Between Honolulu and Fiji, a stretch of 2740 nautical miles — the longest distance ever flown non-stop at that time — the **Southern Cross** was in the air 33 hours. 'Smithy' and his crew landed in Brisbane on June 9 **1928,** after a journey lasting three days, 10 hours, 42 minutes.

Kingsford Smith flew the first trans-Tasman flight in the same aircraft, and later set records by flying from Australia to London in 12 days

18 hours **(1929)** and London via Ireland to New York and San Francisco **(1930).** Later that year he made a solo flight from England to Australia in less than 10 days. In **1933** he cut this time to seven days four hours.

On November 6 **1935** 'Smithy' took off on the last journey of his life, intending to break the England-Australia record set by the winning Comet in the **1934** Centenary air race, and at the same time demonstrate the worth of his new Lockheed Altair plane, **Lady Southern Cross.** He disappeared off the coast of Burma on November 8. Aged 38, he was presumed to have crashed in the Bay of Bengal.

A SPECIAL DUET

Courtesy Weldon Trannies

SOLO FROM BRITAIN

Amy Johnson *was an English girl who flew into Australian history. On May 24* **1930** *she became the first woman ever to fly solo from Britain to Australia. She made the trip in 19 days, to be welcomed by one of the greatest crowds Darwin had seen.*

She was 26 when she took off on that epic flight in a second-hand De Havilland Moth which she had bought for £700. Until then she had never been in the air for more than two hours at a stretch, and had never flown beyond the English Channel.

On her return to England from the solo flight, she was met by a crowd of 100,000. The King presented her with a CBE, and the Daily Mail gave her £10,000.

She made further record solo flights to Japan and back (1931), and to Cape Town and back (1932). Then she crossed the Atlantic with her flier husband **Jim Mollison**, *whom she had met in Australia.*

Amy Johnson *set other records in the* **1930s**, *and became a ferry pilot in World War II. She died in* **1941** *when she bailed out over the Thames estuary after her plane had engine trouble.*

Australia's most celebrated operatic performers have been Dame Nellie Melba (1861–1931) and Dame Joan Sutherland, born in Sydney in 1926.

Melba, born Helen Mitchell in the Melbourne suburb of Richmond, was one of the most colourful Australians of her time ... vain and vulgar at times, a runaway wife, a divorcee and mistress of the Pretender to the French throne. She also gave Australia cause for inspiration as well as pride.

Her American-Czech biographer, Joseph Wechsberg, summed up her greatness: "Melba had everything — commanding presence and beautiful voice, talent and technique, wealth and power. The moment she came on the stage, even before she sang a tone, she could cast a spell ... She was worshipped even by people who had never heard her. She lived at a time that adored its prima donnas, and she was the symbol of that time; the best-known woman in the world, the most applauded and the most highly paid."

Her Australian biographer, Thérèse Radic, describes her this way: "She remains one of the few names that spring to mind when the national myth is discussed; she ranks with Ned Kelly, Don Bradman and Phar Lap in the popular imagination. She made it possible for Australians to be *proud of the quality of what they could produce. With Melba we realised it was possible to stop cringing to the English and get up off our knees."*

Some 60 years after Melba reached international prominence, another magical Australian voice emerged ... that of Joan Sutherland. It has been suggested that the odds against two such voices surfacing from a nation with such a small population are astronomical.

Joan Sutherland joined the Covent Garden Opera Company in 1952. She won great acclaim in many roles, but it was her 1959 performance in the title role of Lucia de Lammermoor which established her as the finest dramatic coloratura soprano in the world.

In 1954 she married the pianist and conductor Richard Bonynge, who collaborated on much of her work and worked hard to develop her voice for the great bel canto roles for which she became famous.

A far less controversial character than Melba, she once shocked the Nobel Prize winning Australian novelist Patrick White by telling him that she had not read a word he had written, but had been unable to put down a less ambitious Australian work, The Thorn Birds.

Courtesy Herald & Weekly Times Limited

Courtesy Weldon Trannies

THE OUTBACK AIRLINE
THAT GREW

Qantas, Australia's international airline, was founded by two young ex-World War I pilots from the Australian Flying Corps — *P.J. McGinness* and *W. Hudson Fysh*. They conceived the idea in 1919, while they were driving in an old T-Ford through the Queensland outback, surveying some of the country over which planes would be flying in the great England to Australia air race later that year. The trip convinced them that an air service should be established to help develop the inland.

On November 16 1920 the Queensland and Northern Territory Aerial Service was founded, and for many years its headquarters was at Longreach in central western Queensland. The first service flew between Charleville and Cloncurry. Later the airline flew between Brisbane and Charleville.

Fysh flew as a pilot early, but became managing director of the company in 1923. In 1928 the company's facilities were used to help launch the Flying Doctor Service, and in 1929 the headquarters moved to Brisbane. In 1934 the company became *Qantas Empire Airways* and joined with *Imperial Airways* (later BOAC) at Singapore to link Australia and Europe. It later expanded into flying boats.

The Commonwealth government bought Qantas in 1947, and *Fysh* became chairman, remaining in that post until 1966. Its first round-the-world route opened in 1958, and by the 1980s Qantas was among the 10 largest world airlines.

The Melbourne Cup, one of the most famous horse-races in the world, was first run in 1861 ... and the prize was not a cup. Archer won the race, and also the same event a year later — and the reward for his owner was prize money plus a hand-beaten gold watch. Sasanof, in 1916, was the first winner of the Melbourne Cup race actually to win a cup.

The heaviest weight carried by a Cup winner was 10st.5lb. (66 kg) — by **Carbine** in **1890**. That was also the year of the biggest Cup field ... 39 horses.

Courtesy VTA

Courtesy Qantas Airways Ltd.

MOMENTS IN AUSTRALI

Courtesy Sun News Pictorial

Bondi confrontation; bikini versus beach inspector 1961.

The mini skirt arrives; Jean Shrimpton, at the Melbourne Cup 1965.

"... THE HERMIT THRUSH"

An extract from Nellie Melba's favourite review, written in Boston in 1907 by Phillip Hale:

Courtesy La Trobe Collection

"There is still no voice like unto that of Madame Melba, and no-one of her sisters on the operatic or concert stage uses voice with the like sponteneity and ease ... It is not so much the voice of a perfect singer as it is the ideal voice of song. The hearer revels in the tonal beauty. The tones themselves are charged with emotion of which, perhaps, the singer is not always conscious. The voice is like that of the hermit thrush ..."

A MAN CALLED "MO"

His real name was Harry van der Sluys, but he adopted the name Roy Rene, after a French clown. They called him 'Mo'. He was Australia's greatest vaudeville comic.

He was born in Adelaide in February 1892, one of seven children of a Dutch-born Jew who worked as a cigar maker. He began in show business very young ... at seven he was already working as a circus bareback rider.

In 1914 he teamed with Nat Phillips to form the 'Stiffy and Mo' double act; they were astonishingly successful, but, after a long and quarrelsome career together, they finally broke up.

Mo played theatres around Australia for more than three decades, plying his own brand of leering, essentially Australian humour. He is credited with having introduced the word 'ratbag' to the language.

In 1946 Mo made the transition to radio, notably with a show called McCackie Mansion. He died in November 1954, before the arrival of television, and he was mourned by millions of Australians.

ASHION

P.M.'s wife shocks the hite House; Sonia cMahon 1971.

OUR PRIME MINISTERS

Prime Minister	Age	Term Commenced	Days in Office
Edmund Barton	51	1/1/1901	996
Alfred Deakin	47	24/9/1903	216
John C Watson	37	27/4/1904	112
George H Reid	59	18/8/1904	321
Alfred Deakin	48	5/7/1905	1227
Andrew Fisher	46	13/11/1908	201
Alfred Deakin	52	2/6/1909	331
Andrew Fisher	47	29/4/1910	1152
Joseph Cook	52	24/6/1913	450
Andrew Fisher	52	17/9/1914	405
William M Hughes	53	27/10/1915	2662
Stanley M Bruce	39	9/2/1923	2447
James H Scullin	53	22/10/1929	806
Joseph A Lyons	52	6/1/1932	2648
Earle C G Page	58	7/4/1939	19
Robert G Menzies	44	26/4/1939	856
Arthur W Fadden	46	29/8/1941	39
John J Curtin	56	7/10/1941	1368
Francis M Forde	54	6/7/1945	7
Joseph B Chifley	59	13/7/1945	1620
Robert G Menzies	54	19/12/1949	5882
Harold E Holt	57	26/1/1966	692
John McEwen	67	19/12/1967	22
John G Gorton	56	10/1/1968	1155
William McMahon	63	10/3/1971	636
E Gough Whitlam	56	5/12/1972	1071
J Malcolm Frazer	45	11/11/1975	2677
Robert J Hawke	53	11/3/1983	

Courtesy Queensland Newspapers

NOTE:
Australia has had 23 Prime Ministers; three of them — **Deakin**, **Fisher** and **Menzies** — led the nation more than once. The longest continuous term served was 16 years, 1 month and 7 days by **Robert Menzies**, the shortest terms were **Francis Forde** 7 days; **Earle Page** 19 days; **John McEwen** 22 days and **Arthur Fadden** 39 days.

John Watson was the youngest, taking office at the age of 37.

John Watson.

P.M. WITH A SECRET

*During his three terms as Prime Minister of Australia, **Alfred Deakin** boosted his income with an unusual, quite secret sideline. He worked as a freelance journalist, writing about Australian politics, as anonymous Australian correspondent for the London Morning Post.*

*Not so surprisingly, **Deakin** the correspondent often made approving comments about the performance of **Deakin** the Prime Minister. But not always. He was sometimes critical, sometimes apparently puzzled. He once wrote of **Deakin** the politician: "To some his course of conduct is thought to be taken always on the line of least resistance, while to others he is a bookish theorist recklessly pursuing impossible dreams."*

***Deakin**, born in Collingwood, Melbourne, in the gold-rush days of 1856, qualified as a barrister, but earned his living mainly as a journalist before he entered politics in 1879. He worked as a leader writer for **David Syme's** Melbourne Age. From federation time, he was Australian correspondent for the London newspaper, and he held the post for 14 years.*

*Very few people knew of his double life ... only the editor and publishers of the London Morning Post, members of his own family, a handful of friends and a taxation official. (**Deakin** always declared his income from the Morning Post.)*

He seemed to delight in the mystery of it all. "The situation is fit for fiction rather than real life," he wrote to a close friend on the Morning Post, "and that is one of its attractions though its responsibilities are hazardous in the extreme."

*Hazardous they were. The knowledge that the Prime Minister was writing as a newspaperman, appraising his own perfomance and those of his contemporaries, would certainly have given great ammunition to his political rivals. One explanation for this bizarre episode is that **Deakin** needed money. When he became Prime Minister, he had no real savings. The Morning Post job paid £500 a year.*

Alfred Deakin.

Courtesy Queensland Newspapers

BENEATH AN OUTBACK TREE, WORLD HISTORY IS FORGED

The Australian Labor Party had its beginnings in the Depression of the 1890s, which brought to a traumatic end the boom period which had followed the gold-rush days of the 1850s. That depression grew from excessive speculation by financial institutions which had been spawned by the boom, and it brought with it mass unemployment and a period of intense industrial unrest.

The trade union movement had begun in the 1850s, with an accent on craft unions and a strong campaign for the eight-hour day. The stonemasons in Sydney were the first to achieve this reform, which was still only a dream elsewhere in the world, and it spread to building workers in Melbourne the same year, 1856.

Soldiers from Brisbane make camp outside Barcaldine, March 1891.

Courtesy John Oxley Library

Australia's first eight-hour-day march; Sydney 1871

By the late 1880s and early 1890s the movement was looking for expansion into direct political involvement. Its first great challenges came with the series of Depression-time strikes which embraced the coal-mining, shipping and pastoral industries. The maritime strike which lasted from August to November 1890 was the largest and most bitter Australia had ever seen. It began with a clash between marine officers engaged on coastal shipping and ship owners, but it quickly spread through a range of unions in the three eastern colonies. In each capital city special constables of militia took arms, and in

Sydney 36 mounted troopers charged a crowd of 10,000 protesters.

*Weeks after the maritime strike had been broken came the shearers' strike of 1891, which was essentially a battle of wills over the issue of unionism versus freedom of contract. The shearers, represented by **W.G. Spence**, president of the Amalgamated Shearers' Union, were determined that there should be a closed shop in the industry. The pastoralists insisted on the right to employ non-unionists. The strike was strongest in Queensland, where 8000 workers formed armed camps ready to oppose 1000 strike-breakers recruited from Victoria and New South Wales; but it spread to other colonies, and various unions joined the shearers.*

*At Barcaldine, about 1000 strikers set up camp under the Eureka flag and marched one night through the town behind a brass band, carrying torches, chanting, "We will not surrender", and finally burning an effigy of the Premier of the time, **Sir Samuel Griffiths**. As strikers clashed with strike-breakers and troops, unionists burned wool and shearing sheds on stations employing 'black' labour. On March 16 1891, militant unionists placed two iron bars across rail tracks in an attempt to derail a troop train on the Clermont line, and on April 1 a wooden bridge on the same line was sabotaged when wooden crosshead girders and piles were sawn through.*

After more provocation, as shearers switched railway points and blocked railway lines with tree trunks to delay trains carrying police and strike-breakers to the battle areas, 400 police invaded Clermont and

Barcaldine. At Clermont, after a police sergeant was struck by one of a volley of stones thrown by unionists, mounted police charged the shearers. At Barcaldine, 200 mounted troopers raided the strike headquarters and arrested 12 union leaders, charging them with conspiracy. Another group arrested at Clermont were taken to Barcaldine in chains, escorted by members of the Queensland Rifle Corps carrying fixed bayonets.

Thirteen of the strike organisers were sentenced to three years' hard labour on St. Helena Island in Moreton Bay. The strikers were defeated, and pastoralists reserved the right to employ non-union workers.

*Many of the strike meetings at Barcaldine took place under a healthy young gum tree near the railway station, and in 1892 a meeting of various unions was held under the same tree to endorse a Labor candidate for parliament. The sitting member for Barcoo, **Frank Murphy**, a conservative and the owner of Northampton Downs Station, had died, and a by-election was to be held.*

*The unionists came from neighbouring regions on horseback, bicycle and on foot to register their votes. **T.J. Ryan** — one of the men arrested in the shearers' strike, but not the **T.J. Ryan** who later became premier of Queensland — was endorsed as a candidate and finally elected to parliament. He was the first parliamentary representative of organised labour in the world. With his election came a firm change in the cause of labour, and ultimately the direction of politics in Australia.*

Courtesy Warwick & District Tourist Association

MAN IN A SINGLET

Some men are remembered in statue, some in song. Mountains are named for some people, and shrubs and trees. The greatest shearer of them all has his name enshrined in a singlet, of a kind he never wore.

The name is Jackie Howe, and in the days when wool was king he was the best, the fastest, of all the men who made a living out of barbering sheep. On October 10 1892, at Alice Downs Station (Queensland), he set the world record by shearing 321 sheep in 7 hours 40 minutes ... with blades, not a shearing machine. He really worked with big scissors.

He was a handsome man, well muscled and around 14 stone, and his father was a circus acrobat. When a eucalyptus company offered a gold medal for the highest tally of sheep shorn by hand and another for the most shorn by machine, he won both.

One week before his record blade tally, Howe skimmed the wool off 1437 sheep in 44½ hours; it is an endurance record which still stands.

The singlet is a shearer's garment, usually blue or black and flannel, always without sleeves. The story goes that a huge shearer once found the sleeves of his flannel 'bluey' restricting, and ripped them off at the shoulder, declaring: "I'll make a Jackie Howe out of it." The name stuck.

When big stores sent out catalogues advertising Jackie Howe singlets, Howe's widow tried to stop them. She claimed he never wore a sleeveless singlet, and she would have known: a dressmaker, she made all his singlets. A lawyer pointed out that no defamation was involved, and the name endured.

Within a few years the tree under which the strikers and the unionists met became known as the Tree of Knowledge. A plaque beneath its aging trunk pays tribute to:

"The loyalty, courage and sacrifice in 1891 of the stalwart men and women of the west from whom, beneath this tree emerged Australia's labour and political movement".

AUSTRALIA GOES TO WAR AGAIN ...

Another call to arms. Another eager rush of brave young men. Another terrible catalogue of casualty lists, this time lasting six years. And this time a real threat to Australia. There was less jingoism in the summer of 1939, and no brass bands and banners to lead men to the recruiting offices. Even the politicians reined back their rhetoric, with no promises about the last man and the last shilling. On the evening of September 3 1939, Australians sitting around mantel model radios in their kitchens and parlours heard Neville Chamberlain broadcast the news that his efforts to preserve peace, in effect to appease Germany, had failed. And 75 minutes later Australia's own Prime Minister, Robert Gordon Menzies, declared that it was his melancholy duty to inform the nation: "In consequence of the persistence of Germany in her invasion of Poland, Great Britain has declared war upon her, and that, as a result, Australia is also at war. No harder task can fall to the lot of a democratic leader than to make such an announcement ..."

There was undoubtedly cause for cynicism among Australians, who had suffered so grievously for Britain's participation in another distant war, another war against Germany, not so long before ... within the lifetime, in fact, of all who had reached adulthood. But cynicism was not apparent. With remarkably little dissent, the Australian nation mobilised again for war. And again, leaders on both sides of politics were united in the notion that Australia must go to the aid of Britain ... that Britain's war was Australia's.

Said *Menzies:* "The history of recent months in Europe has been one of ruthlessness, indifference and inhumanity, which the darkest centuries can scarcely parallel ... It may be taken that Hitler's ambition is not to unite all the German people under one rule, but to bring under that rule as many countries as can be subdued by force. If this is to go on, there can be no security in Europe and no peace for the world." Labor leader *John Curtin* put his party's view: "We stand for the maintenance of Australia as an integral

part of the British Commonwealth of Nations. The party will do all that is possible to safeguard Australia, and at the same time, having regard to its platform, will do its utmost to maintain the integrity of the British Commonwealth."

Courtesy Herald & Weekly Times Limited

Again, a volunteer Australian Imperial Force was recruited for service overseas. There had been five divisions in the First AIF, so the first division formed for the 2nd AIF was the Sixth Division ... and although the mood this time was more sober and purposeful, the first 20,000 quickly volunteered. The Sixth Division marched through Sydney early in January 1940 before half a million people, and sailed for the Middle East. Compulsory military training was introduced for home defence, including Papua New Guinea, and soon the militia numbered 80,000 men.

Events in Europe affected recruiting for the AIF. During the period of the 'phony war', during which Germany took a pause after crushing Poland, only 15,000 more enlisted in the first half of 1940. Then in the three months from June to August 1940, as Germany lunged through Holland and Belgium to France, slaughtering large numbers of innocent civilians, more than 100,000 rushed to join the AIF. New divisions were formed, and the Ninth and Seventh headed also to the Middle East, with the Eighth given the task of assisting British forces to hold Malaya and Singapore.

Australia involved itself enthusiastically in the Empire Air Training Scheme, whose task it was

to produce 50,000 fliers for combat every year. Australian air crews, trained in Australia and Canada, served with Royal Air Force and Royal Australian Air Force squadrons in Europe, the Middle East and the Pacific; seven thousand Australian airmen lost their lives in missions over Europe, and more than 10,000 were lost during the war. The Royal Australian Navy also served in both theatres of war from 1939 to 1945; three cruisers and four destroyers were lost in the conflict, and naval casualties totalled more than 2000.

The 2nd AIF distinguished itself in operations against the Germans, Italians and Vichy French ... the Sixth Division on the African coast and later in Greece and Crete, the Seventh in Syria and Lebanon, and the Ninth (which relieved the Sixth) notably in the 194-day siege of Tobruk. While they were making history in the desert, Australia suddenly found itself in very real peril. The Japanese, after its 'day of infamy' carrier-borne assault on Pearl Harbour on December 7 1941, swept down through the Pacific, inflicting catastrophic defeats on the British in Singapore and Malaya, and sinking the only two British capital ships in the Pacific, the Prince of Wales and Repulse. In the supposedly impregnable fortress of Singapore, the British commander ordered a surrender of his 140,000 troops. The Australian Eighth Division, which had suffered 3000 casualties during the swift 70-day campaign, was lost; nearly 15,400 were taken prisoner, and about one third of the Australians died in captivity, either of illness, on death marches, or on forced labour projects like the Burma railway.

The new Labor Prime Minister John Curtin, who had taken office only two months before Japan entered the war, emerged as a courageous and visionary leader. His nation was virtually defenceless, and he appreciated from the moment he declared war — not waiting, as in other wars, for Britain to act first — that Australia depended not on Britain but on the United States. His historic announcement on December 17 1941 said in part:

"The Australian government ... regards the Pacific struggle as primarily one in which the United States and Australia must have the fullest say in the direction of the democracies' fighting plan.

"Without inhibitions of any kind, I make it quite clear that Australia looks to America, free of any pangs as to our traditional links or kinship with the United Kingdom.

"We know the problems that the United Kingdom faces. We know the constant threat of invasion. We know the dangers of dispersal of strength, but we know, too, that Australia can go and Britain can still hold on.

"We are, therefore, determined that Australia shall not go, and we shall exert all our energies towards the shaping of a plan, with the United States as its keystone, which will give to our country some confidence of being able to hold out until the tide of battle swings against the enemy."

That is what happened, of course. The tide of battle did swing against Japan. But not before *Curtin* had fought hard with *Winston Churchill* for the return of *Australian* divisions from the *Middle East, and Australia had itself become a virtual armed American base, hosting a million GIs under* General Douglas Macarthur.

Australian towns were bombed, with the worst raid occurring at Darwin on February 19 1942 (see box), and Japanese

JAPANESE BOMBS ON DARWIN: 243 DIE

Darwin was the only Australian city heavily and repeatedly attacked by Japanese bombers during World War II. This unfortunate distinction began with two raids on February 19 1942 by 242 carrier-borne and land-based aircraft.

On that day 243 people were killed and 300 wounded. Almost every Australian and American plane in Darwin was destroyed on the ground. Eight ships were sunk and 13 damaged, and on the ships alone 172 were killed.

A missionary on Bathurst Island, **Father John McGrath**, had in fact seen the huge first strike force overhead, and radioed the RAAF control room in Darwin: "I have an urgent message. An unusually large air formation bearing down on us from the north-west. Identity suspect. Visibility not clear."

The message was received, but no alarm was sounded until the bombs began to fall.

In the panic that followed the first raid, much of the civilian population of Darwin fled into the bush. They were joined in disorganised convoys by deserting army and air force personnel, who were convinced that a Japanese invasion was imminent. Bicycles, horses, trucks, a road grader, a sanitary cart, an ice-cream vendor's bicycle cart and 'borrowed' government cars were used in what became known derisively as the Adelaide River Stakes.

A Royal Commission was held into circumstances of the raid and behaviour afterwards. It reported solemnly that some air force deserters had reached Batchelor (62 miles away), others had got to Adelaide River (72 miles away) and one to Daly Waters (400 miles away). One had reached Melbourne (2500 miles away) in 13 days. Inefficient leadership was blamed.

Darwin was bombed on 58 other occasions between March 4 1942 and November 12 1943. Mostly they were nuisance raids, but some attacks were heavy. For most of this time Darwin was defended by Spitfire and Kittyhawk fighters.

Courtesy Australian War Memorial

midget submarines entered Sydney Harbour. A turning point came when American carrier-based planes met a large Japanese naval force in the Battle of the Coral Sea in May 1942, sinking a Japanese carrier and causing an invasion fleet of troopships to turn back. It was later claimed that the 27 troop transports were headed for Port Moresby, Townsville, Noumea, Sydney and Melbourne. Conscripts fought with AIF volunteers in the bitter New Guinea campaign, in which the Japanese were resisted in the most appalling mountain and jungle conditions, and finally vanquished. In that campaign the Australians lost 5700 and the Americans 2800; of the 17,000 Japanese involved in the fighting, about 10,000 died.

When World War II ended, after the atomic bombing of Hiroshima and Nagasaki in August 1945, the Australian dead numbered 33,826, one-third of them airmen. More than 180,000 had been wounded, and 23,000 taken prisoner. The cost was terrible, but not nearly as punishing as it had been in the First World War. For this, improved medical services were partly responsible. But the nature of war had changed. In 1939–45 there was less accent on senseless trench slaughter; there were no Sommes, Passchendaeles, Gallipolis. This was a more mechanised war; true there were bayonet charges and hand-to-hand battles, particularly in the jungles, but the nuclear technology which ended the war was symbolic. This time the innocents suffered more than the combatants ... in the bombardments of British and European cities, in the Nazi concentration and extermination camps, and finally in the use of a weapon which would have a profound effect on war and international politics.

August 1945; World War II ends and the lights go on again all over Australia.

1893

Courtesy John Oxley Library

1974

Courtesy Queensland Newspapers

Courtesy Kevin Diletti/Weldon Trannies

TWO AWFUL FLOODS

The Brisbane River was the centre of the two worst capital-city floods Australia has known. One occurred in 1893, the second in 1974.

In 1893, the river swelled, engulfed whole suburbs, and carried great numbers of houses swiftly with it, crashing them against the Victoria Bridge. Half the Indooroopilly railway bridge, a substantial iron structure, was carried away; the next day the great Victoria Bridge, spanning the river from the city to what is now the area beside Brisbane's Cultural Centre, was destroyed.

Steamers and other craft on the Brisbane River were lifted and deposited high and dry. The gunboat *Gayundah, was left sitting incongruously among the palms and bougainvillaea* of the Botanic Gardens. After a £6000 tender had been accepted for the task of returning her to the river, a second burst of flooding lifted the warship and deposited her back where she belonged.

On Australia Day 1974, in the wake of a cyclone called Wanda, Brisbane was devastated again by terrible flooding. Again, houses were simply picked up and swept away. In Brisbane 13,750 houses were destroyed or damaged, and in neighbouring Ipswich the house casualties totalled 4000. Fifteen people died in the floods.

Courtesy Herald & Weekly Times Limited

A CYCLONE CALLED TRACY

Darwin is a tough town. It has been devastated four times, three by cyclones (in 1897, 1937 and 1974) and once by Japanese bombers (1942). The 1974 cyclone was called *Tracy*; it was a ball of meteorological fury that developed into one of the worst of its kind in recorded history.

It hit on Christmas Day. At that time Darwin had a population of some 47,000. Thirty-five thousand, including most of the women and children, were flown out in the next few days, in the biggest peacetime airlift the nation has known.

About 90 per cent of the city's homes were destroyed, 50 lives were lost in Darwin and at least another 16 at sea. The recorded surface wind speed was 217 km per hour.

THE BATTLE OF BENNELONG POINT

The man who designed the Sydney Opera House was the Danish architect **Joern Utzon** (born 1918), but he was unable to supervise its construction. He resigned from the task after a series of clashes with the New South Wales Government, mainly over construction costs.

Utzon won a competition organised by the NSW Government for construction of a cultural centre at Bennelong Point, Sydney. From 222 entries which came from 32 countries his was judged to be the best ... and he was awarded the $10,000 first prize, with a contract to oversee construction, the first stage of which began in 1959.

The arguments began soon after, with **Utzon** claiming the Government was pushing ahead with construction before the design had been finalised. As costs soared, from the equivalent of $7 million in 1959 to $48 million in 1965, the architect's arguments with the newly elected Liberal government became more heated.

After his resignation, construction went ahead. When the job was completed in 1973, the cost had exceeded $102 million.

THE NATION'S LEADER DISAPPEARS IN SURF

Courtesy Weldon Trannies

Harold Holt, **Australia's 18th Prime Minister, succeeded** *Sir Robert Menzies* **in January 1966. He was 57 years old, trim, affable and energetic.**

Before the end of 1966 he trebled Australia's military commitment to the Vietnam war, took the politically touchy decision to send conscripts to the war, visited Australian and American troops on the Vietnam front, visited the American President *Lyndon Johnson* **and was in turn visited by him, and fought and won an election.**

On December 17 1967, he went swimming in the ocean beach off Portsea, Victoria. He swam strongly for a time, then disappeared in boiling surf. A witness said: "It was like a leaf being taken out. It was so quick, so final." A huge air and sea search was mounted, but his body was never found. He had been Prime Minister for just 692 days.

SLASHING THE RIBBON

The first proposal for a bridge across Sydney Harbour came from the ex-convict architect **Francis Greenway,** *in* **1815.** *When it was built in* **1932,** *after nine years' work, it was described as the greatest bridge of the age.*

One of the longest single-span bridges in the world, the Sydney Harbour Bridge has a length of 1149 metres, with 52 metres clearance for shipping. The actual arch is 503 metres long and its highest point is 134 metres above sea level. It is known fondly as the Coathanger.

Its opening — covered 'as it happened' by a national network of 40 wireless stations — was unconventional. As the New South Wales Premier, **Jack Lang,** *prepared to cut a ribbon with a pair of golden scissors, and declare the bridge open, a horseman rode forward with his sword upraised and slashed the ribbon.*

The interloper, wearing the uniform of the Royal Hussars, was **Captain Francis Edward De Groot,** *a member of the Fascist-inspired New*

Courtesy National Library of Australia

Guard which opposed 'Langism'. **De Groot** *was arrested and charged with being insane. The case was dismissed, and he was fined only for offensive behaviour. After the demise of the New Guard in* **1935,** *De Groot returned to his birthplace of Dublin, where he died in* **1969.**

THE WORST BUSHFIRES

1939.

Australia's two worst bushfires occurred in January **1939** *and February* **1983.** *Both followed long periods of drought, and both occurred in searing temperatures combined with low relative humidity.*

During the **1939** *fires, 71 people died in Victoria and one in South Australia. In* **1983** *the toll was 46 dead in Victoria and 26 in South Australia. Thirteen volunteer firefighters died, and 2000 homes were destroyed.*

In February **1967,** *in similar conditions, bushfires in Tasmania penetrated to within two kilometres of the centre of Hobart, and killed 62 people.*

1967.

Vida Goldstein

Catherine Spence

Courtesy La Trobe Collection

Courtesy National Library of Australia

Courtesy Weldon Trannies

WOMEN ... AND THE RIGHT TO VOTE

Australia — and particularly the colony of South Australia — was something of a pioneer in giving all citizens the right to vote. South Australia's was the first government in the world to give manhood suffrage, to all males over 21, in 1855; the other colonies followed.

In 1894 South Australia introduced the voting right for women, and became the second government in the world (behind New Zealand) to do so. Western Australia followed in 1899, New South Wales in 1902, Tasmania in 1903, Queensland in 1905 and Victoria in 1908.

There was opposition, of course, in the South Australian Parliament. One member, J.L. Stirling, declared that women were "mostly content to trust their husbands in matters political, just as men left household duties to their wives".

The Adelaide Observer commented: "It has always been an anomaly in the colony, that while the most drunken, ignorant man in the community possessed the technical qualifications to vote for members of Parliament and to be a member himself, the most intellectual and noble woman has not enjoyed such rights."

THE FIRST BIG FILM OF ALL

The first full-length film in the world was produced in Melbourne in 1900. It was called Soldiers of the Cross and sponsored by the Salvation Army, which was also responsible for the opening of the first film studio in the country, in 1909.

Bushranging themes dominated two of the nation's earliest feature films, The Story of the Kelly Gang, and Robbery Under Arms.

Two major producers in the 1930s and 1940s were Charles Chauvel and K.G. Hall, and they worked with such actors as Errol Flynn, Peter Finch and Chips Rafferty.

The introduction of television was at first detrimental to the film industry, but its resurgence from the late 1960s was assisted by the formation of bodies like the Australian Film Development Corporation and the Australian Film and Television School.

In recent years Australia has had much international film success ... with performers like Judy Davis, Helen Morse, Wendy Hughes, Mel Gibson, Jack Thompson, Bryan Brown and Sam Neil, directors like Peter Weir and Bruce Beresford, and films like Crocodile Dundee, Breaker Morant, Gallipoli, My Brilliant Career and The Man from Snowy River.

THE FIRST OF A KIND

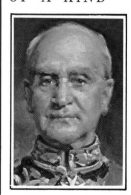

The first Australian-born Governor-General was Sir Isaac Isaacs, an eminent Jew who had been a Victorian and federal politician, federal Attorney-General, a judge of the High Court for 25 years and Chief Justice for two years.

When Lord Stonehaven retired as Governor-General, the Prime Minister, James Scullin, put forward the name of Isaacs and outlined his career. King George V was not impressed, and the historian Manning Clark records that he asked

sharply through his secretary: "Who is Isaac Isaacs?"

Scullin stood firm, and an unwilling King announced with as good grace as possible the appointment of Australia's own representative of His Majesty.

Isaacs was born in 1855, the same year as Ned Kelly. He was Governor-General from 1931 to 1936, and he died in 1948, the year Israel and India became independent.

Courtesy Australian Gallery of Sport

GOLD! GOLD! GOLD!

◁ *"Edwin" Flack.*

Australia's first Olympic gold medallist was the runner *E.H. 'Edwin' Flack,* **who won the 800 and 1500 metres at the inaugural Games at Athens in** *1896,* **and our first woman Olympic champion was the swimmer** *Fanny Durack,* **winner of the 100 metres freestyle at Stockholm in** *1912.*

The youngest Australian Olympic winner was *Shane Gould,* **who was 15 years nine months** when she won three gold medals in Munich in *1972. Claire Dennis* was **16 years five months when she won the 200 metres breaststroke in Los Angeles in** *1932,* **and** *Murray Rose* **was 16 years 10 months when he won gold medals in Melbourne in** *1956.*

The oldest was *Bill Northam,* **a 59-year-old grandfather when he won the 5.5 metres class yachting at the** *1964 Tokyo Games.*

Father-and-son Olympians were *Bill Northam* (yachting, 1964) **and his son** *Rodney* (rowing, 1968); *Bill Roycroft* (equestrian, 1960, 1964, 1968, 1972 and 1976) **and his sons** *Barry* (equestrian, 1964 and 1976), *Wayne* (equestrian, 1968, 1976 and 1984) **and** *Clarke* (equestrian, 1972); *Dick Garrard* (wrestling, 1936, 1948, 1952 and 1956) **and his son** *Dick* (rowing,

1964); *Cecil Pearce* **(rowing 1936) and his son** *Gary* **(rowing, 1964, 1968 and 1972).**

Three Australians have won medals at three consecutive Olympics: rower *Mervyn Wood* **(1948, 1952 and 1956),** athlete *Shirley Strickland* **(1948, 1952 and 1956)** and swimmer *Dawn Fraser* **(1956, 1960 and 1964).**

Courtesy All-Sport Australia

Dean Lukin. △

THE HEROES ... AND THE GOLDEN GIRLS

When Australia's Sporting Hall of Fame was inaugurated three years ago, it was decided that there would be only two first inductees ... a male and a female. After that there would be no rankings. Just to be a member of the elite group, selected from Australia's entire sports history, dating back past the turn of the century, would be honour enough for anyone. In this Bicentennial year, the number of champions represented totals, approximately enough, 200.

The No. 1 sportsman named was Sir Donald Bradman. The first sportswoman was the swimmer Dawn Fraser, and her choice was deserved. She was not only one of the most durable athletes ever, winning the same event — the 100 metres freestyle — at three successive Olympics (a feat which has never been duplicated before or since by any woman). She also had an essentially Australian spirit, a kind of Eureka Stockade spirit.

She was a battler, and at times a lovable larrikin. She bucked the system. She overcame all kinds of odds, some of them physical (she was an asthmatic). They made a movie about her. She defied officials by marching when they told her not to, and she once

pinched an Olympic flag. She was finally forced out of swimming by disqualification.

What she was remarkably good at was winning. She held the world record for her favourite distance from 1956 until 1972 — until it went, fittingly enough, to another Australian, Shane Gould. Dawn won four gold medals and four silver from 11 events over three Olympics.

Dawn was one of Australia's Golden Girls. Just a few of the others have been the swimmers Shane Gould, Michelle Ford, Claire Dennis, Lorraine Crapp and Fanny Durack, the great track and field athletes Betty Cuthbert, Marjorie Jackson, Shirley Strickland and Glynis Nunn, the tennis players Evonne Goolagong Cawley and Margaret Smith Court, the sculler Adair Ferguson, the golfer Jan Stephenson and the squash player Heather McKay.

Since the days when Frank Beaurepaire dominated pools and Norman Brookes courts, Australia has had a steady output of great swimmers and tennis players. At one stage, in Australia's most glorious tennis period during the 1950s and 1960s, the nation won 16 Davis Cup Challenge Rounds; and in 1956 Australia dominated

Courtesy Herald & Weekly Times Limited

the Olympic swimming pool, winning every individual freestyle swimming event, the relays and the men's backstroke.

The tennis greats, masterminded at one stage by the coach and non-playing captain Harry Hopman, have included Rod Laver, Lew Hoad, Ken Rosewall, Frank Sedgman, Jack Crawford, John Newcombe, Roy Emerson and Neale Fraser. Among the finest male swimmers have been Murray Rose, John Konrads, Jon Henricks, John Devitt, John Marshall, David Theile, Michael Wenden, Kevin Barry and John Sieben.

The roll-call of sports heroes includes the runners Herb Elliott, Ron Clarke, John Landy, Robert de Castella, Ralph Doubell, the cyclists Russell Mockridge and Hubert Opperman, the scullers Bobby

◁ *Sandra Morgan, Dawn Fraser, Lorraine Crapp and Faith Leech. Gold medal winners 4x100 1956 Olympics.*

Courtesy All-Sport Australia

Greg Norman. △

Evonne Cawley. △

Pearce, Merv Wood and Stuart MacKenzie, the golfers Greg Norman and Peter Thompson, the yachtsman John Bertrand, the weightlifter Dean Lukin, the squash player Geoff Hunt and boxers like Les Darcy, Jimmy Carruthers, Lionel Rose, John Famechon and Jeff Fenech.

Billiards players like Walter Lindrum, all-rounders like 'Snowy' Baker, racing drivers like Jack Brabham.

The list goes on and on, embracing a legion of cricketers and football players of all codes. Some have made millions from sport, some have paid their own way across the world and settled for just impecunious glory.

Of them all, few have matched the earning power of Greg Norman, the down-to-earth blond golfer with an awesome power game. In 1986 he was unchallenged as the best in the world, and became the first non-American to head the money-winning list in one of the most lucrative fields of all.

CHAPTER SIX

ULMARRA

Ulmarra sits beside a mighty, muscular river, somehow lost in time. There is about its wharf and its serene streets a leisurely, measured mood that reflects a different age. Over the past few decades it hasn't changed much, except to become maybe a little more tranquil. It is hard to imagine, but a hundred years ago this was a bustling, thriving place.

About half a kilometre down the road from what is now the slow-beating heart of town was Lower Ulmarra, downtown Ulmarra, supporting a couple of busy schools, a hospital, three general stores, rival butchers and barbers, a gunsmith and a post and telegraph office. Nothing much remains of all that, except a derelict red-brick school building — 'Public School, 1881, says the inscription — sheltered from the road by a huge, ancient Moreton Bay fig tree.

Stand in the shade of it on a sunny afternoon, day-dream enough to unfetter the imagination, and it is possible to visualise knickerbockered small boys clambering around its inviting branches. Small boys who grew up in time to go off to the trenches in World War I.

◁
Ulmarra slumbers beside the Clarence River dreaming of its bustling past.

Coldstream St., Ulmarra's main thoroughfare, looks to be much busier in 1910 than today.

Courtesy Maclean Historical Society.

△ Patrons of The Commercial, now Ulmarra's only hotel.

△ Nothing's rushed; life has an easy pace in Ulmarra.

△ "Traffic" in one of Ulmarra's few streets.

Ulmarra is, in a sense, a casualty, a rustic victim of the road toll. That river, that river with such broad shoulders, used to be a place of lively traffic, and the wharf was filled with action. The earliest settlers brought cedar to it in bullock-drawn drays as they thinned the magnificent stands that were all around; later, as the farmers moved into the cleared lands, the river boats were laden with maize, wool, sugar cane, bacon and all kinds of dairy produce. One of the first ambitious ventures in town was a sugar mill, in **1868**, then a killing factory and bacon works, and a dairy factory taking milk from hundreds of farms. Blacksmiths were busy here, and tinsmiths too; an SP betting business thrived, and three policemen were posted to maintain law and order. All that river traffic wound down, like a tired toy, in sadly inverse ratio to the steady march through the outback of the roads. That river, the Clarence, was the pulse of Ulmarra and nearby Woodford Island, and as the cars and trucks moved in, its rhythm softened. Fifty years ago steamboats and sailing vessels stopped transporting the butter and bacon.

The town has been classified by the National Trust, which sees it as a unique example of a 19th century river port. But not many motorists on Highway One pause to savour the echoes it evokes, or even to slake a thirst in the Ulmarra pub, which has wide, easy verandahs, and a blackboard in the bar on which are chalked the biggest recent fish catches in the river. Blink, concentrate on the road ahead, and you've gone past Ulmarra. Unsurprisingly, some film makers have seen the township as an ideal setting for period pieces: The Picture Show Man, which required an out-back excursion into the days of the silent movie, was largely filmed there, as was the telemovie Fields of Fire, which focused on another, largely forgotten era.

What makes Ulmarra a special place in **1988**, though, is not just the sense of nostalgia that pervades it, or the prosperity that is obscured now in the mists of time. Ulmarra has a significant link with the First Fleet. In that tiny township which, with

environs, has a population steady around the 550 mark, are a number of families whose direct ancestors accompanied **Captain Arthur Phillip** on the astonishing sea voyage by which he brought 11 vessels 15,000 miles, over 252 days, to an unknown land. Accompanied? That is too grand a word. They were there, uncomprehendingly, fearfully, thrown around below decks in the dark. They had no idea of their destination, on this, the longest trip ever then attempted by so large a group of people. They spent much of their time battened in steaming, stinking holds, even in the tropics, and they survived. In doing so, they moved into Australian history. Forty-eight of their fellow passengers did not.

William and Doreen Bailey in the garden of their Ulmarra home.

*Three of these families are neighbours; two of them, the **Smalls** and the **Baileys**, live next door to each other, and the **Martins** are just down the road, five doors away. Tens of thousands of direct First Fleet descendants exist in Australia today, but few have a more interesting heritage than the **Martins**. Their story goes back to two Negroes, an African and a West Indian, shipped out in the largest transport of the First Fleet, the **Alexander**. This vessel, 114 feet long and 31 feet across the beam, was the most badly crammed of all. Four months before the fleet was due to sail, when 184 male prisoners were already in irons aboard her, **Phillip** complained to the Admiralty about conditions on the **Alexander**: "It will be very difficult to prevent the most fatal illness among men so closely confined; on board that ship which is to receive 210 convicts there is not a space left ... sufficiently large for 40 men to be in motion at the same time." As if to prove him right, typhus broke out in March **1787**, two months before the sailing date, incubated in the congested holds of the **Alexander**. Within a few weeks 11 of the prisoners had died; the rest were hastily disembarked while the ship was fumigated and the convict quarters swabbed with quicklime, but another five died on the **Alexander** before she sailed from Portsmouth.*

*On board her during that awful journey were **John Martin**, a Negro from Africa, sentenced at Middlesex to seven years' transportation for the theft of clothing, and **John Randall**, from the West Indies, sentenced in Manchester, also to seven years, for stealing a watch chain. With them on the **Alexander** was another Negro, a 24-year-old servant called **John Caesar**, who would make his mark on Australian history as the nation's first bushranger. **Randall** was one of the first convicts to be married in Sydney Cove, wedding an oyster pedlar called **Esther Howard** on February 20 **1788** — just 14 days after the female prisoners were brought ashore in longboats to scenes of some debauchery. **Esther Howard**, 28, had made the journey on the **Lady Penrhyn**, aboard which marines were in the habit of buying a woman for a pannikin of rum from their daily rations.*

*About these earliest marriages in Sydney Cove and there were 14 of them in the first couple of weeks — there was no great tinge of romance. Mostly they were matters of convenience, fairly brutal convenience. The Judge Advocate, **David Collins**, was generally critical. "It was soon observed with satisfaction, that several couples were announced for marriage," he wrote. "But on strictly scrutinising into the motive, it was found in several instances to originate in an idea, that the married people would meet with various little comforts and privileges that were denied those in a single state; and some, on not finding these expectations realised, repented, wished and actually applied to be restored to their former situations." Some marriages did survive, though, and yielded the first colonial-born Australians.*

John Martin and his son, unique Australians.

Jack Martin, his wife, daughter-in-law and grandchildren, 5th, 6th and 7th generation Australians.

Tombstones in Ulmarra's cemetery tell their stories . . .

generations of Martins . . .

. . . and Smalls.

Esther Howard died childless on October 11 **1789**, and less than a year later **John Randall** married another convict, an Irish girl called **Mary Butler**, who had been found guilty at the Old Bailey of stealing a basket of beans in the market at Covent Garden. She arrived in June **1790** with the Second Fleet, in the **Neptune**, and within three months she wed **Randall** at St. John's Church, Parramatta. Their first child died as an infant, and the second, **Mary**, was born in **1793**. When **Mary** was 19, she married her father's friend **John Martin**. The two Negroes had both been granted parcels of land on the northern boundary of Sydney after serving their sentences; **Randall** had 60 acres, adjoining **Martin's** 50-acre holding, and each undertook to pay a shilling a year rental.

Martin and **Randall** proved to be men of some substance. **Martin**, 57 when he married, became a constable (on a wage of thirty pence a day), and continued to clear land and cultivate it at Cornwallis and on the Field of Mars. He had three horses and 20 sheep, and at one stage owned a brickyard which employed six men. **Randall**, a good marksman, was appointed official gamekeeper to **Governor Phillip**, and achieved the unlikely distinction of becoming the first person in the colony to kill an emu. It was the first of its kind seen by the settlers, described by **Marine Lieutenant Ralph Clark** as "a remarkably large bird, as big as an Ostrich". **Randall** figured in the news once more, when four Irish convicts with blackened faces broke into his farmhouse at the Northern Boundary Farms and bludgeoned two of his employees. The intruders were later overpowered, and seven Irish convicts finally confessed to having framed a plan to attack and rob a series of homes, including **Governor Phillip's**.

The wedding of the 57-year-old black constable and the 19-year-old daughter of his black friend and neighbour took place at St. John's, Parramatta on July 20 **1812**. They had five children: **John**, **Sophia**, **Francis**, **Henry** and **Hannah**. In the **1828** census, **John Martin** senior was listed as being 73 years old, retired on a pension, with two grandchildren (by his daughter

Sophia and **John Hackett**). He died on December 22 **1837** at the age of 82. It was his son **Henry** who came to Ulmarra, lured like so many of the earliest settlers by stories of the newly discovered river, and the marvellous cedar forests which abounded nearby.

From the time the white man came, they called the Clarence the Big River. It was discovered in the **1830s** by a runaway convict from the Moreton Bay penal settlement, **Richard Craig**. He had come to Australia as a nine-year-old 'free' passenger in **1821** with his father, **William Craig**, who had been sentenced to seven years' transportation. At 16 **Richard** was himself in bad trouble; he was sentenced in **1828** to death for the theft of five head of cattle, but the sentence was later commuted to transport to the Moreton Bay penal settlement for seven years' hard labour. A year later he escaped, headed for the northern rivers area of New South Wales, and spent some years living with a tribe of blacks. Finally the Government granted him a pardon, plus a bonus of 100 gold sovereigns, for information about the whereabouts of the Big River and its entry into the sea at Shoal Bay.

When he heard about the river, and the great troves of cedar growing all around it, a shipbuilder called **Thomas Small** decided to head for the area. His father was **John Small** who had been tried at the Old Bailey in **1784** for stealing a handkerchief valued at one shilling and sentenced to seven years' transportation. He was shipped out with the First Fleet in the **Charlotte**, and in October **1788** he married another convict, **Mary Parker**, who had been sentenced to seven years for stealing; she travelled in the **Lady Penrhyn**. Theirs was one of the First Fleet marriages which lasted. After serving their time, they settled at Eastern Farms, growing wheat and maize, and later set up a 200-acre farm at Cabramatta. While a prisoner, **Thomas** was personal servant to **Governor Phillip**, and his first child **Rebecka** was born at Government House. He later became a constable, a juror and a publican. **Thomas Small** built a 52-ton schooner in his shipyard at Kissing Point on the Parramatta River, named the craft **Susan** after his

second daughter, and set off with his brother **John** to pioneer the Clarence and the cedar industry.

Between them they established something of a dynasty. **Thomas Small** brought the first cattle to the area by water in **1836** and built Ulmarra as a private subdivision, the brothers began the cedar traffic on the Clarence and leased the whole of the first settlement, Woodford Island. Around the area today, the reminders of the first brave venture into the Big River by the sons of a man who stole a handkerchief are many: the sports ground at Ulmarra, called Small Park; the island across the river from Grafton, called Susan Island after the schooner and **Thomas Small**'s daughter; the huge Moreton Bay fig which marks the site of the original Ulmarra homestead, long since burnt down; the graveyards, and particularly the family cemetery wedged behind a picket fence among cane crops on Woodford Island. The stones offer tributes to **Matilda (1860)**, **Hunter (1864)**, **Louisa (1865)**, **Elizabeth (1870)**, **John (1897)** and so many more.

Brian Small is a perky survivor, a kind of custodian of family memories at Ulmarra. He sits in his backyard under a pecan tree, talking about the waves of **Smalls** since his First Fleet ancestor. Mostly, they had big families and lived to ripe ages. **John**, the son of the convict, had 11 children, and **Brian** himself is one of a brood of 10. He is 76, and his father died at 91. "On the family form," he grins, "I reckon I'm good for a fair while yet." He wears a dark blue singlet, blue shorts, a peaked cap and has an alert, at times almost impish face. He spends a lot of time working lovingly on his **1927** Dodge, and is delighted to report that he was asked to drive it for the cameras during the making of Fields of Fire . . . "they paid $100 a day for the car, and $70 a day for me to drive it." **Brian** spent 40 years working at the dairy factory, riding a pushbike to work every day, mainly killing and curing bacon. He slaughtered around 13,000 pigs a year, and when he retired the dairy let him keep the knocking hammer he used. "It's a rare tool," he says. "I'm thinking about giving it to the historical society."

To drive around Ulmarra and Woodford Island with **Brian Small**, to explore the old graveyards and homestead sites with him, is to invite a series of snapshot observations from the past. "That old tree over there, my grandfather Alf saw two tribes of blackfellas fight for a week all around it" . . . "When my dad was born in the place that used to stand over there, the blacks heard him crying and corroboreed around the place for two weeks. He used to tell me they thought he was a new white spirit from the past." . . . "That gravestone over there, she was the midwife who was there for all us kids. That one over there, he won a state lottery one time" . . . "One of my first memories is of the roads crowded with sulkies, hundreds of people heading for the racetrack." The roads are rarely crowded now, except for the highway on which cars stream past between Grafton and the coast.

△ *Brian Small and his adored 1927 Dodge.*

△ *Brian Small beside the graves of his ancestors on Woodford Island.*

△ *Bailey Park beside the muscular Clarence River.*

△ *Lewis Ellem and in the background historic Susan Island.*

Ulmarra is exceptional, a place with a past well worth scratching. But family history is something of a cottage industry all over the district, as it is these days in so many parts of Australia. Not many minutes away in Grafton, in a lovely garden overlooking the Clarence River and Susan Island, a former headmaster, **Lewis Ellem,** *is finalising plans for a Bicentennial Reunion of his own First Fleet family. More than a thousand will attend, a family wine will be distributed, a cricket match will be held between the Sydney* **Ellems** *and all the others. The mullet are jumping in the river, and* **Lewis Ellem** *has assembled all his documents on a table under a jacaranda tree that has won the best-of-its-kind award in Grafton for the past nine years. In a city whose jacaranda festival is renowned throughout the nation, that is some accolade ... a little like a wine being chosen the best Grange Hermitage vintage of all.*

The **Ellem** *family's link with the First Fleet began with a remarkable woman called* **Ann Forbes,** *whose story provides some sort of insight into the tribulations and temptations of the time. Judged from the comfortable distance of 200 years of hindsight, it is deceptively easy to condemn the women who spent more than eight months in the bedlam of the female transport ships, for their promiscuity and often their drunkenness. It helps to consider come of the circumstances: the vulnerability of convict girls, their desire to survive at all costs, the overwhelmingly male community in which they were immersed, the everyday pattern of vice, debauchery, robbery and rape.*

△ *Just up river from Ulmarra the car ferry sedately crosses the broad Clarence.*

Ann Forbes *was 16 years old in* **1786** *when she stole some printed cotton worth 20 shillings in Surrey, in company with another girl. They were sentenced to be hanged, then reprieved and condemned to transportation. In Sydney Cove,* **Ann** *formed a union with a convict,* **George Bannister,** *and had a daughter to him. What happened to the child is not known, but in March* **1790** **Ann** *was sent in the* **Sirius** *with 96 male and 64 other female convicts to Norfolk Island. (Among the males was the troublesome Negro* **Black Caesar**)*. On the island another convict,* **William**

△ *Time glides by ... who wants to rush?*

Dring, *replaced* **Bannister** *in* **Ann's** *affections, and she bore him two children there.* **Dring** *once distinguished himself by getting drunk while unloading stores from the wrecked* **Sirius** *on Norfolk Island, and starting a fire in the hold: he spent two months confined in irons for that.* **Ann's** *obviously affectionate nature caused more problems on Norfolk Island.* **Dring** *was tried, but punished only moderately, when he assaulted a marine private who — according to the commandant,* **Lieut. Philip Gidley King** *— twice 'tempted away'* **Ann Forbes.**

On her return to Sydney in **1792 Ann** *took up with another convict,* **Thomas Huxley,** *who became a successful farmer after he had served his seven years for stealing a pig. She was first his housekeeper and was listed in the* **1828** *census as his wife. Along the way she and* **Thomas Huxley** *had nine children, and when she died in* **1851,** *aged 81, she was the oldest person from the First Fleet ever to die in Australia. When a sixth-generation descendant,* **Bruce Arnett,** *placed a headstone on her grave in a ceremony at Sackville Reach, NSW, in* **1985,** *he said: "Regarding her being wanton, she was but 16 or 17 years old when she was held for six months in prison, in the kind of conditions we could not even begin to imagine, and then sentenced to hang. As a convict girl in Sydney, one of 192 amongst over 1000 unattached men of all kinds, her position again must have been terrifying ... she was a woman to be proud of." Altogether she had 13 children.*

It was one of **Ann**'s daughters, **Charlotte**, who married **Richard Ellem**, Convict 3206, and went on to found a family that ranges from Darwin and Port Augusta across to Barcaldine and the Clarence River. It is particularly vigorous around the Clarence, where the sons of **Richard** began to settle around **1870**. Appropriately enough, the Bicentennial Reunion is to be held on the bank of the Big River. At Ulmarra. At Small Park, which honours another convict who came to a new land in **1788**.

Two little schoolgirls in coral-pink gingham school dresses symbolise more than anyone else the sense of living history that exists in Ulmarra. They are **Kylie** and **Amanda Martin**, nine and six years old respectively. They are the children of **Fred Martin** and his wife **Cheryl**, who used to be **Cheryl Bailey**. The **Bailey** family track their way back to the marriage in **1788** of two First Fleet ancestors, **William Douglas** and **Mary Graves**. **Fred** and his brother **John** are direct descendants of that unlikely marriage between a 57-year-old Negro convict and the 19-year-old daughter of his Negro friend. "Our Grandpa Reuben married his first cousin," says **John**. "Maybe that helped the skin darkness to show a bit." Maybe it does, in the most attractive way. **Kylie** and **Amanda**, two bright kids at Ulmarra State School, seventh-generation Australians on one side and ninth-generation on the other, represent a First Fleet reunion of a special kind. They have much reason to look forward to the future with confidence, and to the past with pride.

MENG KUAV AND THE BIG **V**

Lasiandra Street stretches through deepest Middle Australia, in the outer Melbourne suburb of Nunawading. It is Hill's hoist territory, picket fences at the front and palings at the sides and back. Lots of lemon trees, vegetable garden patches, boys on bikes and telegraph poles which sometimes serve as cricket stumps.

Before it was invaded, before the remorseless march of the brick veneer along the bitumen arteries out of Melbourne, this used to be a place of apple orchards and well-treed cow paddocks. There are still some fine blue gums in front gardens, and trees and shrubs continue to assert themselves in the names of crisscrossing streets: Lasiandra, Oleander, Grevillea, Eugenia, Diosma, Abelia.

In Lasiandra Street lives a Kampuchean family which fled from the capital of Phnom Penh for the best of reasons: if they had remained they would probably have been killed by the bandit army called the Khmer Rouge. They are part of Australia's latest immigration wave ... 95,300 Indo-Chinese, who constitute the greatest per capita intake of post-Vietnam-war refugees of any in the world, and who have offered yet another dimension to multiculturism in Australia. It is a friendly household, one where the mother wears long, colourful Cambodian skirts and where all sorts of enticing spice smells permeate from the kitchen.

What makes the house really different is that in it lives a boy who has already achieved an ambition about which most youngsters in Melbourne dream. He has worn the Big V. He has represented Victoria in the game which grew up in Melbourne but has since expanded throughout most of the nation: Australian Rules football. Not only that. He has captained interstate teams. That does not simply represent the mastering of a strange culture. For a boy who spent his early years amid the almost unspeakable horror of the embattled city of Phnom Penh, it means a triumph of heroic proportion.

When the boy was of an age at which his Australian counterparts are usually coming to terms with sport, his family and other citizens of Phnom Penh were being treated as scapegoats by the bandit army which had been trained by the Viet Cong: the two guerilla armies had had their supply lines and their sanctuaries bombed repeatedly by the Americans, and by some savage logic they felt that the best way to respond was to inflict atrocities on the people of Phnom Penh.

The boy is Meng Kuav, now 14 years old, whose most cherished desire is to play League football with Richmond. He has played for Victoria in under-age football since 1985, and in 1986 after having played the game for only three years — he was appointed captain of Victoria's primary school team. He is slim, wiry and fast, and his time outside school is devoted heavily in winter to the mastery of football; he practises during the week with the Richmond under-15 squad, plays junior football for Richmond on Saturdays, Mitcham on Sundays and Nunawading High School in between.

Meng was seven years old when he and his family made the escape from Phnom Penh under cover of night. He interprets for his mother as she recalls what happened: "The Khmer Rouge were killing all sorts of people, many of our friends, and torturing others. They were using us as slave labour, sending us out in parties to work on farms. We were very hungry and they were very cruel. We knew we had to go, and an escape was organised. We went in two groups, staying very quiet and moving together. A number in the first group were shot, and some people in the second decided it was too dangerous, and stayed behind. We kept going ... my husband, our two sons and my daughter. In the dark we became separated from my daughter, and she didn't get through. She is still in Phnom Penh, and I worry about her a lot. Travelling at night, hiding in the day, we moved through the jungle and crossed the border into Thailand ... then spent 12 months in a refugee camp before being allowed to come to Australia."

She tells about it so matter-of-factly, that transition from an insane nightmare to a tranquil bungalow in Lasiandra Street. Meng was a hesitant nine-year-old, still unable to understand English well, when someone threw him an Australian Rules football at primary school in Nunawading. He didn't know how to hold it. After a while he was kicking it well enough to be invited to try out with a school team. Within two years he was captaining Victoria's under-12 team.

Cricket? "It's boring," says Meng. "All that waiting around to go out and bat. It's not like footy. Even in the summer, I spend a lot of time thinking about football..."

If he realises his ambition to play in the Victorian Football League, Meng Kuav will simply add another ethnic origin to a game which ceased long ago to be the province of sportsmen of Anglo-Saxon descent. Among the names of the very best Australian Rules players these days are Demetriou, DiPierdomenico, Groenewegen, Serafini, Van Der Haar ... and now one from China, Seow.

△ *The Japanese cemetery in Broome; evidence of the town's unusual past.*

△ *Once there were 400 luggers working from Broome, this one is now a monument to that past.*

△ *Broome has style of its own, and nothing is too rushed.*

WHERE ASIA EMBRACED AUSTRALIA

Broome is a town like no other in Australia. Its history stretches back beyond that of Sydney Cove, to the days when the bizarre buccaneer, explorer and travel writer **William Dampier** *was poking around nearby coastland in the* **Cygnet in 1688** *and the* **Roebuck in 1699**. *He landed in the area with a crew of 50 men and boys in the* **Roebuck**, *dug wells for water, thought about kidnapping an Aboriginal to take back to London as a living 'specimen', was attacked by warriors and finally shot one dead. He left, disillusioned, "sorry for what had ... happened", still thirsty. His travels and the landing are remembered constantly in place names: Roebuck Bay, Dampier Creek, Dampier Terrace, the Dampier Peninsula (on which Broome stands), Buccaneer Archipelago, a rock formation called Dampier's Monument, a pastoral property called Dampier Downs.*

What makes Broome really different, though, is the lustiness rather than the length of its history; that, and the utterly cosmopolitan community that history has spawned. It used to be the pearl capital of the world, attracting huge fleets of 400 luggers which hosted 3000 divers and tenders from Japan, Malaya, Koepang, China and the

Philippines. When they came ashore the pearler men gambled, drank huge quantities of liquor, smoked opium, brawled, kept a string of brothels busy, and used pearls as well as sovereigns as currency. The Japanese imported their own prostitutes.

In a sense, during its decades of prosperity before World War I, Broome was a tropical version of an **1850**s *gold-rush town. It offered sudden wealth, and it attracted an army of adventurers ... in moleskins, in white suits, in sarongs, in coolie trousers and baggy pants, in loose white pyjamas with belts, pouches, bandannas around heads, and loose scarves around throats. At the sharp end of the industry were the divers who clumped around ocean floors in great bulbous helmets, canvas suits and leaden boots, groping around sponges and weed for the raw material that would adorn shirts, dresses, ornaments and the necks of beautiful women.*

It was a dangerous job — because of bends or 'diver's paralysis', sharks, faulty air hoses and savage cyclones. Serenely stark testimony to these hazards is offered by the neat forest of tombstones in Broome's large Japanese cemetery.

Broome is where Asia embraced Australia. It is the kind of place which would have appealed to a **Maugham**, *a* **Gauguin**, *a* **Michener**. *Over the years the races blended there, despite the efforts of an administration which tried vainly to protect the notion of White Australia, and which believed that mixed blood represented a menace. For a long time a form of reverse White Australia policy was practised, with the objective of keeping Aboriginals and Asians apart. As part of this policy of segregation, Aboriginals were not allowed on the streets of town after 6pm. It did not work, and Broome today in some ways is an outpost echo of Hawaii, a place where mixed races outnumber so many others.*

Over the years, Broome's pearl market has faded, and the lugger fleet has been reduced to a handful. What the town continues to produce and attract, though, is characters. Australians with a difference. People like **Peter Yu**, **John Jobst** *and* **Richard Bessenfelder**.

THE MAN OF THREE CULTURES

Peter Yu represents as interesting a blend of races as Australia might offer, and one which fits comfortably into the mood of Broome. He is half Chinese, half Aboriginal. He lives easily with three cultures: the two he inherited, and that of white Australia. Unusual? Maybe, somewhere else. But not in Broome, that easy-going settlement which sits decaying a little at the edges, on a lonely belt of coastline facing the Timor Sea and the Indian Ocean. And certainly not in a town where there exist so many products of sexual liaison, some of it hasty and some of it quite lasting, between Aboriginals and Chinese, Japanese, Malays, Filipinos, Cingalese and Koepangers. The fact is that for many generations the Aboriginals have found it easier to relate to other ethnic minorities — and in Broome that term embraces mainly Asians — than they have to white Australians. In the early days, the white pearling masters bore no little resemblance to the colonials of the Raj days of India, or the planters and civil servants of such outposts of the Empire as Penang, Kuala Lumpur and Singapore. They too wore well-laundered tropical suits, they too were clannishly aloof.

What separates *Peter Yu* from so many others of such radically mixed blood is the articulate ease with which he transcends cultures, plus a large degree of sophistication which has not been hindered by world travel ... but more than that, his own version of Australianism, his vision, his positive attitude. It is an attitude which seems to have relevance for all Australians.

Peter Yu has a dark, alert face on which Chinese and Aboriginal features co-exist well, from a cropped hedge of shiny, tufted hair, past angled, Oriental eyebrows to the longish, almost transparent fringe of beard at the very bottom of his chin. At 32, he is married to a white anthropologist who has borne him two children and who is busy on two projects: one involved with Catholic primary education among Aboriginals, the other a history of the Kimberleys. Ten years ago he had another marriage, to an Aboriginal girl who preferred urban life in Perth to the more isolated existence offered by Broome and the Kimberleys. There are two children of that marriage, and they visit Broome on school holidays. "It's important," says *Peter Yu* seriously, "that they maintain links with their extended family in the Bunuba tribe."

That term — "extended family" — crops up often in *Peter Yu's* conversation. For him it covers an astonishing array of geography, south from Broome through the Kimberleys, ranging inland from the north-west coast to places like Fitzroy Crossing and Halls Creek; through villages on Kato Island in southern China, near the New Territories; in Kent, England, where a number of his father's Chinese family have settled. His special people are the Bunuba tribe ... the Aboriginals on his mother's side, a people who were systematically reduced in number and removed from their own territory in the late 19th century by pastoralists, police and an insensitive bureaucracy.

The flexibility of family bonds was demonstrated a few years back when *Peter Yu's* father, a former pearl diver called *Yau Hong Tai*, decided to go back to his old village in China for the On Loong festival, a time when homage is paid to dead ancestors. He had left a wife in the village in 1936, when he went off as a young man to sign up as an indentured worker with the lugger fleet based at Broome. Only once had he been back; during that stay — for two years in the late 1904s — he and his Chinese wife, a wife promised since boyhood, had a daughter. Then he had returned to Broome. When he went back this last time to join the village tribute to ancestors, he felt it only proper that he should take his Aboriginal wife, the mother of his nine children. After all, the children had their ancestors in the village. So it happened that the two wives, the Chinese and the Aboriginal, the mothers of his 10 children, shared a house in a village in China. They got along very well indeed. "Everyone was lovely to me in the village," says the Aboriginal wife, *Madge*, who grew up on a Catholic mission station at Beagle Bay. "They made me feel at home, as if I was one of the family."

By Broome's laissez-faire standards, *Yau Hong Tai's* matrimonial arrangements have not been seen as unconventional. Nor was his eventual marriage 10 years ago to *Madge*, after most of his nine children were grown up.

With his father away on luggers, *Peter Yu* did much of his growing up in company with his Aboriginal grandfather and *Madge*. He attended Chinese festivals, observed Chinese customs, but listened, utterly absorbed, to Aboriginal stories and legends of the Dreaming. He came to see himself basically as Aboriginal, but remained in close touch with his Chinese family. On his way back from a conference in Vancouver, he caught up with his Chinese half-sister, a seamstress who still works in his father's village. On another journey to Europe, he spent time with his father's Chinese wife, now living in Kent with a colony from the same village.

For *Peter Yu*, now executive producer of a film company, Bunuba Productions, the recent years have been studded with achievement. In 1977 he became the first Aboriginal welfare officer in the North, as well as the youngest of any race. He was the first field officer with the Kimberley Land Council, and from 1981 until its demise in 1985 was a member of the National Aboriginal Congress. At 29 he became a Justice of the Peace, and since then has sat on the bench of Broome's Court of Petty Sessions. He has represented his people in various forums overseas, including the United Nations in Geneva and the Russell Tribunal in Rotterdam.

He worked hard for the establishment of a language resource centre, which has been able to define and help keep alive 22 languages in the Kimberleys; he helped found a legal and cultural centre whose aim it is to re-establish tribal ceremonies, traditions and systems of justice. These projects indicate his highest priority: the restoration of pride and dignity to people who were in danger of losing their way.

Is he an activist, a radical? Is he angry? He seems to have enough reason to be that way. When he was sent away to a Church training school in Perth his parents were not consulted. As a high school student in Perth he and his black friends were separated from whites, referred to as "the mission kids". The reason his mother and father took so long to get married was that all sorts of legal barriers were put in their way by authorities. His parents used to have to step off the footpath to make way for white people. His mother was kept indoors at night by a curfew on Aboriginals. His father — "he has more common sense than anyone I know" — has been in court once in his life; he was fined £30 for cohabiting with his mother, who had at that time borne him half a dozen children.

He tells all this quite simply. No anger is apparent. "The skill," he says, "is to harness any resentment you may have. Control it. Use it in a positive manner. When you get knocked back it ought to make you more determined to succeed. We've had setbacks with our film company. All that's done is sharpen our desire to show that we can be as competitive and creative as anyone."

His views about the Bicentennial are interesting. "If Aboriginals don't want to celebrate the arrival of *Captain Phillip* in 1788, they have every right not to participate. If they do choose to celebrate, they should be thinking about the survival of Aboriginal culture in this country for more than 40,000 years, and the last 200 in particular. My own intention is to explain the greatness of Aboriginal culture ... show people it's still very much alive. The Bicentennial could be a time to demonstrate that Aboriginals still have a great contribution to make to the future of Australia ... if white people will let them. It's not a case of trying to make white people feel guilty about the past. What we want them to do is reassess history, recognise our culture, let us participate in the future on an equal, indigenous basis. People should feel guilty only if they want to perpetuate all the bad things that have happened. I see the Bicentennial as a time for looking forward rather than looking back."

Peter Yu's own way of looking forward is to produce a film and a book on an Aboriginal called *Jandamarra*, who used to be called *Pigeon*. He was a guerilla fighter who ran a kind of *Kelly* gang in the Kimberleys 90 years ago, resisting the white invasion of tribal lands. Bunuba Productions, whose board is made up of tribal elders, has had some early funding from the Australian Film Commission and the West Australian Film Council, and already has a fine screenplay by Sydney writer *Ian David*. A young historian, *Howard Pedersen*, is writing a book about *Pigeon*. With luck, Australia could have a new hero before too long. A black one.

△ *Peter Yu (right) and his father, Yau Hong Tai.*

◁ John Jobst the first and only Bishop of Broome.

THE BISHOP AND THE BROTHER

John Jobst and **Richard Bessenfelder** have so much in common, but are a very long way apart. Essentially they are both in the business of saving souls, mainly Aboriginal souls. They have both devoted much of their lives to missionary work, as members of the Pallottine Pious Society of Missions, an order which was founded in Italy in **1835** but which in Australia has long had a German flavour. They both trained at a seminary near Munich, and in the mid-**1930s** knew each other brushingly. **Richard**, nine years the older, was a novitiate then, and **John** was attending a school run by the Pallottines. "He was an eager lad, very energetic and agile," says **Richard** of the younger man. At different times, they both came to the mission in the north-west of Australia which had been taken over in **1901** by the Pallottines, after French Trappists had abandoned it as too difficult. For both men it must have been something of a culture shock, coming from a rustic, verdant, closely settled corner of Germany to 773,000 square kilometres of parched, dry emptiness in the Kimberleys. Both coped with the transition well. The Pallottines are a hardy order, used to challenge, with a long and proud record of handling inhospitable conditions in Africa.

The similarity between the two men ends around that point. They represent very different levels in the structure of the Church. **John Jobst**, the eager 13-year-old, went on to become the Catholic Church's Vicar Apostolic of the Kimberleys in **1959**, and the first and only Bishop of Broome in **1966**. He is a bishop with a mildly unconventional background, having served during World War II with **Hitler's** Panzer Division, in the elite Grosse Deutschland Korps. To add to the incongruity, he has been

honoured by the nation which was once his army's enemy; in **1981** Queen Elizabeth created him a Commander of the Order of the British Empire. He flies his own plane around a beat which includes such lonely outposts as Lombadina, Beagle Bay, Yiyili, Lake Gregory, Balgo Hills, Halls Creek and Turkey Creek, as well as bigger towns like Wyndham and Derby. In his massive diocese are 22,000 people, among them 6500 Catholics. Of the Catholics, at least 5500 are Aboriginals.

Richard Bessenfelder is, by contrast, distinctly earth-bound. His career path has been less ambitious. Born in **1912**, he worked for a time as a cook in the seminary before coming to Australia in **1935**. He is **Brother Richard**, and he has spent more than half a century in the Kimberleys, much of it looking after cattle on missions at Beagle Bay and La Grange. He has had odd trips on leave to his lovely home town of Karlsruhe, very close to the Black Forest. Nothing could have been farther in mood from Karlsruhe than those distant mission stations where mosquitoes and flies flourished, where men from Europe conducted Masses and tried to explain the Gospels to primitive natives. "The heat was never a problem," he says. "I found it difficult to come to terms with distance, and time, and isolation. When you think about the pastoral work you can

perform, the calls you can make on a push-bike in Germany, and compare it with here, it's like multiplying by a hundred." The Bishop and the Brother met for the first time since seminary days when **John Jobst** arrived in Beagle Bay in **1951**. "I took one look around and wanted to go home," says the Bishop. "I promised myself I'd never come back to this godforsaken place again."

Brother Richard also had a rather different kind of war. In **1941** he was rounded up as an enemy alien and put in jail in Broome. While many of his compatriots went to internment camps, and his brother missionaries were given work in Sydney and Melbourne, he was soon back among the Aboriginals and the battle. Which was just as well. In early **1942** he became a hero, leading a rescue team to help survivors of a Dutch plane shot down over Carnot Bay, about 100 kilometres from Broome.

Somebody once asked **Bishop Jobst** if he felt closer to God when he was flying. "I suppose I would if I stepped out," he answered sweetly. He has come just a little closer with the odd flying accident, and on September 14 **1978** he suffered severe head and internal injuries when he crash-landed on the way to Turkey Creek. "Looks like we're out of fuel," said his Aboriginal passenger, **Stephen Albert**, as the plane's engine began to hiccough and sputter. They were: a fuel blockage had occurred, and the Bishop brought the plane down well but hard. **Stephen** stumbled through harsh country for aid, waving his shirt when he saw a cloud of dust from a four-wheel drive. The vehicle went right past him to the Bishop, who finished up spending 10 weeks in hospital. He was still in some pain when he took up his new plane. "I had to do it straight away," he explained. "I had to ensure that I wasn't going to be frightened of flying."

He probably need not have worried. He is not the sort of man who travels with fear. Bavarian-born, he was called up for military service from the seminary. "The Gestapo gave me a hard time when I didn't want to join up," he says. "I trained as a medical orderly for a month, then found myself attached to the Panzers." He was with the Grosse Deutschland Korps as it fought across Europe and into Russia; he was wounded twice, the second time severely. "I got a sliver of steel from a Russian mortar in my head and was unconscious for three days and nights," he says. He woke up in a Russian field hospital, was repatriated to Germany and handed over to the Americans as a prisoner of war. After three months' confinement, he was released and returned to the seminary.

After his dispatch to Australia as a missionary and the first bleak impressions of Beagle Bay, he spent some years lecturing at religious institutions in Sydney before he was posted to Broome. He quickly realised that if he was going to spread himself around the diocese effectively he needed to fly. An appeal was launched, and in 10 days enough money had been raised for the Bishop to buy his first plane. In **1964** he began the series of whistle-stop tours — most of them over several days and several thousand kilometres — which continue to keep him in touch with his flock and his 63 priests, brothers and sisters, who are helped by 50 lay missionaries and teachers. His priority has been education: so far he has built 10 primary schools, a co-educational secondary school, a residential college, seven churches and a cathedral. A tall man who has retained a soldierly bearing and a wry sense of humour, he still has the boundless energy which impressed **Brother Richard** so long ago. He has logged more than 5000 flying hours.

When he went to Broome, only 220 attended Catholic schools. Now the figure is 1400. "It's important for the Aboriginal kids," he says. "If you give them education, you give them some sort of chance for the future." In every sense, **John Jobst** remains at 68 a man with a mission.

Brother Richard can grin now when he talks about being locked up during the war. "Someone must have thought I was dangerous," he says. "When the policeman came to get me he told me I was under arrest, but he had to go and pick up another German a fair distance away. He made me promise not to escape ... as if there was anywhere you could go in that country. When he took me into Broome, they confiscated my high-velocity rifle. I was technically a prisoner, but they didn't even lock the jail doors during the day. Finally they decided I wasn't a menace, and let me go back to Beagle Bay. They gave me my rifle back. You need them, you know ... you can come across some very savage beasts out there, and you have to use a gun to get fresh meat."

On March 3 **1942**, Japanese Zero fighters strafed Broome, killing at least 70 people and destroying all Allied aircraft in the port...16 flying boats, four bombers and three transports. On the way back from Broome to Java, one of the Zeros attacked a Dutch DC3 bringing refugees to Australia. It crash-landed

Courtesy Broome Historical Society.

△ *B17 bomber; victim of the Japanese Zeros.*

on a strip of beach at Carnot Bay, was strafed repeatedly by the Zero, then bombed the next day by a Japanese flying boat. Of the 15 people aboard, four died and several others were badly wounded. When an Aboriginal reported to the Beagle Bay mission that a plane was down, **Brother Richard** set off with a search party. After a journey which took 20 hours, he tended the wounded, provided food and water to the survivors, then headed back for the mission. When this arduous journey was over, and the survivors were receiving treatment at Beagle Bay, he quietly set off again. There was something he had to do, and it meant another exhausting crossing from the mission to the wreckage. He had helped the living. Now he had to attend the dead.

Ulmarra, Broome, Grafton and Nunawading offer interesting vantage points from which to observe Australia and some Australians during the year of the Bicentennial. From them it is possible to take a look at descendants of the people who arrived in that brave, pathetic little armada in 1788, and at people who represent the very latest wave of immigrants. It is possible too to learn something of the culture and the frustrations of those who were here long before 1788, and to appreciate some attitudes of much-later outsiders who became Australians.

The most these diverse viewing platforms can provide, though, are glimpses. No great truths or insights. Just fragments of a complex, contradictory country ... one which is both highly urbanised and yet profoundly, eternally empty. Where it is still possible for young, intelligent people to perish in the outback, in much the fashion of Burke and Wills. Where a New world has tried to come to terms with an Old. A thousand vantage points will offer hundreds of thousands of perceptions of this continent, all of them very different.

Through all the agonies and exultations of the past couple of hundred years, an essential Australian character has been shaping, and all kinds of traditions and cultures emerging. 1988 is a good year to assess them, to see where this country has been since the arrival of the white man. It is a good year, too, to reflect that the shaping process is not finished, that it simply continues ... that Australia has a future every bit as challenging as the past.

The mosaic has many tiles to come.

INDEX

RECOMMENDED FURTHER READING

Triumph of the Nomads, **Geoffrey Blainey** (Macmillan) **1975**.
The Tyranny of Distance, **Geoffrey Blainey** (Macmillan) **1966**.
A Land Half Won, **Geoffrey Blainey** (Macmillan) **1966**.
The Fatal Shore, **Robert Hughes** (Collins Harvill) **1987**.
The Crimes of the First Fleet Convicts, **John Cobley** (Angus and Robertson) **1970**.
1788, The People of the First Fleet, **Don Chapman** (Doubleday) **1986**.
The First Settlement, **Jonathan King** (Macmillan) **1984**.
A Short History of Australia, **Manning Clark** (Mead and Beckett) **1981**.
Australia: History and Horizons, **Roderick Cameron** (Wiedenfeld and Nicolson) **1971**.
The Angus and Robertson Concise Australian Encyclopaedia, (Angus and Robertson) **1986**.
"In the Beginning", edited by **Jonathan King** (Macmillan) **1985**.
The Story of the Australian People, **Donald Horne** (Reader's Digest) **1985**.
A Concise History of Australia, **Clive Turnbull**, with additional text by **Marjorie Tipping** (Currey O'Neil) **1983**.
An Eyewitness History of Australia, **Harry Gordon** (Currey O'Neil) **1986**.
They All Ran Wild, **Eric C. Rolls** (Angus and Robertson) **1969**.
They Dared Mightily, **Lionel Wigmore** (Australian War Memorial) **1986**.
The Inland Sea: Charles Sturt's Expedition, 1844-45, **Edward Stokes** (Hutchinson) **1986**.
Australia's Yesterdays, (Reader's Digest) **1986**.
"I See No End to Travelling", compiled by **Ann Millar** (Bay Books) **1986**.
Dictionary of Australian History, compiled by **Brian Murphy** (Fontana/Collins) **1982**.
The Irish in Australia, **Patrick O'Farrell** (NSW University Press) **1987**.

Gallipoli to the Somme, **Dudley McCarthy** (John Ferguson) **1983**.
Australia Brought to Book, edited by **Kaye Harman** (Boobook Publications) **1985**.
The Shearers, **Patsy Adam-Smith** (Nelson) **1986**.
John Monash, **Geoffrey Serle** (Melbourne University Press) **1982**.
Australian Cricket, **Jack Pollard** (Hodder and Stoughton) **1982**.
Australians at the Olympics, **Gary Lester** (Kingfisher) **1984**.
Australians from Everywhere, (Bay Books) **1986**.
New Ways in an Ancient Land, (Bay Books) **1986**.
Australia Comes of Age, (Bay Books) **1986**.
A Man Called Mo, **Fred Parson** (Heinemann) **1973**.
Melba, **Therese Radic** (Macmillan) **1986**.
Clear Across Australia, **Ann Moyal** (Nelson) **1984**.
A New History of Australia, edited by **Frank Crowley** (Heinemann) **1974**.
The Squatters, **Geoffrey Dutton** (Currey O'Neil) **1985**.
German Speaking Settlers in Australia, **Josef Vondra** (Cavalier Press) **1981**.
The Art of Australia, **Robert Hughes** (Penguin) **1981**.
The Front Door, **Douglas Lockwood** (Rigby) **1974**.
Port of Pearls, **Hugh Edwards** (Rigby) **1983**.
Australia — Spirit of a Nation, **Michael Cannon** (Currey O'Neil) **1985**.
Colonial South Australia, **Michael Page** (J.M. Dent) **1985**.
Great Voyages of Exploration, **Jacques Brosse** (Doubleday) **1983**.
The Rock and the Sand, **Mary Durack** (Corgi) **1985**.
From Deserts the Prophets Come, **Geoffrey Serle** (Heinemann) **1973**.
Captain Cook, **Alan Villiers** (Hodder and Stoughton) **1967**.
The Heroic Journey of John McDouall Stuart, **Ian Mudie** (Angus and Robertson) **1968**.
From the Dreaming to 1915, **Ross Fitzgerald** (University of Queensland Press) **1982**.

ERRATUM
The reproduction on page 66 has been incorrectly captioned in this and other publications as a portrait of 'Dame Nellie Melba'. Research has proven it to be a portrait of the artists wife by Rupert Bunny. Our apologies.

ACKNOWLEDGEMENTS

The compiling of pictorial and historical material used would not have been possible without the kind co-operation of the following people and organizations.
A.A.P. Information Services: A.N.T. Photo Library: Addidas: Alecto Historical Editions, London: Art Gallery of N.S.W.: Australian Bicentennial Authority: Australian Botanic Gardens: Australian Gallery of Sport: Australian National Gallery: Australian War Memorial: Australia Post: B.H.P. Company Limited: Mr. & Mrs. William Bailey: Bay Books Pty. Ltd. and Brooke Twyford: Brisbane City Council: Broken Hill Barrier Truth: Broome Historical Society: Bundaberg Distilling Company Pty. Ltd.: Carlton and United Breweries Darwin: Castlemaine Museum: Chantilly Antiques: Ann Clark, Ann Clarke Agencies: Department of Mines, Queensland: Dixson Galleries: Cassie Doyle & other staff, State Library of Queensland: Lea Dunlea: Mr. Don Eggins: Mr. Fred Ellem: Mr. Lewis Ellem: Malcolm Enright: Stan Greaves: Mr. Rod Henderson, D.P.I. Queensland: Herald & Weekly Times and Don Richards: Horizons and Virginia Goode: John Oxley Library staff: Julian Ashton Art School: Kalbar Colonial Market: Kayell Productions: Lansdowne Press: La Trobe Collection; State Library of Victoria: John Loxton: Mr. & Mrs. Fred Martin & family: Mr. & Mrs. Jack Martin: Mr. & Mrs. John Martin: Melbourne Cricket Club: M.I.M. Holdings Limited: Maclean Historical Society: Macmillan Co. of Australia: Mitchell Library: Mortlock Library of S.A.: Chris Murphy: N.S.W. Historical Society: N.S.W. State Railways: Nan Kivell Collection; State Library of Victoria: National Gallery of Australia: National Gallery of Victoria and Philip Jago: National Library of Australia: News Limited: G. Nicetin, C.S.R. Corporate Affairs: Olympic Federation: Steve Parish: Positive Image Photo Library: Qantas Airways Ltd.: Queensland Australian Football League: Queensland Cricket Association Ltd.: Queensland Cricketers Club: Queensland Lawn Tennis Association: Queensland Museum: Queensland Newspapers and Joanne Burnett: RAAF Association Aviation Museum W.A.: Readers Digest: Rigby Publishing: Rimfire Productions Pty. Ltd.: Royal Flying Doctor Service of Australia: Royal Historical Society of Victoria: Mr. & Mrs. Brian Small: James Stewart: Sydney Maritime Museum: Sydney Opera Centre: Taronga Park Zoo: The Bulletin: The Royal Historical Society of Queensland: The Snowy Mountains Hydro Electric Authority: Trade Union Congress, London: Victoria Barracks Museum & Historical Society: Victorian Police Department: W.A. Museum: W.A. Newspapers: Warwick & District Tourist Association: Weldon Trannies and Debi Wager: White Bay Antiques: Dr. Richard Willan, Queensland University.

THE PRODUCTION TEAM
It would require far more space than that available to individually thank all of the special people involved in this Bicentennial Project. There have been, however, some who have been either involved from the beginning or had some particular role to play. The publishers would like to thank these people as representatives of the entire magnificent production team.
CONCEPT AND PLANNING
Lawry Brindle, Jim McKillop, Keith Buckley, Indy Liepa, Keith Jackson, Alan Podlich, Kev Franklin, Peter Carmody.
The Co-authors Thomas J. Bain, Janice L. Bain, Lawrence M. Fysh.
RESEARCH AND ADVICE
Bep Torkington, Hellen Hough, Christine Imlach, Tom Brandi, Hanne Brandi, Brian Cassidy, Dr. Iraphne Childs (Geography), Prof. John Holmes (Geography), Dr. Ross Johnston (History), George Dean (History), Dr. A.L. Lougheed (Economist), Dr. Sheila Williams (Mathematics).
THE ARTISTS
Maggi Field and Mouse, Peter Moss, Paula Onraet, Terry Straight, Ziya Eris, Keith Howland, Glenda Holyoake.
THE GRAPHIC ARTISTS
Mike Pengilly, Bruce Irwin, Greg Kirkwood, Steven Clark, Peter Holyoake, Mark Hourigan, Cathy Shannon, Billy Bredhauer and Anne Treffene of Press Etching. Bob Russel of Savage Colour, Alan Linton of Savage Type, John Hutton of Haighs and John Bagster for his brilliant computer programme work.
THE PRINTERS
Ted Donaldson, Col Hollaway, Mil Pospisil, Stephen Harper, Barny Bredhauer, Tim Muller and Tony Martin of Prestige Litho. Chris Butterworth and Charles Lawrence of Inprint. George Gatehouse, Bill Elsasser and Max Gardiner of Wilke (Victoria).
THE BINDERS
Norm Kennedy, Barry Bowkett and Noel Podlich of Podlich Enterprises.

Finally the publishers would like to thank Ray Hood for his editorial assistance and patient efforts to maintain typographic consistency.
It's over now. Thank you all.

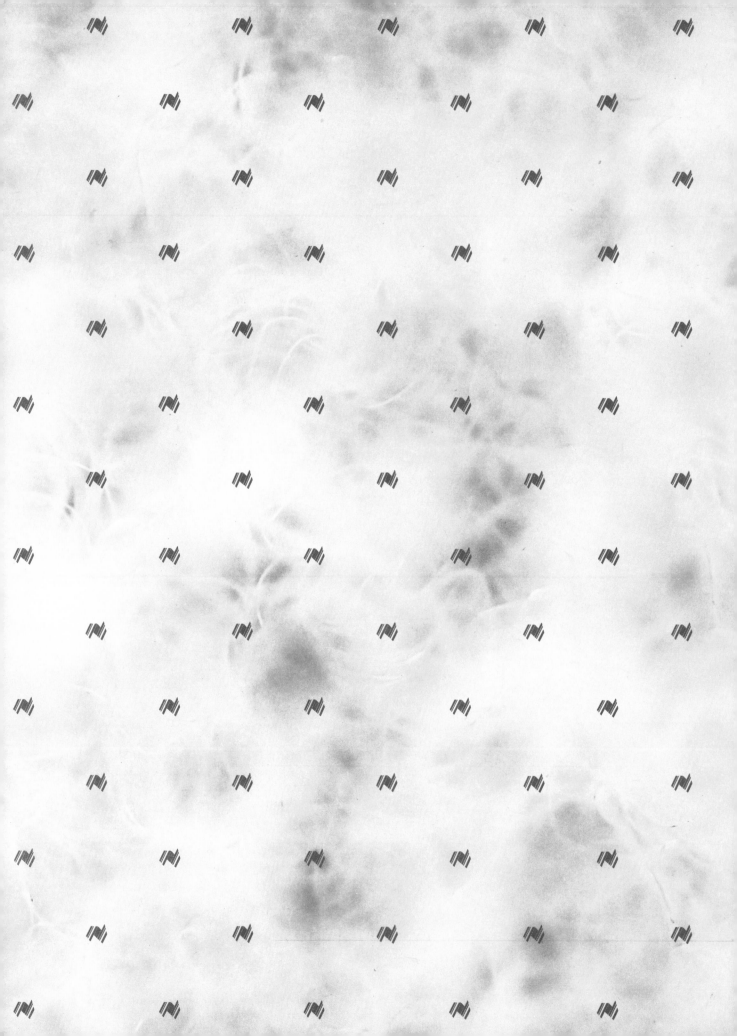